SAP PRESS e-books

Print or e-book, Kindle or iPad, workplace or airplane: Choose where and how to read your SAP PRESS books! You can now get all our titles as e-books, too:

▸ By download and online access
▸ For all popular devices
▸ And, of course, DRM-free

Convinced? Then go to **www.sap-press.com** and get your e-book today.

Object-Oriented Programming with ABAP® Objects

PRESS

SAP PRESS is a joint initiative of SAP and Rheinwerk Publishing. The know-how offered by SAP specialists combined with the expertise of Rheinwerk Publishing offers the reader expert books in the field. SAP PRESS features first-hand information and expert advice, and provides useful skills for professional decision-making.

SAP PRESS offers a variety of books on technical and business-related topics for the SAP user. For further information, please visit our website: *www.sap-press.com*.

Brian O'Neill
Getting Started with ABAP
2015, 452 pages, paperback
ISBN 978-1-4932-1242-2

Paul Hardy
ABAP to the Future
2015, 727 pages, hardcover
ISBN 978-1-4932-1161-6

Puneet Asthana, David Haslam
ABAP 7.4 Certification Guide—SAP Certified Development Associate
(3rd edition)
2015, 663 pages, paperback
ISBN 978-1-4932-1212-5

Schneider, Westenberger, Gahm
ABAP Development for SAP HANA
2013, 609 pages, hardcover
ISBN 978-1-59229-859-4

James Wood and Joseph Rupert

Object-Oriented Programming with ABAP® Objects

Rheinwerk®
Publishing

Bonn • Boston

Editor Hareem Shafi
Acquisitions Editor Kelly Grace Weaver
Copyeditor Julie McNamee
Cover Design Graham Geary
Photo Credit Shutterstock.com/168845210/© wiktord
Layout Design Vera Brauner
Production Kelly O'Callaghan
Typesetting III-satz, Husby (Germany)
Printed and bound in the United States of America, on paper from sustainable sources

ISBN 978-1-59229-993-5
© 2016 by Rheinwerk Publishing, Inc., Boston (MA)
2nd edition 2016

Library of Congress Cataloging-in-Publication Data
Wood, James, 1978- author.
Object-oriented programming with ABAP Objects / James Wood, Joe Rupert. -- 2nd edition.
pages cm
Includes index.
ISBN 978-1-59229-993-5 (print : alk. paper) -- ISBN 1-59229-993-8 (print : alk. paper)
-- ISBN 978-1-59229-994-2 (ebook) -- ISBN 978-1-59229-995-9 (print and ebook : alk. paper) 1. Object-oriented
programming (Computer science) 2. ABAP/4 (Computer program language) I. Rupert, Joe, author. II. Title.
QA76.64.W666 2015
005.1'17--dc23
2015030305

Contents at a Glance

Dear Reader,

Did you pick up this book in the hopes of learning object-oriented programming from experts in the field? Individuals who teach like they were born to it, and write so well that their editor has very little to do? Well, then I am pleased to tell you that you are in good hands; James Wood and Joseph Rupert are all those things and more.

In this second edition of *Object-Oriented Programming with ABAP* these esteemed authors leave no stone unturned as they work to educate readers on object-oriented programming and ABAP objects. From basic concepts, to advanced practical examples, it has never been easier to understand object cleanup and initialization, inheritance, polymorphism, encapsulation, and more. I am sure you will find immense value between the pages of this comprehensive book.

What did you think of the second edition of *Object-Oriented Programming with ABAP*? Your comments and suggestions are the most useful tools to help us make our books the best they can be. Please feel free to contact me and share any praise or criticism you may have.

Thank you for purchasing a book from SAP PRESS!

Hareem Shafi
Editor, SAP PRESS

Rheinwerk Publishing
Boston, MA

hareems@rheinwerk-publishing.com
www.sap-press.com

Contents

3   Encapsulation and Implementation Hiding 121

PART II Case Studies

11 Business Object Development with the BOPF 379

12 Working with the SAP List Viewer 415

Introduction

In the seven-plus years since the first edition of this book was published we've seen a lot of changes in the world of ABAP Objects. These changes are representative of the maturation of ABAP Objects as a language and its continued adoption by developers in the SAP landscape. So, while the core concepts of object-oriented programming (OOP) never really change, we felt the time was right to take a fresh look at OOP with ABAP Objects.

Our goal with this revised and expanded edition of the book remains consistent with the first edition: to teach you how to *think* about writing ABAP-based software from an object-oriented perspective. While it takes a fair amount of time and effort to embrace this way of thinking, we believe that you'll find the investment to be worthwhile from both a personal and professional standpoint.

Target Group and Prerequisites

This book is intended for ABAP developers that have some basic experience writing ABAP programs. Though most of the concepts are presented with lots of background information for developers new to OOP, this book should not be confused as a comprehensive introduction to ABAP. If you haven't worked with ABAP before it's probably a good idea to look for a training course or perhaps read through introductory titles such as *Getting Started with ABAP* (SAP PRESS, 2015); *Discover ABAP, 2nd Edition* (SAP PRESS, 2012); or *ABAP Basics, 2nd Edition* (SAP PRESS, 2011). Aside from that, no prior OOP experience, etc. is expected.

System-wise, we think that you'll find that the majority of the tools/features described in this book are supported on most any AS ABAP system. Indeed, since the object-oriented extensions to ABAP (i.e., the *Objects* part of ABAP Objects) were made available in SAP R/3 4.6C in 1999, it's pretty rare to find a system that doesn't support object-oriented ABAP these days. Still, we will point out release-specific features/additions where appropriate.

Structure of the Book

As we put this book together, we endeavored to strike a balance between theoretical concepts on one hand and practical examples demonstrating the use of ABAP Objects in real-live scenarios on the other. This approach led us to split the book into two parts:

▸ In Part I, we introduce you to core OOP concepts and the ABAP Objects functionality/syntax that corresponds with these concepts.

▸ Then, in Part II, we build on these concepts by presenting case studies that demonstrate how ABAP Objects is used in practical development scenarios.

Despite this logical breakdown, we think that you'll find that we let code do much of the talking throughout the book so that you don't feel like you're reading a college textbook on OOP.

Finally, at the end of each chapter, we've included brief tutorials on the *Unified Modeling Language* (UML). These tutorials show you how to describe your OO designs using a graphical notation that's commonly used throughout the software industry.

Here's an overview of what we'll be covering in the book:

Part I: Introduction

In this part of the book, we introduce basic concepts of OOP in general and ABAP Objects in particular.

▸ **Chapter 1: Introduction to Object-Oriented Programming**
In this chapter, we set the stage for the rest of book by introducing you to object-oriented programming and its basic concepts.

▸ **Chapter 2: Getting Started with Objects**
In Chapter 2 we start getting our hands dirty with classes in ABAP Objects. We spend lots of time exploring ABAP Objects syntax for defining classes, methods, and so on. Along the way we introduce the core development tools we'll be using to develop classes throughout the book: the classic ABAP Workbench and the newer Eclipse-based workbench.

▸ **Chapter 3: Encapsulation and Implementation Hiding**
Though inheritance usually steals all the headlines when it comes to OOP, it could be argued that encapsulation is the most important aspect of OOP. In this

chapter, we review encapsulation concepts by comparing and contrasting the OO-based development approach with the procedural approach. We also introduce the important topic of component visibilities in this chapter.

▶ **Chapter 4: Object Initialization and Cleanup**
In Chapter 4 we explore the lifecycle of objects from the point they're created to the point they're removed by the garbage collector process of the ABAP Runtime Environment. Along the way we'll learn about constructor methods and other ways of influencing the object lifecycle.

▶ **Chapter 5: Inheritance and Composition**
This chapter looks at two common ways of achieving code reuse in OOP: *inheritance* and *composition*. Here, we'll discover that these techniques, when coupled with encapsulation techniques introduced in Chapter 3, allow us to expand our code libraries in dimensions we never thought possible.

▶ **Chapter 6: Polymorphism**
We learn how to take advantage of inheritance relationships to build solutions which rely on interchangeable parts in Chapter 6. Along the way, we also introduce another key OO concept: *interfaces*.

▶ **Chapter 7: Component-Based Design Concepts**
After spending the previous chapters looking at classes underneath the microscope, this chapter broadens the focus a bit by showing you how the ABAP Package Concept can be used to organize class libraries into coarse-grained development components.

▶ **Chapter 8: Error Handling with Exception Classes**
This chapter explains how to deal with exception situations using the ABAP class-based exception handling concept.

▶ **Chapter 9: Unit Tests with ABAP Unit**
Chapter 9 concludes the introductory part of the book by showing you how to develop automated unit tests using the ABAP Unit test framework. These tests help you ensure that your classes deliver on the functionality specified in their API contracts.

Part II: Case Studies

In this part of the book, we'll attempt to reinforce the core concepts learned in Part 1 by looking at some practical examples which demonstrate the use of ABAP Objects and OOP in the real world. These case studies are by no means comprehensive. Instead, we purposefully selected a few scenarios which really help to drive home key concepts.

▶ **Chapter 10: ABAP Object Services**
In this chapter, we show you how to work with ABAP Object Services, a framework that SAP provides to build persistent classes. Besides demonstrating a more OO-based approach to persistence, this case study also allows us to examine how SAP is applying OO design concepts to build out an extensible framework that blends standard functionality with customer enhancements.

▶ **Chapter 11: Business Object Development with the BOPF**
Chapter 11 introduces SAP's *Business Object Processing Framework* (BOPF). Here, we get to see basic OO principles applied on a macro scale towards the development of reusable business objects. Internally, there are lots of OO-related concepts on display—both within the business objects themselves and in the generic API used to interface with the business objects.

▶ **Chapter 12: Working with the SAP List Viewer**
We look at ways of building ABAP report programs which are fully object-oriented based on common design patterns such as the model-view-controller (MVC) pattern in Chapter 12. Here, we build on the OO-based ALV object model to create a reporting framework which provides an excellent demonstration for the use of interfaces and polymorphism in practice.

▶ **Chapter 13: Where to Go From Here**
In this final chapter, we take stock of what we've learned and look at some additional materials you can use to take your OO skills to the next level.

Appendices

▶ **Appendix A: Installing the Eclipse IDE**
This appendix provides detailed instructions for how to install the Eclipse IDE and corresponding ABAP plug-ins for developers that are new to Eclipse.

▶ **Appendix B: Debugging Objects**
In this appendix, we demonstrate ABAP Objects-related features in the ABAP Debugger tool, showing you how to debug object-oriented programs.

Conventions

This book contains many examples demonstrating syntax, functionality, and so forth. Therefore, to distinguish these sections, we use a monospaced font similar to the one used by many integrated development environments (IDEs) to improve code readability:

```
CLASS lcl_test DEFINITION.
  PUBLIC SECTION.

  . . .
ENDCLASS.
```

As new syntax is introduced, we'll highlight the syntax using a bold listing font as demonstrated in the excerpt above with the highlighted PUBLIC SECTION statement. The use of the ellipsis indicates that irrelevant portions of the code were omitted for brevity's sake.

Source Code and Examples

As noted earlier, this book includes a great many code examples which demonstrate the use of ABAP Objects in different settings. Though many of these examples are small and self-contained, we have included all of the more involved examples in a source code bundle that can be downloaded from the book's companion site. Most of the code is presented in text-based mode so that you can easily paste it into your preferred ABAP editor tool and test it out for yourself. For everything else, we've provided detailed instructions which describe how to install/test the relevant development objects.

For the most part, you should be able to try these examples out in any available ABAP system by simply creating the objects in your local development package (i.e., the $TMP package). However, if you don't have access to an ABAP system, then you can obtain access to one by logging onto the SAP store online at *https://store.sap.com*. Here, if you perform a search on the term "SCN", you'll see a search result list come up which contains various AS ABAP trial systems that you can either download locally or install to the cloud using SAP's *Cloud Appliance Library* (CAL). In the latter case, you can roll out an instance in a matter of minutes by linking the CAL with your *Amazon Web Services* (AWS) account. You can find lots of tutorials on how to do this on the SAP Community Network online at *https://scn.sap.com*.

Acknowledgments

Putting a book like this together is no simple feat, and it requires the help and support of lots of important individuals behind the scenes. Throughout the writing process, we were blessed to have the support of two fantastic editors at Rheinwerk Publishing who guided us along our way: Kelly Grace Weaver and Hareem Shafi. We can't thank you enough for the support—we simply couldn't have done it without you.

James would also like to thank another set of unsung heroes in this process: his wife Andrea, and kids Andersen, Paige, Parker and Xander. They've been amazingly patient with me as I've burned the midnight oil putting this book together. I would call them my muse, but alas, I don't think they would appreciate me drawing such nerdy inspiration from them. If only ABAP were cooler in the minds of children...

Joe would like to thank his wonderful and supporting family: his wife Jennifer and his lovely daughters Amelia and Lillian.

PART I
Introduction

This chapter provides an overview of object-oriented programming from a conceptual point of view. The concepts described in this chapter lay the foundation for the remainder of the book.

1 Introduction to Object-Oriented Programming

Object-oriented programming (OOP) is a programming paradigm in which developers approach program design by modeling solutions in terms of a series of *objects* that simulate real-world entities from the problem domain. This shift in design philosophy helps us achieve program designs which more closely resemble the world around them. As a result, object-oriented designs tend to be easier to understand, maintain, and extend. The purpose of this chapter is to introduce you to the basic concepts you'll need to understand in order to effectively design and develop object-oriented programs. These concepts generally apply to most modern OOP languages such as C++, Java, and, of course, ABAP Objects. This chapter will also begin an introduction to the *Unified Modeling Language* (UML), which is the de facto object modeling language used in the software industry today.

1.1 The Need for a Better Abstraction

In the field of software engineering, few topics incite more controversy than object-oriented programming. Loyalists defend the merits of OOP with near religious fervor, while detractors often roll their eyes at the very thought of it. If you're reading this book, it's likely that you find yourself somewhere in the middle of this seemingly endless debate. And if that's the case, probably the most pressing questions on your mind include the following:

▶ Why should I bother learning OOP?

▶ Is OOP really better than procedural programming or other methodologies?

▶ What is it about OOP that makes it so special?

In the sections and chapters to follow, we will attempt to answer these questions by demonstrating how OOP sets itself apart from other programming methodologies by providing a better and more intuitive form of abstraction.

1.1.1 The Evolution of Programming Languages

The quality of a language (spoken or otherwise) is generally measured by its effectiveness in expressing complex thoughts and ideas. If we evaluate programming languages using this criterion, we can easily chart the progression from low-level programming languages such as assembly language to higher-level procedural programming languages such as C (and to some extent ABAP). As programming languages evolve, they become easier to read and write with. Of course, this begs the question: what makes a programming language more expressive?

Though there are many schools of thought here (hence the vast number of programming languages in circulation today), each of the approaches taken over the years shares a common goal: to improve the quality and nature of the abstraction(s) that developers have to work with. If we can improve on that, then developer productivity should undoubtedly increase as well.

To put this into perspective, let's briefly consider the innovations that the C programming language brought to the table back in the days when assembly language programming reigned supreme. In those days, programmers were implementing their designs by twiddling bits of data, manipulating various CPU registers, and so on. With the advent of C, the developer's palette expanded to include:

▸ **Variables** with meaningful names and intuitive data types (e.g. integers and strings of characters)

▸ **Conditional statements** that made it possible to encode program logic using statements that more closely resembled spoken language.

▸ **Callable functions** that allowed developers to break down complex problems into modules that were easier to understand individually.

With these new abstractions in hand, developers were freed from worrying so much about low-level technical details and could focus more on program logic issues.

Despite these early innovations, by the time the 1960s rolled around language researchers had begun to observe a fundamental truth: The abstractions provided by programming languages up to that point still required developers to think about their solutions "in terms of the structure of the computer rather than the structure of the problem they're trying to solve," as Bruce Eckel states in *Thinking in C++*. This is to say that solutions in code bore little resemblance to the problem domain from which they were conceived. For the purposes of this book, we'll refer to this phenomenon as *semantic dissonance*.

The upshot of this trend is that a tremendous burden was placed on developers to ensure that software requirements were accurately *translated* into program code. And, if one of those requirements got lost in the translation or the developer made a mistake somewhere along the way? Well, let's just say that it was going to be a rough couple of days for that developer.

1.1.2   Moving Towards Objects

Around the time software researchers began to wrap their heads around the semantic dissonance problem, several influential language designers took a collective step back and began contemplating what the most ideal type of abstraction would be. Think of it this way: If you could choose *any* kind of element to model your program designs, what would you ask for? Would you stop at abstract data types (ADTs) and functions/subroutines? What if instead someone offered you a series of magical *objects* that look and behave like the entities you interact with in the real world?

While the latter approach may sound too good to be true, it turns out that conjuring up such objects in programs is actually achievable if we begin to think about our program designs just a little bit differently. We'll have an opportunity to explore this thought process in depth beginning in Section 1.2, but before we segue into more practical matters, let's take a moment to understand the *why* in OOP.

At the end of the day, OOP is all about bridging the gap between whatever problem domain we're working with and the solution space where our program code lives and operates. The goal is to model our code in such a way that it resembles (or *simulates*) the problem space we're working in (e.g. purchasing, accounting, and so on). In his book, *Thinking in C++*, Bruce Eckel summarizes the benefits of this approach: "Casting the solution in the same terms as the problem is tremendously beneficial because you don't need a lot of intermediate models to get from a description of the problem to the description of the solution."

Once you begin to see the world through OO glasses, you open yourself up to all kinds of new and exciting possibilities. For example, with objects, it's easier to achieve reuse because you're dealing with self-contained entities that have defined responsibilities as opposed to a scattering of data structures and subroutines. This will all become clearer as we progress through the book, but for now, we would simply ask that you open your mind to the possibility of a system overrun by lots of tiny little objects.

1.2   Classes and Objects

Students learning pure object-oriented languages like Java are often taught that "everything is an object". While this is not necessarily the case in a hybrid language like ABAP Objects (where it's still possible to use procedural constructs), it's still a good way to start thinking about how to design programs using an object-oriented approach. Of course, it helps if you know what an object is. In this section, we'll attempt to unravel the mysteries surrounding objects and also consider a closely related concept in OOP: *classes*.

1.2.1   What Are Objects?

From a technical perspective, an object is a special kind of variable that has distinct characteristics and behaviors. The characteristics (or *attributes*) of an object are used to describe the *state* of an object. For example a Car object might have attributes to capture information such as the color of the car, its make and model, or even its current driving speed. Behaviors (or *methods*) represent the *actions* performed by an object. In our Car example, there might be methods that can be used to drive, turn, and stop the car, for instance.

With all this in mind, our initial definition of an object would read something like this: "An object is a variable that combines data and behaviors together in a self-contained package." However, if we were to leave off here, our definition would be rather limiting. In his book, *Design Patterns Explained: A New Perspective on Object-Oriented Design, 2nd Edition*, Alan Shalloway emphasizes that objects make it possible to "...package data and functionality together by *concept*, so you can represent an appropriate problem-space idea rather than being forced to use the idioms of the underlying machine." This distinction, though subtle, is important in getting us where we really want to go with OOP: to create autonomous entities with defined roles and responsibilities that are able to think and act for themselves.

1.2.2 Introducing Classes

Now that you have a sense for what objects are, you might be wondering how objects are defined in the first place. Unlike other variable types that you might be accustomed to working with, this process requires a fair amount of thought. Since an object, by definition, can literally refer to most anything (i.e. a person, place, thing, or idea), we first need to figure out the *types* of objects we need in order to model our problem domain. For example, if we are building a financial accounting solution, we would probably need objects to represent accounts, ledgers, and so on.

Sometimes this analysis process is intuitive; other times not so much. In these latter cases, we must collect our thoughts using an ordered and methodical process. One fairly typical approach for initiating this process is to identify all of the nouns used to describe various aspects of the problem domain. Then, from here, we can further organize the objects by examining their roles and responsibilities as well as their relationships to other objects. Early OOP researchers observed that the nature of this analysis process bore a number of similarities to the classification techniques used by biologists to identify, categorize and understand the relationships between plants and animals. Consequently, the term *class* was used to describe these abstract data types and over the years the name has stuck.

In practical terms, we can think of a class as being rather like a specialized type declaration. This is to say that a class declaration defines the *type* of an object. As an ABAP developer accustomed to working with structures and internal tables, this typing concept should feel fairly intuitive. For example, in Listing 1.1, you can see how we've defined a structure variable called LS_PERSON in terms of a custom type we've declared called TY_PERSON. This custom type declaration tells the ABAP compiler what the LS_PERSON structure will look like at runtime (i.e. what component fields the structure will have).

```
TYPES: BEGIN OF ty_person,
         first_name TYPE string,
         last_name TYPE string,
       END OF ty_person.

DATA ls_person TYPE ty_person.
```
Listing 1.1 Declaring a Custom Structure Data Type

With class type declarations, we're essentially trying to accomplish the same thing; the only difference is that we're declaring a class of objects as opposed to a structure or internal table. For example, in Listing 1.2, you can see how we've defined a custom class type called LCL_PERSON. We'll have an opportunity to unpack the syntax of this in Chapter 2, but for now, notice the similarities between this class type declaration and the TY_PERSON type declaration from Listing 1.1. This is not by accident since classes are, in many respects, just another form of abstract data type (ADT).

```
CLASS lcl_person DEFINITION.
  PRIVATE SECTION.
    DATA mv_first_name TYPE string.
    DATA mv_last_name TYPE string.
ENDCLASS.

DATA lo_person TYPE REF TO lcl_person.
```
Listing 1.2 Declaring a Custom Class Type

When we look at class type declarations in this light, we can begin to appreciate the relationship between classes and objects. Conceptually speaking, it's appropriate to think of classes as being like templates (or *blueprints*) that an OO runtime environment can use to figure out how to create object instances at runtime. Therefore, the relationship between an object and a class is normally described as *"an object is an instance of a class,"* in OOP lingo.

This relationship is illustrated from a runtime perspective in Figure 1.1. Here, we can see how an arbitrary number of instances of our LCL_PERSON class might be created (or *instantiated*) at runtime. Each created object instance is unique and independent in its own right (i.e. it has its own memory space). For example, notice how each object instance contains its own values for the FIRST_NAME and LAST_NAME attributes. If we were to change the FIRST_NAME attribute for the first object instance, the other object instances would be unaffected because they're independent entities. Indeed, the only thing that these objects really have in common is their shared definition class.

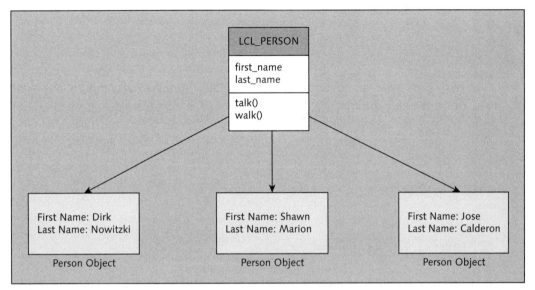

Figure 1.1 Relationship Between Classes and Objects

If all this seems confusing, don't worry; we'll delve into some hands-on examples in Chapter 2 that should make the relationship between classes and objects much clearer.

1.2.3   Defining a Class's Interface

In the previous section, we highlighted some of the similarities between class types and other ADTs such as structures or internal tables. While this analogy is useful in understanding how objects are defined conceptually, it begins to break down when we approach the specification of a class's methods. Methods, which are conceptually similar to subroutines or functions in procedural programming, define the interaction points that make it possible to *communicate* with object instances at runtime. In more formal terms, methods are said to make up a class's *interface*.

To illustrate the idea of a class's interface, consider the revised LCL_PERSON class type declaration shown in Listing 1.3.

```
CLASS lcl_person DEFINITION.
  PUBLIC SECTION.
    METHODS:
      talk,
      walk.

  PRIVATE SECTION.
    DATA mv_first_name TYPE string.
    DATA mv_last_name TYPE string.
ENDCLASS.

CLASS lcl_person IMPLEMENTATION.
  METHOD talk.
    WRITE: / 'Hello'.
  ENDMETHOD.

  METHOD walk.
    ...
  ENDMETHOD.
ENDCLASS.
```

Listing 1.3 Declaring a Class with Methods

With the addition of methods such as talk() and walk(), instances of the LCL_PERSON class all of a sudden take on quite a bit more personality. In effect, we can use these methods to (programmatically) tell our objects what to do. For example, we can tell a person instance to talk by calling the talk() method or to walk around by invoking the walk() method. Such behaviors transform objects from inanimate data structures to living, breathing entities that are self-aware and, to a certain extent, autonomous. Plus, with their attribute data in context, objects inherently know who they are, what their current state is, and what sort of operations they can perform.

1.3   Establishing Boundaries

A fundamental principle of OOP is that objects should rarely exist in isolation. Indeed, if we think of our object-oriented programs as simulations of some real-world problem domain, then it's only natural that there would be some division of labor among the classes/objects that make up the solution architecture. This design approach calls for a series of smaller, more granular classes that specialize in solving a particular piece of the problem as opposed to a handful of "God objects" that are overburdened with many (unrelated) tasks. These smaller, more focused classes are said to have high cohesion in the sense that each of the class's operations are closely related in some intuitive way.

While having such collaboration among objects in a program design is definitely a good thing, it does require that we define some boundaries up front. In this section, we'll learn a bit about how such boundaries are established within classes and why they're important.

1.3.1 An Introduction to Encapsulation and Implementation Hiding

Before we look at the mechanics of boundary definitions within classes, let's briefly take a step back and think about why such boundaries are needed in the first place. After all, this sort of thing is rarely (if ever) a concern in other programming paradigms (such as procedural programming).

To illustrate the importance of boundaries in software design, let's explore an analogy from the world of manufacturing. Here, consider a real-world device (object) that most people are experienced in using: a *smart phone*. This object, much like software objects, has distinct attributes (e.g. form factor and memory size) and behaviors (making/receiving phone calls, sending an e-mail, and so forth). It also has an interface that consumers can interact with. For example, to send a text message, a user simply taps on the appropriate messaging icon and then uses the built-in keyboard to type out their message. With various input gestures, users can tell their smart phone what to do and it will obey their every command.

Design-wise, one of the marvels about smart phones is that, despite of all the wonderful and complex tasks they perform, they're pretty intuitive and easy to use. This begs the question: how is it possible that something so complex could be that easy to use? The answer lies in a technique so obvious you may not have even realized it had a name: *encapsulation*.

As the name suggests, the term *encapsulation* refers to a design approach in which selected elements of an object are hidden together inside of an enclosure (or *capsule*) that's shielded from the outside world. From a manufacturing standpoint, the goal of this technique is simplification. Everything that consumers don't need to know about in a product (object) design is superfluous and gets in the way, so we may as well hide it from them. It's not that the components in question aren't important; it's just that the consumer doesn't need to know about them in order to use the object. In fact, the less the consumer has to know about the internal workings of a particular object, the shorter the learning curve will be in figuring out how the object works.

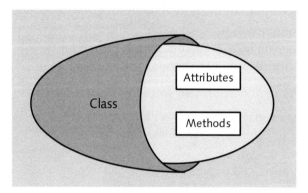

Figure 1.2 Encapsulation of Data and Behavior Inside a Class

Aside from de-cluttering an object's interface, there are several other important benefits to be gained by employing encapsulation techniques in our class/object designs:

▶ From an implementation perspective, encapsulation allows us to hide tender parts of the implementation which are volatile and sensitive to change. In the long run, this approach gives us more flexibility in responding to changes in requirements since we can clearly pinpoint and isolate specific pieces of functionality within the system.

▶ Simplifying the interface promotes *loose coupling* between components. This is to say that it cuts out all of the extraneous wiring required to connect a pair of objects/components. This in turn makes it easier to use (and reuse) our objects in different contexts.

▶ It allows us to modify the implementation behind the scenes without impacting consumers. Getting back to our smart phone analogy, consider the possibility that a smart phone manufacturer might decide to replace its existing processor with a smaller, faster chip in a new product revision. To the consumer, this design change is completely transparent since it doesn't change how they interact with the phone (aside from maybe making it faster and more responsive).

Similarly, with objects, we can achieve the same thing by changing the implementation code hidden behind the class interface. Here, for example, we might decide to speed up a database lookup by utilizing a stored procedure in SAP HANA instead of a normal SQL SELECT statement. To the consumer, nothing has really changed here so long as we continue to uphold our end of the bargain by passing back the data they're expecting.

We'll have an opportunity to expand on these concepts in much more detail in Chapter 3. For now though, the main take-away from all this is that it makes good sense to draw up clear boundaries between the various collaborating objects in our object-oriented designs.

Of course, in order to enforce such boundaries, we're going to need some support from the programming language and its corresponding runtime environment.

1.3.2 Understanding Visibility Sections

In order to clearly define the interface of our classes, there has to be a way for us to differentiate between those elements that we want to share with the public and those that we wish to maintain privately. Most object-oriented languages handle this by grouping selected elements into one of three distinct *visibility sections*:

▸ **Public Section**
Components that we define within this section (e.g. attributes, methods, etc.) can be accessed from any context. The elements in this section make up the class's external interface.

▸ **Private Section**
Components defined in this section are completely shut off and hidden from the outside world. Class consumers cannot access these components in any way. Their sole purpose for being there is to facilitate the inner workings of the class (e.g. helper methods, internal data, and so forth).

▸ **Protected Section**
Components defined in this section are visible only to the superclass and its subclasses. To the outside world, it would seem that these components were defined within the private section of the class. This section will come into play when we discuss inheritance in Chapter 5.

Once we organize our components into these various visibility sections, we can rest assured that the runtime environment will make sure that our boundaries are enforced. In Chapter 3, we'll look at ways of exploiting this functionality to improve the robustness of our designs.

1.4   Reuse

One of the most compelling reasons for adopting an object-oriented approach to program design is the significant capability for reusing code. Of course, while it is easy to allow yourself to become dazzled by promises of huge productivity gains, it's important to keep things in perspective. Learning how to develop reusable classes takes time and experience. The following subsections describe some basic techniques for reusing classes. We'll then circle back and cover these topics at length in Chapters 5 and 6.

1.4.1   Composition

The easiest way to reuse a class is to simply create an instance of it and start calling its methods. Such instances can be created in isolation, or as attributes of new classes that we may decide to build. This latter usage type is often referred to as *composition*, where new classes are *composed* from existing classes. These classes are *aggregates*, using existing classes as building blocks (think LEGO® sets) for constructing arbitrarily complex assemblies. Designs based on composition are easy to understand and highly flexible. Since member objects can be hidden just like any other attribute, it's easy to change the way we utilize these objects both at design time and at run time.

1.4.2   Inheritance

Another way to reuse a class is through *inheritance*. The concept of inheritance is an extension of the classification metaphor used to describe the nature of classes and their relationships. Here, we're interested in defining *specialization* relationships between families of related classes. These relationships begin to reveal themselves as an object-oriented design matures.

The idea of inheritance is best explained by an example. Let's imagine that you're working on an object-oriented design for a banking system. Initially, you come up with a series of classes including one to represent a bank account. After studying the requirements further, you discover that there are certain peculiarities unique to checking and savings accounts. At this point, you're faced with a dilemma. On one hand, you could copy the code you have put together for the account into new checking and savings account classes. However, this seems wasteful since this would introduce a lot of redundant code. Another option would be to use inheritance to describe this specialization relationship. In this case, you still create new checking and savings account classes, but you create them as *subclasses* derived from the original account class (which is the parent or superclass). The checking and savings account subclasses are said to *inherit* the attributes and behaviors (and indeed the type) of the account superclass (see Figure 1.3). Now, the relevant changes can be made to each of the subclasses independently without having to reinvent the wheel.

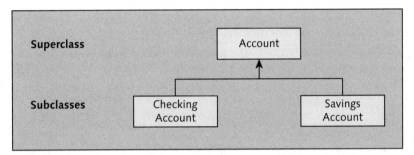

Figure 1.3 Understanding Inheritance Relationships

It's important to understand that inheritance describes a relationship; it's not just a fancy term for "copying-and-pasting" one piece of code into another. Initially, a subclass looks like a clone of the superclass. However, over time, a subclass can be extended to add new attributes and methods as needed. Additionally, changes to the superclass are automatically applied to the subclass (although we'll see exceptions to this rule in Chapter 5). In general, it's possible to create class hierarchies with arbitrarily deep inheritance relationships.

The connection between a subclass and its parent is often described using the "is-a" relationship. Looking at the example above, a checking account *is an* account, etc. The "is-a" relationship is a simple way of saying that the subclass and superclass share the same type. As you may recall from our discussion in Section 1.2.3, a class's type describes how you can communicate with objects of that class. Therefore, since objects of a superclass and subclass share the same type, it is possible to communicate with both of them in the exact same way. Polymorphism exploits this capability, allowing for code reuse in multiple dimensions.

1.4.3   Polymorphism

The definition of an inheritance relationship implies that a subclass is inheriting both the *type* and the *implementation* of its superclass. In the subclass, however, it is possible to *redefine* a method's implementation to further specialize certain behavior. Redefining a method does not change the interface of the method (i.e., the way it's called) in any way. Rather, it simply redefines the behavior of the method to suit the needs/requirements of the subclass.

To the runtime environment, all these class-specific object references look the same. In its eyes, the requirements for calling a particular method on a subclass instance are no different than the requirements to call the same method on the superclass. As programmers, we can take advantage of this relationship to make our designs more flexible.

To put this phenomenon into perspective, let's consider an example. Figure 1.4 depicts an Employee class hierarchy that might be used to model the types of employees managed within an HR system. In this scenario, the Employee superclass is used to describe the basic characteristics and behaviors of all types of employees. The three specialized subclasses (HourlyEmployee, CommissionEmployee, and SalariedEmployee) are extensions of the Employee superclass used to represent employees paid by the hour, employees working on commission, and salaried employees, respectively.

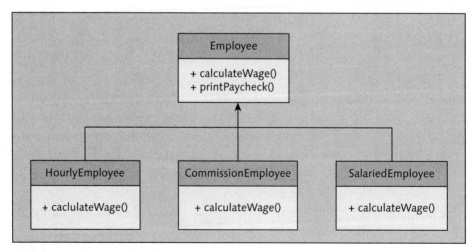

Figure 1.4 An Employee Class Hierarchy

Also, for the purposes of our example, let's assume that the calculateWage() method has been redefined in each of the subclasses to properly calculate the employee's wage based on the actual employee type.

Now, let's imagine that the company wants to use this Employee class hierarchy to enhance their accounts payable (AP) system to automate the creation of monthly paychecks. Listing 1.4 shows an example of the pseudo code for an enhancement such as this.

```
Get Employees
For Each Employee
    Call calculateWage() to calculate the employee's wages
    Call printPaycheck() to print the employee's paycheck
End For
```
Listing 1.4 Pseudocode for Generic Payroll Run Algorithm

Looking closely at the logic contained in Listing 1.4, we can see that there's no real distinction between employee types in the main loop that drives the payment run. This isn't simply a casual omission of detail in the pseudo code. Rather, we're purposefully utilizing the "is-a" relationship between Employee class types to build a generic algorithm that's able to process payments for *any* kind of Employee type. In formal terms, we're exploiting a core object-oriented language feature called *polymorphism*.

The term polymorphism can be translated from its Greek origins as *many forms*. In the example above, each subclass represents a different form (or type) of Employee. However, since the subclasses take part in an inheritance relationship with the Employee superclass, each subclass *is* an Employee. Consequently, since both the superclass and subclass share the same public interface, any method that can be called on the superclass can also be called on the subclass. Our fictitious AP system is taking advantage of this feature by defining its interface to work with generic Employee instances. At runtime, the actual object instances being processed could be of type Employee or any of its subclasses. The runtime system takes care of making sure that the proper method implementation is called behind the scenes. This is another example of how an object is smart enough to know how to do its job.

In Chapter 6, we'll look at ways of utilizing polymorphism to build more intelligent and flexible designs.

1.5   Object Management

At this point, we've hit on the 3 major pillars of OOP: encapsulation, inheritance, and polymorphism. However, before we wrap up this introductory chapter, we should briefly touch on another topic that's of similar importance: *object management*.

As we learned in Section 1.2, objects are specialized variables that are defined in terms of a class type. The class type defines a blueprint which provides the runtime environment with the information it needs to build object instances. Of course, such object instances aren't created automatically. After all, how's the runtime environment supposed to know how many object instances we might need at runtime. Because of the abstract nature of the types we're working with, it's up to us as developers to explicitly tell the runtime environment when and where we want object instances to be created.

Somewhere in between the point when we request that an object instance be created and the point where we actually get our hands on the allocated object reference, the runtime environment provides us with a mechanism for initializing the object. Here, we can define specialized callback methods called *constructors* within our classes that the runtime environment will invoke as instances of a class are being allocated. The constructor's job is to make sure that the object is initialized in a consistent state before it's used. That way, it's ready to perform its requisite tasks when called upon.

We'll investigate the details of object management from a development perspective in Chapter 4. There, we'll also learn a few tricks for improving performance and influencing the object creation process.

1.6   UML Tutorial: Class Diagram Basics

As we've seen, object-oriented software development places a considerable amount of emphasis on design. Before we start coding, it's imperative that we have all of our ducks lined up in a row. In particular, we really need to figure out what kind of objects we'll need as well as how those objects will interact with one another at runtime.

Object-Oriented Analysis and Design (OOAD) is a software development methodology used to analyze system requirements and formulate a system design from an object-oriented perspective. OOAD practitioners often use graphical modelling techniques to communicate their designs more effectively.

The *Unified Modeling Language* (UML) contains a set of graphical notations for building diagrams that depict various aspects of the system model. The UML is used extensively throughout the software development industry, so it's important that you understand how to use UML diagrams to express and interpret object-oriented designs.

Throughout the remainder of this book, we'll examine the usage types of various UML diagrams at the end of each chapter. Our discussions will be based on version 2.0 of the UML standard. We'll begin our introduction to the UML by first looking at the *class diagram*. For now, we will try to keep it simple, reinforcing the concepts covered in this introductory chapter. In Chapters 5 and 6, more advanced features of class diagrams will be considered.

> **Note**
>
> The UML standard is maintained by the *Object Management Group* (OMG). For more information on the OMG, check out their website at *http://www.uml.org*.

1.6.1   What are Class Diagrams?

Class diagrams are used to illustrate the static architecture of an object-oriented system. Here, we can depict the various classes used in the system, as well as their relationships. Figure 1.5 shows a simple class diagram that describes a scaled-down model of a sales order system used to process orders for an e-commerce website. Here, we can observe the basic class types that will make up our sales order system (i.e. the rectangular boxes), their elements, and their relationships to other classes. As simple as this may seem, it's surprising how much information one can glean just by visualizing the key players in an object-oriented design.

In the upcoming sections, we'll explore specific elements of the UML class diagram in more detail.

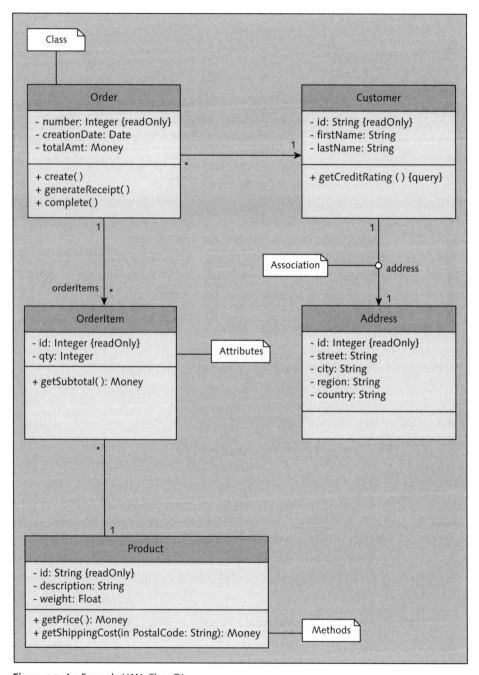

Figure 1.5 An Example UML Class Diagram

1.6.2   Classes

The diagram in Figure 1.5 contains five classes: `Order`, `OrderItem`, `Product`, `Customer`, and `Address`. As you can see, classes are represented in class diagrams as rectangular boxes partitioned into three sections (as shown in Figure 1.6):

▸ The top (shaded) section contains the class name as well as some other optional modifiers that we'll cover in Chapters 5 and 6.

▸ The optional middle section contains some of the more prominent attributes defined by the class

▸ The bottom section contains relevant operations (or methods) of the class

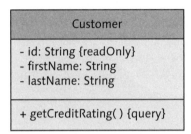

Figure 1.6 Understanding UML Class Notation

As you read through this description, did you notice how we used the terms *some, optional*, and so forth? This is because the UML class diagram notation does not require you to specify *every* element defined within a class. Instead, the goal is to really hit on the key elements that are needed to convey the point of the class. Here, too much detail really can be a bad thing since it clutters up the diagram and makes it difficult to visualize the system at a glance.

The point is to not get too carried away with the details as this can complicate the model to the point that the diagram is unreadable. Some developers new to UML fall into this trap, worrying that there isn't enough information in their class diagram to start writing code. If you find yourself in this position, remember that the UML provides a multitude of diagrams that can be used to express the various aspects of your design; class diagrams only tell one part of the story.

1.6.3   Attributes

Attributes can be specified on the class diagram using the syntax shown in Listing 1.5.

```
visibility name: type-expression = initial-value
                 {property-string}
```
Listing 1.5 Attribute Notation for a UML Class Diagram

Technically speaking, we're only required to provide the name when specifying an attribute in a class diagram. However, the other syntax elements shown in Listing 1.5 can be used to provide some additional information about the attribute:

▸ The `visibility` part of an attribute definition describes the accessibility of the attribute from an external perspective. Possible values for `visibility` include '+' for public attributes, '-' for private attributes, and '#' for protected attributes.

▸ The `type-expression` is used to describe the attribute's type. The UML defines some standard types such as *integer* or *string*, but you can also specify custom types here as well. The `type-expresssion` expression can also be used to express the cardinality of an attribute (e.g. for an internal table), and the initial value of the attribute (if one is assigned).

▸ The `property-string` expression is an optional element that can be used to describe certain additional properties for an attribute. For example, in the `OrderItem` class from Figure 1.5, the `id` attribute has the `readOnly` property assigned to indicate that an item's ID number never changes. Values for these properties can be defined at the discretion of the person designing the class diagram. The primary purpose here is to provide additional details that are helpful to the developer responsible for actually implementing the class using a specific programming language.

1.6.4   Operations

Operations can be expressed using the syntax shown in Listing 1.6.

```
visibility name(parameter-list) : return-type
                                  {property-string}
```
Listing 1.6 Operation Notation in a UML Class Diagram

For brevity's sake, developers will often just specify the name of an operation when creating a class diagram. The remaining optional syntactical elements from Listing 1.6 are typically used strategically to emphasize a certain aspect of the operation:

▶ The `visibility` of an operation defines its accessibility. Possible values include '+' for public operations, '-' for private operations, and '#' for protected operations.

▶ The `parameter-list` in parenthesis can be used to specify a comma-separated list of parameters for the operation. Each parameter is of the form `kind name : type = default-value`. Here, `kind` signifies the type of parameter. Valid values include "in" for inbound parameters passed by value, "out" for outbound parameters passed by value, and "`inout`" for inbound parameters passed by reference. The `name` token symbolizes the parameter name. Each parameter can optionally have a type associated with it using the `type` token. The type can be a generic type, or a type specific to a particular programming language. Finally, you can specify an initial value for the parameter using the `default-value` expression.

▶ The `return-type` element is used to specify the data type of values returned by functional operations.

▶ The optional `property-string` indicates certain properties assigned to an operation. An example of this would be the {query} property string assigned to the `getCreditRating()` operation of class `Customer`. Such operations are *read-only* operations that do not alter the state of the object. Applying these property strings can give hints to aid the developer in implementing the class in a particular programming language.

An example of the syntax described in Listing 1.6 is given in Listing 1.7. This example declares a public operation called `getShippingCost()` that receives a single inbound parameter called `postalCode` (which is of type String). The operation returns a value of type Money to represent the derived shipping cost.

```
+ getShippingCost(in postalCode: String) : Money
```
Listing 1.7 An Example of an Operation Definition

1.6.5   Associations

The lines drawn between classes in a class diagram represent a type of *association*. You can think of an association as another way to specify an attribute for a class.

For example, the directed line drawn between the `Customer` and `Address` classes in Figure 1.5 describes an attribute of type `Address` for class `Customer`. The arrow in the association between classes `Customer` and `Address` indicates that instances of class `Address` can be reached through an attribute defined in class `Customer`. If the association line had contained arrows pointing in both directions, then the association would have been *bidirectional*. In this case, an attribute of type `Customer` would also have been defined for class `Address`, making it possible to navigate between attributes in both directions.

The numbers affixed to each endpoint represents the cardinality of the association from the perspective of the nearby class (see Table 1.1). For example, in Figure 1.5, the association between classes `Order` and `OrderItem` denotes a *one-to-many* relationship between an order and its items. In this case, an order can contain zero or more items and any given item can exist for exactly one order.

Cardinality	Description
`0..1`	Zero or one instances of a class
`1`	Exactly one instance of a class
`*`	Zero or more instances of a class
`m..n`	A range of instances with lower / upper bounds (e.g. 2..4)

Table 1.1 UML Cardinality Notation

At this point, you might be wondering why you would need to build an association when you could just use a simple attribute instead. Generally speaking, there is no hard-and-fast rule for using one approach instead of the other. However, a good rule of thumb is to use an association whenever you are using composition to reuse a class inside of another class. This illustrates the composition relationship more clearly, and makes it easier to rework the diagram as you experiment with your class model.

1.6.6 Notes

We can add comments to our UML diagrams using notes. Notes are represented using an element that resembles a sticky note that has been dog-eared in the top right-hand corner (see Figure 1.7). These notes can be used in any kind of UML diagram to include comments related to a particular element (linked via a dashed line) or to the diagram as a whole. Notes are often used to help clarify a certain requirement that's too difficult to express using standard UML notation.

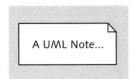

Figure 1.7 UML Note Notation

1.7 Summary

In this chapter, we learned that a class is a type of blueprint that describes how to create object instances. Classes combine attributes and methods together to model real-world phenomena in a software setting. Rules and constraints for these models are enforced using visibility sections which control how attributes and methods within the class are accessed. We also considered some of the basic reuse capabilities associated with classes.

This chapter covered a lot of ground very quickly. So if you are finding yourself a little lost, don't worry, we'll have much more to say about each of these topics in the coming chapters. This begins in Chapter 2 where we'll start to unpack the ABAP Objects syntax used to define and interact with classes/objects.

This chapter introduces you to some basic ABAP Objects syntax and the relevant development tools that you'll need to start building object-oriented programs in ABAP.

2 Getting Started with Objects

Object-oriented programming, like many abstract concepts, is perhaps best learned by example. Therefore, now that we've gotten some of the basic definitions out of the way in Chapter 1, we're ready to turn our attention towards more practical matters and begin looking at some basic syntax and sample code using ABAP Objects.

Because the primary unit of development for object-oriented programs is the class, we'll spend quite a bit of time in this chapter exploring the syntax used to define classes and their internal components. Then, once we come up to speed with basic syntax rules, we'll take a look at the tools used to define and maintain classes. Finally, we'll wrap up our discussion by exploring some new syntax features introduced with Release 7.40 of AS ABAP.

2.1 Defining Classes

Classes in ABAP Objects are declared using the CLASS statement block. This statement block is a wrapper of sorts, grouping all relevant class component declarations into two distinct sections:

- **Declaration Section**
  This section is used to specify all of the components defined within the class including attributes, methods, and events.

- **Implementation Section**
  This section is used to provide implementations (i.e. the source code) for the methods defined within the declaration section.

In the following subsections, we'll unpack the syntax used to build out these sections and fully specify our class types. For the purposes of this introductory section, our focus will be on defining *local classes* (i.e. classes that are defined within ABAP report programs, function group includes, and so on). However, in Section 2.4, we'll learn that this same syntax applies to the definition of global class types as well. The primary difference in the case of global classes is that we have a form-based editor in the Class Builder tool which spares us from typing out some of the declaration syntax longhand.

2.1.1 Creating a Class

To define a new class type, we must declare it within a CLASS...DEFINI-TION...ENDCLASS statement block as shown in Listing 2.1. This statement block makes up the aforementioned declaration section of the ABAP class definition. As we noted earlier, this section is used to declare the primary components that make up a class, such as attributes, methods, etc.

```
CLASS {class_name} DEFINITION [class_options].
   PUBLIC SECTION.
     [components]
   PROTECTED SECTION.
     [components]
   PRIVATE SECTION.
     [components]
ENDCLASS.
```
Listing 2.1 ABAP Class Declaration Section Syntax

Looking closely at Listing 2.1, we can see that the components of a class definition are organized into three distinct *visibility sections*: the PUBLIC SECTION, the PROTECTED SECTION, and the PRIVATE SECTION. Each of these visibility sections is optional, so it's up to us as developers to determine which components go where—a subject that we'll consider at length in Chapter 3.

Naming Conventions

Besides the definition of the components that makeup the class's interface, the next most important task in defining a class is coming up with a good and meaningful name for it. As trivial as it may sound, this task is often harder than it looks. Part of the challenge stems from the fact that ABAP only gives us 30 characters to work with. From here, we must come up with a meaningful name that fits within the confines of the syntax shown in Listing 2.2.

```
[{Namespace}|{Prefix}]CL_{Meaningful_Name}
```
Listing 2.2 ABAP Class Naming Convention

Listing 2.3 shows how this class naming syntax is applied to the various class types that may exist within an ABAP Repository. We'll see many more examples of this naming convention at work as we progress through the book.

```
LCL_LOCAL_CLASS        "Local Customer Class
ZCL_GLOBAL_CLASS       "Global Customer Class
CL_ABAP_MATCHER        "SAP-Standard Class (no namespace)
/BOWDK/CL_STRING_UTILS "3rd-Party Class w/Namespace Prefix
```
Listing 2.3 Class Naming Examples

2.1.2 Component Declarations

As we've seen, the structure and makeup of a class is determined by its component definitions. Therefore, in this section, we'll spend some time learning about the different component types that we can define within a class. Before we get started though, we first need to understand how components are grouped from a scoping perspective. Within a class declaration, we can distinguish between two different types of components:

▶ **Instance Components**
Instance components, as the name suggests, are components that define the state and behavior of individual object instances. For example, an Employee class might have an instance attribute called id that uniquely identifies an employee within a company. Each instance of class Employee maintains its own copy of the id attribute, which has a distinct value. Instance methods operate on these instance attributes to manipulate the object's state and perform instance-specific tasks.

▶ **Class Components**
Class components on the other hand are defined at the class level. This is to say that class components are shared across *all* object instances. Such components can come in handy in situations where we want to share data or expose utility functions on a wider scale. For example, in our Employee class scenario, we might use a class attribute called next_id to keep track of the next available employee ID number. This value could be used as a primitive number range object to assign the id instance attribute for newly-created Employee objects.

In practice, most of the classes we define will contain few class components. After all, it's hard to establish identity at the object level if all the data/functionality resides in global class components. However, in some situations, we'll see that class components can really come in handy when dealing with complex object creation scenarios, finding a home for utility functions, and so forth.

> **Static Components**
>
> Class components are sometimes referred to as *static components* since they are statically defined and maintained at the class level. This is especially the case in other OO languages such as Java or C#.

> **Internal Namespaces**
>
> Regardless of where we decide to define our components, it's important to bear in mind that all component names within an ABAP Objects class belong to the same internal namespace. This means that, for example, it's not possible to define an attribute and a method using the same name – even if they belong to different visibility sections. In the sections that follow, we'll learn that the adoption of good naming conventions makes it easy to avoid such naming collisions.

Attributes

As we learned in Chapter 1, attributes are basically just variables that are defined internally within a class/object. From a definition standpoint, attributes are essentially defined in the same way that variables are defined in other ABAP programming modules. The primary difference in the case of classes is that we have some different contexts to contend with.

To put these contexts into perspective, consider the LCL_CUSTOMER sample class contained in Listing 2.4. Within this class definition, we've defined three different types of attributes:

- ▶ **Instance Attributes**
  To define the properties that are unique to a particular customer instance, we've created several instance attributes such as mv_id, mv_customer_type, mv_name, and ms_address. As you can see in Listing 2.4, these instance attributes are defined using the familiar DATA keyword. Here, we can choose from any valid ABAP data type including structure types, table types, reference types, or even other class types.

- ▶ **Class Attributes**
  The sv_next_id attribute is an example of a class attribute. As you can see, the

only real difference syntax-wise between class attributes and instance attributes is the use of the CLASS-DATA keyword in lieu of the typical DATA keyword.

▶ **Constants**

In the PUBLIC SECTION of our customer class, we've also defined several constants to represent the different customer types modelled in our class: CO_PERSON_TYPE for individuals, CO_ORG_TYPE for organizations, and CO_GROUP_TYPE for customer groups. These constants are defined just like any other constant using the CONSTANTS keyword. However, in the case of class constants, what we're really talking about is a specialized case of a class/static attribute (one that can't be modified at runtime).

```
CLASS lcl_customer DEFINITION.
  PUBLIC SECTION.
    CONSTANTS: CO_PERSON_TYPE TYPE c VALUE '1',
               CO_ORG_TYPE    TYPE c VALUE '2',
               CO_GROUP_TYPE  TYPE c VALUE '3'.
  PRIVATE SECTION.
    DATA: mv_id TYPE i,
          mv_customer_type TYPE c,
          mv_name TYPE string,
          ms_address TYPE adrc.
    CLASS-DATA: sv_next_id TYPE i.
ENDCLASS.
```

Listing 2.4 Declaring Attributes Within a Class

Though the ABAP compiler will generally allow you to define attributes with whatever name you prefer, we strongly recommend that you adopt a naming convention which makes it easier to identify the scope of a given attribute. Table 2.1 describes the naming convention that will be used within this book.

Attribute Type	Naming Convention	Description
Instance Attributes	M{Type}_{Meaningful_Name} Examples: mv_id ms_address mt_contacts	Here, the 'M' implies that we're defining a *member variable*. The {Type} designator helps us more easily determine whether or not we're dealing with elementary variables (V), structures (S), internal tables (T), and so on. Aside from these scoping details, the rest of the instance attribute name is freeform and should be defined in such a way that it conveys meaning.

Table 2.1 Naming Convention for Defining Attributes

Attribute Type	Naming Convention	Description
Class (Static) Attributes	S{Type}_{Meaningful_Name} Examples: sv_next_id	This convention is almost identical to instance attributes. However instead of the 'M' for member variable, static attributes are prefixed with an 'S' to imply that the attribute belongs to the static context.
Constants	CO_{MEANINGFUL_NAME}	Constants are typically defined in all caps using the 'CO_' prefix.

Table 2.1 Naming Convention for Defining Attributes

Methods

Methods are defined using either the METHODS statement for instance methods or the CLASS-METHODS statement for class methods. The syntax for both statement types is given in the syntax diagram contained in Listing 2.5. Here, we can see that a method definition consists of a method name, an optional parameter list, and an optional set of exceptions that might occur. For the purpose of this introductory section, we'll focus on the first two parts of a method definition. We'll have an opportunity to circle back and cover exceptions in Chapter 8.

```
{CLASS-}METHODS {method_name}
    [IMPORTING parameters]
    [EXPORTING parameters]
    [CHANGING  parameters]
    [RETURNING VALUE(parameter)]
    [{RAISING}|{EXCEPTIONS}...].
```
Listing 2.5 Method Definition Syntax

As you can see in Listing 2.5, the first thing we specify in a method definition is the method's name. Since methods define the behavior of classes, it's important that we come up with meaningful names that intuitively describe the method's purpose. Normally, it makes sense to prefix a method name with a strong action verb that describes the type of operation being performed. The sample class contained in Listing 2.6 provides some examples of this convention.

```
CLASS lcl_date DEFINITION.
  PUBLIC SECTION.
    METHODS:
      add IMPORTING iv_days TYPE i,
```

```
      subtract IMPORTING iv_days TYPE i,
      get_day_of_week RETURNING VALUE(rv_day) TYPE string,
      ...
ENDCLASS.
```
Listing 2.6 Defining Meaningful Names for Methods

After we come up with meaningful names for our methods, our next objective is to determine what sort of parameters (if any) the methods will need to perform their tasks. Looking at the syntax diagram from Listing 2.5, we can see that there are four different types of parameters that can be defined within a method's parameter list. Table 2.2 describes each of these parameter types in detail.

Parameter Type	Description
Importing	Importing parameters define the input parameters for a method. The values of an importing parameter cannot be modified inside the method implementation.
Exporting	Exporting parameters represent the output parameters a method.
Changing	Changing parameters are input/output parameters that allow us to update or modify data within a method.
Returning	Returning parameters are used to define *functional methods*. We'll learn more about this parameter type when we look at functional methods in Section 2.2.7.

Table 2.2 Parameter Types for Method Definitions

To distinguish between the various parameter types within a method definition, method parameters are normally prefixed according to the convention described in Table 2.3. Here, the {Type} designator is once again used to differentiate between elementary data types (V), structure types (S), table types (T) and so on.

Parameter Type	Naming Convention
Importing	I{Type}_{Parameter_Name}
Exporting	E{Type}_{Parameter_Name}
Changing	C{Type}_{Parameter_Name}
Returning	R{Type}_{Parameter_Name}

Table 2.3 Method Parameter Naming Conventions

Regardless of the parameter's type, the syntax for declaring a parameter `pl` is given by the syntax diagram contained in Listing 2.7. As you can see, this syntax provides us with a number of configuration options for defining a parameter:

▸ The optional `VALUE` addition allows us to specify that a parameter will be passed by *value* instead of by reference. For more details on this concept, check out the sidebar entitled *Pass-by-Value vs. Pass-by-Reference*.

▸ The `TYPE` addition is used to specify the parameter's data type. The addition is used in this context in the exact same way it's used to define normal variables or form parameters.

▸ The `OPTIONAL` addition can be used to mark a parameter as *optional*. Such parameters can be omitted during method calls on the consumer side.

▸ The `DEFAULT` addition can be used to specify a default value for a given parameter (which makes the parameter optional from a consumer perspective). This value can be overridden by the caller of the method as desired.

```
{ pl | VALUE(pl)} TYPE type [OPTIONAL | {DEFAULT def1}]
```
Listing 2.7 Formal Parameter Declaration Syntax

Pass-by-Value vs. Pass-by-Reference

At runtime, whenever a method that contains parameters is invoked, the calling program will pass parameters by matching up *actual parameters* (e.g. local variables in the calling program, literal values, etc.) in the method call with the *formal parameters* declared in the method signature (see Figure 2.1). Here, parameters are passed in one of two ways: *by reference* (default behavior) or *by value*.

Pass-by-value semantics is enabled via the aforementioned `VALUE` addition. Performance-wise, pass-by-value implies that a *copy* of an actual parameter is created and passed to the method for consumption. As a result, changes made to value parameters inside the method only affect the copy; the contents of the variable used as the actual parameter are not disturbed in any way. This behavior is illustrated at the top of Figure 2.1 with the mapping of parameter a. Here, whenever the method is invoked, a copy of variable x is made and assigned to parameter a. As you might expect, this kind of operation can become rather expensive when dealing with large data objects.

Reference parameters on the other hand contain a reference (or *pointer*) to the actual parameter used in the method call. Therefore, changes made to reference parameters *are* reflected in the calling program. In Figure 2.1, this is illustrated in the mapping of parameter b. Here, if we were to change the value of parameter b inside the method, the change would be reflected in variable y in the calling program.

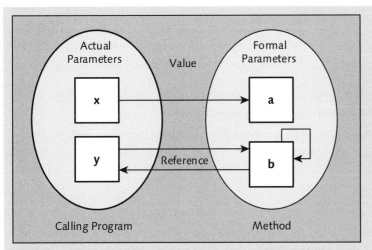

Figure 2.1 Mapping Actual Parameters to Formal Parameters

Since this behavior can potentially cause dangerous side-effects, ABAP allows us to lock down reference parameters for editing inside methods by defining them as importing parameters. So, if we were to define parameter b as an importing parameter, the compiler would complain if we were to try to modify its contents within the method body. In effect, importing parameters allow us to attain all the performance benefits of reference passing without the dangerous side-effects.

Collectively, a method's name and parameter list make up the method's *signature*. From the perspective of class consumers, method signatures determine the exact requirements for calling a particular method: which parameters to pass, the data types of the parameters being exchanged, and so on. As method designers, it's important that we get these details right so that our methods are intuitive and easy to use. To that end, here are some design points to consider when defining method signatures:

▸ In general, we should try to keep the number of parameters being passed to/ from methods to the bare minimum. Here, we should assume that an object already has most of the information it needs (via its instance attributes) to perform a particular task, so only a handful of parameters should ever be required when defining a method.

▸ Methods should be defined to perform one task. Therefore, we should avoid defining methods such as copyDataAndWashCat().

▶ When performing generic operations where specific data types don't matter, it's a good idea to incorporate the use of generic ABAP types so that the methods can be (re)used in a variety of contexts. For a list of available generic types, search on the term *Generic ABAP Types* in the ABAP Keyword Documentation.

Events

Besides the more common attributes and methods that you see in most OO languages, ABAP Objects also allows us to define events that model certain types of occurrences within an object's lifecycle. Here, once again, we can distinguish between instance events that occur within a specific object instance and class events that are defined at the class level.

Listing 2.8 contains the basic syntax used to define instance events and class events. The parameters defined for an event are used to pass additional information about the event to interested event handler methods. Since this is a one-way data exchange, we're only allowed to defined exporting parameters in an event definition. Here, the syntax is pretty much identical to the syntax used to define exporting parameters in methods. The only twist in this case is that event parameters must be passed by value. Aside from the formally defined exporting parameters in an event definition, the system also supplies an implicit parameter called `sender` that contains a reference to the sending object (i.e. the object that raised the event).

```
EVENTS evt [EXPORTING parameters].
CLASS-EVENTS evt [EXPORTING parameters].
```
Listing 2.8 Event Declaration Syntax

Types

Custom data types can be defined within a class using the ABAP `TYPES` statement. These types are defined at the class level, and are therefore not specific to any object instance. We can use these custom types to define local variables within methods, method parameter types, etc. It's also possible to declare the use of global type pools defined within the ABAP Dictionary using the `TYPE-POOLS` statement.

The definition of class `LCL_PERSON` in Listing 2.9 provides an example that demonstrates how types can be declared and used in a class definition. Here, we've defined a custom structure type called `TY_NAME` that's being used to define the person's `ms_name` attribute. The use of the `TY_` prefix in this case is by convention: class-defined types are normally defined using the naming convention `TY_{Type_Name}`.

```
CLASS lcl_person DEFINITION.
   PRIVATE SECTION.
      TYPES: BEGIN OF ty_name,
                first_name TYPE char40,
                middle_initial TYPE char1,
                last_name TYPE char40,
             END OF ty_name.
      TYPE-POOLS: szadr.    "Business Address Services

      DATA: ms_name    TYPE ty_name,
            ms_address TYPE szadr_addr1_complete.
ENDCLASS.
```
Listing 2.9 Defining and Working with Class-Level Types

Looking closely at Listing 2.9, we can also see how type groups from the ABAP Dictionary are declared using the `TYPE-POOLS` statement. In this case, the class has declared the use of the `SZADR` type group from the SAP *Business Address Services* package. Once this declaration is in place, we can use types such as the `SZADR_ADDR1_COMPLETE` type in attribute definitions, method signatures, etc.

2.1.3   Implementing Methods

Anytime we define methods within the declaration section of a class, we need to follow up and provide implementations for them in the implementation section. Such implementations are provided using `METHOD...ENDMETHOD` statement blocks that are nested inside of a `CLASS...IMPLEMENTATION...ENDCLASS` statement block as shown in Listing 2.10.

```
CLASS lcl_date DEFINITION.
   ...
ENDCLASS.

CLASS lcl_date IMPLEMENTATION.
   METHOD add.
     mv_date = mv_date + iv_days.
   ENDMETHOD.

   METHOD subtract.
     mv_date = mv_date - iv_days.
   ENDMETHOD.
```

```
METHOD get_day_of_week.
  "Implementation goes here..
ENDMETHOD.
ENDCLASS.
```
Listing 2.10 Providing Implementations for Methods

As you can see in Listing 2.10, method implementations allow us to jump right into the code. Here, there's no need to provide any further details about the method context since we've already defined its signature in the declaration section. Within the method processing block, we can implement the behavior of the class using regular ABAP statements in much the same way that we would implement subroutines and function modules from the procedural world. We'll see many examples of this in the sections to follow.

Syntax Restrictions

If you're coming to ABAP Objects from a procedural background, we should point out that there are a handful of ABAP language constructs that have been rendered obsolete/deprecated from within the OO context. These changes came about as part of a language cleanup effort whenever SAP first introduced object-oriented extensions to ABAP. Here, SAP saw a golden opportunity to do some internal housekeeping and ensure that deprecated language elements didn't make their way into new ABAP Objects classes.

For the most part, developers following current best practices shouldn't notice any of these statements as their use is generally frowned upon in any context. Still, if you're not sure which statements have become deprecated over the years, don't worry; the compiler will tell you if you get it wrong. For a thorough treatment of best practices though, we highly recommend that you pick up a copy of *Official ABAP Programming Guidelines* (SAP PRESS, 2009). The SAP Help Library also maintains a complete listing of invalided language constructs.

Variable Scoping Rules

Before we wrap up our discussion on method implementations, we should briefly take a moment to talk about variable scoping rules in an OO context. Unlike procedural contexts where the context is pretty cut-and-dry between global variables and local variables, method implementations can actually get their hands on variables at several different scoping levels:

▶ Class attributes which essentially behave like global variables

▶ Local variables whose scope is limited to the method that defines them

▶ Instance variables that sit somewhere in the middle, defining the state of a given object instance

With these additional options in play, it's a good idea to be careful in qualifying the variables so that their usage is clear. Not only does this make the code more readable, it also prevents us from accidentally *hiding* instance or class attributes behind method-local variables with the same name. As you can expect, the hiding of instance or class attributes within a method can have some unexpected and nasty side-effects. Fortunately, as long as you stick to the naming conventions outlined in Section 2.1.2, this shouldn't ever become a concern.

2.2   Working with Objects

Now that you have a feel for how classes are defined in ABAP Objects, let's take a look at how these classes can be utilized from a consumer standpoint. In the sections that follow, we'll learn how to define object reference variables, create new object instances, and put them to work in ABAP programs.

2.2.1   Object References

Before we can begin creating new object instances, we first need to define variables to hold onto these objects so that we can address them within our programs. For reasons that will be explained in Chapter 4, the ABAP runtime environment does not allow us to have direct access to an object within our programs. Instead, we are given indirect access to allocated objects via a special kind of variable called an *object reference variable*.

Listing 2.11 demonstrates the syntax used to define an object reference variable. Here, notice the use of the TYPE REF TO addition to indicate that lo_date is a reference variable. When reading this statement, we would say that lo_date is an object reference variable that can point to objects of (class) type LCL_DATE.

```
DATA lo_date TYPE REF TO lcl_date.
```
Listing 2.11 Syntax to Define an Object Reference Variable

We can use this type of syntax to define object reference variables as instance attributes, local variables within method implementations, local variables within form routines, or even as global variables.

2.2.2 Creating Objects

Once we define the appropriate object reference variable(s), we can begin creating object instances using the CREATE OBJECT statement shown in Listing 2.12. Functionally, this statement is processed behind the scenes as follows:

1. First, the ABAP runtime environment dynamically creates a new object of type LCL_DATE.

2. Then, after the object instance is created, control is handed off to a special method called a *constructor* which provides us with the ability to initialize the object instance before it is used. We'll learn more about constructor methods in Chapter 4.

3. Finally, once the object instance is initialized, the ABAP runtime environment fills in the lo_date variable with a reference that points to the newly-created object.

```
DATA lo_date TYPE REF TO lcl_date.
CREATE OBJECT lo_date.
```
Listing 2.12 Instantiating an Object at Runtime

From a syntax perspective, that's all there is to instantiating objects. Anytime we want a new object reference, we simply use the CREATE OBJECT statement to allocate one on the fly. Of course, if we're not careful in maintaining our object reference variables, these objects can become orphaned. With that in mind, the next section focuses on the important topic of object reference assignments.

2.2.3 Object Reference Assignments

Since object reference variables are basically just a special kind of variable, they can be used in assignment statements using the familiar equals (=) operator. Of course, when assigning object reference variables, it's important to remember *what* we're assigning. To put this concept into perspective, consider the assignment scenario contained in Listing 2.13.

```
DATA lo_date1 TYPE REF TO lcl_date.
DATA lo_date2 TYPE REF TO lcl_date.

CREATE OBJECT lo_date1.
CREATE OBJECT lo_date2.

lo_date1 = lo_date2.
```
Listing 2.13 Understanding Object Reference Assignments

Within the code excerpt contained in Listing 2.13, we have two object reference variables called `lo_date1` and `lo_date2` that point to newly-created `LCL_DATE` objects. Prior to the assignment statement at the bottom of the code excerpt, the variable assignments resemble what is being depicted in Figure 2.2. Here, notice that the objects themselves are not stored within the object reference variables. Instead, the object reference variables simply contain an address for where the object exists in memory.

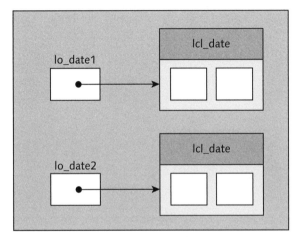

Figure 2.2 Understanding Object-Reference Assignments (Part 1)

The diagram contained in Figure 2.3 illustrates what things look like *after* the object reference assignment is performed at the bottom of Listing 2.13. Here, we can see that the assignment statement has copied the address of the `LCL_DATE` object instance pointed to by the `lo_date2` object reference into `lo_date1`. Now, both `lo_date1` and `lo_date2` point to the same object instance (i.e. the instance at the bottom of Figure 2.3).

Looking closely at the before and after memory snapshots contained in Figure 2.2 and Figure 2.3, we can draw several important conclusions about object reference assignments:

1. First of all, it should be fairly clear that object reference assignments only copy the *addresses* of objects, and not the objects themselves. This implies that object reference assignments are relatively inexpensive from a performance standpoint.

2. Secondly, any time we have two or more object reference variables that point to the same object instance, changes made to the object via one object refer-

ence variable will be reflected in the other object reference variables. This should come as no surprise since the object reference variables all point to the same object instance.

3. Finally, if an object instance is no longer pointed to by any live object reference variables, the object instance becomes *orphaned* and no longer accessible from a programming context. In Chapter 4, we'll see how a special service of the ABAP runtime environment called the *garbage collector* cleans up these orphaned objects to re-coup unused memory.

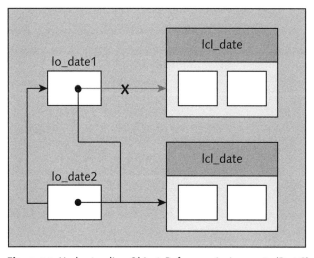

Figure 2.3 Understanding Object-Reference Assignments (Part 2)

With time and a little bit of practice, these concepts should become second nature to you. In the meantime though, we would recommend taking a methodical approach to creating object instances and performing object reference assignments. For example, consider the code excerpt contained in Listing 2.14. Here, the intent was to create 10 date objects but, since there's only one object reference variable, the first 9 date objects are created and then subsequently orphaned.

```
DATA lo_date TYPE REF TO lcl_date.
DO 10 TIMES.
  CREATE OBJECT lo_date.
ENDDO.
```

Listing 2.14 An Invalid Idiom for Creating a Collection of Objects

Listing 2.15 corrects the error from Listing 2.14 by introducing an internal table of object references. Now, each new date object that's gets created is stored in a separate object reference variable within the table. As obvious as this may seem, these are the types of issues that can occur if we aren't careful with our object handling.

```
DATA lt_dates TYPE STANDARD TABLE OF REF TO lcl_date.
FIELD-SYMBOLS <lo_date> LIKE LINE OF lt_dates.

DO 10 TIMES.
  APPEND INITIAL LINE TO lt_dates ASSIGNING <lo_date>.
  CREATE OBJECT <lo_date>.
ENDDO.
```

Listing 2.15 Defining a Collection Objects

Thinking (Object)ively

For many ABAP developers, the notion of reference variables is a foreign concept. So, if you happen to find yourself getting tripped up by all this indirection, perhaps an analogy will help. Here, consider the relationship between a remote control and a TV set.

As you know, remote controls are small, lightweight devices that make it easy for us control a TV set. As long as we have our remote control, we can turn on the TV, change the channel, and control the volume as desired. However, if we were to lose the remote, then we'd no longer be able to access the TV (at least, not without getting off the couch). To guard against such occurrences, we could buy a universal remote to provide us with a backup. That way, we could program the universal remote to point to the TV's remote frequency. Once the universal remote is programmed, we would be able to control the TV using either remote since they both effectively point to the same TV.

Relating this back to our object reference discussion, we can see that object reference variables are rather like remote controls. As long as an object reference variable points to a particular object instance, we can use the object reference to control the object it points to. However, if we reassign the object reference or clear it out using the ABAP CLEAR statement, then we can no longer use it to access the object instance. This doesn't mean the object is deleted any more than a TV would simultaneously explode if a remote control is lost. What it does mean though is that we may no longer be able to access the object if we don't have another object reference variable on hand that happens to point to that object. This is the OO equivalent of losing all the remotes in the couch cushions.

At the end of the day, the moral of the story here is to treat object references with care and make sure that you're really done with an object before blowing away its object reference variables.

2.2.4 Accessing Instance Components

As we learned in the previous sections, object reference variables provide us with a handle for addressing object instances. Using this handle, we can access the instance components of an object by building compound expressions using the object component selector operator (->) as shown in Listing 2.16. Here, we can see that the object component selector allows us to specify which instance component we want to access within a given object instance.

```
oref->attribute
oref->method()
CALL METHOD oref->method( )
```

Listing 2.16 Working with the Object Component Selector (Part 1)

What's the Proper Syntax for Calling a Method?

As you can see in Listing 2.16, there are actually two different ways to call methods. These days, the direct oref->method() option is generally the preferred option as it more closely resembles syntax used in other OO languages. The CALL METHOD statement is still valid of course, but should be avoided as a rule. In Section 2.2.7 and Section 2.2.8, we'll see some reasons why it's a good idea to get into the habit of calling methods directly.

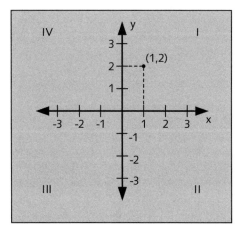

Figure 2.4 Modeling a Point Object in the Cartesian Coordinate System

To demonstrate the use of the object component selector operator, let's take a look at an example. Imagine that we're modeling a 2D graphics system and want to create an object to represent points in the Cartesian coordinate system. If you've slept since your last high school geometry class, a Cartesian coordinate system (or plane) is a two-dimensional grid that contains a horizontal x-axis and vertical y-axis (see Figure 2.4). To plot points on the graph, all we have to do is specify an x-coordinate and a y-coordinate. This is demonstrated in Figure 2.4 where we've plotted a point at (1,2).

To model our point object, we'll create a new class called LCL_POINT as shown in Listing 2.17. This class contains three instance components: two instance attributes called mv_x and mv_y to represent the x and y coordinates, respectively, and an instance method called get_distance() that can be used to calculate the Euclidian distance between the current point and some other point within the plane.

```
CLASS lcl_point DEFINITION.
    PUBLIC SECTION.
        DATA: mv_x TYPE p DECIMALS 2    "X-Coordinate
              mv_y TYPE p DECIMALS 2.   "Y-Coordinate

        METHODS get_distance IMPORTING io_point2
                                       TYPE REF TO lcl_point
                             RETURNING VALUE(rv_distance) TYPE f.
ENDCLASS.

CLASS lcl_point IMPLEMENTATION.
    METHOD get_distance.
        DATA: lv_dx TYPE f,         "Diff. X
              lv_dy TYPE f.         "Diff. Y

        "Calculate the Euclidean distance between the points:
        lv_dx = io_point2->mv_x - me->mv_x.
        lv_dy = io_point2->mv_y - me->mv_y.

        rv_distance =
            sqrt( ( lv_dx * lv_dx ) + ( lv_dy * lv_dy ) ).
    ENDMETHOD.
ENDCLASS.
```
Listing 2.17 Working with the Object Component Selector (Part 2)

Looking closely at the implementation of the get_distance() method, we can see that the object component selector is used to access the instance attributes of two different objects: the io_point2 object passed to the method and the current point object. In the latter case, we're referring to the current point object's instance attributes using the me self-reference variable described in the sidebar below.

The me self-reference variable is a special instance attribute that's implicitly defined by the ABAP runtime environment whenever an object instance is created. As its name implies, the me reference variable points back to its containing object. If you've worked with other object-oriented languages such as Java, you can think of the me reference variable as being equivalent to the this self-reference variable.

From a usage perspective, the me self-reference variable can be used just like any other object reference variable. For example, in Listing 2.17 we used me to access the mv_x and mv_y instance attributes of the LCL_POINT class. Technically speaking, we didn't have to use me to access these attributes. Instead, we could have simply referenced the attributes directly and the system would have quietly resolved the reference behind the scenes. The advantage of qualifying these references directly is that we make our intentions clear to the reader.

Another place where the me reference variable is used is in situations where we want to pass the current object instance as a parameter to another method. In this case, me provides us with a convenient mechanism for accessing the current object directly within a method implementation.

The code excerpt contained in Listing 2.18 demonstrates how to use the object component selector is used to access attributes and methods from outside of a class. Here, we're using the selector to:

▶ Initialize the instance attributes of a pair of point objects (lo_point_a and lo_point_b, respectively).

▶ Invoke the get_distance() method to calculate the distance between the two points.

```
DATA: lo_point_a  TYPE REF TO lcl_point,
      lo_point_b  TYPE REF TO lcl_point,
      lv_distance TYPE f.

"Instantiate both of the point objects:
CREATE OBJECT lo_point_a.
lo_point_a->mv_x = 1.
lo_point_a->mv_y = 1.

CREATE OBJECT lo_point_b.
lo_point_b->mv_x = 3.
lo_point_b->mv_y = 3.

"Calculate the distance & display the results:
lv_distance = lo_point_a->get_distance( lo_point_b ).
```

```
WRITE: 'Distance between point a and point b is: ',
       lv_distance.
```
Listing 2.18 Working with the Object Component Selector (Part 3)

2.2.5   Accessing Class Components

To demonstrate how to access class components, let's enhance the LCL_POINT class we developed in the previous section to incorporate a couple of class components. Here, we'll introduce a new class method called create_from_polar() that can be used to create point objects using polar coordinates. To drive the conversion routine, we've also created a constant called CO_PI to represent the value of pi.

```
CLASS lcl_point DEFINITION.
  PUBLIC SECTION.
    CONSTANTS CO_PI TYPE f VALUE '3.14159265'.

    CLASS-METHODS:
      create_from_polar IMPORTING iv_r TYPE f
                                  iv_theta TYPE p
                        RETURNING VALUE(ro_point)
                                  TYPE REF TO lcl_point.
    ...
ENDCLASS.

CLASS lcl_point IMPLEMENTATION.
  METHOD create_from_polar.
    "Convert the angle measure to radians:
    DATA lv_theta_rad TYPE f.
    lv_theta_rad = ( iv_theta * CO_PI ) / 180.

    "Create a new point object and calculate the
    "X & Y coordinates:
    CREATE OBJECT ro_point.

    ro_point->mv_x = iv_r * cos( lv_theta_rad ).
    ro_point->mv_y = iv_r * sin( lv_theta_rad ).
  ENDMETHOD.
  ...
ENDCLASS.
```
Listing 2.19 Defining Class Components

Since our new create_from_polar() method is defined at the class level, we don't require an object reference to access it. Instead, we can access it via the static/class context using the class component selector operator (=>) as shown in Listing 2.20. Here, you can see how we're also accessing the CO_PI constant using the same kind of syntax: {class_name}=>{class_component}.

```
DATA lo_point TYPE REF TO lcl_point.
DATA lv_message TYPE string.

lo_point = lcl_point=>create_from_polar( iv_r = '3.6'
                                         iv_theta = '56.31' ).
lv_message =
   |Coordinates: ({ lo_point->mv_x }, { lo_point->mv_y })|.
WRITE: / lv_message.
lv_message = |PI is { lcl_point=>CO_PI }|.
WRITE: / lv_message.
```
Listing 2.20 Working with the Class Component Selector

Looking back at Listing 2.19, you'll notice that we didn't qualify the use of the CO_PI constant within the create_from_polar() method. Within the class itself, such qualifications are optional since the class context is implicitly known. Whether or not you choose to formally qualify such references is strictly a matter of preference.

2.2.6 Working with Events

For developers coming into ABAP Objects with a background in other OO languages such as Java or C#, the concept of events as first-class citizens of class definitions may seem a bit foreign. However, once you see how events work, it's pretty easy to see how they relate to common object synchronization patterns employed in those environments (e.g. the observer pattern, for instance).

From a conceptual perspective, events are a special kind of component that can be used to model important milestones that might occur during an object's lifecycle. Such milestones could be unique to a particular object instance (instance events) or to the class itself (class events). In either case, whenever a particular milestone is reached, we can highlight the occurrence by *raising* an event. Interested parties (i.e. other objects) can listen for these events by registering themselves as *event handlers*. This allows the objects to be notified of the event automatically by the ABAP runtime environment.

This exchange is illustrated by the diagram contained in Figure 2.5. Here, we have a class called LCL_PUBLISHER that defines an instance event called MESSAGE_

ADDED. This event is triggered whenever the publisher receives a new message via its add_message() instance method. On the other end of the exchange, we have another class called LCL_SUBSCRIBER that has registered itself as a *listener* for the MESSAGE_ADDED event. Now, whenever a new message arrives at the publisher, instances of LCL_SUBSCRIBER will be notified via the on_message() event handler method.

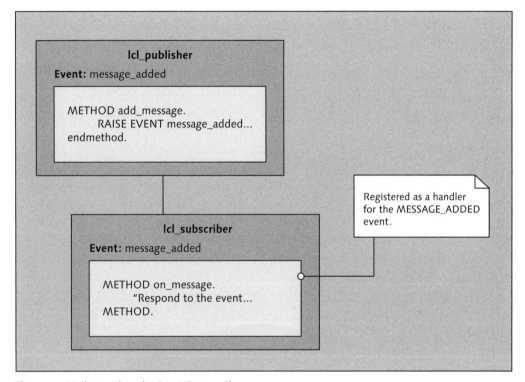

Figure 2.5 Understanding the Event Process Flow

Event-Related Syntax

Looking at the event process flow at Figure 2.5, you might be wondering how the on_message() method was fired in response to the MESSAGE_ADDED event. Unlike the methods we've seen thus far, the on_message() method is defined as an *event handler method*. As you might expect, event handler methods are specialized methods which register themselves as listeners for particular types of events. You can define event handler methods within the same class that declared the event or in a completely separate class.

To declare event handler methods, we must once again enlist the aid of the METH-ODS statement as shown in Listing 2.21. Here, the FOR EVENT...OF CLASS addition links the method with the corresponding event it's defined to handle. As you would expect, the importing parameter list must match up with the exporting parameter list defined by the event it's listening for.

```
METHODS {method_name}
   FOR EVENT {event} of CLASS {class_name}
   [IMPORTING p1 p2 ... [sender]].
```
Listing 2.21 Declaring Event Handler Methods

Once an event handler method is defined, we can register it to listen for events using the SET HANDLER statement whose syntax is shown in Listing 2.22. Here, the handler tokens refer to event handler methods (without quotes) that are defined within the class from which the SET HANDLER statement emanates. The remaining additions are defined as follows:

▶ When registering event handler methods for instance events, we have a couple of options for identifying the scope of the event binding:

   ▶ The optional FOR oref addition is used to bind an event handler method to a specific object instance.

   ▶ Alternatively, we can use the ALL INSTANCES addition to bind an event handler method to all object instances.

▶ When registering event handler methods for class events, we don't have to specify an object context so neither the FOR oref and ALL INSTANCES additions apply.

▶ Finally, for both instance and class event bindings, we have the option of activating and deactivating an event registration using the ACTIVATION addition. Here, we can activate an event handler method using the true ('X') value or deactivate the method using the false (space) value.

```
SET HANDLER handler1 handler2 ... [FOR oref|{ALL INSTANCES}]
                                  [ACTIVATION {'X'|' '}].
```
Listing 2.22 Registering Event Handler Methods

The final piece to the event syntax puzzle is the RAISE EVENT statement whose syntax is shown in Listing 2.23. As you can see, the syntax here is pretty straightforward: we simply specify the event being raised and pass along any parameters that event handlers will use to process the event downstream.

```
RAISE EVENT evt [EXPORTING p1 = a1 p2 = a2 ...].
```
Listing 2.23 Syntax for Raising Events

Putting It All Together

To see how all this comes together in real-life ABAP code, let's see how we might build the LCL_PUBLISHER and LCL_SUBSCRIBER classes depicted in Figure 2.5. The code for the LCL_PUBLISHER class is contained in Listing 2.24. Here, you can see how we've defined the message_added event using the EVENTS keyword introduced in Section 2.1.2. This event is then triggered from within the add_message() method using the RAISE EVENT statement.

```
CLASS lcl_publisher DEFINITION.
  PUBLIC SECTION.
    METHODS:
      add_message IMPORTING iv_message TYPE string,
      confirm_receipt IMPORTING iv_subscriber TYPE string.

    EVENTS:
      message_added
        EXPORTING VALUE(ev_message) TYPE string.
ENDCLASS.

CLASS lcl_publisher IMPLEMENTATION.
  METHOD add_message.
    DATA lv_message TYPE string.
    lv_message = |Publishing message: [{ iv_message }].|.
    WRITE: / lv_message.

    RAISE EVENT message_added
      EXPORTING
        ev_message = iv_message.
  ENDMETHOD.

  METHOD confirm_receipt.
    DATA lv_message TYPE string.
    lv_message = |Message processed by { iv_subscriber }.|.
    WRITE: / lv_message.
  ENDMETHOD.
ENDCLASS.
```
Listing 2.24 Defining and Raising Events

Listing 2.25 contains the definition of the LCL_SUBSCRIBER class which is listening for messages issued from the LCL_PUBLISHER class. Here, you can see how we've defined an event handler method called on_message() that will be used to process

publication events at runtime. The event binding takes place within the con-
structor() method using the SET HANDLER statement. We'll learn more about
constructor methods in Chapter 4, but for now simply know that this method is
invoked automatically whenever an LCL_SUBSCRIBER instance is created.

```
CLASS lcl_subscriber DEFINITION.
  PUBLIC SECTION.
    METHODS:
      constructor,

        on_message FOR EVENT message_added
                   OF lcl_publisher
                   IMPORTING
                   ev_message sender.

ENDCLASS.

CLASS lcl_subscriber IMPLEMENTATION.
  METHOD constructor.
    SET HANDLER on_message FOR ALL INSTANCES.
  ENDMETHOD.

  METHOD on_message.
    DATA lv_message TYPE string.
    lv_message = |Received message [{ ev_message }]|.
    WRITE: / lv_message.

    sender->confirm_receipt( 'LCL_SUBSCRIBER' ).
  ENDMETHOD.
ENDCLASS.
```

Listing 2.25 Defining and Registering an Event Handler Method

With both classes in place, we can run a test by passing a message to the add_mes-
sage() method of the LCL_PUBLISHER class. This will trigger the MESSAGE_ADDED
event and allow us to see how the LCL_SUBSCRIBER class responds. Once you play
around with this and learn how to interact with the event processing loop, you'll
find that this feature offers many interesting possibilities.

```
DATA lo_publisher TYPE REF TO lcl_publisher.
DATA lo_subscriber TYPE REF TO lcl_subscriber.

CREATE OBJECT lo_publisher.
CREATE OBJECT lo_subscriber.

lo_publisher->add_message( 'Ping...' ).
```

Listing 2.26 Testing the Event Processing Loop

2.2.7 Working with Functional Methods

As we've stated from the outset, one of the main goals with OOP is to develop code that's intuitive and easy to read. One of the ways that OO languages achieve this is by providing a syntax that resembles the sentence structure of spoken languages. For example, if you think about a method call, you have a subject (either an object or a class) and a verb (the method being called). With a little bit of creativity and proper naming, we can build statements that even non-technical types can read and understand (at least conceptually).

To make our code flow even better, we can employ the use of *functional methods*. As the name suggests, functional methods are used to compute a single discrete value. The value in this approach is that we can plug in functional methods in the operand positions of various ABAP statements to build powerful expressions.

Listing 2.27 illustrates the basic syntax used to declare functional methods. Here, as before, we can declare IMPORTING parameters to provide inputs to the method. The lone output of the method is provided in the form of the RETURNING value parameter. As is the case with other parameter types, we're generally free to define the type of the returning parameter using the same rules that apply for EXPORTING parameters. However, type selection does play a role in determining whether or not a functional method can be used as an operand in selected ABAP statements.

```
METHODS func_method
   [IMPORTING parameters]
   RETURNING VALUE(rval) TYPE type
   [EXCEPTIONS...].
```
Listing 2.27 Functional Method Declaration Syntax

To demonstrate how functional methods are used in ABAP code, let's take a look at an example. In Listing 2.28, we've created a string tokenizer class called LCL_STRING_TOKENIZER that can be used to parse through delimited records and make it easy to access individual string tokens. This class defines two functional methods:

▶ The has_more_tokens() method is a Boolean method which can be used to determine if there are more tokens in the sequence.

▶ The next_token() method provides a simple mechanism for accessing the next token in the sequence.

```
CLASS lcl_string_tokenizer DEFINITION.
  PUBLIC SECTION.
    METHODS:
      constructor IMPORTING iv_string TYPE csequence
                            iv_delimiter TYPE csequence,

      has_more_tokens RETURNING VALUE(rv_result) TYPE abap_bool,

      next_token RETURNING VALUE(rv_token) TYPE string.

  PRIVATE SECTION.
    DATA mt_tokens TYPE string_table.
    DATA mv_index TYPE i.
ENDCLASS.

CLASS lcl_string_tokenizer IMPLEMENTATION.
  METHOD constructor.
    SPLIT iv_string AT iv_delimiter INTO TABLE me->mt_tokens.

    IF lines( me->mt_tokens ) GT 0.
      me->mv_index = 1.
    ELSE.
      me->mv_index = 0.
    ENDIF.
  ENDMETHOD.

  METHOD has_more_tokens.
    IF me->mv_index LE lines( me->mt_tokens ).
      rv_result = abap_true.
    ELSE.
      rv_result = abap_false.
    ENDIF.
  ENDMETHOD.

  METHOD next_token.
    READ TABLE me->mt_tokens INDEX me->mv_index INTO rv_token.
    ADD 1 TO me->mv_index.
  ENDMETHOD.
ENDCLASS.
```
Listing 2.28 Working with Functional Methods (Part 1)

The code excerpt contained in Listing 2.29 demonstrates how we can use our string tokenizer class within regular ABAP code. Here, notice how we're using the has_more_rows() method as the basis of the logical expression that drives the WHILE loop that processes the string tokens. At runtime, this method will be invoked prior to the evaluation of the logical expression and the returned value will be used to determine if the WHILE loop should continue. Not only does this save us a few lines of code, it also makes the code much more intuitive.

```
DATA lo_tokenizer TYPE REF TO lcl_string_tokenizer.
DATA lv_token TYPE string.

CREATE OBJECT lo_tokenizer
  EXPORTING
    iv_string = '09/13/2005'
    iv_delimiter = '/'.

WHILE lo_tokenizer->has_more_tokens( ) EQ abap_true.
  lv_token = lo_tokenizer->next_token( ).
  WRITE: / lv_token.
ENDWHILE.
```
Listing 2.29 Working with Functional Methods (Part 2)

Table 2.4 provides some further examples of places where functional methods can be used in common ABAP expressions.

ABAP Expression	Where Used

Conditional Expressions (e.g. IF and WHILE statements)	As an operand in a logical expression.
	Example:
	`IF oref->get_weight( ) GT 100.`
	`...`
	`ENDIF.`

CASE	As the operand in logical expressions.
	Example:
	`CASE oref->get_type( ).`
	`WHEN oref->get_value1( ).`
	`...`
	`ENDCASE.`

LOOP AT /
DELETE /
MODIFY
	As part of the logical expression in a WHERE clause.
	Example:
	`LOOP AT itab`
	`   WHERE field EQ oref->get_val( ).`
	`...`
	`ENDLOOP.`

Table 2.4 Using Functional Methods in Expressions

New in Release 7.40: Enhancements to Functional Methods

As of Release 7.40 of the AS ABAP, the signature of functional methods has been enhanced to support exporting and changing parameters in addition to the singular returning parameter. Such methods can still be used inline within regular ABAP expressions; the extra exporting/changing parameters simply come along for the ride.

Another helpful addition in Release 7.40 is the introduction of *predicative method calls*. As the name suggests, predicative method calls are functional method calls where the result is used as a predicate in logical expressions. To put this into perspective, consider the way that we're using predicative method calls to refactor the WHILE loop from Listing 2.29 below. Here, notice that we no longer have to compare the result of the has_more_tokens() method using a logic expression. In this context, if the returning value parameter of has_more_tokens() is initial, then the result is false; all non-initial values evaluate to true. So, we can define the signature of methods using Boolean approximation types such as ABAP_BOOL or pretty much any other data type. Of course, for readability's sake, we would encourage you to define your functional methods using familiar Boolean types wherever possible.

```
WHILE lo_tokenizer->has_more_tokens( ).
  ...
ENDWHILE.
```

Note that no syntactical changes are required in the implementation of methods such has_more_tokens() in order to exploit this functionality. You can continue to develop functional methods as per usual, only now you can incorporate them into functional expressions in a more concise and readable manner.

2.2.8   Chaining Method Calls Together

Enhancement Pack 2 (EhP2) of Release 7.0 of the AS ABAP brought with it a language feature that many OO developers had been yearning for since ABAP Objects first came onto the scene: support for chained method calls. This little bit of syntactic sugar makes it easy to consolidate a handful of operations into a single line of code.

In order to understand how chained method calls work, let's consider an example. In Listing 2.30, we've created a simple string utilities class called LCL_STRING. Within this class, we've defined a number of functional methods which perform various operations on a string value: converting the string to upper case, trimming of leading/trailing whitespace, and replacing characters. This is all pretty much standard fare until we get to the part where each of these methods passes back a copy of the me self-reference variable. This subtle addition to the code is what makes method chaining possible.

```
CLASS lcl_string DEFINITION.
  PUBLIC SECTION.
    METHODS:
      constructor IMPORTING iv_string TYPE csequence,

      trim RETURNING VALUE(ro_string) TYPE REF TO lcl_string,

      upper RETURNING VALUE(ro_string)
               TYPE REF TO lcl_string,

      replace IMPORTING iv_pattern TYPE string
                        iv_replace TYPE string
              RETURNING VALUE(ro_string)
                  TYPE REF TO lcl_string,

      get_value RETURNING VALUE(rv_value) TYPE string.

  PRIVATE SECTION.
    DATA mv_string TYPE string.
ENDCLASS.

CLASS lcl_string IMPLEMENTATION.
  METHOD constructor.
    me->mv_string = iv_string.
  ENDMETHOD.

  METHOD trim.
    me->mv_string =
      condense( val = me->mv_string from = `` ).
    ro_string = me.
  ENDMETHOD.

  METHOD upper.
    me->mv_string = to_upper( val = me->mv_string ).
    ro_string = me.
  ENDMETHOD.

  METHOD replace.
    REPLACE ALL OCCURRENCES OF REGEX iv_pattern
        IN me->mv_string WITH iv_replace.

    ro_string = me.
  ENDMETHOD.

  METHOD get_value.
    rv_value = me->mv_string.
  ENDMETHOD.
ENDCLASS.
```
Listing 2.30 Working with Chained Methods (Part 1)

The code excerpt in Listing 2.31 demonstrates how chained method calls are implemented from a code perspective. Here, you can see how we're taking an existing string and performing multiple operations on it in one go. This starts with the call to the `trim()` method. This method strips off the leading/trailing whitespace and then passes back a copy of the `me` self-reference. The resultant object reference is then used as the basis for the subsequent call to the `upper()` method which follows the same kind of pattern. The call chain ultimately terminates with the call to `get_value()`, at which time we receive the formatted text "PAIGE_A_PUMPKIN".

> **Note**
>
> The line break between the calls to `upper()` and `replace()` was added so that the statement would fit onto a printed page in the book. Within the ABAP Editor, this sort of line break would result in a syntax error.

```
DATA lo_string TYPE REF TO lcl_string.
DATA lv_new_value TYPE string.

CREATE OBJECT lo_string
  EXPORTING
    iv_string = `  Paige A Pumpkin  `.

lv_new_value =
  lo_string->trim( )->upper( )->
    replace( iv_pattern = `\s` iv_replace = '_' )->get_value( ).

WRITE: / lv_new_value.
```
Listing 2.31 Working with Chained Methods (Part 2)

As you can see in the example above, chained method calls make it easy to string together related operations in one condensed statement. For simple operations like the ones demonstrated in Listing 2.31, this makes logical sense. For more complex statements though, chained method calls are probably a bad idea. We leave it to you as responsible developers to know when it makes sense to sacrifice readability in order to save a few keystrokes.

2.3 Building your First Object-Oriented Program

In the previous section, we looked at several examples which demonstrated how to work with objects. However, since these code excerpts were isolated, you might be wondering how all these pieces fit together in actual ABAP programs. With that in mind, this section will demonstrate the creation of a simple report program that utilizes a local class. As you'll come to find out, these concepts apply equally to the incorporation of local classes to function group definitions, module pool programs, and so on.

2.3.1 Creating the Report Program

To get things started, let's create the report program that will drive our demo. If you're new to ABAP development, this can be achieved by performing the following steps:

1. To begin, log onto the system and open up the Object Navigator (Transaction SE80).

2. In the object list selection box in the Repository Browser on the left-hand side of the screen, choose the LOCAL OBJECTS list option (see Figure 2.6).

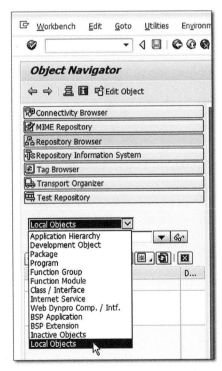

Figure 2.6 Selecting the Local Objects Repository View

3. This will pull up a tree view of locally-defined development objects for your user account as shown in Figure 2.7. To create a new report program, simply right-click on the top-level object node (i.e. $TMP DEVELOPER shown in Figure 2.7) and select the CREATE • PROGRAM menu option.

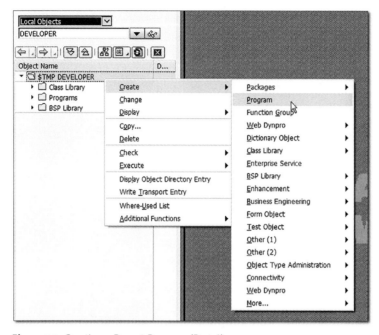

Figure 2.7 Creating a Report Program (Part 1)

4. Next, you'll be presented with the CREATE PROGRAM dialog box shown in Figure 2.8. At this step, you can simply specify the name of the report program (we called our report YDATE_DEMO) and press the enter key to continue. Note that the CREATE WITH TOP INCLUDE checkbox should not be selected in this case since we're just building a simple report.

Figure 2.8 Creating a Report Program (Part 2)

5. Figure 2.9 shows the next dialog box that will be displayed during the creation process. Here, you can provide a program title and additional attributes concerning the program setup. For the purposes of our simple demonstration, you can accept the defaults and click on the SAVE button to continue.

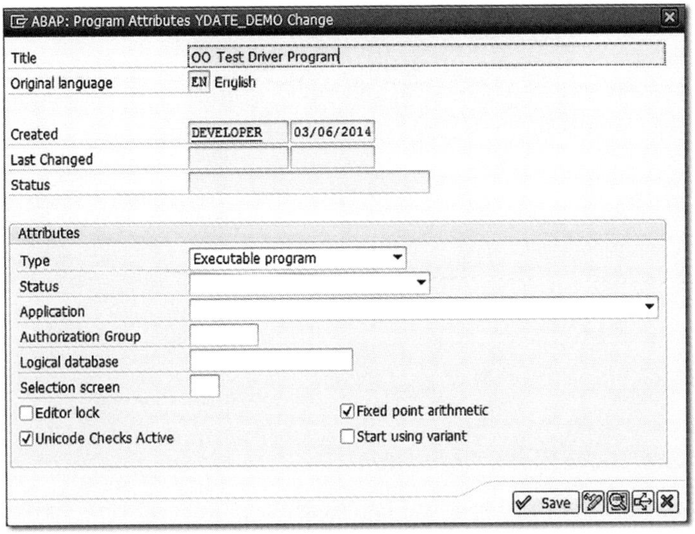

Figure 2.9 Creating a Report Program (Part 3)

6. At the next step, you'll be asked to select a package to store the object in within the ABAP Repository. Since this is a demo program, we'll leave the default $TMP package selection and click the SAVE button to continue. That way, the program will only be defined locally and can't be transported.

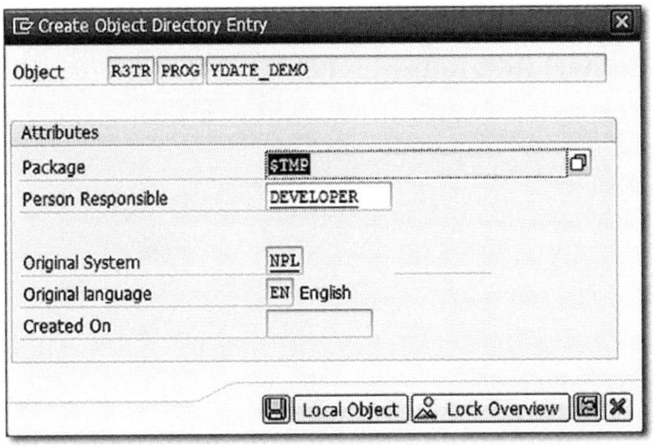

Figure 2.10 Creating a Report Program (Part 4)

7. Finally, if all goes well, you should end up at an editor screen like the one shown in Figure 2.11. From here, we can get started with our coding exercise.

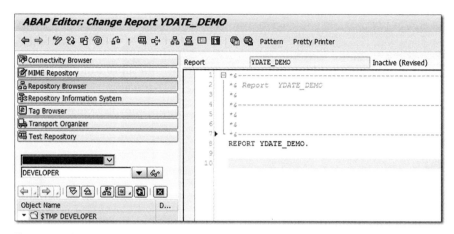

Figure 2.11 Creating a Report Program (Part 5)

2.3.2 Adding in the Local Class Definition

Once the report program is created, we can begin defining our local class in one of two ways:

- We can start keying in the class definition directly underneath the REPORT statement just like we would for other type definitions.

- Or, we can create an INCLUDE program and key in the class definition over there.

The ABAP compiler doesn't care which option we choose, so it's up to us to decide how best to organize our code. For now, we'll keep things simple and define the class directly within the report program (see Listing 2.32). In Section 2.4, we'll take a closer look at some logistical implications when defining classes.

```
REPORT ydate_demo.
CLASS lcl_date DEFINITION.
  ...
ENDCLASS.

CLASS lcl_date IMPLEMENTATION.
  ...
ENDCLASS.
```

Listing 2.32 Defining Local Classes within a Report Program

Once the local class is defined, we can use access it from within the report program in several different ways:

▸ We could define global object reference variables and then use those variables to create and use objects from within report events such as START-OF-SELECTION and END-OF-SELECTION.

▸ We could define local object reference variables within subroutines called from within the report program and access the objects that way.

▸ If the class defines a "main" class method, we could simply invoke that directly and let the class itself drive the main program logic.

Since this is a book about OO programming, we'll tend to prefer the 3rd option as it frees us from having to mix-and-match programming paradigms. The code excerpt in Listing 2.33 demonstrates this approach. Here you can see how the main program logic is driven by the main() class method which is accessed directly within the START-OF-SELECTION event module. From here, it's OO programming as per usual. Figure 2.12 shows what the program output looks like. If you want to try this out for yourself, you can download a complete version of the program within the book's source code bundle online.

```
REPORT zoopbook_date_demo.
CLASS lcl_date DEFINITION.
  PUBLIC SECTION.
    CLASS-METHODS:
      main.
      ...
ENDCLASS.

CLASS lcl_date IMPLEMENTATION.
  METHOD main.
    DATA lo_birth_date TYPE REF TO lcl_date.
    DATA lv_message TYPE string.

    CREATE OBJECT lo_birth_date
      EXPORTING
        iv_date = '20030113'.

    lv_message =
    |Andersen was born on a
      { lo_birth_date->get_day_of_week( ) }.|.
    WRITE: / lv_message.

    lv_message =
```

```
     |Official birth date:
        { lo_birth_date->get_long_format( ) }.|.
    WRITE: / lv_message.
  ENDMETHOD.
ENDCLASS.

START-OF-SELECTION.
  lcl_date=>main( ).
```

Listing 2.33 Integrating Local Classes Inside Report Programs

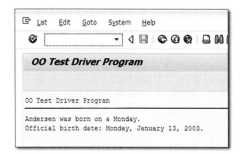

Figure 2.12 Output of the Example Program

2.4   Working with Global Classes

As we've noted at several points throughout this chapter, ABAP distinguishes between two different types of classes:

- ▶ **Local Classes**
  These are the types of classes that we've looked at thus far. As we observed in Section 2.3, these classes are defined within some other ABAP module such as a report program, include program, etc. This implies that local classes have limited visibility within the system.

- ▶ **Global Classes**
  Global classes on the other hand are standalone ABAP Repository artifacts that are visible across the system. In this regard, you can think of global classes as being on equal footing with globally-defined function modules.

From a syntax perspective, local and global classes are the same. However, as we'll learn in this section, the way that we go about developing global classes is a little bit different. So with that in mind, let's jump in and take a look at global classes.

2.4.1 Understanding the Class Pool Concept

From a technical perspective, global classes are stored within the ABAP Repository inside of a special repository object called a *class pool*. Class pools are special ABAP program types that define a single global repository class along with related local type definitions used to support the implementation of the class. Class pools are similar to function groups in the sense that they cannot be executed directly. Instead, runtime object instances are created using the familiar CREATE OBJECT statement and then processed from there.

2.4.2 Getting Started with the Class Builder Tool

Class pools are maintained within a specialized tool in the ABAP Workbench called the *Class Builder*. To access the Class Builder from within the ABAP Workbench, simply choose the CLASS / INTERFACE list option in the object list selection box of the Repository Browser shown in Figure 2.13.

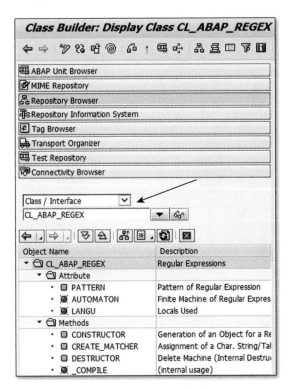

Figure 2.13 Accessing the Class Builder from the ABAP Workbench

Outside the ABAP Workbench, you can access the Class Builder directly using Transaction SE24, or via the menu path shown in Figure 2.14.

Figure 2.14 Accessing the Class Builder from the SAP Easy Access Menu

Figure 2.15 shows what the initial screen of the Class Builder looks like when accessed in standalone mode.

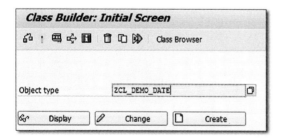

Figure 2.15 Initial Screen of the Class Builder Tool

2.4.3 Creating Global Classes

To create a new class pool in the Class Builder, perform the following steps:

1. From the initial screen shown in Figure 2.15, type in the name of the class you want to create and hit the Create button. Alternatively, from within the Object

Navigator, you can key in the class name in the input field shown in Figure 2.13 and press the Enter key.

2. In either case, you'll end up at the CREATE CLASS dialog box shown in Figure 2.16. Here, we must fill in the following attributes:

  ▷ In the CLASS field, we confirm the name of the class that we're creating. Since this class is part of the overall ABAP Repository, we must give it a unique name using the {Namespace}CL_ prefix as shown in Figure 2.16.

  ▷ In the DESCRIPTION field, we can provide a brief description of what the class is used for, etc.

  ▷ The INST. GENERATION drop-down list is used to determine the class's *instantiation context*. We'll explore this concept beginning in Chapter 4.

  ▷ The CLASS TYPE radio button group allows us to specify what type of class we're building. For now, we'll stick to the default USUAL ABAP CLASS option. The remaining class types will be described in Chapters 8, 11, and 9, respectively.

  ▷ Finally, the FINAL checkbox allows us to determine if the class is closed off from inheritance. We'll explore this concept in Chapter 5.

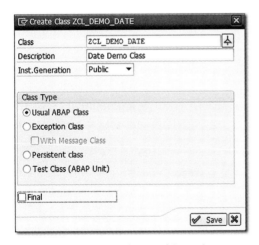

Figure 2.16 Creating a Class Pool (Part 1)

3. Once the class definition details are established, you can proceed with the creation process by clicking on the SAVE button (see Figure 2.16).

4. At this point, you'll be prompted to choose the development package where the class will be stored. For the purposes of our demo classes, we'll stick with the default $TMP local package.

5. If all goes well, you should end up at the form editor screen shown in Figure 2.17. From here, we can begin rounding out the class definition by defining attributes, methods, and so on.

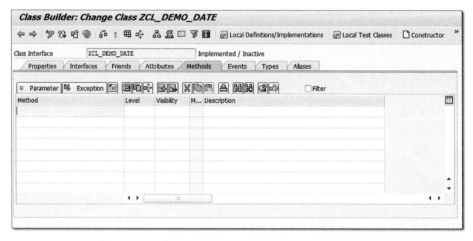

Figure 2.17 Main Editor Screen of the Class Builder Tool

2.4.4 Using the Form-Based Editor

As you can see in Figure 2.17, the default view of the Class Editor tool provides us with a form-based view for defining various types of components. For the most part, these forms simply provide an input mask for entering the component declaration details described in Section 2.1.2. In the following sections, we'll take a look at these forms and see how they're used to declare class components.

Defining Attributes

Attributes are defined on the ATTRIBUTES tab of the Class Editor. This tab of the Class Editor provides an entry table in which you can specify all of the various attributes for a class (see Figure 2.18).

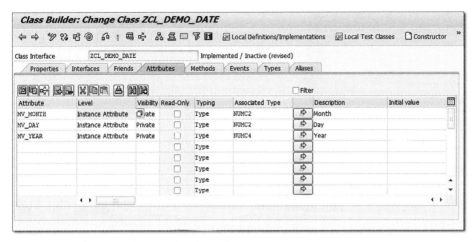

Figure 2.18 Defining Attributes in the Class Editor

As you can see in Figure 2.18, the attributes table defines a number of columns that we can use to specify attribute definitions:

▸ The name of an attribute is specified in the ATTRIBUTE column.

▸ The LEVEL column is used to define the declaration type of the attribute. Figure 2.19 contains a list of the possible declaration types available in the input value help for this column. As you can see, global class attributes can be declared as an *Instance Attribute*, a *Static Attribute*, or a *Constant*.

Figure 2.19 Setting the Declaration Type for an Attribute

▸ The VISIBILITY column is used to assign the attribute to a specific visibility section within the class (for a list of possible values, see Figure 2.20).

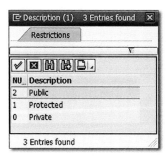

Figure 2.20 Assigning the Visibility Section for an Attribute

▸ In the READ-ONLY column, we can specify that the attribute has read-only access from outside the class.

▸ The TYPING and ASSOCIATED TYPE columns are used to specify the attribute's data type. The pick list values for the TYPING field are shown in Figure 2.21. Once this context is determined, the ASSOCIATED TYPE column can be used to complete the type declaration using built-in types, ABAP Dictionary types, or even custom types/type pools defined within the class itself.

Figure 2.21 Specifying the Attribute's Type

▸ The DIRECT TYPE ENTRY button directly to the right of the ASSOCIATED TYPE column provides us with another option for specifying an attribute's type. Whenever you click on this button, you'll be taken to a source code editor view in which you can edit the attribute definition directly using ABAP code as described in Section 2.1.2. Once you've specified the type, you can click on the BACK button to navigate back to the ATTRIBUTES tab.

▸ The DESCRIPTION column allows us to type in an optional short text description of the attribute so that users will understand what the attribute is used for. To improve code readability, we highly recommend that you utilize this feature.

▸ Finally, in the INITIAL VALUE column, we can provide a value that will be used to initialize the attribute before it is first accessed.

Defining Methods

Methods are defined on the METHODS tab in the Class Editor. Here, much like we saw on the ATTRIBUTES tab, the Class Editor provides us with an input table for defining the methods of a class. As you can see in Figure 2.22, most of the attributes here are self-explanatory. The lone exception to this is the LEVEL field. This field is used to determine if the method is defined at the instance level or the class level (see Figure 2.23).

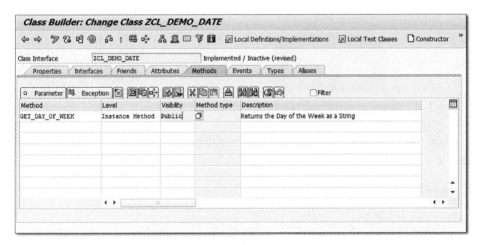

Figure 2.22 Defining Methods in the Class Editor

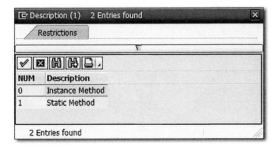

Figure 2.23 Setting the Declaration Type for a Method

To define the parameters for a method, simply place your cursor on the name of the method you wish to edit in the Method column and click on the Parameters button in the toolbar directly above the method input table. This will open up the Method Parameters input screen shown in Figure 2.24. From here, we can fill in parameter details in much the same way that we define attributes on the Attributes tab.

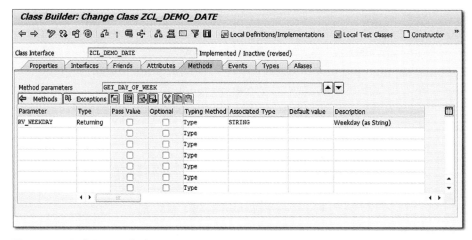

Figure 2.24 Defining Method Parameters

To edit the method's implementation, you can either double-click on the method name, or click on the Source Code button highlighted in Figure 2.25.

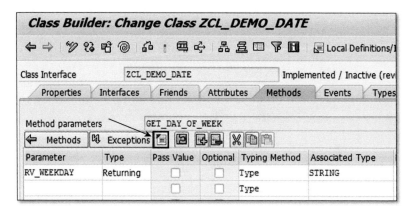

Figure 2.25 Navigating to the Method Source Code Editor

In the source code editor, you can implement the method inside of a
METHOD...ENDMETHOD processing block within the ABAP Editor as per usual (see
Figure 2.26).

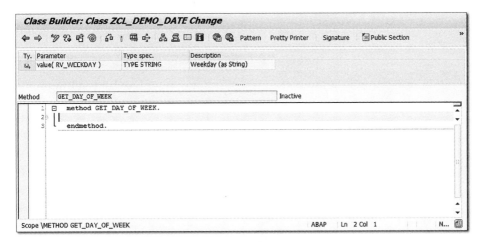

Figure 2.26 Implementing a Method in the ABAP Editor

Defining Events

Events are defined on the EVENTS tab of the Class Editor. Here, you are provided
with an input table similar to the ones used to specify components on the ATTRI-
BUTES and METHODS tabs (see Figure 2.27).

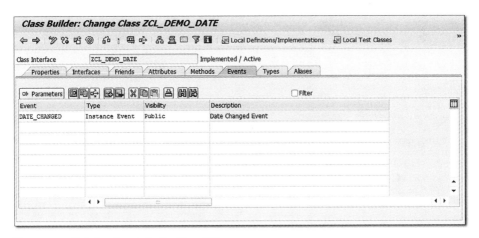

Figure 2.27 Defining Events in the Class Editor

To declare parameters for an event, place your cursor on the name of the target event in the EVENT column and click the PARAMETERS button in the toolbar above the input table. This will open up the EVENT PARAMETERS input screen shown in Figure 2.28. Here, you can specify the exporting parameters of the event in much the same way that you learned how to define method parameters in the previous section.

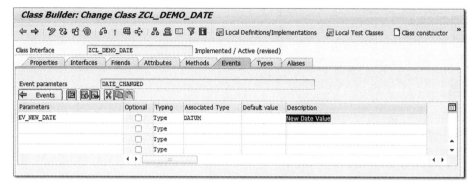

Figure 2.28 Defining Event Parameters

Defining Custom Data Types

Custom data types can be defined on the TYPES tab of the Class Editor. As you can see in Figure 2.29, the TYPES tab has a similar look-and-feel to the ATTRIBUTES tab shown in Figure 2.18.

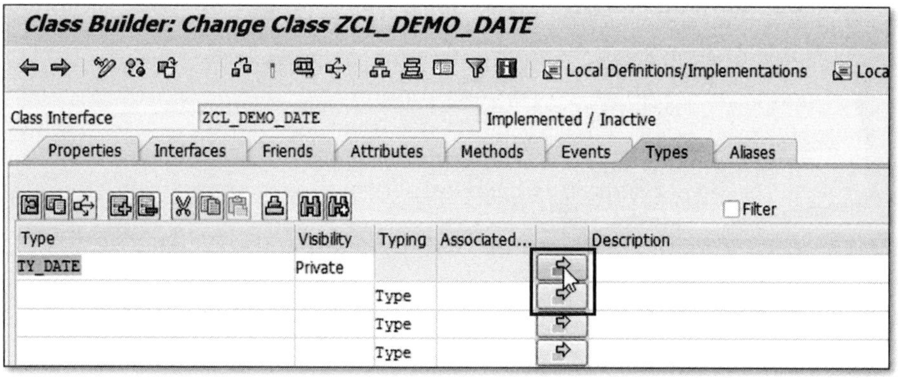

Figure 2.29 Defining Custom Types in the Class Editor

Here, once again, we can use the DIRECT TYPE ENTRY button (highlighted in Figure 2.29) to jump into an ABAP editor and refine the type definition using the TYPES statement as necessary (see Figure 2.30).

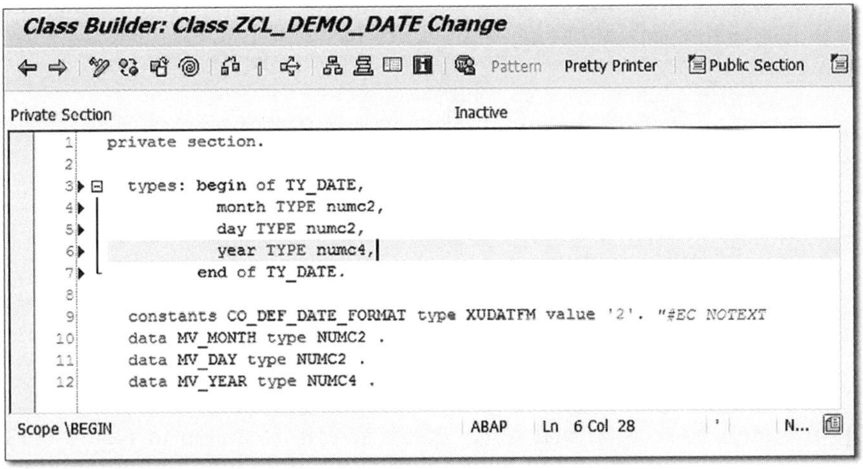

Figure 2.30 Defining Custom Types Using Direct Type Entry

Local Definitions / Implementations

Besides the various components considered thus far, class pools can also be defined with various local types that can be used to aid in the implementation of the global class. These local types could be used to define local variables in methods, etc. To access this section of the code, simply click on the LOCAL DEFINITIONS/ IMPLEMENTATIONS button shown in Figure 2.31. From here, you'll be taken to a code-based editor in which you can define local data types and even local class types as desired. In the latter case, you simply define the local classes using the same syntax demonstrated in Section 2.1.

Figure 2.31 Accessing the Local Definitions Include of a Class Pool

2.4.5 Using the Source Code Editor

Beginning with the SAP NetWeaver 7.02 release, the Class Builder also comes with an alternative to the form-based editor: the source code-based editor. To access this mode, simply click on the SOURCE CODE-BASED button in the main toolbar as shown in Figure 2.32.

Figure 2.32 Accessing the Source Code-Based Editor (Part 1)

This will bring you to a normal ABAP editor screen as shown in Figure 2.33. From here, you can work with the basic ABAP Objects syntax covered over the course of this chapter. You can stick with this mode to write the code, or toggle back to the form-based view by clicking on the FORM-BASED button highlighted in Figure 2.33.

| Pattern | Pretty Printer | | Local Definitions/Implementations | Local Test Classes | Form-Based | Class documentation |

Class Source   Active

```
 1  class ZCL_DEMO_DATE definition
 2    public
 3    create public .
 4
 5  public section.
 6
 7    methods CONSTRUCTOR
 8      importing
 9        !IV_DATE type DATUM .
10    methods GET_DAY_OF_WEEK
11      returning
12        value(RV_WEEKDAY) type STRING .
13    methods AS_NATIVE_DATE
14      returning
15        value(RV_DATE) type D .
16    methods SET_MONTH
17      importing
18        !IV_MONTH type NUMC2 .
```

Figure 2.33 Accessing the Source Code-Based Editor (Part 2)

2.5 Developing Classes Using the ABAP Development Tools in Eclipse

Up until very recently, the only way to develop classes in ABAP Objects was to use the ABAP Workbench tools. Beginning with the SAP NetWeaver 7.03 release though, we now have a new and exciting toolset to work with: the *ABAP Development Tools in Eclipse* (AIE). In this section, we'll take an introductory look at some of the basic features of the AIE toolset.

2.5.1 What is Eclipse?

Before we start looking into specific features of the AIE toolset, we should first provide a brief introduction to Eclipse. Eclipse is a flexible, Java-based integrated development environment (IDE) that was initially developed by IBM and then subsequently donated to the open source community in 2001. From there, the project picked up a lot of steam as other major vendors (or "stewards") jumped on board and added their contributions to the project. These efforts culminated in the launch of the Eclipse Foundation in 2004.

In and of itself, Eclipse is basically just like any other IDE: it provides functionality to edit source code, organize code into projects, and so forth. What sets Eclipse apart is its flexible plug-in system. Here, software vendors and individuals alike can create plug-ins to extend the core functionality of the IDE in all kinds of interesting ways. Indeed, if you look online, you can generally find plug-ins that allow you to develop in just about any programming language imaginable using Eclipse. With the advent of the AIE toolset, this list of programming languages now includes ABAP.

From a strategy perspective, moving towards an Eclipse-based IDE makes a ton of sense for SAP. Technology-wise, it's fair to say that SAP has reached the limits of what can be achieved using classic Dynpro technology in the ABAP Workbench. Indeed, we daresay that you'll be stunned by some of the Eclipse-based features demonstrated in Section 2.5.3. These capabilities simply weren't possible using the old technology stack. Plus, as new developers come onto the scene, it's in SAP's best interest to offer a familiar development platform that's on par with competing IDEs such as Microsoft's Visual Studio, etc.

> **Note**
>
> Even though we think most users will never want to go back to the ABAP Workbench once they get their hands on AIE, we should point out that the ABAP Workbench is not going away anytime soon. The great news for developers is that we now have more choices to work with. We can stick with the ABAP Workbench, jump over to AIE, or toggle back-and-forth. Indeed, since the two IDEs can be used simultaneously, developers can dip their toes in the water and decide which IDE works best for them over time.

2.5.2   Setting Up the AIE Environment

Since the ABAP Development Tools (ADT) are bundled as a series of plug-ins, they can generally be installed on top of most any recent Eclipse installation. This could include Eclipse installations used to develop software outside of the SAP landscape, or other SAP-based Eclipse installations such as the SAP HANA Studio. If you're an experienced Eclipse developer, then you can find instructions for setting up the AIE plug-ins at *https://tools.hana.ondemand.com/#abap*. Otherwise, check out Appendix A for step-by-step instructions that walk you through the installation process.

> **Release Compatibility**
>
> At the time of this writing, AIE requires that the AS ABAP backend must be on SAP Kernel 7.20 or higher and the SAP BASIS component at version 7.31 with support pack stack 04. Though this may change over time, suffice it to say that you're probably not going to be able to use AIE with an old AS ABAP system running on SAP NetWeaver 7.0. For more details about the particular requirements and instructions for verifying/establishing AIE connectivity, check out *https://scn.sap.com/docs/DOC-47656*.

Once you have your Eclipse installation in place, you can access the ADT by launching the IDE and performing the following steps:

1. From the top-level FILE menu choose the PROJECT... menu option as shown in Figure 2.34.

2. This will launch the NEW PROJECT wizard shown in Figure 2.35. Here, you'll want to expand the ABAP folder and choose the ABAP PROJECT node. Click the NEXT button to continue.

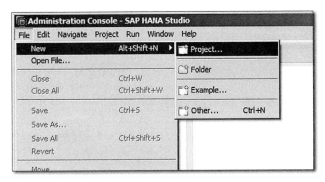

Figure 2.34 Creating an ADT Project (Part 1)

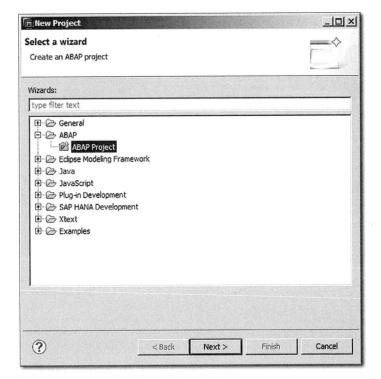

Figure 2.35 Creating an ADT Project (Part 2)

1. At the NEW ABAP PROJECT dialog box shown in Figure 2.36, you choose the AS ABAP system you want to connect to by clicking on the BROWSE... button. In the SELECT EXISTING SYSTEM popup, you can choose from available system con-

nections established within the SAP logon pad. Click the OK button to confirm your selection and click the NEXT button to continue.

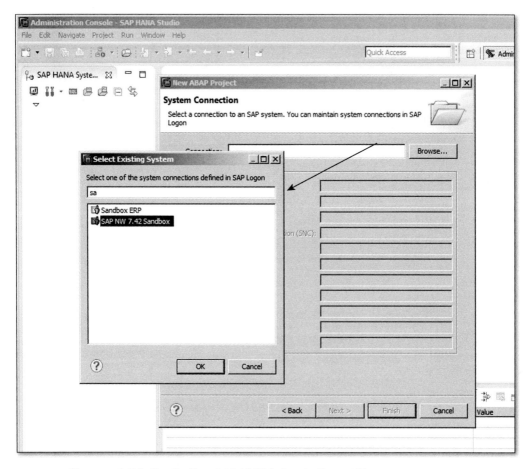

Figure 2.36 Selecting the Target AS ABAP System to Connect To

2. At the next step, you'll be prompted to provide logon credentials so the ADT plug-ins can log onto the AS ABAP backend (see Figure 2.37). Click the NEXT button to continue.

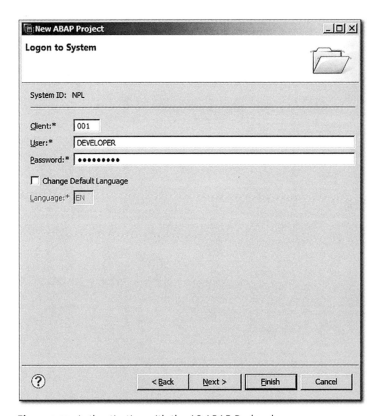

Figure 2.37 Authenticating with the AS ABAP Backend

3. Figure 2.38 shows the last step in the ABAP Project setup wizard. Here, you are provided with a couple of options for tweaking the experience once the project is created:

 ▸ In the FAVORITES PACKAGES area, you can click on the ADD... button to pre-select the ABAP package(s) that you want to work with in your project. Note that this favorites list can be created and/or amended later on if you prefer to wait.

 ▸ In the WORKING SETS area, you can add the project to the set of Eclipse working sets. This is an organizational feature that's native to the Eclipse IDE.

Once you've confirmed your settings, you can click on the FINISH button to create the project.

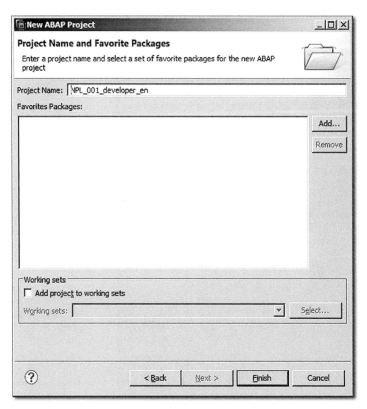

Figure 2.38 Confirming the Project Setup

4. At this point, you'll likely be presented with the OPEN ASSOCIATED PERSPECTIVE? prompt shown in Figure 2.39. In Eclipse, a *perspective* is an arrangement of related windows and views that are used to tandem to perform a particular type of development. In the case of AIE, we have the ABAP perspective which groups together various ADT functions together to improve developer productivity. As you become more proficient in using Eclipse features, you can tweak this perspective as needed and even create your own customized perspectives.

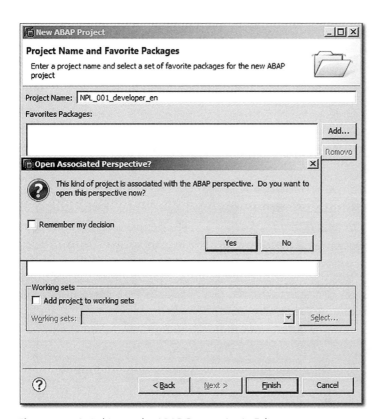

Figure 2.39 Switching to the ABAP Perspective in Eclipse

A Word on Workspaces and Projects

As you create new ABAP projects in Eclipse, there are a couple of things going on behind the scenes that you should be aware of:

1. Eclipse stores project files in a directory on your local machine referred to as the Eclipse *workspace*. You can find this directory from within Eclipse by choosing WINDOW • PREFERENCES in the top-level menu bar and then expanding GENERAL • WORKSPACE. From here, a link should be provided to find the current settings.

2. For ABAP-based projects, the files stored in the workspace are limited to project files and metafiles. These files are used to keep track of your project settings and preferences. Source code remains within the ABAP Repository on the AS ABAP backend. This is different than most other project types (e.g. Java projects) where the source code is maintained locally and then checked into some kind of software revision control system such as Perforce or CVS.

2.5.3 Working with the AIE Class Editor Tools

Once an ABAP Project is created and a connection is established within the AS ABAP backend, we can begin creating and editing ABAP-related artifacts as shown in Figure 2.40. Here, you can see that the editor screen within the ABAP perspective is split into four editor panes:

▶ On the top left-hand pane, we have the PROJECT EXPLORER window which resembles the tree-based Repository Browser that allows us to search for development objects from within the ABAP Workbench.

▶ The top right-hand pane consists of a tabbed pane that contains one or more editor views. So, for example, we can open up a class, a report, and a function module on different tabs and toggle back-and-forth. Eclipse also supports split-screen views so that you can perform side-by-side comparisons.

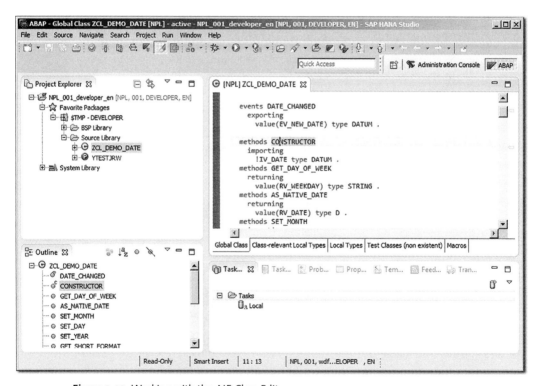

Figure 2.40 Working with the AIE Class Editor

▶ In the lower left-hand pane, we have the OUTLINE view which makes it easy to navigate directly to specific modules within the development object we happen to be editing.

▶ Finally, the lower right-hand pane is generally reserved for secondary views, properties views, and so on.

Since each of these editor panes are contained within a splitter pane, you can shrink or expand particular panes by dragging along the separator bars with your mouse. You can also expand/hide panes by clicking the corresponding icons in the top right-hand corner of the pane.

Once you become acquainted with the ABAP perspective, you can begin experimenting with the various Eclipse-based editors by either opening up an existing object (by double-clicking on it in the Project Explorer) or creating a new one. In the latter case, this can be achieved using the provided context menus. Since we're most interested in editing ABAP classes, the steps required to create a new class are as follows:

1. Within the desired ABAP development package, right-click on the SOURCE LIBRARY folder and choose the NEW • ABAP CLASS menu option (see Figure 2.41).

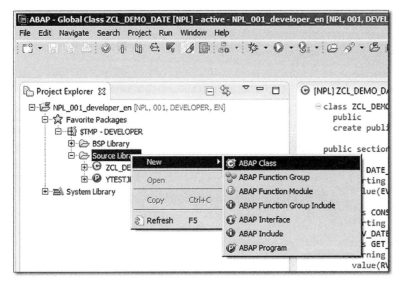

Figure 2.41 Creating a Global Class Using the AIE Class Editor (Part 1)

2. This will open up the NEW ABAP CLASS dialog box shown in Figure 2.42. Here, you must specify the class name and a brief description. From here, you can follow the wizard to completion to create the new class by accepting all defaults.

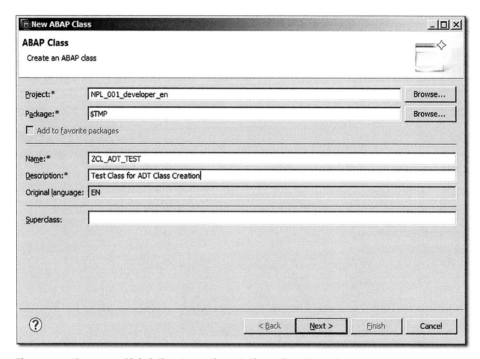

Figure 2.42 Creating a Global Class Using the AIE Class Editor (Part 2)

Once a class is opened, we can begin editing it using normal ABAP Objects syntax. To maximize the editor area, we recommend double-clicking on the top-level tab for the class you're editing. This will expand the editor area as shown in Figure 2.43. Along the top of the editor, you can access all of the familiar toolbar functions available in the normal Class Builder tool: syntax check, save, activate, and so on.

Within the editor itself, there are quite a number of useful features. For example, in Figure 2.43, you can see how the editor is equipped with intelligent code completion features. These features can be accessed on demand as you're coding by clicking the Ctrl + Space keys.

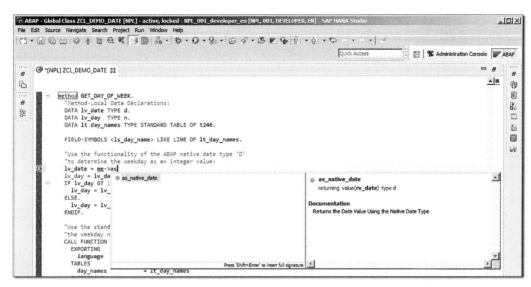

Figure 2.43 Working with the Expanded Editor Area

Besides the normal code-completion features already available in the new source code editor of the ABAP Workbench, AIE also taps into a powerful feature of the Eclipse IDE: *templates*. As the name suggests, templates refer to pre-defined code templates that make it easy to drop in familiar code blocks/idioms. For example, in Figure 2.44, you can see how we're using a template in Eclipse to build out an ABAP CASE statement. As you're typing familiar ABAP keywords, you can try this out by once again clicking the ⎡Ctrl⎤+⎡Space⎤ keys.

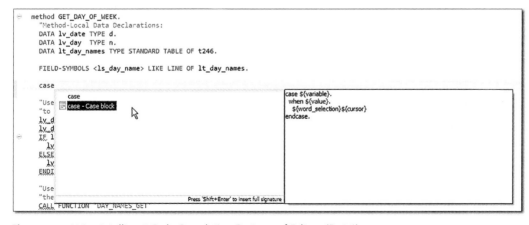

Figure 2.44 Using Intelligent Code Completion Features of Eclipse (Part 1)

Looking closely at the template being inserted in Figure 2.44, you can see how the template code contains a number of variables that are contained within the ${} blocks (e.g. ${variable}). As you insert a template, these variables can help further define a code block and give you more than just a simple piece of boilerplate code.

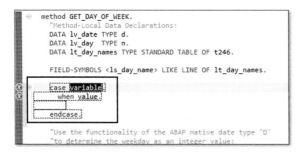

Figure 2.45 Using Intelligent Code Completion Features of Eclipse (Part 2)

To see what templates are available, you can choose the WINDOW • PREFERENCES menu option as shown in Figure 2.46. From here, select ABAP DEVELOPMENT • EDITORS • SOURCE CODE EDITORS • TEMPLATES to access the template editor table shown in Figure 2.47. Here, you can view/edit existing templates or create new ones as desired.

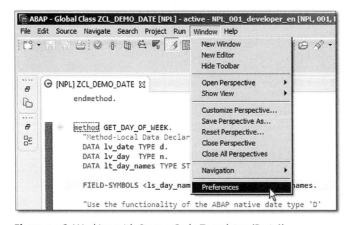

Figure 2.46 Working with Source Code Templates (Part 1)

While you're in there looking at ABAP development preferences, you might want to consider turning on another useful feature. Under the MARK OCCURRENCES preferences, there's a checkbox called MARK OCCURRENCES OF THE SELECTED ELEMENT (see Figure 2.48). If you select this checkbox and confirm your selection, you'll notice a subtle difference in the behavior of the editor as highlighted in Figure 2.49. Here, whenever you put your cursor on the name of a variable or code module, the editor will highlight all occurrences of that element with a gray background.

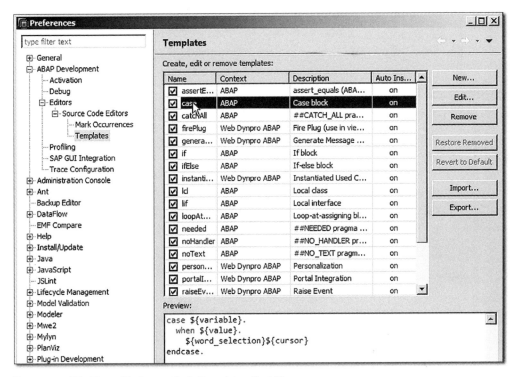

Figure 2.47 Working with Source Code Templates (Part 2)

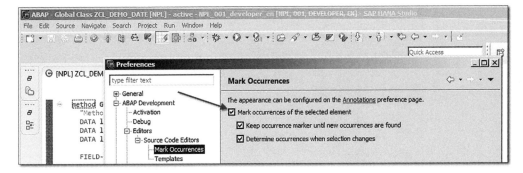

Figure 2.48 Turning on the Mark Occurrences Feature

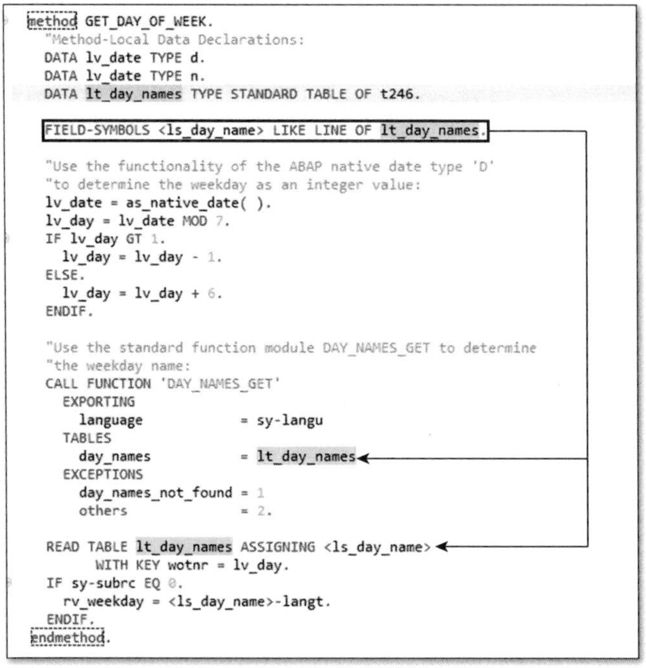

```
method GET_DAY_OF_WEEK.
  "Method-Local Data Declarations:
  DATA lv_date TYPE d.
  DATA lv_date TYPE n.
  DATA lt_day_names TYPE STANDARD TABLE OF t246.

  FIELD-SYMBOLS <ls_day_name> LIKE LINE OF lt_day_names.

  "Use the functionality of the ABAP native date type 'D'
  "to determine the weekday as an integer value:
  lv_date = as_native_date( ).
  lv_day = lv_date MOD 7.
  IF lv_day GT 1.
    lv_day = lv_day - 1.
  ELSE.
    lv_day = lv_day + 6.
  ENDIF.

  "Use the standard function module DAY_NAMES_GET to determine
  "the weekday name:
  CALL FUNCTION 'DAY_NAMES_GET'
    EXPORTING
      language              = sy-langu
    TABLES
      day_names             = lt_day_names
    EXCEPTIONS
      day_names_not_found = 1
      others                = 2.

  READ TABLE lt_day_names ASSIGNING <ls_day_name>
       WITH KEY wotnr = lv_day.
  IF sy-subrc EQ 0.
    rv_weekday = <ls_day_name>-langt.
  ENDIF.
endmethod.
```

Figure 2.49 Working with the Mark Occurrences Feature

Besides making it easy to visualize where certain elements are used in the code, the mark occurrences feature also allows us to tap into some powerful refactoring features built into editor. To access these features, simply highlight the code element you want to refactor and click on the $\boxed{\text{Ctrl}}$+$\boxed{1}$ key sequence (this sequence is called the Quick Fix sequence in Eclipse). For example, in Figure 2.50, you can see how we're using this feature to rename the variable lt_day_names.

Selecting the RENAME sequence highlighted in Figure 2.50 causes the RENAME FIELD dialog box shown in Figure 2.51 to open up. To rename the variable, we simply key in the new name in the NEW NAME field and click the NEXT button to continue.

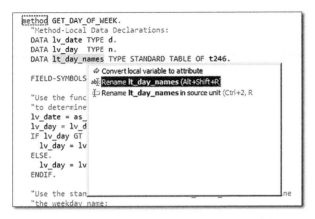

Figure 2.50 Using the Built-in Refactoring Features of the ADT (Part 1)

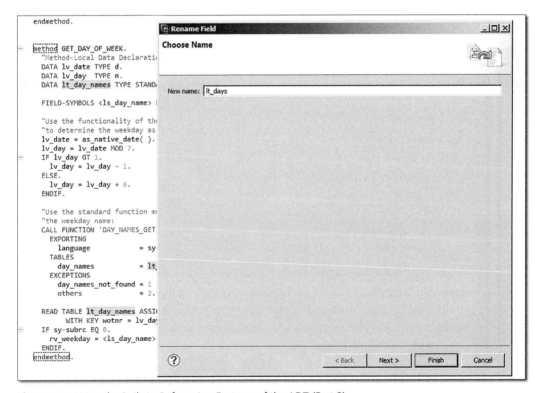

Figure 2.51 Using the Built-in Refactoring Features of the ADT (Part 2)

At the end of the rename wizard, we are presented with a split-screen editor that previews what the changes will look like if we decide to proceed. If we change our mind, we can click on the CANCEL button and the source code will be left untouched. Otherwise, we can confirm the selection by clicking on the FINISH button.

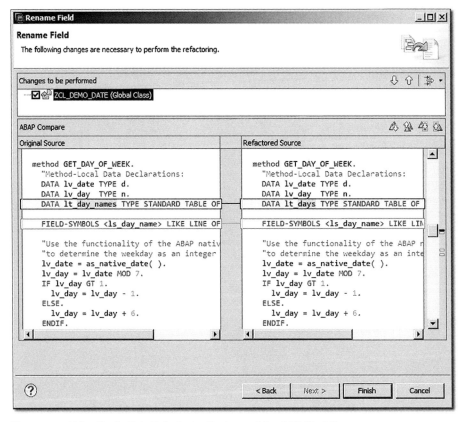

Figure 2.52 Using the Built-in Refactoring Features of the ADT (Part 3)

Menu-based access to these features and more can be found in the SOURCE menu highlighted in Figure 2.53. Here, for example, we can clean up unused variables, format portions of the code according to preferences/project standards, and much, much more.

As you're editing development objects using these features, keep in mind that most of the changes being made are made in-memory. This means that the changes are not synchronized with the ABAP Repository until you save and/or activate the code. At that point, the changes are committed and available for subsequent editing in Eclipse or the backend ABAP Workbench.

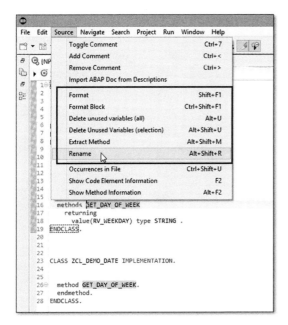

Figure 2.53 Accessing Other Refactoring Features

2.5.4   Where to Go to Find More Information about AIE

Realistically, the introduction to Eclipse offered in this section barely scratches the surface of the features offered by this tool. If you're eager to learn more about what's possible with AIE, we highly recommend that you tour the AIE community page at *http://scn.sap.com/community/abap/eclipse*. A number of useful video tutorials are also provided at *http://scn.sap.com/docs/DOC-31815*.

Finally, we're starting to see some custom-developed Eclipse plug-ins for AIE which are definitely worth investigating. Here, you can find plug-ins to help you generate ABAP classes from UML diagrams, create documentation bundles, and integrate with the popular SAPlink project used for code migration. Most of these plug-ins are featured on the aforementioned AIE community page on the SAP Community Network, so we'd encourage you to take a look around and see what sort of goodies you can find.

2.6 New Syntax Features in Release 7.40

For years, one of the primary complaints for developers coming to ABAP Objects from other contemporary OO languages was that ABAP Objects syntax is simply too verbose. For example, consider the code excerpts contained in Listing 2.34 and Listing 2.35. Both of these code excerpts carry out the task of instantiating a "point" object. In Listing 2.34, you can see how the Java programming language allows us to accomplish this in one line of code using the Java `new` operator. When compared with the ABAP-based equivalent in Listing 2.35, you can see that the several more keystrokes are involved. First, we have to declare an object reference variable, then we have to instantiate the object using the familiar `CREATE OBJECT` statement. Both approaches get us to the same place, but the ABAP way leads to early onset carpal tunnel syndrome.

```
Point p = new Point(2, 3);
```
Listing 2.34 Instantiating an Object in the Java Programming Language

```
DATA lo_point TYPE REF TO lcl_point.
CREATE OBJECT lo_point
  EXPORTING
    x = 2
    y = 3.
```
Listing 2.35 Instantiating an Object in ABAP Objects

In an effort to make the ABAP Objects language more developer-friendly, SAP introduced a new operator type in Release 7.40 that allows ABAP developers to build expressions similar to those they might be accustomed to creating in other OO languages such as Java or C#: *constructor expressions*.

The syntax diagram contained in Listing 2.36 demonstrates the syntax used to create constructor expressions. In order to understand this syntax, it helps to have a feel for the types of constructor operators that are available. Table 2.5 highlights some of the more relevant operator types offered with Release 7.40. Here, we can see that operator types help clarify the context of a particular constructor expression. For example, the presence of the `NEW` operator type tells us that the constructor expression is used to instantiate a data object. The rest of the expression syntax is then used to specify the type of the object being created and any parameters needed to carry out the instantiation process.

```
... operator [type|#]( ... ) ...
```
Listing 2.36 Syntax Diagram for Constructor Expressions

Operator	Description
Instance Operator (NEW)	This operator type is used to create/instantiate objects. Here, the term object refers to object instances in the OO context as well as anonymous data objects.
Value Operator (VALUE)	This operator is used to construct complex values that are used in initialization expressions, as method arguments, and so forth.
Reference Operator (REF)	This operator's used to create data references on the fly. So, for example, if there's a method that expects a data reference, we can use the REF operator to create that reference without having to use the GET_REFERENCE OF dobj INTO... statement to copy the data reference into a helper variable first.
Conversion/Casting Operators (CONV and CAST)	These operators are used to perform type conversions on the fly in order to reduce the number of helper variables needed to work with various API signatures, etc.
Conditional Operators (COND and SWITCH)	These operators are used to streamline conditional initialization statements into a single expression.

Table 2.5 Selected Constructor Operator Types Introduced with Release 7.40

So what do real world constructor expressions look like? Well, consider the code excerpt contained in Listing 2.37. Here, we've refactored the ABAP code excerpt from Listing 2.35 using the NEW operator as well as the new inline declaration feature introduced with Release 7.40 (e.g. the DATA(variable) part). From a compilation/runtime perspective, both code excerpts work exactly the same. However, it goes without saying that the newer approach is much more concise.

```
DATA(lo_point) = NEW lcl_point( x = 2, y = 3 ).
```
Listing 2.37 Working with the NEW Operator

From a pure OO programming perspective, the NEW operator is perhaps the most compelling. However, while the other operator types were not designed exclusively for OO programming, they certainly make for more streamlined coding. For instance, consider the code excerpt contained in Listing 2.38. Here, we're using the new syntax features in Release 7.40 to reduce the number of lines it takes to build a SQL query using the object-oriented *ABAP Database Connectivity* (ADBC) library. Without these features, the number of lines of code required to implement this example would nearly double to accommodate all of the helper variable declarations, etc.

```abap
DATA(lv_program_id) = 'R3TR'.
DATA(lv_object_type) = 'CLAS'.
DATA(lv_pattern) = 'CL_ABAP%'.

DATA(lo_stmt) = NEW cl_sql_statement( ).
lo_stmt->set_param( REF #( lv_program_id ) ).
lo_stmt->set_param( REF #( lv_object_type ) ).
lo_stmt->set_param( REF #( lv_pattern ) ).

DATA(lo_rs) =
  lo_stmt->execute_query(
    `SELECT obj_name, author ` &&
      `FROM tadir ` &&
      `WHERE mandt = ? AND pgmid = ? AND object = ? ` &&
        `AND obj_name LIKE ?` ).

DATA(lt_rsmd) = lo_rs->get_metadata( ).
DATA(lr_line_type) = lo_rs->get_struct_ref( md_tab = lt_rsmd ).
DATA(lo_line_descr) = CAST cl_abap_structdescr(
  cl_abap_structdescr=>describe_by_data_ref( lr_line_type ) ).
DATA(lo_table_descr) = CAST cl_abap_tabledescr(
  cl_abap_tabledescr=>create( p_line_type = lo_line_descr ) ).

DATA lr_results_tab TYPE REF TO data.
CREATE DATA lr_results_tab TYPE HANDLE lo_table_descr.
lo_rs->set_param_table( lr_results_tab ).
lo_rs->next_package( ).
lo_rs->close( ).

FIELD-SYMBOLS <lt_results> TYPE INDEX TABLE.
FIELD-SYMBOLS <ls_result> TYPE any.

ASSIGN lr_results_tab->* TO <lt_results>.
LOOP AT <lt_results> ASSIGNING <ls_result>.
  WRITE: / <ls_result>.
ENDLOOP.
```

Listing 2.38 Using Constructor Expressions to Simplify an ADBC Query

At the end of the day, constructor expressions, inline declarations and the other Release 7.40-specific functions described in this chapter are merely syntactic sugar. If you happen to be working on a Release 7.40 system, then we think that you'll find these statements to be useful from a productivity perspective. However, if your system is not quite there yet, don't worry; you're not missing out on any core functionality. You just might want to invest in a wrist brace or two in the meantime.

2.7   UML Tutorial: Object Diagrams

In the previous chapter, we learned how class diagrams could be used to specify the static architecture of an object-oriented system. Most of the time, these diagrams are straightforward and easy to interpret. However, sometimes the relationship between certain classes is not so intuitive. In these cases, *object diagrams* can be used to depict a snapshot or simulation of the actual objects created in reference to these classes at runtime. Oftentimes, just seeing an example of how the actual objects are configured at runtime can shed some light on the nature of complex class relationships.

Figure 2.54 illustrates a portion of a class diagram that shows the recursive aggregation relationship between a bill of material (BOM) document and its components/items. The diamond on the `MaterialBOM` side of the association is used to indicate that the BOM is an *aggregate*, containing 0 or more items.

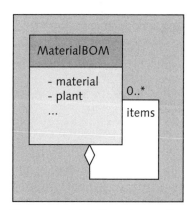

Figure 2.54 UML Class Diagram Showing Material BOM Aggregation

The static class diagram contained in Figure 2.54 is useful for identifying the basic relationship between a BOM and its items, but it doesn't really help us visualize just how complex the relationships might be between BOMs and items at runtime. For example, in complex engineering scenarios, it's not uncommon for a

BOM to contain items that are also complex assemblies. Depending on the nature of what we're building, this hierarchy can be nested arbitrarily deep.

In order to visualize what's going on at runtime, what we really need is a diagram to show the relationship between the actual object instances that will be created. Within the UML, this task is performed by the *object diagram*.

As you can see in Figure 2.55, object diagrams depict a snapshot of object instances and their interrelationships. Here, we can see how the BOM object for a laptop computer explodes out into a multi-level hierarchy. If we're developing algorithms to process this hierarchy, it can be useful to have this view of the data in order to visualize how we might go about traversing nodes, etc.

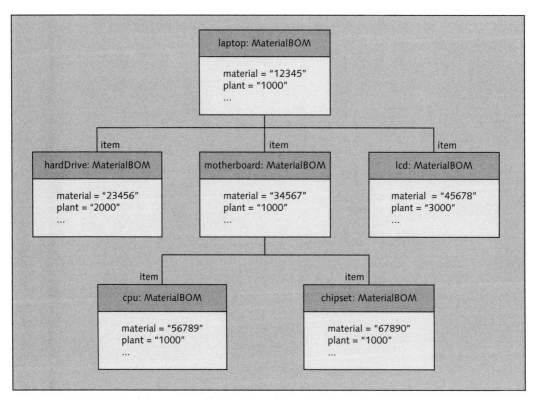

Figure 2.55 Object Diagram Showing BOM for a Laptop Computer

As you can see from Figure 2.55, object diagrams are very similar to class diagrams in many respects. However, in object diagrams, the rectangular boxes represent object instances instead of classes. Figure 2.56 shows the basic notation for specifying objects in an object diagram. In the top box, you provide the name of the object as well as the type of class the object is created in reference to. The lower box is optional, allowing you to provide additional runtime details about the object (i.e. its current state).

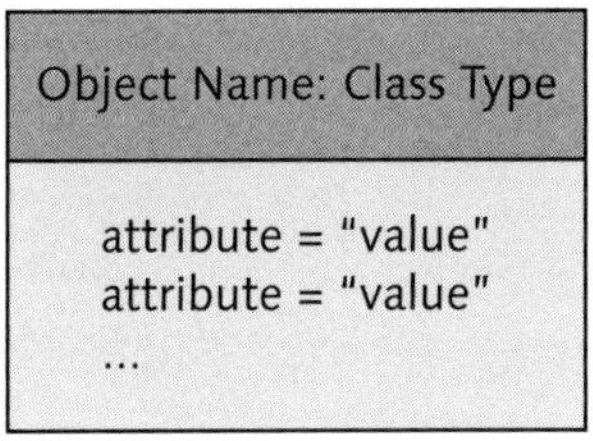

```
Object Name: Class Type

   attribute = "value"
   attribute = "value"
   ...
```

Figure 2.56 Object Instance Notation in Object Diagrams

Object diagrams can display as many objects as needed to illustrate the class/object relationships. The diagram is considered to be a viewport into the system at a particular point in time. Objects are created and destroyed in programs all the time, so it's important not to get hung up on trying to illustrate every possible object that will be created in the system at runtime. If one diagram cannot fully describe the relationship, additional diagrams can be used to show the progression of the object configuration as the program continues to run.

2.8 Summary

This chapter covered a lot of ground, exposing you to the basic syntax and tools you'll need to begin writing object-oriented programs in ABAP. However, while we've given a nuts-and-bolts description of classes and objects in this chapter, we've only begun to scratch the surface with regards to the potential benefits that can be obtained by adopting an object-oriented approach in our program designs. Therefore, in the next chapter, we'll begin to explore some of these features by examining the concepts of *encapsulation* and *implementation hiding*.

Classes are abstractions that are used to extend the functionality of a programming language by introducing user-defined types. Encapsulation and implementation hiding techniques are used to simplify the way that developers interface with these user-defined types, making object-oriented program designs easier to understand, maintain, and enhance.

3 Encapsulation and Implementation Hiding

One of the most obvious ways to speed up the software development process is to leverage pre-existing code. However, while most projects strive to create reusable source code artifacts, few actually succeed in delivering modules that can be classified as *reusable*. In most cases, this lack of (re)usability can be traced back to the fact that the module(s) become too tightly coupled with their surrounding environment. With so many "wires" getting in the way, it's hard to pick up a module and drop it in somewhere else. Therefore, in order to improve reusability, we need to cut the cords and figure out ways of building autonomous components that can *think* and *act* on their own.

In this chapter, we'll learn how to breathe life into objects by exploring the benefits of combining data and behavior together under one roof. Along the way, we'll explore the use of access control mechanisms and see how they can be used to shape the *interfaces* of the defining classes to make them easier to modify and reuse in other contexts.

3.1 Lessons Learned from Procedural Programming

Contrary to popular belief, many core object-oriented programming concepts are based on similar principles rooted in the procedural programming paradigm. In both paradigms, the basic goal is to provide developers with the tools they need to translate requirements from the physical world into software-based solutions. However, while both programming models share in this goal, they go about achieving it in vastly different ways. In this section, we'll take a closer look at the procedural approach and consider some of the limitations which ultimately caused many language designers to move in the direction of an object-oriented approach.

3.1.1 Decomposing the Functional Decomposition Process

Typically, procedural developers formulate their program designs using a process called *functional decomposition*. The term "functional decomposition" is taken from the world of mathematics, where mathematical functions are broken down into a series of smaller discrete functions that are easier to understand on their own. From a development perspective, functional decomposition refers to the process of *decomposing* a complex program into a series of smaller modules (e.g. procedures or subroutines).

One common approach for discovering these procedures is to scan through the functional requirements and highlight all the verbs used to describe the actions a program must take to meet its objectives. After all of the steps have been identified, they are then *composed* into a main program that's responsible for making sure that the procedures are executed in the right sequence. This process of organizing and refining the main program is sometimes called *step-wise refinement*.

For small to medium-sized programs, this strategy works pretty well. However, as programs start to branch out and grow in complexity, the design tends to become unwieldy as the main program becomes saddled with too many responsibilities. Here, besides keeping track of all of the different procedures and making sure that they're processed in the right order, the main program is also normally responsible for managing all of the data used by the various procedures. For this reason, such programs are often referred to as "God programs".

> **Note**
>
> In his book, *Design Patterns Explained: A New Perspective on Object-Oriented Design, 2nd Edition*, Alan Shalloway suggests that the term "God program" stems from the fact that only God can understand these programs.

With functional decomposition, the level of abstraction is the *subroutine*. Within a given subroutine definition, we can implement logic to perform a particular task using data that's provided from one of two places:

- Parameters that are passed into the subroutine from the calling program
- Global variables which are visible from within the subroutine

Regardless of the approach we use to supply subroutines with data, the reality is that there's no clean way of doing this without introducing some undesirable dependencies. For example, if we make liberal use of global variables, we open ourselves up to the possibility of data corruption errors. Here, imagine the impacts of switching out the call sequence of a pair of subroutines which make changes to the same global variable(s). If subroutine b depends on subroutine a to initialize the data and the call sequence gets flipped based on a requirements change, it's very likely that we'll start seeing strange data-related errors in the processing (see Figure 3.1).

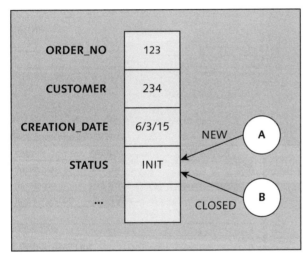

Figure 3.1 Data Collision Errors between Subroutines and Global Variables

Conversely, replacing global variables by passing around lots of parameters places additional burden on the main program to keep track of the parameters. Plus, we end up cluttering up the subroutine's parameter interface, which in turn leads to the tight coupling problem we described earlier.

Ideally we'd like for our modules to assume more responsibilities internally so that they are less reliant on controlling programs/modules when carrying out their tasks. Think of it this way, if we were to compare the organization of a software program with organizational (org) structures in an enterprise, which of the two org structures depicted in Figure 3.2 and Figure 3.3 would we want our programs to look like? In the case of the flat org structure depicted in Figure 3.2, we have one centralized module that's responsible for (micro)managing lots of submodules. On the other hand, the tall org structure shown in Figure 3.3 is much more balanced with higher level modules delegating responsibilities down to specialized submodules.

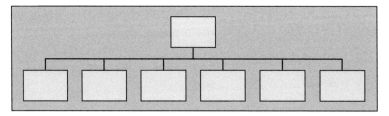

Figure 3.2 Example of a Flat Organizational Structure

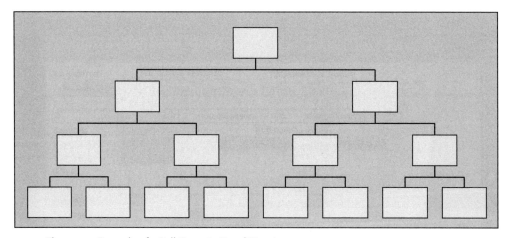

Figure 3.3 Example of a Tall Organizational Structure

In programming, just like business, it's important that we delegate responsibilities so that our programs remain flexible. In order for that to happen, the (sub)modules need to be smart enough to figure certain things out on their own — and that requires data. In the sections to come, we'll find that combining data and behavior together within a class helps us develop modules that can attain the kind of autonomy we're looking for.

3.1.2 Case Study: A Procedural Code Library in ABAP

To better illustrate some of the procedural programming challenges noted in Section 3.1.1, let's consider an example. In this section, we'll sketch out the development of a date utility library using ABAP function modules.

If you've worked with function modules before, then you know that they're defined within the context of a *function group*. In some respects, function groups bear some similarities to classes in that you can use them to define data and behaviors together within a self-contained unit (called a *function pool*). However, this analogy breaks down when you consider the fact that you cannot load multiple instances of a function group inside your program. This limitation makes it difficult for developers to work with the (global) data inside of a function group since additional logic is required to partition the data into separate work areas (or instances).

Because of this shortcoming, most function module developers tend to design their functions as *stateless* modules which operate on data that's maintained elsewhere. In this context, the term "stateless" implies that the function modules have no recollection of prior invocations and don't maintain any sort of internal state. As a result, function module developers need only worry about implementing the procedural logic—keeping track of the data/sessions is someone else's problem.

> **Note**
>
> Whenever you call a function module from a particular function group inside your program, the global data from the function group is loaded into the memory of the internal session of your program. Any subsequent calls to function modules within that function group will share the same global data allocated whenever the first function module was called.

> **Blame it on the BAPIs**
>
> The stateless approach to function module development increased in popularity quite a bit in the late 1990s/early 2000s whenever SAP started introducing *BAPIs* (the term "BAPI" stands for Business Application Programming Interface). At that time, SAP rolled out loads of function modules which promoted a stateless architecture. To call these BAPIs, one would generally have to define a slew of (global) variables that would be used to process BAPI calls. This is illustrated with the commonly used BAPI_USER_GET_DETAIL used to read user details. In the function signature shown in Figure 3.4, you can see that there's quite a bit of data about a user that has to be maintained outside of the function module. It's also interesting to note that the same variables would be needed to perform other operations on users such as create, change, and so forth.

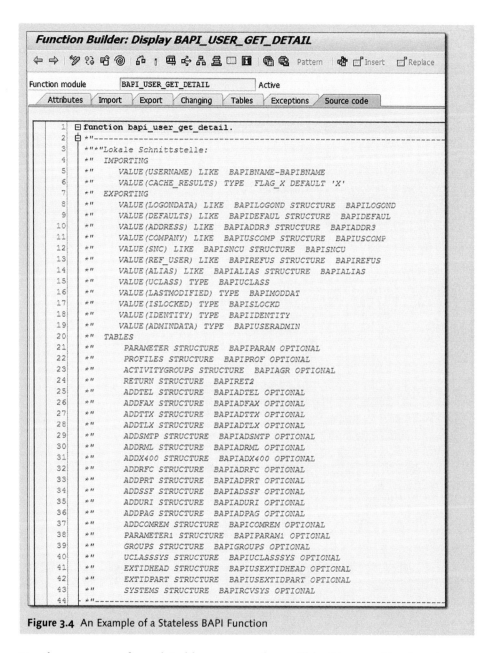

Figure 3.4 An Example of a Stateless BAPI Function

For the purposes of our date library example, we'll build our utility functions as stateless function modules. Within these functions, we'll operate on a date value represented by the SCALS_DATE structure shown in Figure 3.5. Here, though we could have just as easily used the internal ABAP date (D) type, we elected to use a structure type so that we could clearly address the individual components of a date (e.g. month, day, or year) without using offset semantics.

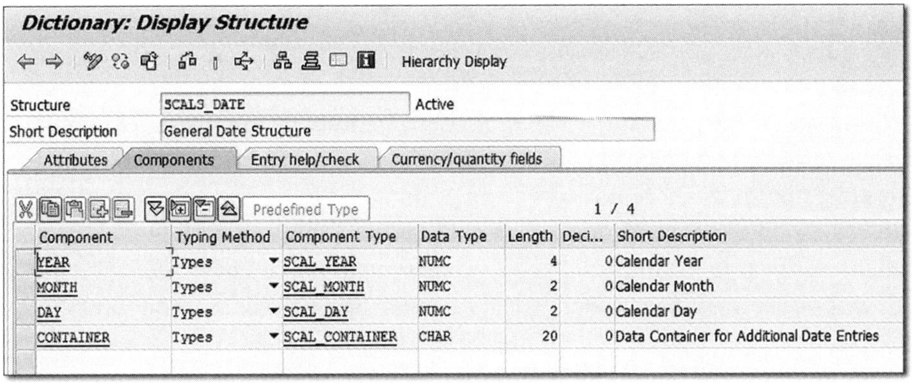

Figure 3.5 Modeling the Data Used for the Date Library

The code excerpt contained in Listing 3.1 sketches out the date API in a function group called ZDATE_API. Here, we've defined a handful of utility methods that can be used to perform date calculations, format dates according to different locales, and so forth.

```
FUNCTION-pool zdate_api.
FUNCTION z_add_to_date.
  * Local Interface IMPORTING VALUE (iv_days) TYPE i
  *                 CHANGING (cs_date) TYPE scals_date
  ...
ENDFUNCTION.
FUNCTION z_subtract_from_date.
  * Local Interface IMPORTING VALUE (iv_days) TYPE i
  *                 CHANGING (cs_date) TYPE scals_date
  ...
ENDFUNCTION.
FUNCTION z_get_day_name.
  * Local Interface IMPORTING VALUE (is_date) TYPE scals_date
  *                 EXPORTING ev_day TYPE string
  ...
ENDFUNCTION.
FUNCTION z_get_week_of_year.
  * Local Interface IMPORTING VALUE (is_date) TYPE scals_date
  *                 EXPORTING ev_week TYPE i
  ...
ENDFUNCTION.
```

```
FUNCTION z_format_date.
  * Local Interface IMPORTING VALUE (is_date) TYPE scals_date
  *                          VALUE (iv_format) TYPE csequence
  *                 EXPORTING ev_formatted TYPE string
  ...
ENDFUNCTION.
```
Listing 3.1 Building a Date Utility Library Using Function Modules

Within an ABAP program, we might use functions in the ZDATE_API function group to operate on date values being evaluated as part of a data processing routine like the contrived reporting example contained in Listing 3.2. With this kind of scenario in mind, in the upcoming sections we'll think about how our date API might stand up to maintenance requests that might pop up over time. This analysis will set the stage for Section 3.1.3 when we begin thinking about objects.

```
REPORT zsome_report.
START-OF-SELECTION.
  PERFORM get_data.

FORM get_data.
  DATA ls_date TYPE scals_date.
  DATA lt_itab TYPE STANDARD TABLE OF ...
  FIELD-SYMBOLS <ls_wa> LIKE LINE OF lt_itab.

  SELECT *
    INTO TABLE lt_itab ...

  LOOP AT lt_itab ASSIGNING <ls_wa>.
    ls_date = ...

    CALL FUNCTION 'Z_ADD_TO_DATE'
      EXPORTING
        iv_days = <ls_wa>-work_days
      CHANGING
        cs_date = ls_date.
    ...
    CALL FUNCTION 'Z_SUBTRACT_FROM_DATE'
      EXPORTING
        iv_days = <ls_wa>-offset
      CHANGING
        cs_date = ls_date.
    ...
    CALL FUNCTION 'Z_FORMAT_DATE'
      EXPORTING
        is_date = ls_date
        iv_format = `MM/DD/YYYY`
      IMPORTING
        ev_formatted = lv_formatted.
```

```
    . . .
  ENDLOOP.
ENDFORM.
```
Listing 3.2 Incorporating the Date API into an ABAP Report Program

Expanding the Scope of the Date API

For the first scenario, imagine that we discover a need to expand the date API to also keep track of time. While this seems easy enough in principle, this could prove challenging since the structure used to model the date value doesn't contain components to capture a time stamp.

Looking at the SCALS_DATE structure in the ABAP Dictionary (in Figure 3.6), we discover that this structure cannot be enhanced/appended to. Maybe we could get away with using the unused CONTAINER field, but this wouldn't be obvious to developers who weren't intimately familiar with the internal workings of our date API.

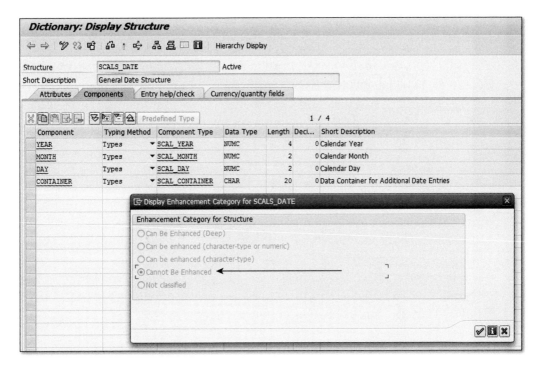

Figure 3.6 Looking at the Enhancement Category of the SCALS_DATE Structure

To implement this change correctly, we'd probably have to change the signature of our function modules to utilize a new structure. Besides requiring a fair amount of rework within the functions themselves, this also requires that we make wholesale changes to the programs that call them.

Though you might be saying to yourself that the choice of the SCALS_DATE structure for the date API's data model was a poor one (and you're right to say so), that's really not the issue here. The point of this demonstration is to illustrate the fact that our date API exposes way too much information about its internal representation. Consumers of our date API shouldn't know (or care) whether we use the native ABAP date type (D), a structure, or something else entirely.

By exposing this kind of information in the function signatures, we've effectively coded ourselves into a corner. For better or worse, we have to stick with the design choices we've made and try our best to enhance around them. With stateless modules, this is about the best we can hope for.

Dealing with External Data Corruption

For the next scenario, imagine that you receive a defect report which indicates that the Z_FORMAT_DATE function is producing invalid output. After much investigation, you determine that the invalid output isn't a function of the logic in Z_FORMAT_DATE, but rather due to fact that an invalid day value has been specified in the SCALS_DATE structure's DAY field. Here, you discover that the invalid value is set within the calling report program which is accessing the SCALS_DATE structure outside of the ZDATE_API function group.

Though such errors might be easy to fix once you find them, they can be difficult to find. Since the ZDATE_API function group doesn't technically own the data, there's nothing stopping other modules from overwriting and/or corrupting the API's data model. In a perfect world, we'd like all accesses to the date API's data model to go through functions in the ZDATE_API function group so that we can isolate them and enforce the necessary validation rules (e.g. you can't have a date value of 20160231). However, this is something the procedural model simply can't guarantee. To really enforce these rules, we need some support from the underlying language implementation to control access.

3.1.3   Moving Toward Objects

The ZDATE_API function group introduced in Section 3.1.2 is an example of an *abstract data type* (ADT). As the name suggests, ADTs are data types which provide an abstraction around some entity or concept (e.g. a date). Included in this abstraction is the data itself as well as a set of operations that can be performed on that data.

In order for ADTs to be effective, we must keep the data and operations as close to one another as possible. As we observed in Section 3.1.2, such cohabitation is virtually impossible to achieve with procedural programming techniques. Because of this divide, our date API (though admittedly contrived) was awkward to use and quite error prone. These problems become even more pronounced as the size and complexity of such code libraries expand.

In many ways, all of the problems we've considered in this section can be traced back to one central theme: poor support for data. While it would seem obvious that data is the foundation upon which any successful computer program runs, the stark reality is that data takes a back seat to actions in the procedural programming paradigm. As a result, procedural programs tend to decay at a much faster pace than programs built using programming models which place a greater emphasis on the data.

3.2   Data Abstraction with Classes

Recognizing many of the limitations outlined in Section 3.1, software researchers developed the OOP paradigm from the ground up with a strong emphasis on data *and* behavior. As you've already learned, classes are the vehicle that drives this equilibrium, encapsulating data (attributes) and behavior (methods) together inside a self-contained unit.

Encapsulation improves the organization of the code, making object-oriented class libraries much easier to understand and use than their procedural counterparts. To put this into perspective, consider the clumsiness of the function module-based date library we created in Section 3.1.2. Each time we accessed one of the API functions, we had to pass in an externally-managed structure which contained all of the date information needed to handle the request. Plus, if we wanted to work with multiple dates, then we had to define multiple variables and track those variables manually outside of the function group.

Let's compare that experience with a reimagined date API built using an ABAP Objects class. In Listing 3.3, we've created a class called LCL_DATE which provides the same functionality of the ZDATE_API function group. As you look over the class definition, notice the simplification in the signature of the API methods. Instead of passing around an SCALS_DATE structure, the date information is being stored internally in an instance attribute called MS_DATE_INFO. Besides simplifying the interface, this design change also allows us to get out of the business of tracking date information externally. Now, our date API is truly an ADT which provides a *complete* abstraction around a date value as opposed to a loosely associated set of stateless function modules.

```
CLASS lcl_date DEFINITION.
  PUBLIC SECTION.
    DATA ms_date_info TYPE scals_date.
    METHODS:
      add IMPORTING iv_days TYPE i
          RETURNING VALUE(ro_date) TYPE REF TO lcl_date,
      subtract IMPORTING iv_days TYPE i
               RETURNING VALUE(ro_date) TYPE REF TO lcl_date,
      get_day_name RETURNING VALUE(rv_day) TYPE string,
      get_week_of_year RETURNING VALUE(rv_week) TYPE i,
      format IMPORTING iv_pattern TYPE csequence
             RETURNING VALUE(rv_date) TYPE string.
      ...
ENDCLASS.
```
Listing 3.3 Reimagining the Date Utilities API as an ABAP Objects Class

The code excerpt contained in Listing 3.4 demonstrates how we can work with our refactored date library. Once an LCL_DATE instance is created, we no longer have to worry about handling the date value. Instead, we can use methods like add() and subtract() to apply the changes in-place. From a code readability standpoint, this is much easier to follow because the context of an operation like add() is clearly the object referenced by lo_date.

```
DATA lo_date TYPE REF TO lcl_date.
DATA lv_message TYPE string.

CREATE OBJECT lo_date
  EXPORTING
    iv_date = '20150913'
lo_date->add( 30 ).
lv_message = |{ lo_date->subtract( 15 )->format( 'YYYYMMDD' ) }|.
```
Listing 3.4 Working with an OO-Based API

Ultimately, objects created in reference to encapsulated classes take on their own *identity*, allowing developers to start thinking about their designs in more conceptual terms (e.g. a date). Consumers of these classes don't have to worry about low-level implementation details; to the end user the LCL_DATE class is like a black box which performs various date manipulations. We don't have to supply the LCL_DATE class with lots of data/context/instructions; it intrinsically *knows* how to do its job.

In the next section, we'll learn how to round out ADTs like the LCL_DATE class by closing off access to internal components such as the MS_DATE_INFO attribute. This safeguard ensures that *all* operations on date values are mediated through API methods which rigorously validate incoming requests to ensure that the integrity of date values is maintained. As we'll see, this approach offers several important benefits.

3.3 Defining Component Visibilities

The term "encapsulation" refers to the idea of enclosing something inside of a *capsule*. The verbal imagery associated with words like "capsule" implies that we're setting some kind of boundary between the internal components of a class and the outside world. The purpose of this boundary is to protect (or hide) the inner mechanisms of the object that are sensitive to change. Most of the time, the most vulnerable parts of an object are its attributes since these define the object's state. However, in this book, we'll look at ways to hide *any* design decisions that are subject to change.

In this section, we'll describe the ABAP Objects language constructs that you can use to establish boundaries within your classes. Then, in the section that follows, we'll consider how to use these boundaries to build robust classes that can easily be adapted to ever-changing functional requirements.

3.3.1 Working with Visibility Sections

ABAP Objects provides three visibility sections for controlling access to the components defined within a class: the PUBLIC SECTION, the PROTECTED SECTION, and the PRIVATE SECTION. Within a CLASS DEFINITION statement, all component declarations must be defined within one of these three visibility sections. The code excerpt contained in Listing 3.5 demonstrates the syntax used to define components within these sections.

```
CLASS lcl_visibility DEFINITION.
  PUBLIC SECTION.
    DATA x TYPE i.
  PROTECTED SECTION.
    DATA y TYPE i.
  PRIVATE SECTION.
    DATA z TYPE i.
ENDCLASS.
```
Listing 3.5 Working with Visibility Sections

As you might expect, components defined within the PUBLIC SECTION of a class are accessible from any context in which the class itself is visible (i.e., anywhere you can use the class type to declare an object reference variable). These components make up the *public interface* of the class.

Components defined within the PRIVATE SECTION of a class are only accessible from within the class itself. Note that this is more than just a mere suggestion; this is something that's strictly enforced by the ABAP compiler/runtime environment. For example, the code excerpt contained in Listing 3.6 would produce a compilation error because the z attribute of the LCL_VISIBILITY class is defined as a private attribute. The only way to get our hands on z is through a method defined in the LCL_VISIBILITY class.

```
DATA lo_visible TYPE REF TO lcl_visibility.
CREATE OBJECT lo_visible.
IF lo_visible->z GT 0.
  ...
ENDIF.
```
Listing 3.6 Attempting Access to Private Components of a Class

For now, we'll defer a discussion on the PROTECTED SECTION until we have a chance to cover inheritance in Chapter 5. For now, simply note that components defined in the PROTECTED SECTION are only accessible within a class and its subclasses.

When working in the form-based view of the Class Builder tool, you can assign components of global classes to visibility sections using the VISIBILITY column highlighted in Figure 3.7.

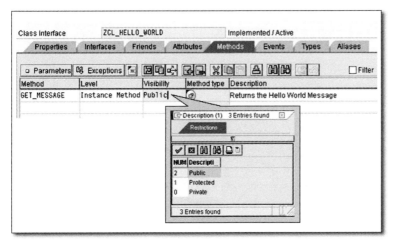

Figure 3.7 Setting the Visibility of Components Using the Form-Based View of the Class Builder Tool

Designing Across Multiple Dimensions

Choosing the right visibility section for a given component can be tricky, and it requires a fair amount of thought. Here, rather than thinking about the individual components, we need to think in terms of the class's overall interface. If we want to make our class simple and easy to use, then we'll need to strip down the public interface to just the essentials. This makes the interface less busy and therefore easier to consume.

In general, clients of a class should be on a "need-to-know" basis. In other words, if a client doesn't require direct access to a component, then there's no need for them to even be aware of its existence. Declaring such components within the PRIVATE SECTION of a class makes life easier for everyone: clients get to work with a simplified interface and the owners of the class have the freedom to change/improve the internal implementation of a class without fear of breaking existing client code.

With this concept in mind, we'd suggest that most attributes should be defined within the PRIVATE SECTION of a class. The primary reason for hiding attributes is to ensure that the state of the object cannot be tampered with haphazardly. If a client needs to update the state of an object, then they can do so through a method defined in the PUBLIC SECTION. The advantage of this kind of indirection is that we can control the assignment of the attribute using business rules that are defined inside the method. This eliminates a lot of the guesswork in troubleshooting data-related errors since we know that any and all changes to an attribute are brokered through a single method. Methods that update the value of private attributes are sometimes called *setter* (or *mutator*) methods. To access these values (or formatted versions of these values), clients can invoke *getter* (or *accessor*) methods which broker access in the other direction.

This getter/setter method approach to indirect data access is demonstrated in the LCL_TIME class contained in Listing 3.7. Here, the state of the time object is being represented by three private attributes called mv_hour, mv_minute, and mv_second. Any updates to these attributes are controlled through setter methods such as set_hour() or set_minute(). Within these methods, we've included logic to ensure that the attributes remain consistent (e.g. we don't have an hour value of 113). Clients can obtain copies of these values by calling the corresponding getter methods (e.g. get_hour()).

```
CLASS lcl_time DEFINITION.
  PUBLIC SECTION.
    METHODS:
      set_hour IMPORTING iv_hour TYPE i,
      get_hour RETURNING VALUE(rv_hour) TYPE i,
      set_minute IMPORTING iv_minute TYPE i,
      get_minute RETURNING VALUE(rv_minute) TYPE i,
      set_second IMPORTING iv_second TYPE i,
      get_second RETURNING VALUE(rv_second) TYPE i.

  PRIVATE SECTION.
    DATA: mv_hour TYPE i,
          mv_minute TYPE i,
          mv_second TYPE i.
ENDCLASS.

CLASS lcl_time IMPLEMENTATION.
  METHOD set_hour.
    IF iv_hour BETWEEN 0 AND 23.
      me->mv_hour = iv_hour.
    ELSE.
      "TODO: Error handling...
    ENDIF.
  ENDMETHOD.

  METHOD get_hour.
    rv_hour = me->mv_hour.
```

```
ENDMETHOD.
  ...
ENDCLASS.
```
Listing 3.7 Working with Getter and Setter Methods

As an alternative to the getter method approach, ABAP also allows us to define read-only attributes within a class definition. This is achieved using the READ-ONLY addition to the DATA keyword. The code excerpt below demonstrates how we might refactor the LCL_TIME class from Listing 3.7 to use this feature.

```
CLASS lcl_time DEFINITION.
  PUBLIC SECTION.
    DATA: mv_hour TYPE i READ-ONLY,
          mv_minute TYPE i READ-ONLY,
          mv_second TYPE i READ-ONLY.
  ...
ENDCLASS.
```
Listing 3.8 Defining Read-Only Attributes in a Class

While this feature can come in handy for simple classes which are primarily used for transferring data, we'd encourage you to use this option sparingly since it exposes the internal implementation details of your class.

3.3.2 Understanding the Friend Concept

In the previous section, we learned that components defined within the private and protected sections of a class are not visible outside of that class (or subclasses in the case of protected components). However, in some cases, it might be advantageous to be able to grant special access to certain classes of our choosing. Such classes are called *friends* of the class that grants them access.

Listing 3.9 illustrates the syntax used to create friend relationships between a defining class CL_SOME_CLASS and its friends: C1, C2, and so on. Here, the FRIENDS addition is added to a CLASS DEFINITION statement to declare this relationship up front to the ABAP compiler. As you can see, we can specify multiple friend classes after the FRIENDS addition (not to mention interfaces, which are covered in Chapter 6).

```
CLASS cl_some_class DEFINITION FRIENDS c1 c2 i3 i4.
  ...
ENDCLASS.
```
Listing 3.9 Defining Friendship Relationships in Classes

To demonstrate how friendship relationships work between classes, consider the example code contained in Listing 3.10. Here, we have a pair of classes called LCL_PARENT and LCL_CHILD which have entered into a friendship relationship. The LCL_CHILD class is taking advantage of this relationship by accessing the LCL_PARENT class's mv_credit_card_no attribute in a method called buy_toys(). Since mv_credit_card_no is defined as a private attribute, the only way for LCL_CHILD to access this value is through the friendship relationship. Without this addition, the code below would produce a syntax error.

```
CLASS lcl_child DEFINITION DEFERRED.
CLASS lcl_parent DEFINITION FRIENDS lcl_child.
  PRIVATE SECTION.
    DATA mv_credit_card_no TYPE string.
ENDCLASS.

CLASS lcl_child DEFINITION.
  PUBLIC SECTION.
    METHODS buy_toys.
ENDCLASS.
CLASS lcl_child IMPLEMENTATION.
  METHOD buy_toys.
    DATA: lo_parent TYPE REF TO lcl_parent,
          lo_store TYPE REF TO lcl_toy_store.
    lo_parent = ...
    lo_store = ...

    lo_store->checkout( lo_parent->mv_credit_card_no ).
  ENDMETHOD.
ENDCLASS.
```

Listing 3.10 Bypassing Access Control Using Friends

We can achieve the same effect for global classes maintained in the form-based view of the Class Builder tool by plugging the target friend classes on the Friends tab as shown in Figure 3.8.

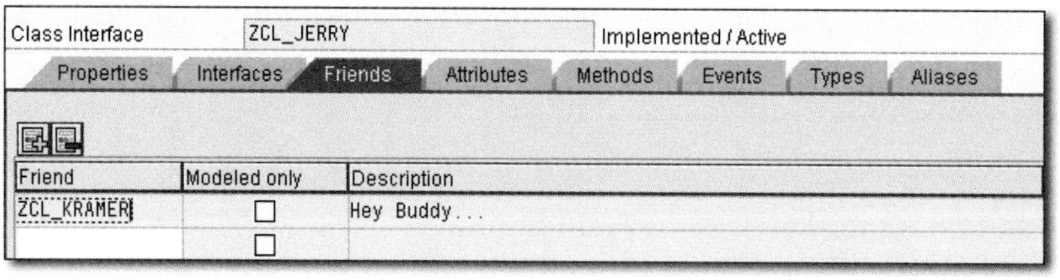

Figure 3.8 Defining Friendship Relationships Between Global Classes

As you begin working with friendship relationships, there are a couple of important things to consider. First of all, it's important to note the direction and nature of the friendship relationship. In Listing 3.10, class LCL_PARENT explicitly granted friendship access to class LCL_CHILD. This relationship definition is not reflexive. For example, it would not be possible for class LCL_PARENT to access the private components of class LCL_CHILD without the LCL_CHILD class granting friendship access to LCL_PARENT first. Secondly, notice that classes cannot arbitrarily declare themselves friends of another class. For instance, it would not be possible for class LCL_CHILD to surreptitiously declare itself a friend of class LCL_PARENT. If this were the case, access control would be a waste of time since any class could bypass this restriction by simply declaring themselves a friend of whatever class they were trying to access.

The example shown in Listing 3.10 also introduced a new addition to the CLASS DEFINITION statement that we have not seen before: the DEFERRED addition. In a scenario like this, the DEFERRED addition used in the first CLASS DEFINITION statement for LCL_CHILD is needed to instruct the compiler of the existence of the LCL_CHILD class in the CLASS DEFINITION statement for the LCL_PARENT class. Without this clause, the compiler would have complained that class LCL_CHILD was unknown whenever we tried to establish the friendship relationship in the definition of class LCL_PARENT.

To Friend or Unfriend

Many purists argue that the use of friends should not be allowed in object-oriented languages since they bypass traditional access control mechanisms. Whether you agree with this sentiment or not, we would recommend that you use friendship relationships sparingly in your designs because it truly is rare that you would need to open up access like this.

3.4 Designing by Contract

As we've learned, encapsulation and implementation hiding techniques can be used to define very precise public interfaces for a class. These interfaces help to form a *contract* between the developer of a class and users of that class. The contract metaphor is taken from the business world, where customers enter into contractual agreements with suppliers providing goods or services. In his book, *Object-Oriented Software Construction*, Bertrand Meyer described how this concept could be adapted into object-oriented software designs in order to improve the reliability of software components that are "...implementations meant to satisfy well-understood specifications."

In this context, objects are subject to a series of *invariants* (or constraints) that specify the valid states for the object. To maintain these invariants, methods are defined using *preconditions* (what must be true before the method is executed) and *postconditions* (what must be true after the method is executed). In Chapter 8, we'll look at ways to deal with exceptions to these rules.

The primary goal when applying the *Design by Contract* approach in your software designs is to produce components that deliver *predictable* results. The boundaries set by the visibility sections ensure that *loopholes* are not introduced into the contract. For instance, the date library that we first introduced in Section 3.1.2 had many loopholes that made it possible to bypass the business rules implemented inside the function module(s). The encapsulation techniques we applied in the class-based reimplementation of this library eliminated these loopholes by encapsulating the date data as a private attribute that's cut off from external tampering.

Client programmers using classes based on these principles know what to expect from the class based on the provided public interface. Similarly, class developers are free to change the underlying implementation so long as they continue to honor the contract outlined in the public interface. Over time, the duel nature of this relationship helps to increase trust as we accumulate reusable modules that clients know will work.

3.5   UML Tutorial: Sequence Diagrams

So far, our study of the UML has been focused on diagrams that are used to describe the static architecture of an object-oriented system. In this chapter, we will introduce the first of several *behavioral diagrams* that are used to illustrate the behavior of objects at runtime. The *sequence diagram* depicts a message sequence chart between objects that are interacting inside a software system.

Figure 3.9 shows a simple sequence diagram that is used to illustrate a cash withdrawal transaction in an ATM machine. A sequence diagram is essentially a graph in two dimensions. The various objects involved in the interaction are aligned along the horizontal axis. The vertical axis represents time. Sequence diagrams are initiated by a request message from some kind of external source. In the example in Figure 3.9, the external source is a user interfacing with the ATM machine. This initial message is called a *found message*. In object-oriented terms, a message is analogous to a method call. Messages are sent to objects (depicted in the familiar object boxes seen on the object diagrams described in Chapter 2). The dashed line protruding from underneath the object box represents the object's *lifeline*.

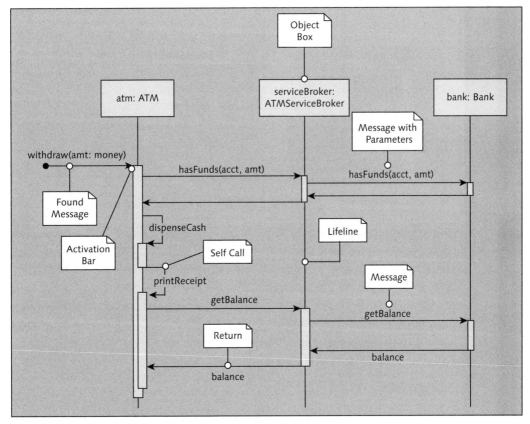

Figure 3.9 Sequence Diagram for Withdrawing Cash from an ATM

The intersection of a message and an object's lifeline is depicted with a thin rectangular box called an *activation bar*. The activation bar shows when an object is active during the interaction. Objects are activated via messages (i.e. method calls). Messages can include parameters that help clarify the operation to be performed by the object. However, it's not a good idea to try and fully specify the method interface in a sequence diagram—that's what a class diagram is for. Here, we only use parameters for emphasis or clarity. Synchronous method calls can have a *return* message that can also have optional parameters.

In some cases, a method might need to call other local helper methods to complete its task. In this case, a *self call* can be illustrated by drawing a circuitous arrow to another activation bar that is stacked on top of the current activation bar. For example, in Figure 3.9, messages `dispenseCash` and `printReceipt` are both represented as self calls on the `atm` object inside method `withdraw`.

Sequence diagrams are very useful for explaining complex interactions where the order of operations is difficult to follow. One of the reasons that sequence diagrams are so popular is that the notation is very intuitive and easy to read. To maintain this readability, it's important to avoid cluttering a sequence diagram with too many interactions. In the coming chapters, we'll look at other types of interaction diagrams that can be used to illustrate fine-grained behavior within an object or more involved interactions that span multiple use cases.

3.6 Summary

In this chapter, you learned about the many advantages of applying encapsulation and implementation hiding techniques to your class designs. Encapsulating data and behavior in classes simplifies the way that users/clients work with classes. Hiding the implementation details of these classes strengthens the design even further, making classes much more resistant to change and/or data corruption. The combination of these two design techniques helps you to design intelligent classes that are highly self-sufficient. Such classes are easy to reuse in other contexts since they are loosely coupled to the outside world.

In the next chapter, we'll examine the basic lifecycle of an object. We'll also learn about special methods called *constructors* that can be used to ensure that object instances are always created in a valid state.

Some of the most elusive bugs to trap are the ones that can be traced back to missing or invalid variable initializations. With that in mind, this chapter takes a deep dive into the lifecycle of objects and explores techniques for ensuring that objects are properly initialized before consumers ever get their hands on them.

4   Object Initialization and Cleanup

In the previous chapter, we learned how encapsulation and implementation hiding techniques can be used to protect the integrity of an object. Such objects produce consistent and reliable results, freeing developers from constantly worrying about data correctness issues in their programs. However, all these measures are wasted if we fail to properly initialize the object in the first place.

In this chapter, we'll consider some techniques for ensuring that objects are always created in a valid state. We'll also examine the overall object lifecycle, paying particular attention to how object resources are managed by the automatic memory management functionality of the ABAP runtime environment.

4.1   Understanding the Object Creation Process

One of the primary goals of the object-oriented design process is to identify ways to delegate responsibilities to objects. This approach transfers complexity from the main program into objects that are intelligent enough to handle the tasks they're assigned.

In order to coordinate these efforts, the main program needs to be able to create and destroy objects on demand. While the ABAP runtime environment takes care of most of the low-level technical details related to object allocation, there are some costs associated with creating objects dynamically. To recognize how these costs can affect the performance of your programs, it's important to understand what's going on behind the scenes whenever you request the creation of an object using the CREATE OBJECT statement.

To put all this into perspective, let's consider an example of a simple ABAP report program that needs to create objects at runtime. For the purposes of our discussion, we'll assume that this report is running in the foreground in an SAP GUI session. However, the basic principles remain the same for background processes, etc.

As you can see in Figure 4.1, our report program is running inside of a logical memory frame called an *internal session*. Conceptually, you can think of internal sessions as being part of a call stack of sorts that gets created as programs call other programs (e.g. using the CALL TRANSACTION or SUBMIT statements). Here, a given internal session manages the data objects of the program that is running, as well as the data objects of other programs (e.g. function pools, class pools, etc.) that are being used by that program. The call stack itself is contained within a *main session* that gets allocated whenever we open up the SAP GUI (or create a new session).

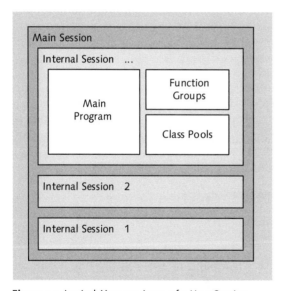

Figure 4.1 Logical Memory Areas of a User Session

If we broaden our focus a bit further, we can see that main sessions are stored within another logical memory area called a *user session* (also sometimes referred to as a *context*). As the name suggests, user sessions contain state information about users that are logged onto the system: basic user information, assigned authorizations, etc. They also keep track of the program(s) a user is running along with the data objects used by those programs.

Internally, user sessions are stored with a special section of shared memory on the AS ABAP application server host called the *roll buffer*. As you can see in Figure 4.2, the roll buffer is separated from the local memory area allocated to service work processes such as the one that's processing our report program. Why implement such separation? Well, since the AS ABAP is a time-sharing system designed to support multiple users, there has to be a way to swap users in and out between tasks in order to maximize work process utilization. In SAP terms, this swap process is referred to as a "roll-out" (when a user is evicted from a work process) and "roll-in" (whenever a user request is assigned to a work process).

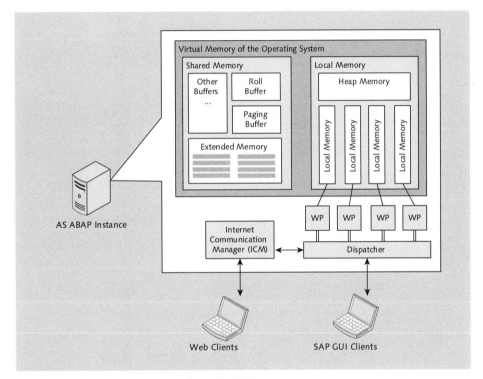

Figure 4.2 Basic Memory Structure of an AS ABAP Instance

Since roll-outs/roll-ins are happening all the time during normal operation, they must execute swiftly to avoid system latency. This means that SAP has to keep the user session itself small so that it can be copied quickly and easily. The upshot of all this from an object-management perspective is that SAP can't afford to carry around object data within a user session. So, to get around this limitation, SAP decided to create a layer of separation between object instances and the programs that allocate them. This is where the object reference variables introduced in Chapter 2 come into play.

Figure 4.3 illustrates how this separation is achieved from a memory allocation perspective. Here, our ABAP report is operating within a work process and our user session has been copied (rolled-in) to the roll area of the work process.

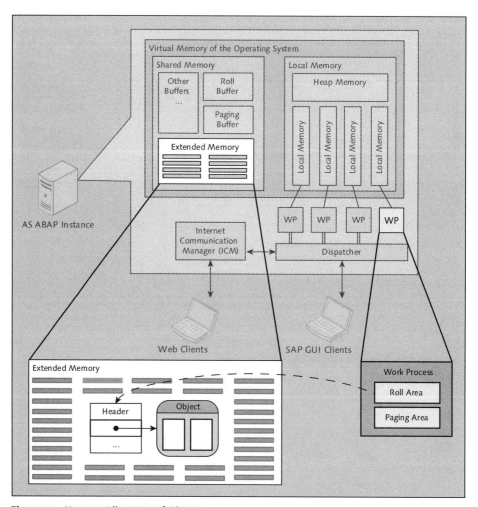

Figure 4.3 Memory Allocation of Objects

Whenever we request the creation of an object at runtime (using the CREATE OBJECT statement), the ABAP runtime environment will carry out the allocation request as follows:

1. First, it looks at the class definition referenced by our object reference variable and determines how much memory it needs to allocate an object instance of this type.

2. Then, once it knows how much memory it needs, it will scan through the extended memory area in order to find a chunk of memory large enough to store the object and its data.

3. During this memory allocation process, the runtime environment will also set aside some additional memory to create a *header* data structure that is used to keep track of various administrative details about the object (see Figure 4.3).

4. Finally, once the object instance is allocated, the address of the header structure is copied into the object reference variable the CREATE OBJECT statement is performed against.

The primary consequence of this approach for dynamically generating objects is the additional time required to allocate the proper amount of memory for an object. As multiple programs create and destroy objects, the extended memory area can become fragmented, making it difficult to locate a contiguous chunk of memory large enough to hold an object. Skeptics sometimes point to these performance costs as a reason for not using objects in their programs, claiming that they can't afford the additional overhead at runtime.

However, if you look carefully at your existing programs, you'll likely find that you are already using many types of dynamic data objects. For example, internal tables are dynamic data objects that require additional memory to be dynamically allocated as additional rows are appended to them. Most design decisions involve some kind of trade-off, and in the case of objects, you might have to sacrifice a little bit of performance in order to realize the many benefits of object-oriented programming. Fortunately, SAP has optimized the performance of the ABAP runtime environment such that these performance issues are rarely a concern. Still, we'll investigate some basic guidelines for tuning performance in Section 4.5.

> **Note**
>
> For an excellent description of dynamic data objects, check out Horst Keller's web log entitled "ABAP Geek 12—The Deep" at *https://www.sdn.sap.com/irj/sdn/weblogs?blog=/pub/wlg/2016*.

4.2 Working with Constructors

Encapsulated objects rely on data stored in private/hidden attributes to keep track of their internal state so that they can respond to method requests intelligently. So, it goes without saying that it's crucial that we ensure that an object's attributes are properly supplied with the data it needs to perform its duties when called upon. Otherwise, we end up back in procedural hell where methods are stateless and we have to go to great lengths to fetch data before we can do any useful work.

In order to avoid these kinds of situations, we need to figure out a way to *guarantee* that the attributes of an object are properly initialized before *any* calls are made to methods that depend on these attributes. Of course, we could try to be disciplined in our approach and make sure that we call all of the appropriate "setter" methods before we use the object, but then we have to remember to do it every time we instantiate an object. Here, in the best case, we have introduced a lot of redundant code. In the worst case, we forget to call a method here and there and therefore create an even bigger problem for ourselves. Clearly, we need a better method for initializing objects. To take the guesswork out of this process, OO languages such as ABAP Objects allow us to define special initializer methods within a class definition called *constructors*. These specialized callback methods are invoked automatically by the ABAP runtime environment *after* an object is allocated but *before* control is handed back to a consumer. Therefore, they represent an ideal place for injecting the relevant logic needed to initialize an object.

4.2.1 Defining Constructors

Constructors are defined using essentially the same syntax we use to define regular instance methods (see Listing 4.1). The notable difference is that we can only define importing parameters in the method signature. If you think about it, this makes sense since the constructor is called by the ABAP runtime environment in response to a CREATE OBJECT statement as opposed to the normal CALL METHOD statement. Here, we should point out that it's not possible to invoke constructors directly using the CALL METHOD statement.

```
METHODS constructor
          IMPORTING [VALUE(]i1 i2 ...[)]
                TYPE type [OPTIONAL]...
          EXCEPTIONS ex1 ex2.
```

Listing 4.1 Syntax for Defining an Instance Construtor

Constructors can be created in global classes by pressing the CONSTRUCTOR button in the Class Editor as shown in Figure 4.4.

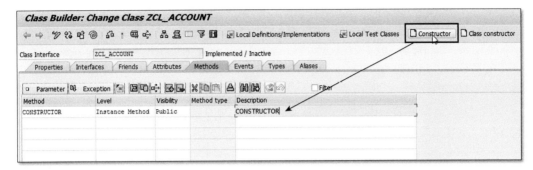

Figure 4.4 Creating Constructors for Global Classes

4.2.2 Understanding How Constructors Work

To demonstrate how constructors work, let's consider an example based on an account class used to model a bank account. In Listing 4.2, we've created a local class called LCL_ACCOUNT that allows us to view the current balance of the account and withdraw or deposit funds. The account details are stored in private attributes that do not have associated "setter" methods. Instead, we'll assume that these attributes are initialized via a database lookup inside the constructor() method. This implies that consumers must supply a valid account number whenever they create an account object. In Chapter 8, we'll see how class-based exceptions can be used to enforce this rule; for now we'll simply assume that this is the case.

```
CLASS lcl_account DEFINITION.
  TYPE-POOLS: abap.
  PUBLIC SECTION.
    METHODS:
      constructor IMPORTING iv_account_no
                   TYPE string,
      get_balance RETURNING VALUE(rv_balance)
                   TYPE bapicurr_d,
      deposit     IMPORTING iv_amount
                   TYPE bapicurr_d,
      withdrawal  IMPORTING iv_amount
                   TYPE bapicurr_d
                  RETURNING VALUE(rv_result)
                   TYPE abap_bool.
  PRIVATE SECTION.
    DATA: mv_account_no TYPE string,
```

```
           mv_balance     TYPE bapicurr_d.
ENDCLASS.

CLASS lcl_account IMPLEMENTATION.
  METHOD constructor.
*    Query database tables to retrieve account details:
*    SELECT FROM ...
*     WHERE account_no = iv_account_no.
  ENDMETHOD.

  METHOD get_balance.
    rv_balance = me->mv_balance.
  ENDMETHOD.

  METHOD deposit.
    me->mv_balance = me->mv_balance + iv_amount.
  ENDMETHOD.

  METHOD withdrawal.
    IF iv_amount LE me->mv_balance.
      me->mv_balance = me->mv_balance - iv_amount.
      rv_result = abap_true.
    ELSE.
      rv_result = abap_false.
    ENDIF.
  ENDMETHOD.
ENDCLASS.
```

Listing 4.2 Working with Constructors (Part 1)

The code excerpt in Listing 4.3 shows how we access our new constructor using the CREATE OBJECT statement. Here, notice how the addition of the constructor() method has effectively put a lock on the front door of our LCL_ACCOUNT class. Since the mv_balance instance attribute is initialized before the object is ever handed over to consumers, we no longer have to worry about making sure that the account balance is up-to-date: it gets initialized internally and updates can only occur through the deposit() and withdraw() methods that have built-in logic to guard against overdraws, etc. We also no longer have to worry about passing around account numbers since this detail is established up front during the object allocation process.

```
DATA lo_checking TYPE REF TO lcl_account.
CREATE OBJECT lo_checking
  EXPORTING
    iv_account_no = '1234567890'.

"Assume the opening balance is zero:
```

```
lo_checking->deposit( '100.00' ).
IF lo_checking->withdraw( '200.00' ) NE abap_true.
  WRITE: / 'Insufficient funds.'.
ENDIF.
lo_checking->deposit( '300.00' ).
```
Listing 4.3 Working with Constructors (Part 2)

4.2.3 Class Constructors

Most of the time, whenever we talk about constructors, we're typically talking about *instance constructors* that are used to initialize an instance of an object that is being created. However, it's also possible to define a *class constructor* for a class. Class constructors provide a mechanism for initializing class/static attributes and are implicitly called by the system before any accesses are made to the class inside a program.

> **Note**
>
> In this sense, class constructors are functionally equivalent to static initializer blocks from Java or C#.

Class constructors are defined using the syntax shown in Listing 4.3. As you can see, we're not allowed to define parameters for class constructors since they're implicitly called by the system.

```
CLASS-METHODS class_constructor.
```
Listing 4.4 Syntax for Defining a Class Constructor

Class constructors can be created for global classes by clicking the CLASS CON-STRUCTOR button on the Class Editor screen (see Figure 4.5).

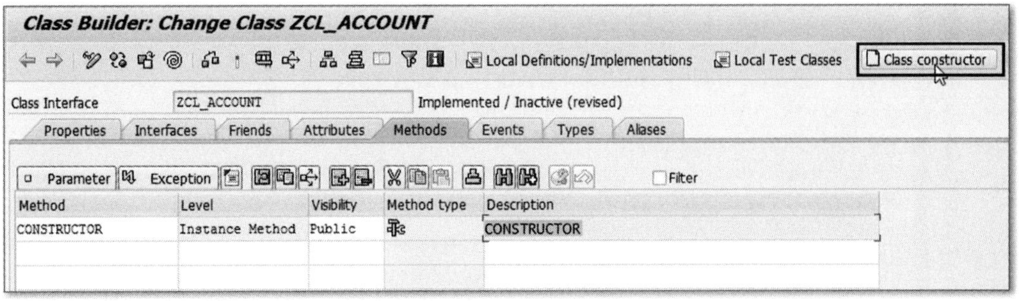

Figure 4.5 Creating Class Constructors for Global Classes

From an implementation perspective, class constructors are defined just like any other class method. Here, we can pre-allocate and initialize shared resources to eliminate overhead and speed up the object instantiation process. We'll observe some practical benefits of these capabilities in Section 4.3.

> **Note**
>
> Since class constructors are defined at the class level, we cannot access instance components within a class constructor since no instances of the class exist in that context. Of course, it *is* possible to instantiate an object of the class within the class constructor and then use that object reference to access instance components. We'll see examples of this technique in Section 4.3.

4.3   Object-Creational Patterns

Most of the classes that we've looked at up to this point in the book are trivial and easy to instantiate. However, as we get into more complex designs, we may run into situations where object instantiation becomes a bit trickier. Here, for example, we may find that we want to constrain the number of object instances users can create. Or, we may run into situations where there might be multiple ways to construct an object.

In this section, we'll look at a couple of common object-creational patterns that you can use to deal with complex object creation requirements. These patterns were originally documented in the classic software engineering text entitled *Design Patterns: Elements of Reusable Object-Oriented Software* (Addison-Wesley, 1995). For an excellent ABAP-based treatment on these concepts, we highly recommend that you pick up a copy of *Design Patterns in Object-Oriented ABAP, 2nd Edition* (SAP PRESS, 2009).

4.3.1   Controlling the Instantiation Context

By default, users are able to create instances of classes whenever and wherever they like using the CREATE OBJECT statement. Sometimes though, this sort of wide-open access is undesirable. For example, imagine that we have an object that needs to acquire a shared resource such as an external database connection or lock. For these types of objects, we would definitely want to control the number of object instances that are created in order to prevent resource contention issues.

In order to assert this kind of control, we must modify the instantiation context at the class definition level using the CREATE addition highlighted in Listing 4.5. Table 4.1 describes each of the possible instantiation contexts in detail.

```
CLASS lcl_db_connection DEFINITION
  CREATE {PUBLIC | PROTECTED | PRIVATE}.
  ...
ENDCLASS.
```

Listing 4.5 Specifying the Instantiation Context of an ABAP Objects Class

Instantiation Context	Visibility
PUBLIC	Classes with this (default) instantiation context can be instantiated anywhere that the class itself is visible without restrictions. This means that instances of the class can be created internally via instance/class methods or externally from any normal ABAP programming context: e.g. subroutines, functions, report programs, and so forth.
PROTECTED	Instances of these classes can only be created inside methods of the class itself and its subclasses.
PRIVATE	Instances of these classes can only be created inside methods of the class itself.

Table 4.1 Instantiation Contexts for Classes

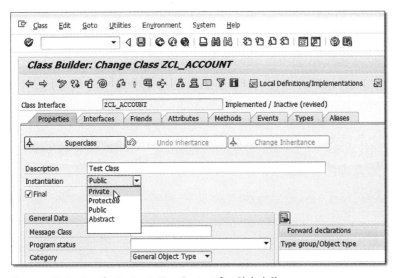

Figure 4.6 Setting the Instantiation Context for Global Classes

The instantiation context can be set for global classes by opening up the Class Builder tool and navigating to the PROPERTIES tab. Here, the instantiation context can be set using the INSTANTIATION drop-down list shown in Figure 4.6.

In the upcoming sections, we'll look at a couple of widely-used creational patterns which utilize this feature to control the way that object instances are created.

4.3.2 Implementing the Singleton Pattern

As we mentioned earlier, there may be times whenever we want to restrict the number of object instances that are created at runtime. For example, if we were to design a proxy class to broker database connections, we might want to design the class in such a way that a finite number of connections are maintained in a connection pool. Here, rather than creating a separate object instance per connection request, we would want to create a pool of objects and only provide users with access to one of the available connection objects from the pool.

In the most extreme case, we might only want a single object instance to exist at any one time within the system. This single object instance is referred to as a *singleton*. As a result, the software design pattern that describes how such objects are created is called the *singleton pattern*.

To demonstrate how the singleton pattern works, let's consider an example. Let's imagine that we need to build a number generator class that can be used to obtain a unique sequential number within some arbitrary range. In order to guarantee that the next number in the range is unique, we have to ensure from an implementation perspective:

▸ Only one instance of our number generator object can exist within the system at a given time.

▸ All number requests must be brokered through that single object.

▸ The state of that single object must remain consistent. In other words, we must keep track of the next available number in the sequence.

> **Note**
>
> Since SAP systems usually consist of multiple application server instances distributed across multiple host systems, keep in mind that further synchronization measures would be required to implement this pattern in a production setting (e.g. shared memory objects and/or enqueue locks).

In Listing 4.6, we've created a class called `LCL_NUMBER_GEN` that provides an implementation of our number generator. Here, notice how we're using the `CREATE PRIVATE` addition to ensure that instances of the number generator can only be created from within the `LCL_NUMBER_GEN` class. This forces clients to go through a class method called `get_instance()` that contains conditional logic to ensure that only one instance of `LCL_NUMBER_GEN` exists at a time. With that mechanism in place, we can easily implement the `get_next()` instance method to simply return the next number in the sequence.

```abap
CLASS lcl_number_gen DEFINITION CREATE PRIVATE.
  PUBLIC SECTION.
    CLASS-METHODS:
      get_instance RETURNING VALUE(ro_generator)
                            TYPE REF TO lcl_number_gen.

    METHODS:
      get_next RETURNING VALUE(rv_number) TYPE i.

  PRIVATE SECTION.
    CLASS-DATA so_instance TYPE REF TO lcl_number_gen.

    DATA mv_current_num TYPE i.

    METHODS:
      constructor.
ENDCLASS.

CLASS lcl_number_gen IMPLEMENTATION.
  METHOD get_instance.
    IF so_instance IS NOT BOUND.
      CREATE OBJECT so_instance.
    ENDIF.

    ro_generator = so_instance.
  ENDMETHOD.

  METHOD constructor.
    me->mv_current_num = 0.
  ENDMETHOD.

  METHOD get_next.
    me->mv_current_sum = me->mv_current_sum + 1.
    rv_number = me->mv_current_num.
  ENDMETHOD.
ENDCLASS.
```

Listing 4.6 Implementing the Singleton Pattern

The code excerpt contained in Listing 4.7 demonstrates how to consume our singleton number generator class within ABAP code. Here, notice that the ABAP compiler will not allow us to create instances of the number generator via the `CREATE OBJECT` statement. Instead, we're forced to go through the `get_instance()` method to create/access the number range instance. Once we obtain a reference to the current number range object, it's pretty much business as usual from there.

```
DATA lo_generator TYPE REF TO lcl_number_gen.
DATA lv_number TYPE i.

*CREATE OBJECT lo_generator. "Syntax error...
lo_generator = lcl_generator=>get_instance( ).

DO 5 TIMES.
  lv_number = lo_generator->get_next( ).
  WRITE: / 'Number #', lv_number.
ENDDO.
```
Listing 4.7 Accessing Singleton Objects from Consumer Code

4.3.3 Working with Factory Methods

Unlike other OO languages such as Java, ABAP Objects does not provide support for overloading methods. This is to say that we can't define multiple versions of the same method with different parameter lists. Though this is usually not a concern when defining normal methods, it does present us with a bit of a dilemma if we happen to be working with objects that need to be created in lots of different ways.

To put this scenario into perspective, let's imagine that we're tasked with building a data transfer object (DTO) for storing information about a person. In order to maximize the use of our person class, we'd like to make it easy to create instances of it using all kinds of different data sources including user master records, HR personnel records, business partner records, and so forth.

So how do we support all these different creation scenarios? Well, one option would be to cram the various input parameters into the signature of the `constructor()` method as shown in Listing 4.8. This approach works, but is messy and hard to follow.

```
CLASS lcl_person DEFINITION.
  PUBLIC SECTION.
    METHODS:
      constructor IMPORTING iv_user_id TYPE sy-uname OPTIONAL
```

```
                             iv_empl_no TYPE hrobjid OPTIONAL
                             iv_partner TYPE bu_partner OPTIONAL
                             ...
      ...
   PRIVATE SECTION.
      DATA mv_first_name TYPE string.
      DATA mv_last_name TYPE string.
      DATA mv_phone_num TYPE string.
      DATA mv_email TYPE string.
ENDCLASS.
```

Listing 4.8 Cluttering up the Constructor Method Signature

A better approach calls for the creation of *factory methods* which encapsulate the various creation contexts into a series of class methods that are easy to understand and use. This approach is demonstrated in Listing 4.9. Here, the various create_from_...() methods assume the responsibility of creating person objects in terms of users, employees, and so on. This makes the code more readable and provides us with the structure for adding additional creation scenarios down the road.

```
CLASS lcl_person DEFINITION.
   PUBLIC SECTION.
      CLASS-METHODS:
         create_from_user IMPORTING iv_user_id TYPE sy-uname
                          RETURNING VALUE(ro_person)
                                    TYPE REF TO lcl_person,
         create_from_employee IMPORTING iv_empl_no TYPE hrobjid
                              RETURNING VALUE(ro_person)
                                        TYPE REF TO lcl_person,
         create_from_partner IMPORTING iv_partner TYPE bu_partner
                             RETURNING VALUE(ro_person)
                                       TYPE REF TO lcl_person,
         ...
      METHODS:
         constructor,
         set_first_name IMPORTING iv_first_name TYPE string,
         get_first_name RETURNING VALUE(rv_first_name) TYPE string,
         ...
   ...
ENDCLASS.
```

Listing 4.9 Working with Factory Methods

4.4   Garbage Collection

Once we've finished using an object in our programs, we need to make sure that we restore its resources to the system. In early OO languages, it was the programmer's responsibility to make sure that objects were properly destroyed. Fortunately, the runtime environments of modern languages like ABAP Objects come equipped with a special memory management service called a *garbage collector* to take care of these housekeeping duties behind the scenes.

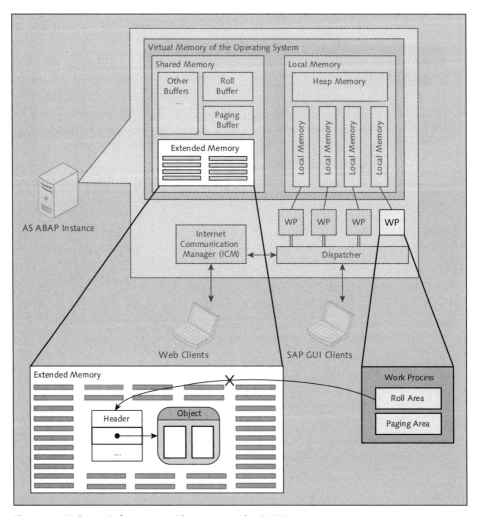

Figure 4.7 Deleting References to Objects Using the CLEAR Statement

The garbage collector's job is to scan through memory and delete orphaned object instances that no longer have any references associated with them. Much of the time, these references are destroyed automatically whenever an object reference variable passes out of scope (i.e. when a subroutine or method termi- nates). However, if you're done with an object early on in a long-running routine, it's not a bad idea to explicitly remove the reference using the CLEAR statement (see Figure 4.7).

4.5 Tuning Performance

The advanced memory management features of the ABAP runtime environment provide a safe environment for creating and destroying objects. However, it's important to remember that these features do not provide a safeguard against poor design decisions that consume excessive amounts of memory, etc. In this section, we'll provide some basic tips that you can use to avoid these performance traps.

4.5.1 Design Considerations

Even if you don't anticipate performance problems for a given class, it's always a good idea to modularize the initialization logic of the class so that you can imple- ment performance tuning measures later without disturbing core functionality, etc. The following list contains some basic modularization tips that you should consider when developing your classes:

▶ Keep the logic inside the constructor() method to a minimum by delegating initialization tasks to modularized private helper methods.

▶ If you're using your class as a data transfer object (DTO), provide yourself with a public reset() method that can be used to clear the values of a class's instance attributes.

▶ Avoid adding too many parameters to the constructor() method's interface. Instead, encapsulate the initialization process inside of a series of creational methods as described in Section 4.3.3.

4.5.2 Lazy Initialization

Sometimes, we may be working with large composite objects that contain lots of lower-level details that aren't frequently used. To put this scenario into perspec- tive, consider a SalesOrder class that contains a list of SalesOrderItem objects that also in turn contain a list of ScheduleLine objects. Depending on the usage scenario, we may or may not need to have all of the line item/schedule line level detail in context in order to do our job. For example, if we're using the SalesOrder class to create a sales order summary report, we probably only need to report on the header-level data. Bringing the item-level data in only slows the report down and consumes a lot more memory. In this case, it makes sense to delay the initialization of the lower-level details until they're actually needed. This technique is referred to as *lazy initialization*.

The code excerpt contained in Listing 4.10 demonstrates how lazy initialization works. Here, you can see that we're not actually fetching sales order line item information until a consumer invokes the get_items() method. By using encapsulation techniques to funnel item lookup requests through the get_items() method, we can defer the performance hit associated with fetching the line items until we actually need them.

```
CLASS lcl_sales_order DEFINITION.
  PUBLIC SECTION.
    TYPES: ty_item_tab TYPE STANDARD TABLE OF
                       REF TO lcl_order_item.
    METHODS:
      get_items RETURNING VALUE(rt_items) TYPE ty_item_tab.

  PRIVATE SECTION.
    DATA ms_header TYPE ...
    DATA mt_items TYPE ty_item_tab.
ENDCLASS.

CLASS lcl_sales_order IMPLEMENTATION.
  METHOD get_items.
    IF lines( mt_items ) EQ 0.
      "Build the line items table on demand...
    ENDIF.

    rt_items = me->mt_items.
  ENDMETHOD.
ENDCLASS.
```
Listing 4.10 Implementing Lazy Initialization

The lazy initialization technique, though powerful, can lead to some undesired side-effects if we're not careful. Typically, such side-effects are the result of private methods accessing instance attributes directly instead of going through the appropriate getter method(s). In this case, unexpected results might occur as a result of missing data.

Like most performance tuning measures, you have to weigh the benefits against the risks. For example, for objects whose data is fetched from a relational database, you *might* be better off taking the up-front performance hit as opposed to sprinkling in lots of little ad hoc SQL queries in "getter" methods - it really depends on your usage scenario.

4.5.3   Reusing Objects

The easiest way to avoid the performance hits associated with creating/destroying objects is to simply avoid this process altogether by recycling objects. Some typical candidates for recycling include temporary objects created inside loops, as well as objects created in utility methods. Here you may discover that you could have created an object in a higher scope that could be reused in the loop or method calls. In other cases you might be working with a lightweight object in a loop that simply needs to be reinitialized based on the loop index, etc. Rather than create a new object each time, you might be able to call a `reset()` method to reuse the object, etc.

4.5.4   Making Use of Class Attributes

As you design your classes, you should think about whether or not each object instance will require their own local copy of an attribute. If a local copy of an object is not required for an object instance, defining the attribute as a class attribute can help to avoid the creation of a lot of redundant data objects.

4.6   UML Tutorial: State Machine Diagrams

The sequence diagrams introduced in the previous chapter are good for showing the behavior of multiple objects interacting in a particular use case. Another type of behavioral diagram in the UML is the *state machine diagram*. State machine diagrams are useful for showing the behavior of a single object throughout its lifetime.

Figure 4.8 shows a state machine diagram for a class that could be used to represent a batch job that is created using the SAP Job Scheduler tool. Whenever a new job object is created, it is initialized in the `Scheduled` status. This is depicted on the diagram by an *Initial Pseudostate* node that points to the `Scheduled` state box.

Each of the possible statuses of a job are shown using rounded boxes called *states*. Changes in state are represented with directed *transition* arrows. Transitions can optionally be labelled with special transition label strings using the syntax shown in Listing 4.11.

```
event(s) [guard conditions]/activity
```
Listing 4.11 Syntax Diagram for Defining Transition Labels

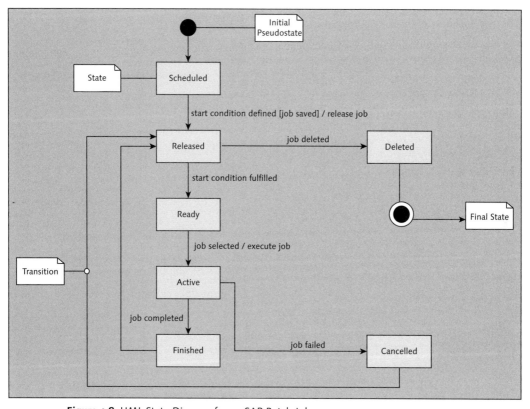

Figure 4.8 UML State Diagram for an SAP Batch Job

The event(s) portion of the transition label is used to describe the event (or events) that would trigger a change in state for the object. If guard conditions are included in the transition label (within the square brackets), then those conditions must be true in order for the transition to occur. The activity option can be used to specify some behavior that takes place during the transition. As an example, let's consider the transition between the Scheduled and Released statuses in

Figure 4.8. In this case, the triggering event occurs whenever a user defines a start condition for the job in Transaction SM36. However, in order for the job to be released in the system, it must first be saved.

If a job is deleted in the system, then the state machine (i.e. the object) will reach its *final state*. This is shown via the arrow that points to the circular node with a dot in it (see Figure 4.8).

Like many of the diagrams that we'll see throughout this book, the state machine diagram fulfills a distinct purpose. In this chapter, we investigated some of the various ways that objects are created in the system. Most of the time, the lifecycle of an object is pretty straightforward. However, for objects with complex lifecycles, state machine diagrams can be very useful in showing how an object will interact with the environment around it.

4.7   Summary

In this chapter, we learned various techniques for ensuring objects are always properly initialized before they are used in a program. When we combine these methods with the encapsulation techniques described in Chapter 3, we're able to build reliable and robust class libraries that function in a deterministic manner. In the next chapter, we'll investigate ways for reusing these classes in other contexts.

One of the more compelling features of OOP is its support for inheritance.
In this chapter, we'll introduce this concept and also look at other ways of
achieving code reuse with classes.

5   Inheritance and Composition

As we noted in Chapter 3, one of the primary reasons it's so difficult to achieve code reuse is because there are usually (implicit) assumptions made along the way which inextricably link the code to specific usage contexts. Here, while the use of encapsulation and implementation hiding techniques can go a long way towards preventing us from coding ourselves into a corner, there will be times when we come to the realization that a particular class simply can't be stretched any further.

At this point, we've got a major dilemma on our hands. Do we try to enhance/ rework the classes to accommodate the new requirements? Or do we cut our losses and try to salvage as much of the code as possible by copying-and-pasting it into a new set of classes? Realistically, neither approach is ideal:

- ▶ Enhancing/reworking the existing classes to handle the requirements threatens the integrity of pre-existing programs since it's quite possible that our enhancements could compromise existing functionality. Indeed, even the most gifted of code surgeons typically have a hard time pulling off a seamless transition.

- ▶ The copy-and-paste approach might be less risky initially, but ultimately increases the cost of long-term maintenance efforts since redundant code makes the overall code footprint bigger. Over time, we may end up finding ourselves having to apply the same set of changes to lots of classes which unofficially share this same code line.

In this chapter, we'll explore how the object-oriented concept of *inheritance* offers a third option for adapting to changes. Here, we'll find that by inheriting from a class, we can effectively make a copy of that class without disturbing the source class or introducing redundant code. As we explore this concept, we'll also learn about another technique called *composition* that provides an alternative way to reuse classes in situations where inheritance either isn't possible or doesn't make sense.

5.1　Generalization and Specialization

One of the most difficult parts of the object-oriented design process is trying to identify all of the classes that are needed to model a problem domain. During the OO analysis process, we might take several passes through the requirements before we can settle on what classes are needed, what the relationships between those classes should look like, and how instances of those classes will interact with one another at runtime. Depending on the problem domain, this analysis process can become so challenging that even the most experienced object-oriented developers rarely get it all right the first time. This begs the question: what happens if we get the cut of our class model wrong?

When you think about it, there are lots of potential mistakes we can make as we formulate our class model. For example, after several rounds of analysis, we might discover that we've failed to identify several key entities. Or, perhaps we've identified the entities, but defined them too generically.

To put this phenomenon into perspective, let's imagine that we've been tasked with designing a human resources (HR) system. Early on, we quite naturally identify a need for an `Employee` entity class, among others. However, as we dig deeper, more requirements come out which describe specific functionalities relevant for certain types of employees. At this point, we could try to incorporate a lot of conditional logic into the `Employee` class to deal with the specialized cases, but this runs contrary to the ideal that we don't want to clutter up our classes with too many responsibilities. On the other hand, abandoning the `Employee` class altogether in favour of lots of specialized classes (e.g., `HourlyEmployee`) leads to the kind of code redundancy issues we want to avoid with OOP. Fortunately, OO languages like ABAP Objects provide a better and more natural way of dealing with these kinds of specialization problems: *inheritance*.

5.1.1　Inheritance Defined

Using the concept of inheritance, we can *extend* a class in such a way that we can reuse what's already developed (and hopefully tested) while at the same time expanding the class model to better fit specialized cases. The newly-created class is called a *subclass* of the original class; the original class is referred to as the *superclass* of the newly-created class. As the term "inheritance" suggests, subclasses *inherit* components from their superclass. These relationships allow us to build out hierarchical inheritance trees with superclasses as parent nodes and subclasses as child nodes (see Figure 5.1). In Chapter 6, we'll learn how members of this inheritance tree can be used interchangeably, providing for some very compelling generic programming options.

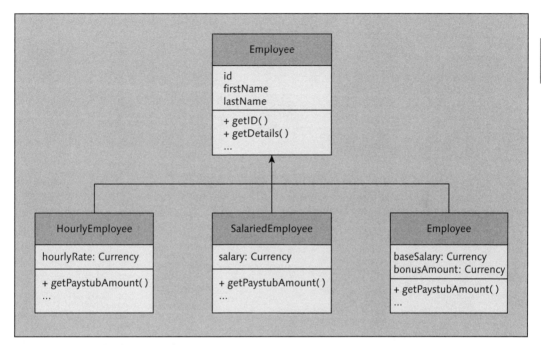

Figure 5.1 A Sample Class Hierarchy

The Generic OBJECT Type in ABAP Objects

Though not depicted in Figure 5.1, the root of any inheritance tree in ABAP Objects is the predefined (empty) OBJECT class. So, even though you may not have realized it, all of the custom classes that we've created thus far have implicitly inherited from this standard base class.

5.1.2 Defining Inheritance Relationships in ABAP Objects

To understand how inheritance works in ABAP Objects, let's see how we might go about building out a portion of the Employee class hierarchy depicted in Figure 5.1. As you can see in Listing 5.1, we've defined three classes: LCL_EMPLOYEE, LCL_HOURLY_EMPLOYEE, and LCL_SALARIED_EMPLOYEE. The LCL_EMPLOYEE class is

the base class in the hierarchy, while the LCL_HOURLY_EMPLOYEE and LCL_SALA-
RIED_EMPLOYEE classes are subclasses that inherit the basic features of the LCL_
EMPLOYEE superclass.

```
CLASS lcl_employee DEFINITION.
  PUBLIC SECTION.
    DATA: mv_id TYPE pernr_d READ-ONLY, "Public for demo only!!!
          mv_first_name TYPE ad_namefir,
          mv_last_name TYPE ad_namelas.

    METHODS:
      constructor IMPORTING iv_id TYPE pernr_d
                            iv_first_name TYPE ad_namefir
                            iv_last_name TYPE ad_namelas,

      get_id RETURNING VALUE(rv_id) TYPE pernr_d,

      get_details RETURNING VALUE(rv_details) TYPE string.
ENDCLASS.

CLASS lcl_employee IMPLEMENTATION.
  METHOD constructor.
    me->mv_id = iv_id.
    me->mv_first_name = iv_first_name.
    me->mv_last_name = iv_last_name.
  ENDMETHOD.

  METHOD get_id.
    rv_id = me->mv_id.
  ENDMETHOD.

  METHOD get_details.
    rv_details =
      |Employee #{ mv_id }: { mv_first_name } { mv_last_name }|.
  ENDMETHOD.
ENDCLASS.

CLASS lcl_hourly_employee DEFINITION
        INHERITING FROM lcl_employee.
  PUBLIC SECTION.
    CONSTANTS:
      CO_WORK_WEEK TYPE i VALUE 40.

    METHODS:
      constructor IMPORTING iv_id TYPE pernr_d
                            iv_first_name TYPE ad_namefir
                            iv_last_name TYPE ad_namelas
                            iv_hourly_rate TYPE bapicurr_d,
```

```abap
      get_paystub_amount RETURNING VALUE(rv_wages)
                                  TYPE bapicurr_d.

  PRIVATE SECTION.
    DATA mv_hourly_rate TYPE bapicurr_d.
ENDCLASS.

CLASS lcl_hourly_employee IMPLEMENTATION.
  METHOD constructor.
    super->constructor(
      EXPORTING
        iv_id = iv_id
        iv_first_name = iv_first_name
        iv_last_name = iv_last_name ).

    me->mv_hourly_rate = iv_hourly_rate.
  ENDMETHOD.

  METHOD get_paystub_amount.
    rv_wages = me->mv_hourly_rate * CO_WORK_WEEK.
  ENDMETHOD.
ENDCLASS.

CLASS lcl_salaried_employee DEFINITION
        INHERITING FROM lcl_employee.
  PUBLIC SECTION.
    METHODS:
      constructor IMPORTING iv_id TYPE pernr_d
                            iv_first_name TYPE ad_namefir
                            iv_last_name TYPE ad_namelas
                            iv_salary TYPE bapicurr_d,

      get_paystub_amount RETURNING VALUE(rv_wages)
                                  TYPE bapicurr_d.

  PRIVATE SECTION.
    DATA mv_salary TYPE bapicurr_d.
ENDCLASS.

CLASS lcl_salaried_employee IMPLEMENTATION.
  METHOD constructor.
    super->constructor(
      EXPORTING
        iv_id = iv_id
        iv_first_name = iv_first_name
        iv_last_name = iv_last_name ).

    me->mv_salary = iv_salary.
  ENDMETHOD.
```

```
METHOD get_paystub_amount.
  rv_wages = me->mv_salary / 52.
ENDMETHOD.
ENDCLASS.
```

Listing 5.1 Defining an Employee Class Hierarchy in ABAP Objects

For the most part, the LCL_EMPLOYEE base class contained in Listing 5.1 looks like most any local class we've considered up to this point. Where things get interesting is with the definition of the LCL_HOURLY_EMPLOYEE and LCL_SALARIED_ EMPLOYEE subclasses. Here, notice how we're using the INHERITING FROM addition of the CLASS DEFINITION statement to define the inheritance relationship to LCL_ EMPLOYEE. With this simple inclusion, we've defined new subclasses that come pre-equipped with all of the instance attributes/methods of LCL_EMPLOYEE. This means, for example, that we could call the get_details() method on an LCL_ HOURLY_EMPLOYEE instance and the code defined in the LCL_EMPLOYEE class's implementation would fire automagically. Similarly, instances of LCL_SALARIED_ EMPLOYEE inherit/have access to public instance attributes such as mv_id, mv_ first_name, and mv_last_name.

> **Note**
>
> The new subclasses may come pre-equipped with all of the instance attributes/methods of LCL_EMPLOYEE, but we should qualify this by saying that the subclasses only inherit components that the LCL_EMPLOYEE class makes visible to them. We'll expand on this concept further in Section 5.2.

After the INHERITING FROM addition, the definition of the LCL_HOURLY_EMPLOYEE and LCL_SALARIED_EMPLOYEE subclasses proceeds pretty much as per usual. Here, the new components we create are unique to the subclasses; LCL_EMPLOYEE isn't retrofitted/altered by any of the changes we make at the subclass level.

Defining Inheritance Relationships in the Class Builder Tool

Technically speaking, the inheritance definition syntax is the same for local or global classes. However, if you prefer to work in the form-based view of the Class Builder, then you must configure the inheritance relationship manually. If you're building a new subclass from scratch, this can be achieved via the CREATE CLASS wizard screens as shown in Figure 5.2 and Figure 5.3, respectively.

Here, the highlighted CREATE INHERITANCE button shown in Figure 5.2 reveals the SUPERCLASS field shown in Figure 5.3. Once we plug in the appropriate superclass and hit the SAVE button, the Class Builder tool will take care of building out the appropriate syntax.

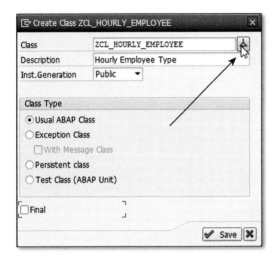

Figure 5.2 Specifying an Inheritance Relationship in the Class Builder Tool (Part 1)

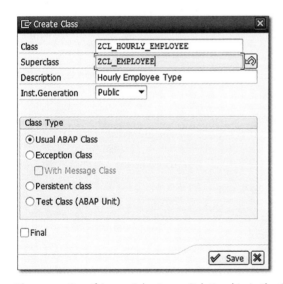

Figure 5.3 Specifying an Inheritance Relationship in the Class Builder Tool (Part 2)

If the inheritance relationship isn't specified up front during the class creation process, then we can always maintain it after the fact on the PROPERTIES tab of the

Class Builder as shown in Figure 5.4. Here, there are three buttons that we can use to adjust the inheritance relationship for the class:

▶ SUPERCLASS

This button is used to specify a superclass for a given subclass when there isn't one defined yet. Once this button is selected, you can fill in the new superclass in the correspondingly-named field as shown in Figure 5.4.

▶ UNDO INHERITANCE

This button can be used to remove an inheritance relationship from a subclass. Note that this will remove all inherited components from the class, so be careful when performing this step on classes that may have methods in place that depend on these components.

▶ CHANGE INHERITANCE

As the name suggests, this button can be used to change the inheritance relationship from one superclass to another. As you might expect, this can get very tricky depending on the compatibility of the two superclasses, so we'd recommend that you exercise caution when performing this change.

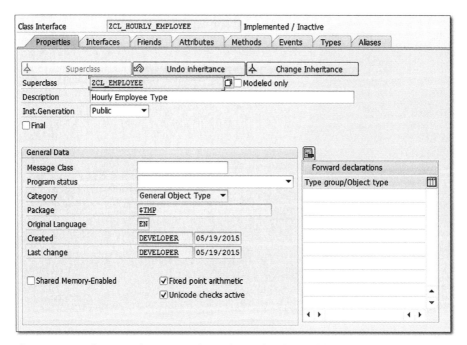

Figure 5.4 Specifying an Inheritance Relationship in the Class Builder Tool (Part 3)

5.1.3 Working with Subclasses

The code excerpt contained in Listing 5.2 demonstrates how we can work with subclass instances. As you can see, there's no special syntax required to interface with the subclass instances: we instantiate them using the CREATE OBJECT statement and access instance attributes/methods as per usual. Behind the scenes, the ABAP runtime environment is able to interpret incoming requests and route them appropriately. This means that calls to get_paystub_amount() are routed to the subclasses while calls to get_details() are routed to the superclass. To the end user, all this sleight of hand is completely transparent.

```
DATA lo_hourly_emp TYPE REF TO lcl_hourly_employee.
DATA lo_salary_emp TYPE REF TO lcl_salaried_employee.

CREATE OBJECT lo_hourly_emp
  EXPORTING
    iv_id = '12345678'
    iv_first_name = 'Andersen'
    iv_last_name = 'Wood'
    iv_hourly_rate = '80.00'.

CREATE OBJECT lo_salary_emp
  EXPORTING
    iv_id = '23456789'
    iv_first_name = 'Paige'
    iv_last_name  = 'Wood'
    iv_salary = '150000'.

IF lo_hourly_emp->get_paystub_amount( ) GT
     lo_salary_emp->get_paystub_amount( ).
  WRITE: / lo_hourly_emp->get_details( ), `makes more money.`.
ELSE.
  WRITE: / lo_salary_emp->get_details( ), `makes more money.`.
ENDIF.
```
Listing 5.2 Working with Subclass Instances

5.1.4 Inheritance as a Living Relationship

Before we move on to more involved inheritance concepts, we should (re)emphasize the fact that inheritance is more than just a fancy way of copying classes into new classes. Inheritance defines a natural relationship that will likely evolve over time. To appreciate the nature of this relationship, imagine that we're asked to start keeping track of employee addresses using our fictitious Employee class model.

Depending on when we're asked to apply this change, it could be that our Employee class hierarchy has expanded to include many type-specific subclasses. However, even if that's the case, the subclasses are not cut off from the root Employee class. So, if we need to make a fundamental change to the way that we model employees, we can simply add an instance attribute containing the address information to the Employee root class and each of the subclasses will inherit this attribute automatically.

This phenomenon is sketched out in the code excerpt contained in Listing 5.3. Here, we've introduced a new class called LCL_ADDRESS which models a simple address record. With this class in place, we then enhance the LCL_EMPLOYEE root class originally defined in Listing 5.1 to include an instance attribute and getter/setter methods which allow us to get our hands on this address record from an Employee object. Finally, since the getter/setter methods were defined as part of the public interface of LCL_EMPLOYEE, you can see how we can access this inherited functionality from subclasses such as LCL_HOURLY_EMPLOYEE without having to make any changes to the downstream classes themselves. Once we apply the change to the base class, the (exposed) functionality is available immediately downstream within the subclasses.

```
CLASS lcl_address DEFINITION.
  PUBLIC SECTION:
    METHODS:
      as_string RETURNING VALUE(rv_value) TYPE string,
      get_street1 RETURNING VALUE(rv_street) TYPE ad_street,
      set_street1 IMPORTING iv_street TYPE csequence,
      get_street2 RETURNING VALUE(rv_street) TYPE ad_strspp1,
      set_street2 IMPORTING iv_street TYPE csequence,
      get_city RETURNING VALUE(rv_city) TYPE ad_city1,
      set_city IMPORTING iv_city TYPE csequence,
      ...
  PRIVATE SECTION.
    DATA: mv_street1 TYPE ad_street,
          mv_street2 TYPE ad_strspp1,
          mv_city TYPE ad_city1,
          mv_region TYPE regio,
          mv_country TYPE land1.
ENDCLASS.

CLASS lcl_address IMPLEMENTATION.
  METHOD as_string.
    ...
  ENDMETHOD.
  ...
ENDCLASS.
```

```
CLASS lcl_employee DEFINITION.
  PUBLIC SECTION.
    METHODS:

      . . .
      get_address RETURNING VALUE(ro_address)
                  TYPE REF TO lcl_address,
      set_address IMPORTING io_address TYPE REF TO lcl_address.

  PRIVATE SECTION.
    DATA mo_address TYPE REF TO lcl_address.
ENDCLASS.

CLASS lcl_employee IMPLEMENTATION.
  . . .
  METHOD get_address.
    ro_address = me->mo_address.
  ENDMETHOD.

  METHOD set_address.
    me->mo_address = io_address.
  ENDMETHOD.
  . . .
ENDCLASS.

DATA lo_hourly_emp TYPE REF TO lcl_hourly_employee.
DATA lo_address TYPE REF TO lcl_address.

CREATE OBJECT lo_address.
. . .
CREATE OBJECT lo_hourly_emp
  EXPORTING ...

lo_hourly_emp->set_address( lo_address ). "Inherited method
WRITE: / lo_hourly_emp->get_address( )->as_string( ).
```
Listing 5.3 Understanding the Effects of Base-Level Class Refactoring

5.2   Inheriting Components

Much like inheritance in the classical sense (i.e., where you inherit property from a friend or loved one upon their death), inheritance relationships in the OOP space are pretty tightly regulated. Here, the creators of parent classes get to choose which components they wish to pass down to subclasses and which components they want to keep under wraps. This is, of course, usually for the subclass's own good because inheriting too much of a good thing can oftentimes become a bad thing.

In this section, we'll take an up-close look at the rules that govern inheritance relationships. Once you wrap your head around these basic concepts, we think you'll find the overall inheritance definition process to be relatively straightforward and intuitive.

5.2.1 Designing the Inheritance Interface

Up to this point in the book, our discussions on the subject of component visibility have been focused on designing a class's public and private interface from the perspective of an external client (e.g. another class or function module). However, inheritance adds a new dimension into the mix since we now also need to consider how to define the interface between a superclass and its subclasses. Here, for example, we might run into situations where we want to provide access to selected components to subclasses without having to expose the components to the outside world via the superclass's public interface.

To put this into perspective, let's revisit the LCL_EMPLOYEE class hierarchy that we introduced in Listing 5.1. There, as you may recall, we included the base-level instance attributes (e.g. mv_id, mv_first_name and mv_last_name) for the employee within the public interface of the LCL_EMPLOYEE class. Why? Well, partly for demonstration purposes, but also because we wanted to provide access to these instance attributes within subclasses such as LCL_HOURLY_EMPLOYEE. Sure, we could have provided getter/setter methods to provide such access but even then one could argue that this is exposing more details than we want to share with the outside world via the LCL_EMPLOYEE class's public interface.

To address problems like this, most modern OO languages introduce a third visibility section: the *protected section*. Components defined within this section are visible only to the superclass and its subclasses. To the outside world, it's as if these components were defined within the private section of the class.

In ABAP Objects, the protected section is defined in much the same way that public/private sections are defined. There's a PROTECTED SECTION statement and all of the components defined within that section are assigned the protected level scope. This is demonstrated in the code excerpt contained in Listing 5.4. Here, notice how we've moved the instance attributes for LCL_EMPLOYEE to the protected section. With this change, we've effectively cut off access to these components to the LCL_EMPOYEE class and its subclasses. Now, the only way that external clients can get their hands on these attributes is if we purposefully expose them via public methods, etc.

```
CLASS lcl_employee DEFINITION.
  PUBLIC SECTION.
    METHODS:
      constructor IMPORTING iv_id TYPE pernr_d
                            iv_first_name TYPE ad_namefir
                            iv_last_name TYPE ad_namelas,

      get_id RETURNING VALUE(rv_id) TYPE pernr_d,

      get_details RETURNING VALUE(rv_details) TYPE string.

  PROTECTED SECTION.
    DATA: mv_id TYPE pernr_d READ-ONLY,
          mv_first_name TYPE ad_namefir,
          mv_last_name TYPE ad_namelas.
ENDCLASS.
```

Listing 5.4 Moving Inherited Components to the Protected Section

Collectively, the components that we include in the protected and public sections of a class define its *inheritance interface*. When defining this interface, it's important not to get too carried away with adding components to the protected section on the off chance that we might want to expose those components to subclasses. Here, we recommend that you apply the encapsulation concept of *least privilege* when designing your inheritance interface.

Understanding the Concept of "Least Privilege"

The concept of "least privilege" implies that if a subclass doesn't really need to access a component, then it shouldn't be granted access to it. For example, imagine that you want to make some fundamental changes to the implementation of a base-level class that sits at the root of an inheritance tree. If the components that you want to change are defined in the protected visibility section of the superclass, then it's quite possible that the changes cannot be carried out without affecting some/all of the subclasses that may be using these components.

With that being said, the general rule of thumb would be to prefer to define sensitive components in the private visibility section unless you have a compelling reason to do otherwise. If a subclass needs to be granted access to these components, then access can be provided in the form of getter and setter methods that are defined in the PROTECTED SECTION of the class. This little bit of additional work ensures that a base class remains fully encapsulated.

5.2.2   Visibility of Instance Components in Subclasses

Subclasses inherit the instance components of *all* of the superclasses defined in their inheritance tree. However, not all of these components are *visible* at the subclass level.

A useful way of understanding how these visibility rules work is to imagine that you have a special instance attribute pointing to an instance of the superclass inside of your subclass. You can use this reference attribute to access public components of the superclass, but access to private components is restricted just as it would be for any normal object reference variable.

As it turns out, this imaginary object reference metaphor is not too far off from what's actually implemented in subclasses behind the scenes. Subclasses contain a special *pseudo reference* variable called super that contains a reference to an instance of an object of the superclass's type. This reference is used to access components of a superclass inside a subclass. The primary difference between the super pseudo reference variable and a normal reference variable is that the super pseudo reference can also be used to access components defined in the protected section of the superclass it points to.

The use of the super pseudo reference variable is optional (as was the case with the me self-reference variable discussed in Chapter 2), but can be used in situations where explicit reference to superclass components is needed. Normally, you'll simply access the components of the superclass directly, but it's important to remember that the compiler is implicitly plugging in the super pseudo reference behind the scenes in order to properly address these components. If you operate in this mindset, the visibility rules for accessing superclass components should become second nature to you.

> **Inheritance Namespace Concepts**
>
> Public and protected components of classes in an inheritance tree all belong to the same internal namespace. This implies that you cannot create a component in a subclass using the same name that was used to define a component in a superclass. There's no such restriction on the naming of private components, however. For example, if you define a private component called comp in a superclass, you can reuse this same name to define components in subclasses without restriction.

5.2.3   Visibility of Class Components in Subclasses

In addition to all of the instance-level components, subclasses also inherit all of the class components of their superclasses. As was the case with instance components though, only those components that are defined in the public or protected visibility sections of a superclass are actually visible at the subclass level.

In terms of inheritance, class attributes are not associated with a single class, but rather with the overall inheritance tree. The change in scope makes it possible to address these class components by binding the class component selector operator with any of the classes in the inheritance tree. This can be confusing since class components are defined in terms of a given class, and probably don't have a lot of meaning outside of their defining class's context. To avoid this kind of confusion, we'd recommend that you always address class components by applying the class component selector to the defining class's name (e.g. `lcl_superclass=>compo-nent`). That way, your intentions are always clear.

5.2.4   Redefining Methods

Frequently, the implementation of inherited methods needs to be changed at the subclass level in order to support more specialized functionality. To put this concept into perspective, imagine that we decide to refactor the `Employee` class hierarchy by moving the definition of the `get_paystub_amount()` method up to the `LCL_EMPLOYEE` base class level. Here, we might provide a bare bones implementation in the base class, but our real objective is to associate this behavior with all employee types and not redundantly define the same method over and over in the various subclasses.

Of course, this doesn't change the fact that the calculation of the paystub amount differs between the specific employee types. Clearly, the implementation will be type-specific but, when you think about it, the signature of the method remains static in any case. So, we *define* the method in the `LCL_EMPLOYEE` base class and then *redefine* (or override) the implementation of the method in each of the type-specific subclasses.

The code excerpt contained in Listing 5.5 shows how we can redefine methods like this using ABAP Objects syntax. Here, notice how we've refactored the `LCL_EMPLOYEE` base class to define the method `get_paystub_amount()`. This definition fully specifies the method signature which will not change. Then, at the LCL_ HOURLY_EMPLOYEE subclass level, we're using the REDEFINITION addition to declare our intention to redefine/re-implement the get_paystub_amount() method to include type-specific calculation logic. Finally, within the implementation section of the LCL_HOURLY_EMPLOYEE subclass, it's pretty much business as usual as we're free to redefine the logic of the get_paystub_amount() method in any way we see fit.

```
CLASS lcl_employee DEFINITION.
  PUBLIC SECTION.
    METHODS:
      ...
      get_paystub_amount RETURNING VALUE(rv_wages)
                                 TYPE bapicurr_d.
  ...
ENDCLASS.

CLASS lcl_employee IMPLEMENTATION.
  ...
  METHOD get_paystub_amount.
    "Empty for now...
  ENDMETHOD.
ENDCLASS.

CLASS lcl_hourly_employee DEFINITION
      INHERITING FROM lcl_employee.
  PUBLIC SECTION.
    ...
    get_paystub_amount REDEFINITION.
ENDCLASS.

CLASS lcl_hourly_employee IMPLEMENTATION.
  ...
  METHOD get_paystub_amount.
    rv_wages = me->mv_hourly_rate * CO_WORK_WEEK.
  ENDMETHOD.
ENDCLASS.
```

Listing 5.5 Redefining Methods in Subclasses

We can achieve the same thing for global classes maintained in the form-based view of the Class Builder by selecting the target method and clicking on the REDE-FINE button as shown in Figure 5.5.

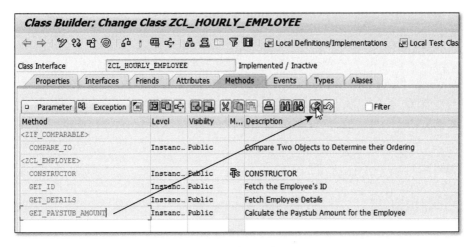

Figure 5.5 Redefining Methods in the Class Builder Tool

Misleading Terminology

Even though the REDEFINITION addition sounds like it might change the definition of a method, we should once again emphasize that it has absolutely no effect on the definition of a method's signature. This implies that we can't add/remove parameters to the method, change its visibility section assignment, and so on. In Chapter 6, we'll learn that there's a very important reason why this interface must remain intact, but for now, the main take-away is that we can only use the REDEFINITION addition to change a method's implementation in a subclass.

Reusing the Superclass Implementation

Whenever we redefine methods using the REDEFINITION addition, we're effectively choosing to abandon the superclass's implementation in favor of our own custom one. While this is clearly what we want, there may be times when we merely want to tweak the implementation of the superclass, not replace it altogether. In these situations, we can use the super pseudo reference within the redefined method to invoke the superclass implementation and then adjust the output as needed.

This technique is demonstrated in the code excerpt contained in Listing 5.6. Here, we've defined a simple estimating class and a subclass which redefines its get_estimate() method. In the subclass implementation, we're delegating most of the heavy lifting to the superclass and then adjusting the estimate by 10% after the fact. If the get_estimate() method defined importing parameters, we could have also influenced the behavior by adjusting the parameter values on the fly before handing them off to the superclass implementation.

```
CLASS lcl_estimator DEFINITION.
  PUBLIC SECTION.
    METHODS:
      get_estimate RETURNING VALUE(rv_estimate) TYPE f.
ENDCLASS.

CLASS lcl_estimator IMPLEMENTATION.
  METHOD get_estimate.
    rv_estimate = ...
  ENDMETHOD.
ENDCLASS.

CLASS lcl_conservative_estimator DEFINITION
        INHERITING FROM lcl_estimator.
  PUBLIC SECTION.
    METHODS:
    get_estimate REDEFINITION.
ENDCLASS.

CLASS lcl_conservative_estimator IMPLEMENTATION.
  METHOD get_estimate.
    rv_estimate = super->get_estimate( ).
    rv_estimate = rv_estimate + ( rv_estimate * '0.10' ).
  ENDMETHOD.
ENDCLASS.
```
Listing 5.6 Invoking the Superclass's Implementation of a Redefined Method

5.2.5 Instance Constructors

Unlike regular instance components such as attributes or methods, constructors *are not* inherited. If you think about it, this makes sense since each class only knows how to initialize objects of its own type.

Despite the fact that constructor methods exist independently in each class within an inheritance hierarchy, the signature of the constructor() method in subclasses needs to remain relatively stable. Here, while it's perfectly acceptable to add new type-specific parameters to the signature of the method, we'll want to leave the pre-existing parameter interface intact. This is because constructor methods in subclasses are required to call the constructor of their superclass within the implementation of the constructor() method.

We saw an example of this with the `LCL_EMPLOYEE` class hierarchy defined in Listing 5.1. Here, you can see how type-specific subclasses such as `LCL_HOURLY_EMPLOYEE` expand the interface of the `constructor()` method to include additional parameters as needed. The rest of the parameters are passed onto the superclass's constructor via the call to `super->constructor()` to facilitate the initialization of the base-level employee instance. Then, after that initialization is complete, the subclass's constructor method logic kicks in to complete the initialization of the type-specific employee instance.

5.2.6 Class Constructors

Each subclass is also allowed to define its own unique class constructor. This constructor gets called right before the class is addressed in a program for the first time. However, before it's executed, the ABAP runtime environment will work its way up the inheritance tree to make sure that the class constructor has been called for each superclass in the inheritance hierarchy. These class constructor calls are guaranteed to occur in the proper order.

For example, let's imagine that you have a class hierarchy with four classes A, B, C, and D. When a program tries to access class D for the first time, the runtime environment will first check to see if the class constructors have been called for classes A, B, and C. If the class constructor has already been called for class A, but not for B and C, then the order of class constructor calls will be B, C, and D. This ensures that the class attributes of a superclass are always properly initialized before a subclass is loaded into context.

5.3 The Abstract and Final Keywords

As we've observed, inheritance adds a dimension to our class design which forces us to take a hard look at *where* we should define certain components within a class hierarchy. As we come to these decisions, it's important to be able to lock the hierarchy down such that these design choices are honored in subclasses. In this section, we'll look at a couple of keywords that make this possible in ABAP Objects.

5.3.1 Abstract Classes and Methods

In Section 5.2.4, we told you how there was some potential value in moving the `get_paystub_amount()` up the `Employee` class hierarchy to the `LCL_EMPLOYEE` root class. Though we'll explore the details of this in Chapter 6, this refactoring job does identify an important point: the higher we make our way up the inheritance tree, the more generic things become. Indeed, when we get to the `LCL_EMPLOYEE` root class, things are so generic that there's not really a reasonable implementation to provide for the `get_paystub_amount()` method. That's why we ended up leaving the implementation empty in Listing 5.5.

While this approach might seem harmless enough, it can actually be quite dangerous in practice. For example, imagine that we neglected to redefine the `get_paystub_amount()` method in type-specific subclasses such as `LCL_HOURLY_EMPLOYEE`. If this were to happen, all calls to this method on type-specific employee instances at runtime would be routed to the implementation in the `LCL_EMPLOYEE` superclass which does nothing.

Rather than leave all this to chance, ABAP Objects allows us to identify these gaps in a class definition using the `ABSTRACT` keyword. Using this keyword, we can explicitly delegate undefined features to subclasses.

To understand how this works, let's once again refactor the `LCL_EMPLOYEE` class from Listing 5.5 by redefining the `get_paystub_amount()` method as abstract. As you can see in Listing 5.7, this minor change was carried out by strategically plugging in the `ABSTRACT` keyword in two places within the class definition:

▶ First, we included the `ABSTRACT` keyword in the overall `CLASS DEFINITION` statement. This is necessary for any class which will contain one or more abstract methods. We'll learn more about what this means in just a moment.

▶ Next, we added the `ABSTRACT` keyword to the definition of the `get_paystub_amount()` method.

Aside from these two syntactical changes, the only other notable change is to the implementation section of the `LCL_EMPLOYEE` class. Here, notice that we've no longer included an empty implementation of the `get_paystub_amount()` method. This is not an accidental omission in the source code. Whenever we declare a method as abstract, we can no longer provide an implementation for it in the class that defines it. Instead, the implementation must come from subclasses such as `LCL_HOURLY_EMPLOYEE` which, as you can see in Listing 5.7, redefine the method as per usual.

```
CLASS lcl_employee DEFINITION ABSTRACT.
  PUBLIC SECTION.
    METHODS:
```

```
     ...
     get_paystub_amount ABSTRACT RETURNING VALUE(rv_wages)
                                            TYPE bapicurr_d.
   ...
ENDCLASS.

CLASS lcl_employee IMPLEMENTATION.
   ...
ENDCLASS.

CLASS lcl_hourly_employee DEFINITION
        INHERITING FROM lcl_employee.
  PUBLIC SECTION.
     ...
     get_paystub_amount REDEFINITION.
ENDCLASS.

CLASS lcl_hourly_employee IMPLEMENTATION.
   ...
  METHOD get_paystub_amount.
     rv_wages = me->mv_hourly_rate * CO_WORK_WEEK.
  ENDMETHOD.
ENDCLASS.
```

Listing 5.7 Defining Abstract Classes and Methods

For global classes maintained in the form-based view of the Class Builder tool, you can define abstract methods by performing the following steps:

1. First, highlight the target method on the METHODS tab of the form-based view as shown in Figure 5.6 and click on the highlighted DETAIL VIEW button.

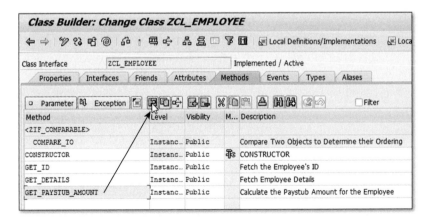

Figure 5.6 Defining an Abstract Method in the Class Builder Tool (Part 1)

2. Then, in the CHANGE METHOD dialog box, click on the ABSTRACT checkbox to declare the method as abstract. This will open up the INFORMATION dialog box shown in Figure 5.7 advising that the implementation of the method will be deleted.

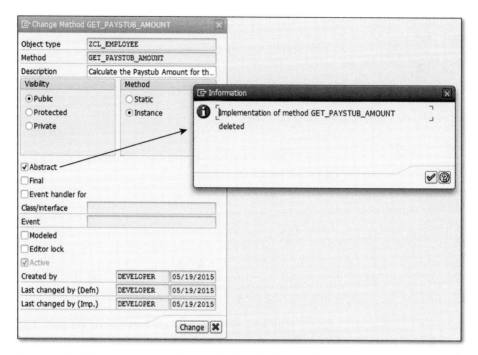

Figure 5.7 Defining an Abstract Method in the Class Builder Tool (Part 2)

3. Finally, after confirming the information message, click on the CHANGE button to complete the assignment. At this point, the Class Builder will implicitly change the instantiation context to *abstract*, indicating that the class itself is now abstract. You can view and/or set this context directly on the PROPERTIES tab as shown in Figure 5.8.

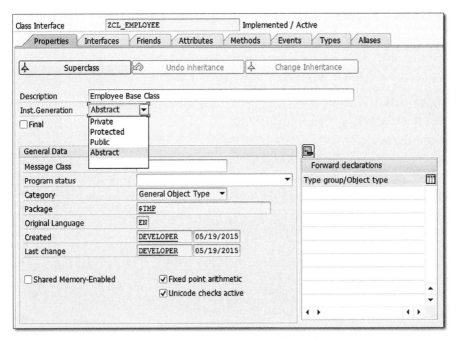

Figure 5.8 Defining an Abstract Method in the Class Builder Tool (Part 3)

While these abstract declarations might seem rather cosmetic, we should point out that the use of the ABSTRACT keyword has some pretty significant effects on the way these classes are utilized at runtime. For example, by declaring the get_ paystub_amount() method as abstract in Listing 5.7, we're implying that the LCL_ EMPLOYEE class is incomplete from an implementation perspective. While LCL_ EMPLOYEE can (and does) define many other fully-implemented methods, there are certain elements of its design that are abstract in nature. Therefore, by extension, we say that LCL_EMPLOYEE is an *abstract class*.

Because their implementation is incomplete, abstract classes like LCL_EMPLOYEE cannot be instantiated on their own. Instead, their purpose is to provide a common *template* that makes it easier to implement specialized subclasses. For instance, by stubbing out core behaviors such as the get_paystub_amount() method in the abstract LCL_EMPLOYEE superclass, we've more accurately provided a template for what an employee should look like—regardless of type.

5.3.2 Final Classes

As we build out our class inheritance trees, we may sometimes reach a point where a class shouldn't be extended any further. In these situations, we can use the FINAL keyword to lock the class down such that it can no longer be inherited.

The code excerpt contained in Listing 5.8 shows how the FINAL keyword is being used to finalize a class called LCL_PASSWORD_UTILS. Here, we simply add the FINAL keyword to the CLASS DEFINITION statement. Once this designator is set, it's no longer possible to inherit from LCL_PASSWORD_UTILS. Indeed, if you paste this code excerpt into the ABAP editor and try to activate it, you'll receive a syntax error indicating that class LCL_PASSWORD_UTILS may not have any subclasses.

```
CLASS lcl_password_utils DEFINITION FINAL.
  PUBLIC SECTION.
    METHODS:
      is_valid_password RETURNING VALUE(rv_valid) TYPE abap_bool,
      ...
ENDCLASS.

CLASS lcl_password_utils IMPLEMENTATION.
  METHOD is_valid_password.
    ...
  ENDMETHOD.
ENDCLASS.

CLASS lcl_malware DEFINITION   "<== Syntax error
        INHERITING FROM lcl_password_utils.
  PUBLIC SECTION.
    METHODS:
      is_valid_password REDEFINITION.
ENDCLASS.

CLASS lcl_malware IMPLEMENTATION.
  METHOD is_valid_password.
    "Try to bypass core behavior through inheritance...
    rv_valid = abap_true.
  ENDMETHOD.
ENDCLASS.
```

Listing 5.8 Marking a Class as Final

We can achieve the same effect for global classes maintained in the form-based view of the Class Builder tool by selecting the FINAL checkbox on the PROPERTIES tab as shown in Figure 5.9.

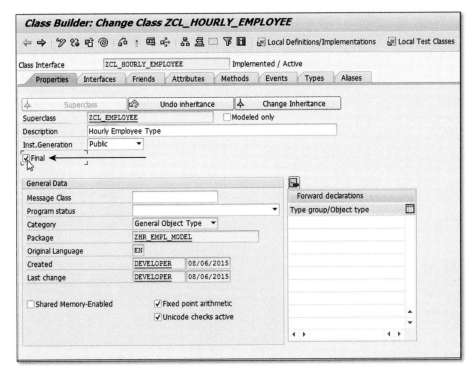

Figure 5.9 Setting the Final Indicator on a Global Class in the Class Builder

Though you don't see the FINAL indicator used as much with custom classes developed at customer sites, it's very common to see SAP and their partners apply this flag in order to prevent customers from making further changes to their standard-delivered content.

5.3.3 Final Methods

Sometimes, we may find ourselves in situations where we want to lock down certain methods of a class for inheritance without locking down the entire class. To accommodate these kinds of scenarios, ABAP Objects also allows us to apply the `FINAL` keyword to individual method definitions.

This approach is demonstrated in Listing 5.9. Here, you can see how we've reopened the `LCL_PASSWORD_UTILS` class for inheritance, but kept the `is_valid_password()` method locked down.

```
CLASS lcl_password_utils DEFINITION.
  PUBLIC SECTION.
    METHODS:
      is_valid_password FINAL RETURNING VALUE(rv_valid)
                                    TYPE abap_bool,
      ...
ENDCLASS.

CLASS lcl_password_utils IMPLEMENTATION.
  METHOD is_valid_password.
    ...
  ENDMETHOD.
ENDCLASS.

CLASS lcl_malware DEFINITION   "<== This is now allowed
      INHERITING FROM lcl_password_utils.
  PUBLIC SECTION.
    METHODS:
      is_valid_password REDEFINITION. "<== But this isn't
ENDCLASS.

CLASS lcl_malware IMPLEMENTATION.
  METHOD is_valid_password.
    "Try to bypass core behavior through inheritance...
    rv_valid = abap_true.
  ENDMETHOD.
ENDCLASS.
```

Listing 5.9 Marking Individual Methods as Final

You can achieve the same effect for methods maintained in the form-based view of the Class Builder tool by selecting the target method, clicking on the DETAIL VIEW button, and checking the FINAL checkbox as shown in Figure 5.10. Be sure to click the CHANGE button to confirm your changes.

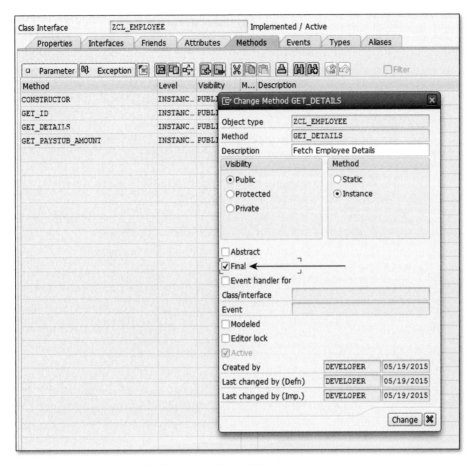

Figure 5.10 Setting the Final Indicator for a Method Using the Form-Based View of the Class Builder Tool

5.4 Inheritance vs. Composition

With all the hype surrounding inheritance, novice OO developers sometimes assume that if they're not using inheritance extensively that they must be doing something wrong. Here, it's important to realize that while inheritance is powerful, it's not always the best solution for reusing code from existing classes. Indeed, one of the worst mistakes you can make is to try to stretch classes to fit into some sort of contrived inheritance relationship.

Whenever you're thinking of defining a new class in terms of some pre-existing class, the first question you should ask yourself whether or not the relationship between the subclass and superclass fits into the "is-a" relationship mold. To illustrate this, let's consider an inheritance tree for various types of orders (see Figure 5.11). At each level of the tree, you should be able to apply the "is-a" relationship between a subclass and its superclass and it should make sense. For example, a SalesOrder *is an* Order, a CashOrder *is a* SalesOrder, and so on.

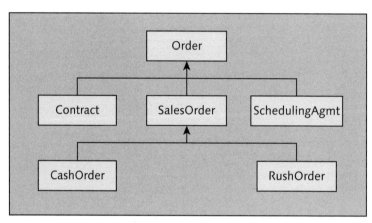

Figure 5.11 Inheritance Tree for Order Types

Most of the time, the application of the "is-a" test should make inheritance relationships between classes pretty obvious. For example, if we try to extend the Order class in Figure 5.11 to define a Delivery subclass, the "is-a" relationship wouldn't make sense because a Delivery is not an Order.

While the "is-a" test should be intuitive enough even for novice developers, it's not uncommon to encounter situations where developers have tried to stretch inheritance relationships like this in an effort to leverage classes that have useful features or similarities to the ones they are trying to implement. Whenever you find yourself stuck trying to figure out ways to define an inheritance relationship between two classes, it's a good idea to take a step back and think about the relationship between the classes from a logical perspective. If you think about it, a Delivery is not an Order, but an Order does have one or more Deliveries associated with it. This "has-a" association is commonly referred to as a *composition* relationship.

The term *composition* is basically just a fancy word used in OO circles to describe the reuse of existing functionality in classes by integrating objects of those classes as attributes in your new class. You can use these attributes in the same way that you use ordinary attributes based on elementary types, structures, etc.

The code excerpt contained in Listing 5.10 demonstrates how the composition technique is used to model the "has-a" relationship between a delivery class called LCL_DELIVERY and an order class called LCL_ORDER. As you can see, we're not really doing anything special here syntax-wise. Instead, we're just incorporating functionality from the LCL_DELIVERY class into LCL_ORDER so that we don't have to reinvent the wheel.

```
CLASS lcl_delivery DEFINITION.
    PUBLIC SECTION.
        METHODS:
            constructor,
            get_delivery_date RETURNING value(rv_date)
                                        TYPE sydatum.

    PRIVATE SECTION.
        DATA: mv_delivery_date TYPE sydatum.
ENDCLASS.

CLASS lcl_delivery IMPLEMENTATION.
    METHOD constructor.
        mv_delivery_date = sy-datum.
    ENDMETHOD.

    METHOD get_delivery_date.
        rv_date = mv_delivery_date.
    ENDMETHOD.
ENDCLASS.

CLASS lcl_order DEFINITION.
    PUBLIC SECTION.
        METHODS:
            constructor IMPORTING iv_id TYPE i,
            release,
            track.

    PRIVATE SECTION.
        DATA: mv_id        TYPE i,
              mo_delivery TYPE REF TO lcl_delivery.
ENDCLASS.

CLASS lcl_order IMPLEMENTATION.
```

```
METHOD constructor.
   mv_id = iv_id.
ENDMETHOD.

METHOD release.
   "Create an outbound delivery for the order...
   CREATE OBJECT mo_delivery.
   ...
ENDMETHOD.

METHOD track.
   DATA lv_message TYPE string.
   lv_message =
      |Order #{ me->mv_id } was shipped on | &&
      |{ mo_delivery->get_delivery_date DATE = user}|.
   WRITE: / lv_message.
ENDMETHOD.
ENDCLASS.
```

Listing 5.10 Reusing Classes using the Composition Technique

In many respects, composition is rather like building with LEGO® building blocks: we're just stacking classes together to build sub-assemblies that are more powerful than the sum of their parts. Sometimes, the easiest way to achieve code reuse is to simply reuse the classes directly. Indeed, unless the inheritance relationship is obvious, we generally favor the use of composition over inheritance in day-to-day development because it ends up providing us with more flexibility. In the next chapter, we'll shed some further light on this choice as we show you how inheritance brings along some unwanted baggage that can clutter up the design if we're not careful.

5.5   Working with ABAP Refactoring Tools

As we've seen, inheritance provides a natural way for extending classes to adapt to changing functional requirements. Of course, while this all sounds good on paper, there will be times when we discover that modelling an inheritance relationship may require more than just creating a subclass or two. Indeed, depending on when we discover the relationship(s), we might end up having to modify other classes in the inheritance hierarchy to make the relationships work.

We've seen a couple of instances of this throughout this chapter as the LCL_ EMPLOYEEclass hierarchy has evolved. For example, in Section 5.2.4, we decided to move the `get_paystub_amount()` out of type-specific subclasses such as `LCL_HOURLY_EMPLOYEE` and into the `LCL_EMPLOYEE` root class since this is an operation that exists for any employee type. While this may seem like a simple cut-and-paste code modification, structural changes like this are normally described using a more official term in OO circles: *refactoring*.

What is Refactoring?

In his famous book *Refactoring: Improving the Design of Existing Code*, Martin Fowler describes refactoring as a process whereby selective code modifications are applied to improve the underlying structure of a system without affecting its external behavior. While many would argue that you should never touch code that's not "broken", proponents of refactoring refute this claim by pointing out that small structural improvements actually extend the lifespan of the code.

In *Refactoring to Patterns*, Joshua Kerievsky puts it this way: "By continuously improving the design of code, we make it easier and easier to work with. This is in sharp contrast to what typically happens: little refactoring and a great deal of attention paid to expediently adding new features. If you get into the hygienic habit of refactoring continuously, you'll find that it is easier to extend and maintain code". If you've ever stumbled across shared ABAP modules such as BAdI implementation classes or function modules that have lots of different cross-cutting functions cobbled together, then you probably have some appreciation for just how messy code can become if it isn't cleaned up periodically.

While we won't attempt to sell you on the merits of refactoring in this book, we would simply offer that Fowler's *Refactoring* describes a series of *refactorings* (or patterns) that can guide you in making good design decisions whenever you need to alter the structure of your classes. Though these refactorings can be performed manually using cut-and-paste style code changes, it turns out the Class Builder tool offers a much better alternative: the *Refactoring Assistant*.

The *Refactoring Assistant* tool can be used to automatically perform some of the most common refactorings. Besides saving you some keystrokes, the automation of this process helps to ensure that you don't accidentally make a mistake by missing a manual step or two along the way.

You can start the Refactoring Assistant tool from within the form-based view of the Class Builder by selecting UTILITIES • REFACTORING • REFACTORING ASSISTANT in the top-level menu bar. This will open up the REFACTORING ASSISTANT dialog box shown in Figure 5.12.

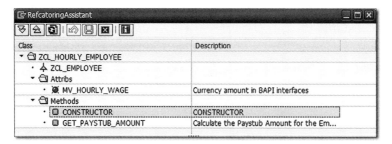

Figure 5.12 Working with the Refactoring Assistant Tool

Within the REFACTORING ASSISTANT, we can implement various move refactorings by simply dragging-and-dropping components from one class onto another. For example, Figure 5.13 shows how we're implementing the move method refactoring described in Section 5.2.4 to move the get_paystub_amount() method up to the ZCL_EMPLOYEE base class level. After we drop the method onto ZCL_EMPLOYEE, we simply hit the SAVE button and the Refactoring Assistant will take care of making all the necessary changes. From here, all that's left to do is activate the changes in the respective classes.

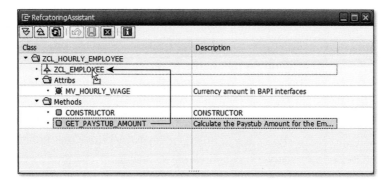

Figure 5.13 Performing a Move Method Refactoring Using the Refactoring Assistant

In addition to the more class-specific refactorings provided via the ABAP Workbench-based Refactoring Assistant, the ABAP Development Tools for Eclipse provide automated support for lots of useful refactoring patterns for renaming variables and methods, extracting methods, and so forth. Many of these patterns are provided via the contextual Quick Fix features described in Section 2.5.3. Others are included in the contextual source code features accessible via the SOURCE menu shown in Figure 5.14.

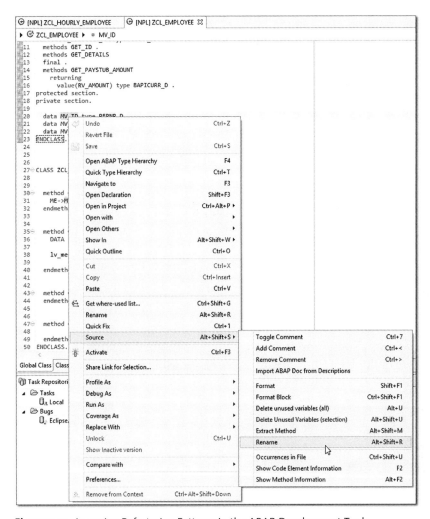

Figure 5.14 Accessing Refactoring Patterns in the ABAP Development Tools

Over time, it's likely that we'll see the Eclipse-based refactoring feature list grow to eclipse (no pun intended) that of the ABAP-based Refactoring Assistant. Indeed, Eclipse has long included many useful refactoring tools for other supported languages such as Java that it's only a matter of time before these make their way into the ABAP world. For up-to-date information on new features in the ABAP Development Tools, we'd encourage you to visit the ABAP in Eclipse community page at *http://scn.sap.com/community/abap/eclipse*.

5.6   UML Tutorial: Advanced Class Diagrams

In Chapter 1, we introduced some of the basic elements of a class diagram, show-ing you how to model rudimentary classes along with their attributes and behav-iors. In this chapter and the next one, we'll expand our discussion of class dia-grams to incorporate some of the more advanced concepts that we've covered in the past several chapters.

5.6.1   Generalizations

Most of the time, our discussions on inheritance tend to focus on specializations at the subclass level. However, if we look up the inheritance tree, we see that superclasses become more generalized as we make our way upwards towards the top of the tree. Perhaps this is why the creators of the UML decided to describe the notation used to depict inheritance relationships between classes in a class diagram as a *generalization* relationship.

Figure 5.15 shows a basic class diagram that depicts a superclass called Account along with two subclasses (CheckingAccount and SavingsAccount). Notice that each subclass has a connector drawn upward towards their superclass. The trian-gle at the top of the association identifies the relationship between the two classes as a generalization.

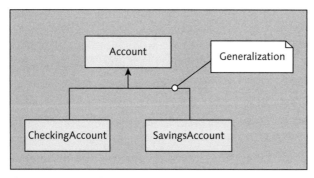

Figure 5.15 UML Class Diagram Notation for Generalizations

5.6.2   Dependencies and Composition

In Section 5.4, we described the concept of composition in terms of a "has-a" rela-tionship between two classes. Up until now, the only way we've had to represent this kind of relationship is via a UML association. However, an association depicts a fairly loose relationship between two classes. In the case of composition, the terms of the relationship between the classes are much more pronounced. To model these relationships, the UML provides us with *dependency associations*.

Dependency associations are depicted using directed lines with an arrow pointing towards the class that the source class depends on. Figure 5.16 shows how dependencies are depicted using the notation. Here, we can follow the direction of the association to determine that the Order class is dependent on the Delivery class.

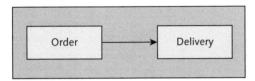

Figure 5.16 Defining a Dependency Relationship Between Classes

The UML also provides a specific notation for depicting composition relationships. In Figure 5.17, we've used this notation to show that an instance of class Address can be embedded inside either class Customer or class Vendor, but not both. This notation also implies that any instances of class Address will be deleted whenever the instance of the composing Customer or Vendor class is deleted.

Figure 5.17 Defining Composition Relationships in Class Diagrams

Because the UML interpretation of composition relationships is a bit more detailed than the common view of composition applied in practice, most developers prefer to model these relationships using dependencies since this leaves more flexibility to the implementer regarding how the actual relationships are realized from a code perspective.

5.6.3   Abstract Classes and Methods

Figure 5.18 shows the UML notation for depicting abstract classes and methods. As you can see, the only requirement here is to italicize the class or method name to indicate that the class or method is to be defined as abstract. However, since the italics are sometimes hard to read, you'll sometimes see developers tag abstract classes using the non-normative <> keyword as shown in Figure 5.19.

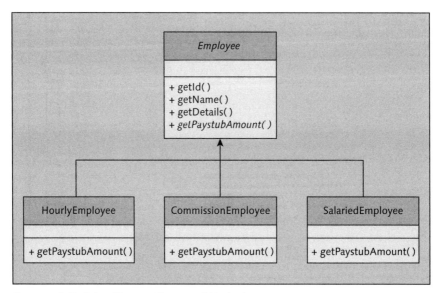

Figure 5.18 Defining Abstract Classes and Methods

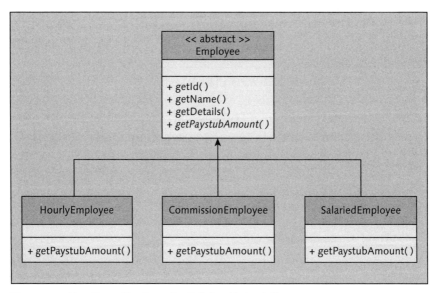

Figure 5.19 Non-Normative Form for Defining Abstract Classes

5.7   **Summary**

In this chapter, you've learned how inheritance and composition techniques can be used to quickly and safely reuse the implementations of existing classes. In this chapter, we concentrated our focus on inheriting a class's implementation. However, there's another dimension of the inheritance relationship that we have not yet considered. In the next chapter, we'll see how *type inheritance* can be used to further exploit inheritance relationships in order to make our designs even more flexible.

The term polymorphism literally means "many forms". From an object-oriented perspective, polymorphism works in concert with inheritance to make it possible for various types within an inheritance tree to be used interchangeably. In this chapter, we'll learn how to harness this power to create highly flexible program designs using ABAP Objects.

6 Polymorphism

In the previous chapter, we learned how to define inheritance relationships between related classes. From there you will recall that the basic litmus test we used to identify these relationships was to ask ourselves whether or not a given class was a more specific type of a particular superclass. For example, a `Dog` is a specific type of `Mammal`. So, instead of creating a standalone `Dog` class, it makes sense to define the `Dog` class as a *subclass* of `Mammal` so that it can inherit selected features from `Mammal`.

When we look at inheritance in this light, it's easy to see its obvious benefits in terms of code reuse. However, as it turns out, there's another (and arguably more important) dimension of the "is-a" relationship that we haven't yet considered.

Since the classes in an inheritance tree share a common public interface, it's technically possible for a given subclass to respond to any request (i.e., method call) directed at its superclass. This aspect of the inheritance relationship is referred to as *interface inheritance*. When we combine interface inheritance with the ability for subclasses to redefine/override the implementation of their inherited methods, we end up in a situation where clients no longer have to worry about the types of objects they're interfacing with: they simply issue requests (method calls) and let the objects themselves figure out how to process the requests in type-specific ways. In other words, types within an inheritance tree become interchangeable from a client perspective.

In this chapter, we'll see how we can exploit this functionality to simplify our OO designs and improve flexibility. Along the way, we'll also introduce you to another powerful tool in the OO developer's toolkit: *interfaces*.

6.1   Object Reference Assignments Revisited

In Chapter 2, we learned how to use the assignment operator (=) to perform assignments between object reference variables. As you may recall, object reference assignments copy the pointer stored in the source object reference variable into the target object reference variable. After the assignment is complete, both object reference variables point to the same object instance.

Though we sort of glossed over the details at the time, there's an important rule that we must follow when making object reference assignments: the assignments must be made using *compatible types*. For example, an assignment between an object reference variable pointing to a Material class and an object reference variable pointing to a Customer class doesn't make sense because these two types are not compatible with one another. This is demonstrated in the code excerpt contained in Listing 6.1.

```
DATA lo_material TYPE REF TO lcl_material.
DATA lo_customer TYPE REF TO lcl_customer.
CREATE OBJECT lo_material.
lo_customer = lo_material.   "<== Syntax error
```

Listing 6.1 Type Compatibility Issues with Object Reference Assignments

Strictly speaking, two variables are only compatible if they share the same type. In spite of this though, we routinely make assignments between variables having incompatible types (e.g. between built-in types such as an integer and a floating point number). Such types are said to be *convertible* in the sense that there exists some kind of conversion rule that tells the ABAP runtime environment how to convert the contents of the source variable into a format compatible with the target variable.

In the case of object reference assignments, conversions don't make sense because an object reference stores a pointer to an object and not the object itself. Therefore, in order for an object reference variable to point at an object that has a different type it must be *enhanced* with additional type information that provides visibility to the components of the actual object that it points to. In this section, we'll learn how to achieve this and perform object reference assignments between families of related types. Understanding how these assignments work is a prerequisite for learning how to implement generic designs using polymorphism.

6.1.1 Static and Dynamic Types

Up until now, the object reference assignment examples that we've considered have been between object reference variables that share the same *static type*. The static type of an object reference variable is the class type (or interface type as we'll learn in Section 6.3) used to define the object reference variable. For example, the `lo_oref` object reference variable depicted in Listing 6.2 has the class type `LCL_SOME_CLASS`.

```
DATA lo_oref TYPE REF TO lcl_some_class.
```
Listing 6.2 Determining the Static Type of an Object Reference Variable

Frequently, we may want to perform assignments between object reference variables that do not share the same static type. For example, since instances of a superclass and its subclasses are intended to be interchangeable, it should be possible to perform an assignment between object reference variables whose static types are part of the same inheritance tree. The code excerpt contained in Listing 6.3 provides an example of the kind of assignment we might want to perform between related types.

```
CLASS lcl_parent DEFINITION.
   PUBLIC SECTION.
      METHODS: a,
               b.
ENDCLASS.

CLASS lcl_parent IMPLEMENTATION.
   METHOD a.
      WRITE: / 'In method a.'.
   ENDMETHOD.

   METHOD b.
      WRITE: / 'In method b.'.
   ENDMETHOD.
ENDCLASS.

CLASS lcl_child DEFINITION
               INHERITING FROM lcl_parent.
   PUBLIC SECTION.
      METHODS: c.
ENDCLASS.

CLASS lcl_child IMPLEMENTATION.
   METHOD c.
      WRITE: / 'In method c.'.
```

```
    ENDMETHOD.
ENDCLASS.

DATA: lo_parent TYPE REF TO lcl_parent,
      lo_child  TYPE REF TO lcl_child.

CREATE OBJECT lo_parent.
CREATE OBJECT lo_child.
lo_parent = lo_child.
```

Listing 6.3 Performing a Cast with an Object Reference Assignment

To understand how an object reference assignment like the one depicted in Listing 6.3 works, we need to revisit the remote control/TV set metaphor we first introduced in Chapter 2. There, we noted that object reference variables are like remote controls which can be used to interface with object instances of a particular type. By default, object reference variables, like remote controls, are only able to communicate with a specific type of object.

Now, imagine that you decide to purchase a universal remote to replace the default remote that came with the TV. In this case, even though the *static type* of the universal remote is more generic than the one provided by the manufacturer, it's still *compatible* with the public interface provided by the TV (i.e., it supports common operations such as *Turn On*, *Adjust Volume*, and so forth). However, before you can use the universal remote with the TV, it must be *programmed* with information about the actual TV model it's interfacing with. Similarly, object reference variables that are (re)assigned to point to objects that have a different static type must be (re)programmed with dynamic type information at runtime.

The *dynamic type* of an object reference variable refers to the class type of the actual object instance pointed to by the reference variable. In the example given in Listing 6.3, the statement CREATE OBJECT lo_parent instantiates an object of type LCL_PARENT and assigns a pointer to that object to the lo_parent object reference variable. At this point, the static and dynamic type of the lo_parent reference variable is the same. However, when we perform the assignment statement lo_parent = lo_child, the dynamic type of the lo_parent reference is changed by the ABAP runtime environment to point to the LCL_CHILD class type. This information is crucial for the ABAP runtime environment to be able to interact with the compatible components of the LCL_CHILD object instance that's now being pointed to by the lo_parent reference variable.

It's worth mentioning that we cannot arbitrarily set the dynamic type of an object reference to just any class type. In other words, these kinds of assignments don't make sense without some kind of an inheritance relationship between the source and target object reference variables. In Section 6.1.2, we'll explore the rules that determine how these assignments work.

6.1.2   Casting

If the static type of the source and target object reference variables is not the same in an assignment operation, a special operation called a *cast* must occur in order for the assignment to work. A cast operation is allowed whenever the static type of the target object reference is the same as or more general than the dynamic type of the source object reference. There are two different types of cast operations: a *narrowing cast* and a *widening cast*.

Narrowing Casts

A narrowing cast occurs in an object reference assignment statement whenever the static type of a target object reference variable is more generic than the static type of the source object reference variable. Here, since we're moving upwards in the inheritance tree, these narrowing casts are also sometimes referred to as *up casts*.

The assignment statement from Listing 6.3 provided an example of a narrowing cast between the reference variables lo_parent and lo_child. We refer to this type of assignment as a narrowing cast because the class type LCL_PARENT is more general than LCL_CHILD, effectively *narrowing* the scope of the components that can be accessed in the LCL_CHILD object to those defined in the LCL_PARENT superclass.

This reduction in scope prevents the target object reference variable (i.e., LO_PARENT) from accessing components that are not defined in its static type definition. For example, the method call that is commented out in Listing 6.4 would cause a syntax error since method c() is not defined in class LCL_PARENT. Of course, this reduction in scope does not imply that the object itself is changed or truncated in some way. The LCL_CHILD object instance in Listing 6.4 is still a full-fledged object of type LCL_CHILD, it's just that the lo_parent object reference variable doesn't have visibility to the components defined in LCL_CHILD.

```
DATA: lo_parent TYPE REF TO lcl_parent,
      lo_child  TYPE REF TO lcl_child.
CREATE OBJECT lo_parent.
CREATE OBJECT lo_child.
lo_parent = lo_child.
lo_parent->c( ).    "Syntax Error!
```
Listing 6.4 Attempting to Call a Method That's Out of Scope

In addition to normal object reference assignments, it's also possible to perform narrowing casts using inline syntax. For example, if we know that we want to perform an up cast up front during the object instantiation process, then we can carry out the narrowing cast using the TYPE addition of the CREATE OBJECT statement. This syntax is demonstrated in Listing 6.5. Here, the CREATE OBJECT statement is creating an object of type LCL_CHILD and then performing a narrowing cast as it assigns a pointer to the object back to the lo_parent object reference.

```
DATA lo_parent TYPE REF TO lcl_parent.
CREATE OBJECT lo_parent TYPE lcl_child.
```
Listing 6.5 Performing a Narrowing Cast During Object Creation

Beginning with Release 7.40 of the AS ABAP, we also have the option of performing up casts using the new CAST operator. The code excerpt contained in Listing 6.6 demonstrates how this syntax can be used to implement the same casting scenario that we demonstrated in Listing 6.4. Here, we simply plug in the static type of the source object reference and the CAST operator takes care of the rest.

```
DATA(lo_child) = NEW lcl_child( ).
DATA(lo_parent) = CAST lcl_parent( lo_child ).
```
Listing 6.6 Performing an Up Cast Using the CAST Operator

Widening Casts

In cases where the static type of the target object reference variable is *more* specific than the static type of the source object reference variable, a *widening cast* has to be applied in order for the assignment statement to pass muster with the ABAP compiler. Widening casts allow us to take control of the assignment process by telling the compiler that we know what we're doing when we're performing an assignment between object references that have different static types.

Of course, this delegation doesn't mean that a validity check never takes place; it just means that the check is deferred until runtime when the dynamic type of the source object reference is known. Here, as we stated before, the static type of the target object reference must be the same as or more general than the dynamic type of the source object reference - otherwise, an exception will occur. In Chapter 8, we'll look at how to recover from these types of exceptions a bit more gracefully. Nevertheless, we strongly recommend that you use widening casts carefully as they can be somewhat confusing (and indeed, dangerous).

Because of the dangerous nature of widening casts, the ABAP language specification requires that we formally declare our intent to perform a widening cast by using a special assignment operator called the *casting operator*. As of Release 7.40 of the AS ABAP, there are actually *two* casting operators that we can use for performing widening casts: the legacy casting operator (?=) and the aforementioned new CAST operator.

The code excerpt contained in Listing 6.7 shows how to perform a widening cast using the legacy casting operator. This contrived example performs an up cast to copy an object reference of type LCL_CHILD into an object reference variable with static type LCL_PARENT. Then, we assign the object reference back to the lo_child object reference variable using a widening cast. During all of this shuffling, the LCL_CHILD object created via the CREATE OBJECT remained intact, so after the widening cast, we can access the object via the lo_child object reference variable as per usual.

```
DATA: lo_parent TYPE REF TO lcl_parent,
      lo_child TYPE REF TO lcl_child.

CREATE OBJECT lo_child.
lo_parent = lo_child.
* lo_child = lo_parent.    "<== Syntax Error
lo_child ?= lo_parent.
```
Listing 6.7 Performing Widening Casts Using the Legacy Casting Operator

The code excerpt contained in Listing 6.8 shows how we can achieve the same effect using the new CAST operator introduced with Release 7.40 of the AS ABAP. Here, notice how the usage is pretty much the same whether we're performing an up cast or a down cast. This approach improves readability by keeping the syntax consistent for any type of cast operation.

```
DATA(lo_child) = NEW lcl_child( ).
DATA(lo_parent) = CAST lcl_parent( lo_child ).
lo_child = CAST lcl_child( lo_parent ).
```
Listing 6.8 Performing a Down Cast Using the CAST Operator

6.2   Dynamic Method Call Binding

Now that you have a better idea of how to use casting operations to perform assignments between related class types, we're ready to start examining how polymorphism really works. Here, everything starts with an OO language's ability to support dynamic method call binding.

In order to understand how dynamic method call binding works, let's consider an example. The report program ZPOLYTEST included in Listing 6.9 contains an abstract class called LCL_ANIMAL, a pair of subclasses called LCL_CAT and LCL_DOG, and a test driver class called LCL_SEE_AND_SAY. The LCL_SEE_AND_SAY class is modeled loosely after the "See-n-Say®" educational toys manufactured by Mattel, Inc. Here, we want to build a simulation in which the LCL_SEE_AND_SAY class can play the sounds made by many different animals.

```
REPORT zpolytest.
CLASS lcl_animal DEFINITION ABSTRACT.
  PUBLIC SECTION.
    METHODS:
      get_type ABSTRACT RETURNING VALUE(rv_type) TYPE string,
      speak ABSTRACT RETURNING VALUE(rv_message) TYPE string.
ENDCLASS.

CLASS lcl_cat DEFINITION
        INHERITING FROM lcl_animal.
  PUBLIC SECTION.
    METHODS: get_type REDEFINITION,
             speak REDEFINITION.
ENDCLASS.

CLASS lcl_cat IMPLEMENTATION.
  METHOD get_type.
    rv_type = 'Cat'.
  ENDMETHOD.

  METHOD speak.
    rv_message = 'Meow'.
  ENDMETHOD.
ENDCLASS.

CLASS lcl_dog DEFINITION
        INHERITING FROM lcl_animal.
  PUBLIC SECTION.
    METHODS: get_type REDEFINITION,
             speak REDEFINITION.
```

```
ENDCLASS.

CLASS lcl_dog IMPLEMENTATION.
  METHOD get_type.
    rv_type = 'Dog'.
  ENDMETHOD.

  METHOD speak.
    rv_message = 'Bark'.
  ENDMETHOD.
ENDCLASS.

CLASS lcl_see_and_say DEFINITION.
  PUBLIC SECTION.
    CLASS-METHODS:
      play IMPORTING io_animal
                   TYPE REF TO lcl_animal.
ENDCLASS.

CLASS lcl_see_and_say IMPLEMENTATION.
  METHOD play.
    DATA(lv_message) =
      |The { io_animal->get_type( ) } | &&
      |says "{ io_animal->speak( ) }".|.
    WRITE: / lv_message.
  ENDMETHOD.
ENDCLASS.

START-OF-SELECTION.
  DATA(lo_cat) = NEW lcl_cat( ).
  DATA(lo_dog) = NEW lcl_dog( ).

  lcl_see_and_say=>play( lo_cat ).
  lcl_see_and_say=>play( lo_dog ).
```
Listing 6.9 Dynamic Binding with Method Calls

Looking at the sample code contained in Listing 6.9, you can see how the various classes are implemented and the inheritance relationships are formed between the abstract LCL_ANIMAL base class and the animal-specific subclasses. Where things start to get interesting is in the definition of the LCL_SEE_AND_SEE class. Here, if you look closely at the signature of method play(), you can see that it receives an importing parameter of type LCL_ANIMAL. However, in the START-OF-SELECTION event of program ZPOLYTEST, notice how we're calling this method with object reference parameters of type LCL_CAT and LCL_DOG. In this case, the

ABAP runtime environment is performing an implicit narrowing cast during the assignment of the importing parameter io_animal.

Within the play() method, the logic is purposefully generic. From the perspective of the LCL_SEE_AND_SAY class, it doesn't really matter what the dynamic type of the io_animal parameter is because any LCL_ANIMAL object is guaranteed to provide implementation for methods get_type() and speak(). So, the play() method calls these methods on the io_animal parameter and the requests are routed to the type-specific subclasses. This subtle feature makes it possible for the code inside the play() method to be implemented 100% generically.

The driving force behind all this is dynamic method call binding. Here, the dynamic type information associated with an object reference variable allows the ABAP runtime environment to dynamically bind a method call with the implementation defined in the static type of the object instance pointed to by the object reference variable. This is crucial since the io_animal parameter points to an abstract type that could never be instantiated on its own. The implementation must come from a concrete subclass such as LCL_CAT or LCL_DOG.

Dynamic binding provides for tremendous flexibility in designs. In the simple example from Listing 6.9, we only considered an implementation for a cat and a dog. In the future though, we may decide to implement subclasses for lots of other types of animals such as a horse, a cow, a pig, etc. However, since the LCL_SEE_AND_SAY class works with the generic LCL_ANIMAL type, we can integrate these new types into the "See-n-Say" service quite seamlessly. Such designs are said to be *extensible* in the sense that we can easily introduce new functionality by simply creating a new subclass and plugging it in at runtime.

6.3   Interfaces

Throughout this book, we've used the term *interface* quite a bit to describe the various interaction points between classes and their clients. For example, a method's signature defines an interface that's used by clients wishing to call that method. From an object-oriented perspective, you can think of an interface as a type of *protocol* that defines rules for communicating with objects.

This protocol analogy should be familiar since we interact with many types of protocols every day. For instance, the *HyperText Transfer Protocol* (HTTP) defines the rules that web clients (i.e., browsers such as Mozilla Firefox or Google Chrome) and web servers must adhere to in order to be able to reliably publish and retrieve content on the World Wide Web. These rules make it possible for web browsers to request web pages from many different types of web server implementations (e.g. Microsoft IIS, Apache, etc.) without having to worry about how these servers are implemented. Similarly, we've seen how polymorphism can be used to dynamically bind many different types of implementations to a single interface.

As OO theory evolved, many language designers began to see the value in being able to define an interface independently from any particular class. Such interfaces do not have an implementation associated with them and therefore cannot be instantiated on their own. While this may seem like a stretch at first, suffice it to say that we can do a lot of interesting things with interfaces. In this section, we'll look at how interfaces can be used expand a class's scope into multiple dimensions.

6.3.1   Interface Inheritance vs. Implementation Inheritance

Some object-oriented languages support a *multiple inheritance* model, allowing you to define several inheritance relationships within a given class. As you may have guessed by now, ABAP Objects only supports a *single inheritance* model. This is a design decision that has been employed by many modern object-oriented languages in an effort to avoid some of the ambiguity that can arise with complex inheritance hierarchies.

To illustrate some of the potential problems associated with a multiple inheritance model, let's consider an example. The class diagram in Figure 6.1 depicts a diamond-shaped class hierarchy. In this case, let's imagine that classes B and C have both redefined method someMethod() from class A. If class D does not redefine method someMethod(), from which implementation does it inherit: B or C? This problem is known as the *diamond problem*.

A single-inheritance model avoids these kinds of vagaries since a subclass always inherits from a single superclass. However, interfaces can enhance this model by providing a way to extend the *type* of a class without having to bring along all of the implementation baggage associated with multiple inheritance. In Section 6.3.4, we'll see how the implementation of an interface allows a class to be used polymorphically wherever a reference of that interface type is used.

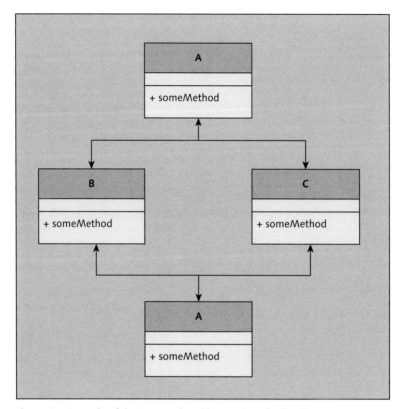

Figure 6.1 Example of the Diamond Problem with Multiple Inheritance

6.3.2   Defining Interfaces

The syntax required to define an interface is very similar to the syntax that is used in the declaration part of a class definition. Listing 6.10 shows an example of how to define a local interface called LIF_IFACE. Notice that none of the interface components have been defined within a visibility section. This is because all components of an interface are implicitly defined within the public visibility section. If you think about it, this makes sense because the purpose of an interface is to expand the public interface of implementing classes.

```
INTERFACE lif_iface.
  DATA a TYPE string.
  METHODS: m.
  EVENTS: e.
ENDINTERFACE.
```

Listing 6.10 Syntax for Defining a Local Interface

Most of the time, interfaces are used to add additional methods to the public interface of a class. However, you can technically define all of the same types of components that you can define for classes in an interface: attributes, methods, events, types, and so on.

Just like classes, interfaces can be defined as local objects and global ABAP Repository objects. In the latter case, we can create/edit interfaces using the familiar Class Builder tool. To illustrate how this works, let's create a new global interface called ZIF_COMPARABLE that can be used to specify an arbitrary ordering for implementing classes. Here, the steps are as follows:

1. From within the ABAP Workbench, select the appropriate package, right-click, and select the CREATE • CLASS LIBRARY • INTERFACE menu option (see Figure 6.2).

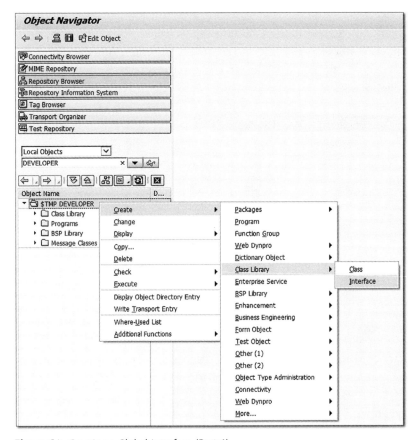

Figure 6.2 Creating a Global Interface (Part 1)

2. This will open up the CREATE INTERFACE dialog box shown in Figure 6.3. Here, we simply enter a name for the interface and a brief description. The name of the interface should be defined according to the convention {namespace}IF_ {meaningful_name}. In the example given, we have ZIF_COMPARABLE which is being defined in the customer Z namespace.

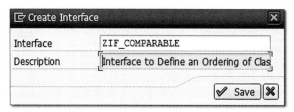

Figure 6.3 Creating a Global Interface (Part 2)

3. After we fill out the details in the CREATE INTERFACE dialog box shown in Figure 6.3, we can click on the SAVE button to create the interface. At this point, we'll be prompted with the familiar CREATE OBJECT DIRECTORY ENTRY dialog box shown in Figure 6.4.

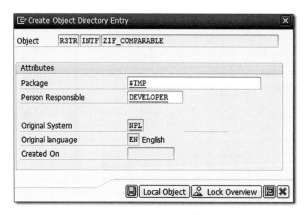

Figure 6.4 Creating a Global Interface (Part 3)

4. Finally, after confirming the Repository/transport details, the interface will be created and opened up in the Class Builder tool as shown in Figure 6.5. Here, just like classes, we can edit interfaces in the form-based view or the source code-based view.

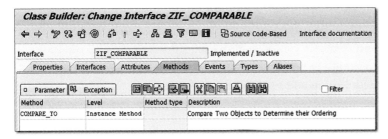

Figure 6.5 Editing a Global Interface in the Class Builder Tool

Within the ZIF_COMPARABLE interface, we've defined a single method called com-pare_to() which can be used to compare two objects to determine their relative ordering. Figure 6.6 shows the signature of this method. As you can see, it defines two parameters:

▶ IO_OBJECT
This importing parameter represents the object that's being compared with the host object (i.e., the object that drives the comparison). Here, notice that we've defined the type of this parameter using the generic OBJECT type. This will allow us to compare *any* type of object using this interface.

▶ RV_RESULT
This returning parameter specifies the ordering of the two objects as an integer value. The resulting value will be a negative integer, zero, or a positive integer depending on whether or not the host object is less than, equal to, or greater than the object passed via io_object parameter.

Class Builder: Change Interface ZIF_COMPARABLE							
Interface	ZIF_COMPARABLE		Implemented / Inactive (revised)				
Properties	Interfaces	Attributes	Methods	Events	Types	Aliases	

Method parameters			COMPARE_TO					
Parameter	Type	Pass Value	Optional	Typing Method	Associated Type	Default value	Description
IO_OBJECT	Importing	☐	☐	Type Ref To	OBJECT		Object to be Compared
RV_RESULT	Returning	☑	☐	Type	I		Result Value
		☐	☐	Type			

Figure 6.6 Building out the ZIF_COMPARABLE Interface

Listing 6.11 shows the source code generated for the ZIF_COMPARABLE interface. Since interfaces don't contain any sort of implementation, that's all there is to our ZIF_COMPARABLE interface. In Section 6.3.3 and Section 6.3.4, we'll see how this interface is used to build a container class which collects a series of related objects together and provides value-add operations such as sorting.

```
interface ZIF_COMPARABLE
  public .

  methods COMPARE_TO
    importing
      !IO_OBJECT type ref to OBJECT
    returning
      value(RV_RESULT) type I .
endinterface.
```
Listing 6.11 Source Code for Interface ZIF_COMPARABLE

6.3.3   Implementing Interfaces

Interfaces are not all that interesting until we start implementing them in classes. Within a class definition, we can implement an interface using the INTERFACES keyword. Here, we can specify one or more interfaces that we want to implement in a comma-separated list. Logically, this has a similar effect to adding the INHERITING FROM addition to the CLASS DEFINITION statement: the components from the selected interfaces will be inherited in the implementing class.

To demonstrate how interface implementation works, let's consider a brief example. Listing 6.12 shows how a local class called LCL_IMPLEMENTER is implementing an interface called LIF_IFACE. As you can see, implementing the LIF_IFACE interface in LCL_IMPLEMENTER requires that we provide implementation for the methods defined in LIF_IFACE: m1() and m2().

```
INTERFACE lif_iface.
  METHODS: m1,
           m2.
ENDINTERFACE.

CLASS lcl_implementer DEFINITION.
  PUBLIC SECTION.
    INTERFACES: lif_iface.
ENDCLASS.

CLASS lcl_implementer IMPLEMENTATION.
  METHOD lif_iface~m1.
    ...
```

```
ENDMETHOD.

METHOD lif_iface~m2.
   ...
ENDMETHOD.
ENDCLASS.
```
Listing 6.12 Implementing an Interface in a Class Definition

Looking closely at the implementation of the LCL_IMPLEMENTER class, you can see that the inherited methods are qualified with a prefix of the source interface (LIF_IFACE) and the tilde character (~). The "~" between the interface name and the interface component name is called the *interface component selector* operator. This qualification makes the inheritance relationship(s) clear in cases where a class might implement multiple interfaces which happen to have components that share the same name.

When working with the form-based view of the Class Builder tool, we can implement interfaces by simply plugging in the interface name(s) on the INTERFACES tab as shown in Figure 6.7. Behind the scenes, the Class Builder will automatically add the inherited components to the class definition and stub out the implementation section.

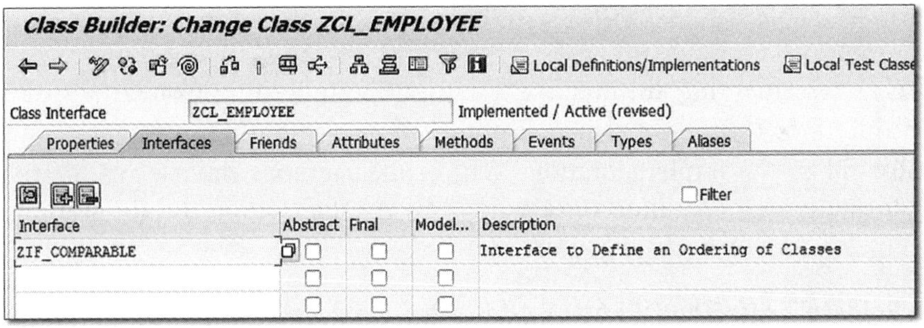

Figure 6.7 Implementing an Interface Using the Form-Based View of the Class Builder Tool

Now that you have a better understanding of the nuts-and-bolts of implementing interfaces, let's turn our attention back to the implementation of our ZIF_COMPARABLE interface which we've been working on in this section. As you can see in Figure 6.7, we've implemented this interface in the ZCL_EMPLOYEE entity object that we developed in Chapter 5. The intent here is to provide a means of comparing employee objects so that we can sort them.

The code excerpt contained in Listing 6.13 provides a demonstration of how we might implement the `compare_to()` method for our `ZCL_EMPLOYEE` class. Here, we chose to define the sort ordering in terms of the employee's ID value, but we could have just as easily defined the order in terms of the employee's last name, etc. As you can see in the code, the actual comparison is pretty straightforward. The only trick to make this work is in implementing the widening cast on the generic `io_object` parameter. By performing a down cast on the object, we're able to address its components (e.g. the `get_id()`method) in the evaluation logic.

```
method ZIF_COMPARABLE~COMPARE_TO.
  "Perform a widening cast on the comparison object
  "so that we can access its components during the
  "comparison process:
  DATA(lo_employee) = CAST zcl_employee( io_object ).

  "Compare the two employees based on their ID number:
  IF me->get_id( ) > lo_employee->get_id( ).
    rv_result = 1.
  ELSEIF me->get_id( ) < lo_employee->get_id( ).
    rv_result = -1.
  ELSE.
    rv_result = 0.
  ENDIF.
endmethod.
```

Listing 6.13 Implementing the compare_to() Method

Ultimately, implementing an interface is rather like inheriting from an abstract class: the interface defines the structure of the components and the implementing class must fill in the implementation. Within the methods themselves, there's nothing really special going on—just regular ABAP Objects code as per usual.

New in Release 7.40—The DEFAULT Addition

Over the years, one of the pain points of working with interfaces in ABAP Objects is that you have to provide an implementation for every method defined by the interface in the implementing class. While purists would no doubt argue that this is proper, it does make our job as developers a bit tedious at times.

To address this phenomenon, SAP introduced a new addition to the METHODS statement in Release 7.40 which can be used to specify whether or not a given method must be implemented by an implementing class. The code excerpt contained in Listing 6.14 shows how this addition works.

```
INTERFACE lif_big_interface.
  METHODS:
    important_method DEFAULT FAIL,
    optional_method DEFAULT IGNORE.
  ...
ENDINTERFACE.
```

Listing 6.14 Working with the DEFAULT Addition

In the code excerpt contained in Listing 6.14 we have an interface called LIF_ BIG_INTERFACE which defines a pair of methods called important_method() and optional_method(), respectively. In the case of important_method(), we want to ensure that any implementing class does provide an implementation for this method. With the DEFAULT FAIL addition, the behavior works as it would under normal circumstances.

In the case of optional_method(), the DEFAULT IGNORE addition makes it possible for implementing classes to skip over the implementation of this method if desired. At runtime, if a polymorphic call is made to this method, we won't see a runtime error. Instead, the ABAP runtime environment will silently skip over the method as if the call never took place.

The use of the DEFAULT addition is optional, supporting complete backwards compatibility with previously-defined interfaces. Whether you choose to use it to define your interfaces is up to you, but it can simplify the implementation process in certain cases.

6.3.4   Working with Interfaces

At this point, we don't have a lot to show for all the hard work we put into defining and implementing the ZIF_COMPARABLE interface. However, this doesn't mean that interfaces are a waste of time—we just have to learn how to harness their capabilities in our designs. In this section, we'll look at a practical example which uses the ZIF_COMPARABLE interface to create a generic collection class that aggregates/organizes a set of related object instances.

At first blush, you might think that creating a custom collection class is a waste of time since ABAP already defines a built-in container for object instances with internal tables. Here, we can create collections of object instances using syntax like that contained within Listing 6.15. However, while internal tables like lt_employees provide a convenient mechanism for storing and looping through object references, there are certain things they can't do. For example, this internal table has no idea how to sort the employee records it contains. A custom collection class on the other hand can be enhanced to include this kind of expanded functionality. This is where the ZIF_COMPARABLE interface begins to show its value.

```
DATA lt_employees TYPE STANDARD TABLE OF REF TO zcl_employee.
```
Listing 6.15 Defining an Internal Table with an Object-Based Line Type

If we build our collection class to accept objects that implement the ZIF_COMPARA-BLE interface, then we have everything we need to build out a generic sort function within the collection. However, before we get into the nuts and bolts of this, let's first take a look at the basic design of our custom collection class. For our first pass at this, we'll create a new class called ZCL_COLLECTION which defines three methods whose names are pretty self-explanatory: add_element() adds an element to the collection, remove_element() removes an element from the collection, and sort() performs an in-place sorting on the elements. As you can see in the method signatures as well as the mt_elements internal table attribute which stores the elements internally, all element references are defined in terms of the generic OBJECT type. This design choice allows us to store *any* type of object within our collection.

```
CLASS zcl_collection DEFINITION.
  PUBLIC SECTION.
    TYPE-POOLS abap.

    METHODS:
      add_element IMPORTING io_element TYPE REF TO object,
      remove_element IMPORTING io_element TYPE REF TO object
                     RETURNING VALUE(rv_result) TYPE abap_bool,
      sort.

  PRIVATE SECTION.
    DATA mt_elements TYPE STANDARD TABLE OF REF TO object.
ENDCLASS.
```
Listing 6.16 Defining the Shell of the ZCL_COLLECTION Class

With this basic framework in place, we can now turn our attention to the sort() method's implementation. Listing 6.17 contains an implementation based on the familiar *Insertion Sort* algorithm. This simple (though somewhat inefficient) algorithm operates in similar fashion to the way you might sort a hand of playing cards. Assuming the cards are in unsorted order and lying face down on the table, you begin sorting by picking up cards one-by-one and inserting them into the proper position within your hand (i.e., based on the value of the card). When applied to the sorting of collection elements, the Insertion Sort algorithm gets the ordering from the `compare_to()` method of the `ZIF_COMPARABLE` interface.

```
method SORT.
  DATA: lo_key     TYPE REF TO object,
        lo_element TYPE REF TO object,
        lo_compare TYPE REF TO zif_comparable,
        lo_temp    TYPE REF TO object,
        lv_i       TYPE i,
        lv_j       TYPE i VALUE 2,
        lv_index   TYPE i.

  "Sort the collection elements using the Insertion Sort
  "algorithm:
  LOOP AT me->mt_elements INTO lo_key FROM 2.
    lv_i = lv_j - 1.
    READ TABLE me->mt_elements INDEX lv_i INTO lo_element.
    lo_compare ?= lo_element.

    WHILE lv_i GT 0 AND
          lo_compare->compare_to( lo_key ) EQ
            zif_comparable=>co_greater_than.
      READ TABLE me->mt_elements INDEX lv_i INTO lo_temp.
      lv_index = lv_i + 1.
      MODIFY me->mt_elements FROM lo_temp INDEX lv_index.

      lv_i = lv_i - 1.
      READ TABLE me->mt_elements INDEX lv_i INTO lo_element.
      lo_compare ?= lo_element.
    ENDWHILE.

    lv_index = lv_i + 1.
    MODIFY me->mt_elements FROM lo_key INDEX lv_index.
    lv_j = lv_j + 1.
  ENDLOOP.
endmethod.
```

Listing 6.17 Implementing a Generic Sort Algorithm in the ZCL_COLLECTION Class

Looking closely at the implementation of the `sort()` method in Listing 6.17, you can see that we never refer to any particular type of element class within the sorting logic. Instead, we use a widening cast on the element objects in order to reference them as `ZIF_COMPARABLE` instances. The target of this widening cast is an *interface reference variable* called `lo_compare` whose static type is defined as `ZIF_COMPARABLE`. This interface reference variable allows us to address the object in exactly the same way we use object reference variables to address object components: via the familiar instance selector operator (->). This is evidenced by the call to the compare_to() method which drives the sorting logic.

Since the logic in the sort() method is focused on the implementation of the ZIF_COMPARABLE interface, the only requirement for incorporating element classes into the collection is that the element class implements the ZIF_COMPARABLE interface. How that element class chooses to implement the comparison logic is completely irrelevant to the ZCL_COLLECTION class; it just assumes the element classes know what they're doing.

> **Note**
>
> The ZIF_COMPARABLE implementation validation is enforced in the add_element() method using features that we haven't yet covered in this book. You can find detailed information about the approach we're taking here in the ZCL_COLLECTION class contained within the book's online source code bundle.

Though we could have achieved similar results using regular class-based inheritance, such a design approach would have limited the usefulness of the collection because it would have restricted us from being able to incorporate element classes that already have inheritance relationships in place. For example, since the ZCL_HOURLY_EMPLOYEE class introduced in Chapter 5 already inherits from ZCL_EMPLOYEE, it couldn't also inherit from an abstract class such as ZCL_COMPARABLE. However, since we can implement as many interfaces as we want in an ABAP Objects class, it's a trivial matter to incorporate the ZIF_COMPARABLE interface to extend a class to make it *comparable*.

6.3.5   Nesting Interfaces

So far, we've only considered simple, elementary interfaces. However, it's possible to *nest* interfaces inside of a compound or *nested interface*. Interfaces embedded inside of a nested interface are called *component interfaces*. Listing 6.18 shows an example of the syntax used to nest the component interface LIF_COMPONENT inside of the nested interface LIF_NESTED. As you can see, interfaces are themselves nested using the familiar INTERFACES statement.

```
INTERFACE lif_component.
  METHODS: c1,
           c2.
```

```
ENDINTERFACE.

INTERFACE lif_nested.
  INTERFACES: lif_component.
  METHODS: n1,
           n2.
ENDINTERFACE.
```
Listing 6.18 A Nested Interface Example

We can achieve the same effect for Repository-based interfaces in the form-based view of the Class Builder tool by plugging in the component interface(s) in the INCLUDES column of the INTERFACES tab as shown in Figure 6.8.

Each of the component interfaces within a nested interface exists at the same level. So, if a given component interface happens to be nested more than once, there will only be a single set of the components defined within that component interface inside the nested interface.

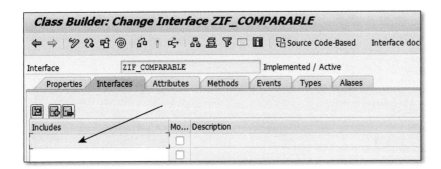

Figure 6.8 Nesting Interfaces in the Form-Based View of the Class Builder

By default, components of component interfaces are not directly visible within the nested interface. To make these components visible via the public interface, we must define *alias names* for the components. Listing 6.19 shows how the ALIASES statement is being used in the LIF_NESTED interface definition to define aliases for a pair of methods inherited from the LIF_COMPONENT component interface. With this promotion, the class LCL_NESTED_IMPL is now able to address/implement the nested methods provided via the LIF_COMPONENT interface even though it only formally implements the overarching LIF_NESTED interface.

```
INTERFACE lif_component.
  METHODS: c1,
           c2.
```

```
ENDINTERFACE.

INTERFACE lif_nested.
  INTERFACES: lif_component.
  ALIASES: c1 FOR lif_component~c1,
           c2 FOR lif_component~c2.
  METHODS: n1,
           n2.
ENDINTERFACE.


CLASS lcl_nested_impl DEFINITION.
  PUBLIC SECTION.
    INTERFACES: lif_nested.
ENDCLASS.


CLASS lcl_nested_impl IMPLEMENTATION.
  METHOD lif_nested~n1.
  ENDMETHOD.

  METHOD lif_nested~n2.
  ENDMETHOD.

  METHOD lif_nested~c1.
  ENDMETHOD.

  METHOD lif_nested~c2.
  ENDMETHOD.
ENDCLASS.
```

Listing 6.19 Working with Alias Names

Much like we observed in Section 6.1.2, we can also perform casts in assignments between interface reference variables. For example, Listing 6.20 shows an example of how we can perform a narrowing cast between interface reference variables defined using the static types LIF_COMPONENT and LIF_NESTED introduced in the code excerpts contained in Listing 6.18 and Listing 6.19. In this case, the narrowing cast is allowed because LIF_COMPONENT is a component interface of LIF_NESTED.

```
DATA: lo_component TYPE REF TO lif_component,
      lo_nested    TYPE REF TO lif_nested.
CREATE OBJECT lo_nested TYPE lcl_nested_impl.
lo_component = lo_nested.
lo_component->c1( ).
```

Listing 6.20 Performing Narrowing Casts Using Interface References

6.3.6 When to Use Interfaces

Since interfaces are expressions of pure design, it can be difficult at times to figure out when and where to employ them in your own designs. Rest assured you're not alone in this: OO enthusiasts have been debating this point for quite some time. On one side of the argument, you have those who advocate widespread use of interfaces. Indeed, in the introductory title *The Java Programming Language, 4th Edition*, the authors assert that "every major class in an application should be an implementation of some interfaces that captures the contract of that class." The other side of the debate takes a softer stance, preferring to use interfaces more on an as-needed basis (e.g. to implement multiple inheritance).

While we won't attempt to persuade you one way or another in this debate, we would be remiss if we didn't at least highlight a couple of the more common design scenarios where you might want to consider the use of interfaces. Over time, we think you'll find that these design choices will become second nature, but it helps early on to examine these scenarios up close.

Interfaces vs. Abstract Classes

Since abstract classes are basically interfaces with a bit of reusable implementation content in tow, it's only natural for developers to tend to gravitate towards the use of abstract classes over interfaces. From an implementation perspective, there's no doubt about it: abstract classes are definitely easier to work with. Nevertheless, there are times when the extra effort associated with going the interface route definitely pays off.

Since ABAP Objects doesn't support multiple inheritance, the only way we can utilize abstract classes is by directly inheriting from them. This works well when we're clearly dealing with main types such as Employee, SalesOrder, or Delivery, but what about secondary types like the Comparable type we considered in Section 6.3? For certain class types, the "is-a" relationship might apply to multiple types, not just the main type.

To illustrate this concept further, let's look at a fairly typical example of interface usage in ABAP Objects: SAP Business Workflow. In Business Workflow, the processing logic behind workflow tasks can be defined using the instance methods of ABAP Objects classes. In order for the workflow engine to be able to communicate with these objects, there's a requirement that these workflow classes implement the SAP standard IF_WORKFLOW interface which defines callback methods the workflow engine can use to load objects, etc. Though SAP could have opted to define this functionality in an abstract class (e.g. CL_WORKFLOW), such a design choice would have limited developers from plugging in just any old ABAP Objects class into workflow scenarios since such classes might already inherit from some other base class. On the other hand, adding an implementation of the IF_WORK-FLOW interface on top of an existing class is relatively easy and doesn't disturb any of the existing functionality.

In general, we'd recommend that you model any sort of secondary type using interfaces. You can usually identify these secondary types by considering whether they represent a core concept in the object model, or cross-cutting concepts which are more secondary in nature. For example, when we implemented the ZIF_COMPARABLE interface in the ZCL_EMPLOYEE in Section 6.3.3, we didn't change the main concept of employee types; we just said that these employee types are *also* comparable. You can think of this as an "is also" relationship.

Using Interfaces to Hide Implementation Details

As we learned in Section 6.3.4, clients can use interface reference variables to address object instances polymorphically. While this may not seem all that interesting at first, it turns out that there are lots of interesting things we can do with this capability.

One common way that developers exploit this feature is by creating *factories* which clients can use to obtain instances of objects that implement a particular interface. If you've ever worked with the iXML library for XML parsing in ABAP, you've seen an example of this design pattern in practice. The code excerpt contained in Listing 6.21 demonstrates how the CL_IXML factory class is used to obtain access to the iXML library. As you can see, on the client side we deal exclusively with the interfaces defined by the iXML library: IF_IXML, IF_IXML_DOCU-MENT, and so forth. Such interfaces define the core functionality of the iXML library in abstract terms.

```
DATA lo_ixml TYPE REF TO if_ixml.
DATA lo_document TYPE REF TO if_ixml_document.
lo_ixml = cl_ixml=>create( ).
lo_document = lo_ixml->create_document( ).
...
```

Listing 6.21 The Factory Pattern Applied to the SAP iXML Library

The reason SAP went to the trouble of creating all of these interfaces was to provide an abstraction around a delicate XML parsing library that's built on top of kernel modules (i.e., modules written using C/C++ native code in lieu of ABAP). By defining the API in terms of interfaces, SAP is able to shield customers from the underlying implementation details. As a result, if SAP decided to scrap the kernel module approach and re-write the library, they could easily do so and simply plug in the new concrete classes at runtime via the create() factory method of class CL_IXML.

While customers might be less likely to encounter direct requirements like this in practice, we'd encourage you to think about how the use of interfaces might improve the flexibility of APIs you decide to develop in-house. As we progress further in the book, we'll encounter several other examples of this to give you a better sense of the benefits of this kind of design pattern.

6.4   UML Tutorial: Advanced Class Diagrams Part II

In this section, we'll complete our coverage of UML class diagrams by introducing the notation for working with interfaces and their components.

6.4.1   Interfaces

The notation for defining interfaces in a UML class diagram is almost identical to the one used to define classes. The only difference is the addition of the << interface >> tag in the top name section of the interface notation (see Figure 6.9).

Figure 6.9 Notation for Defining Interfaces

The relationship between a nested interface and its component interfaces is shown using the same generalization notation used to depict inheritance relationships. For example, in Figure 6.10, the Nested interface is inheriting the components from interface Component.

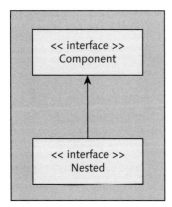

Figure 6.10 Notation for Defining Nested Interfaces

6.4.2 Providing and Required Relationships with Interfaces

Figure 6.11 shows the two kinds of relationships that a class can have with an interface. The dashed line between class Employee and interface Comparable indicates that class Employee *provides* (or implements) the Comparable interface. Notice how the notation for this relationship is similar to the one we've seen for generalization relationships. In this case, the interface Comparable represents one kind of generalization for class Employee. Implicitly, this tells us that we can substitute instances of class Employee in places where the interface Comparable is used. The dashed arrow between class Collection and interface Comparable represents a dependency, indicating that class Collection *requires* the Comparable interface in some way. As we witnessed in Section 6.3.4, this dependency exists in method sort(), which performs comparisons between collection elements using the compareTo() method defined in interface Comparable.

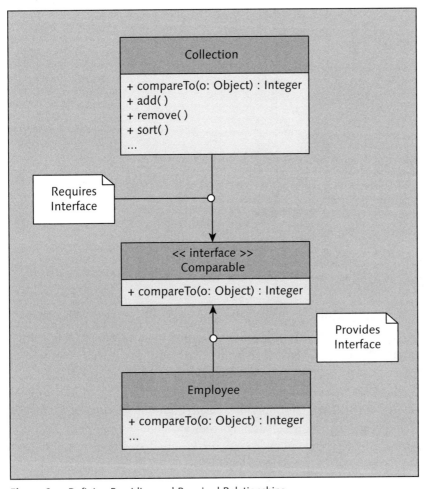

Figure 6.11 Defining Providing and Required Relationships

6.4.3 Static Attributes and Methods

Whether we're defining them at the class level or the interface level, we can identify static components within a class diagram by simply underlining them. Figure 6.12 illustrates this notation for a standard utilities class provided by SAP called CL_ABAP_CHAR_UTILITIES.

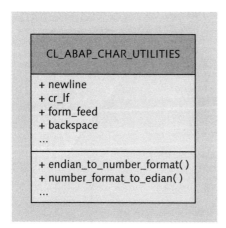

Figure 6.12 Defining Static Attributes and Methods

6.5   Summary

This chapter concludes our basic introduction to object-oriented programming. In many ways, the powerful designs that we learned to implement in this chapter represent part of the big payoff for all of the hard work that goes into designing families of abstract data types. As we progress further throughout the book, we'll see many more examples that demonstrate how the three main pillars of OOP (encapsulation, inheritance, and polymorphism) allow us to implement designs that can stand up to any changes that may come along over time. In the world of business software, such flexibility is vital for keeping pace with ever-changing business requirements.

In the next chapter, we'll look at ways to take these abstractions to the next level as we consider how to organize our class libraries into high-level software components using the SAP *package concept*.

A component-based approach to software design breaks a system down into a series of logical components that communicate using well-defined interfaces. When designed properly, these components become reusable software assets that can be mixed and matched to rapidly adapt to ever-changing business processes. In this chapter, we'll look at ways to implement component-based designs in ABAP.

7 Component-Based Design Concepts

Now that you've learned the basic principles of object-oriented software development, we can begin to broaden our focus by looking at ways of organizing class libraries and their related resources into reusable *software components*. This process begins with the assignment of classes to modular software units called *packages*. Packages bring structure to the ABAP development process, transforming fine-grained code libraries into more coarse-grained development components.

In this chapter, you'll learn how to create and work with packages. You'll also see how packages fit into the overall SAP component-based software logistics model. Collectively, these concepts will help you keep your software catalog organized as class libraries evolve over time.

7.1 Understanding the SAP Component Model

To understand how to effectively implement component-based software designs in an ABAP development environment, it's helpful to spend a little bit of time reviewing the component model that SAP uses to manage their own software logistics. As you can see in Figure 7.1, SAP assembles its software products using high-level software units called *software components*. Software components are comprised of a series of *packages* which organize the development objects that provide the actual implementation part of the system (e.g., classes, function groups, ABAP Dictionary objects, etc.).

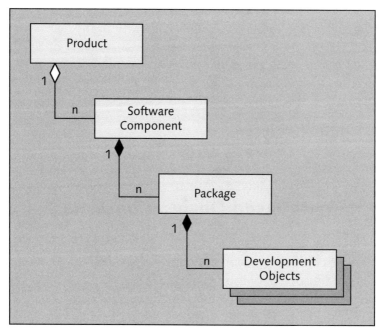

Figure 7.1 The SAP Component Model for ABAP Software Logistics

Each of the component model elements depicted in Figure 7.1 exist in *versions*. To put this into perspective, let's consider the architecture of one of the more well-known products in the SAP landscape: *SAP ERP*. At the time of this writing, most SAP customers are running version 6 of this product, with various enhancement packages and support packages installed on top of it. Underneath the hood, an SAP ERP product installation consists of a series of installed software components which also exist in versions: SAP_APPL, SAP_HR, and so forth. You can see which software component versions are installed on any SAP Business Suite system by selecting SYSTEM • STATUS in the top-level menu bar and clicking on the COMPONENT INFORMATION button as shown in Figure 7.2.

Software Component Versioning Concepts

Looking closely at Figure 7.2, you can see that there are multiple dimensions to a software component's version:

▶ Release Number

▶ Support Package (SP) Level

▶ Support Package Patch (SPP) Level

This versioning scheme is consistent with the major, minor, build, revision scheme you've probably seen in other software products. With such a large customer base, SAP needs to be able to issue periodic support packs which bundle together a series of fixes for a particular software component version. Such changes are meant to be of the break/fix variety and shouldn't disturb day-to-day activities within the enterprise. Support pack patches are similar to hot fixes where SAP issues a patch to correct a reported product defect.

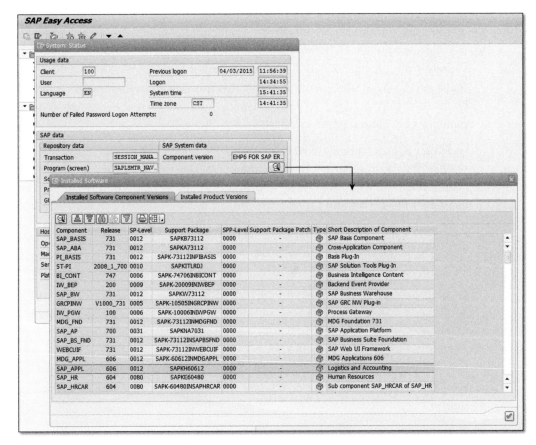

Figure 7.2 Browsing the Installed Software Components in an SAP System

If we dissect a particular software component version, we'll find a series of ABAP development objects which are organized into packages. Since each of these development objects exist in versions, we can think of a software component version as a snapshot of related development objects which were bundled together to create an installation unit. Such software components are then logically grouped together into a product version.

From a logistics perspective, adopting a layered approach to system design offers many advantages. First of all, it helps organize the software into logical pieces that are encapsulated and therefore easier to work with. This is particularly important for large organizations like SAP which employ development teams working on interrelated projects around the globe. Secondly, it promotes the reuse of common components in other systems. Within the SAP Business Suite, we see many examples of this with foundational components such as the SAP_ BASIS and SAP_ABA components being reused across SAP Business Suite solutions such as SAP Customer Relationship Management (SAP CRM), SAP Supply Chain Management (SAP SCM), and so on. Finally, it makes the software more extensible because defined dependencies between components make it easier to determine how to integrate new or revised components into the system.

In the sections to follow, we'll see how these concepts can also be applied on a smaller scale to custom ABAP development performed at customer sites. Here, even though the goal may not be to produce a commercial product, the need for component-based encapsulation applies just the same.

7.2   The Package Concept

Prior to Release 6.10 of the SAP Web Application Server (today called the AS ABAP), all development objects within the ABAP Repository were grouped together into logical containers called *development classes*. Development classes (which are in no way related to classes in the OO paradigm) provided a simple way for organizing related development objects by functional area. In Release 6.10, SAP replaced development classes with packages and the so-called *package concept*.

At the time, the introduction of the package concept was not met with much fanfare because most developers mistakenly assumed that the term "package" was just a new name given to development classes. However, as we'll learn in this section, the package concept brings much more to the table than just a folder-like organizational structure. When used properly, the package concept allows developers to organize development objects into coarse-grained and reusable development components.

7.2.1 Why Do We Need Packages?

Throughout this book, we've seen how the OO development approach lends itself towards the creation of lots of small, individualized classes, interfaces, and related artifacts. This is a far cry from the old days of ABAP where the main units of development were large, monolithic ABAP report programs, classic Dynpro-based module pool programs, and the occasional subroutine pool or function group.

While such decomposition is undoubtedly a good thing, there is a natural side-effect: modern ABAP development projects produce lots of custom development objects that we must account for. So much so that it's no longer realistic to think that we can organize objects using specialized naming conventions or functional area-specific development classes/packages (e.g., ZFI for financial accounting-related artifacts, ZHR for human resources, and so forth).

This phenomenon is brought into sharp relief when you consider the number of artifacts generated in say a Web Dynpro ABAP (WDA) application. Here, in even the simplest of application scenarios, we might produce upwards of 25-30 custom objects when you consider the WDA-related artifacts themselves, ABAP Dictionary objects, helper classes, and so forth. If we multiply that number by the number of custom applications we might build in a particular functional area (e.g., logistics), it's plain to see how a given package can fill up in a hurry. For developers unfamiliar with the history of the development objects contained within these packages, it can be very difficult to figure out what goes with what after the fact. Even if we try to re-organize such large packages into smaller sub-packages, this approach eventually breaks down too because it fails to address the main problem: the development objects within a package require boundaries.

In many ways, these logistical problems are not unlike the ones we observed in Chapter 3 when we looked at encapsulation concepts. For example, if we compare the organization of development objects into development classes/packages with the functional decomposition process used to break large, monolithic programs into subroutines/procedures, we can see that neither process really establishes any sort of boundaries. Whenever we build applications and libraries, we definitely want to group related development objects together, but we also want to be able to restrict access to objects which are part of the underlying implementation and subject to change. Packages allow us to achieve both of these objectives. We'll see how this works in the sections to come.

7.2.2   Introducing Packages

Within the Package Concept, there are three types of packages we can use to organize development objects: *structure packages*, *main packages*, and *development packages*. These package types and their interrelationships are depicted in Figure 7.3. We'll describe each of these package types in detail in the following subsections.

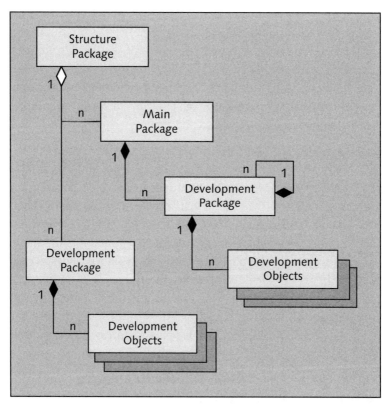

Figure 7.3 Structure of the ABAP Package Hierarchy

Structure Packages

Structure packages, as the name suggests, are used to provide *structure* around lower-level packages within the hierarchy. Within the Package Concept, structure packages are closely aligned with the encapsulating software component (refer back to Figure 7.1). For example, the structure package ABA encapsulates all of the packages/development objects contained within the SAP_ABA software component. Though this is the typical use case, we should point out that structure packages can generally be used any time you want to organize a large scale development effort. For customers who aren't interested in re-selling software components, this might imply the use of structure packages to organize development objects by functional area (having the same general positioning as the development classes of old).

Regardless of how they're used, it's important to bear in mind that structure packages are not *extensible* in the sense that you can't embed development objects directly beneath them. Instead, we can only embed other packages within a given structure package.

Main Packages

Underneath structure packages, we can further organize our development into high-level modules called *main packages*. Main packages are typically used to group development objects by *function*. Development objects embedded inside a main package are logically related in some way. Often, a main package is used to group together modules related to the development of complex applications. However, main packages, just like structure packages, cannot have development objects embedded directly beneath them (refer to Figure 7.3).

Development Packages

At the bottom of the package hierarchy, we have *development packages*. It's at this level that we can begin embedding ABAP development objects (e.g., classes, function groups, ABAP Dictionary objects, and so forth). Such assignments occur within the ABAP Workbench tools whenever new development objects are created. This is highlighted in Figure 7.4 where you can see that a package assignment is a required attribute in the CREATE OBJECT DIRECTORY ENTRY screen.

Within the package concept, development packages are used to organize development objects that are closely related to one another. For example, if we were to use ABAP Objects classes to model some business object (e.g. a material) then it would probably make sense to bundle these classes, their related ABAP Dictionary objects, and so on within the same development package.

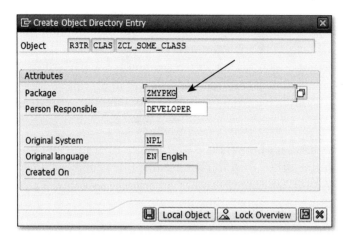

Figure 7.4 Assigning ABAP Repository Objects to Packages

Ultimately, the goal in defining development packages is to maintain a reasonable level of cohesion with the underlying development objects. There's no restriction on the number of development packages that we can create within the system, so developers shouldn't be afraid to create as many of these packages as they need to keep things organized.

Over time, these package assignments may change as the software architecture evolves, and that's OK. At the end of the day, we want to make it easy for developers to find development objects without having to consult naming convention guides and the like. If we get the right cut for our development packages, the process of locating development objects should be rather intuitive.

7.2.3 Creating Packages Using the Package Builder

Packages can be maintained in one of two places: directly within the ABAP Workbench (Transaction SE80) or in the standalone *Package Builder* transaction (Transaction SE21). Figure 7.5 shows the initial screen of the Package Builder with the familiar CREATE, CHANGE, and DISPLAY functions. Once you get past this initial screen of the Package Builder, the look-and-feel is largely the same in both transactions. As such, most developers will prefer to work within the ABAP Workbench directly due to its handy context-sensitive features.

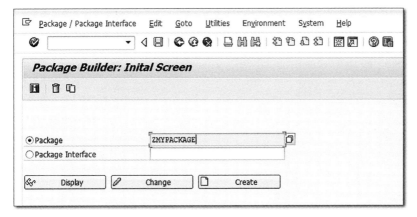

Figure 7.5 Package Builder Transaction: Initial Screen

Within the ABAP Workbench, you can create a new package by performing the following steps:

1. On the left-hand side of the screen, select the REPOSITORY BROWSER view if it's not selected already. From here, select the PACKAGE option in the object list as shown in Figure 7.6.

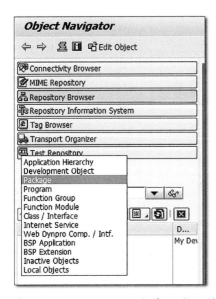

Figure 7.6 Creating a New Package (Part 1)

2. Next, in the input field directly beneath the object list box, enter the name of your new package (e.g., ZPKGDEMO) and press the ⌈Enter⌋ key. This will open up the CREATE PACKAGE dialog box shown in Figure 7.7. In this case, we want to click on the YES button to proceed with the creation of the new package.

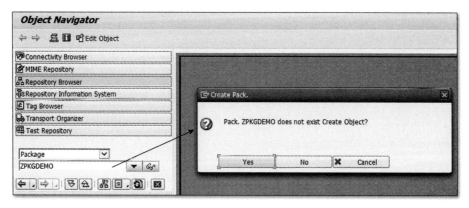

Figure 7.7 Creating a New Package (Part 2)

3. At the CREATE PACKAGE screen shown in Figure 7.8, we must specify the basic attributes for our new package. We'll explore the purpose of these attributes momentarily. In any case, once the attributes are set, we can click on the button with the green checkbox on it to continue.

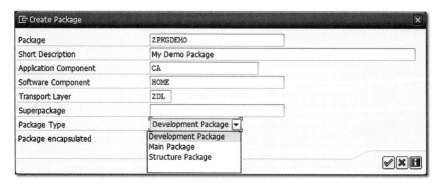

Figure 7.8 Creating a New Package (Part 3)

4. Finally, after assigning the package to a transport request, we'll end up with an empty package in the object list as shown in Figure 7.9. To edit this package,

we can simply double-click on it just like any other object in the ABAP Workbench.

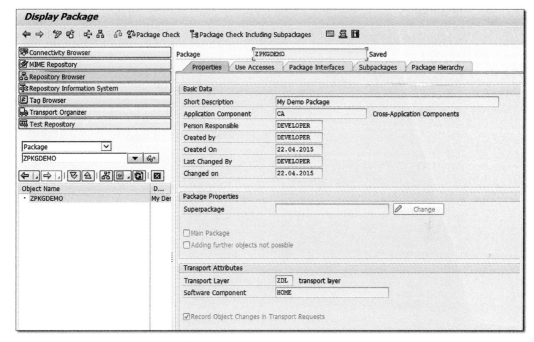

Figure 7.9 Creating a New Package (Part 4)

Now that you know how packages are created within the ABAP Workbench, let's now examine some of the various attributes that make up a package definition. These attributes correspond with the ones entered on the input screen shown in Figure 7.8.

Attribute Name	Description
Short Description	This attribute is used to provide a short text description for the package and its intended use.
Application Component	This attribute is used to align a package within an application component in the SAP Application Hierarchy. We'll explore the benefits of this assignment a little bit later on in this section.

Table 7.1 Attributes of Packages

Attribute Name	Description
Software Component	This attribute is used to assign the package to a software component (refer back to Figure 7.1 to visualize this relationship).
Transport Layer	This attribute is used to link a package (and by extension its embedded development objects) with a transport layer definition in the SAP *Change and Transport System* (CTS). If you're not familiar with the CTS, suffice it to say that a transport layer definition defines the transport path which guides changes through the landscape (e.g., from development to QA to production).
Superpackage	This attribute is used to embed a given package underneath an existing one. We'll explore this concept further in Section 7.2.4. Here, we'll also find that the ABAP Workbench will implicitly fill this attribute out for us whenever we create sub-packages using the contextual flyout menus.
Package Type	As the name suggests, this attribute is used to define the package type. Here, we can choose between structure packages, main packages, or development packages (see Figure 7.8).
Package Encapsulated	This Boolean attribute was added in the SAP NetWeaver 7.3x release. Whenever this flag is set, the ABAP development tools enforce strict encapsulation within the package. This implies that ABAP clients cannot address development objects within the package unless the objects are exposed via the package's interface. In object-oriented terms, this setting introduces the concept of visibility sections within a package definition. We'll explore this idea in further detail in Section 7.2.5 and Section 7.2.6, respectively.

Table 7.1 Attributes of Packages (Cont.)

Aligning Packages with the SAP Application Hierarchy

If you've worked around SAP software very long, then you've probably encountered the SAP Support Portal (available online at *https://support.sap.com*). Among other things, this portal provides customers with links to download SAP software products, search for notes/knowledge base articles, and report product defects. Though the portal is designed to make it easy for customers to search for relevant items, it certainly helps to understand how the SAP software catalog is organized. Otherwise, it can feel like you're searching for a needle in a haystack.

Internally, SAP organizes its software catalog into logical *application components* which are in turn organized into a hierarchy called the *SAP Application Hierarchy*. Using this hierarchy, we can quickly narrow down the scope of our search to components within a particular application area. For example, when searching for SAP Notes related to purchase orders, we could plug in the MM-PUR-PO application area as shown in Figure 7.10 and Figure 7.11. Here, we're narrowing down the search to *Materials Management* application area first, then the *Purchasing* application area, and then specifically *Purchase Orders*. Of course, if you don't know the target area(s) offhand, you can also use wildcards (e.g., the asterisk "*" character) to broaden the scope of your selection.

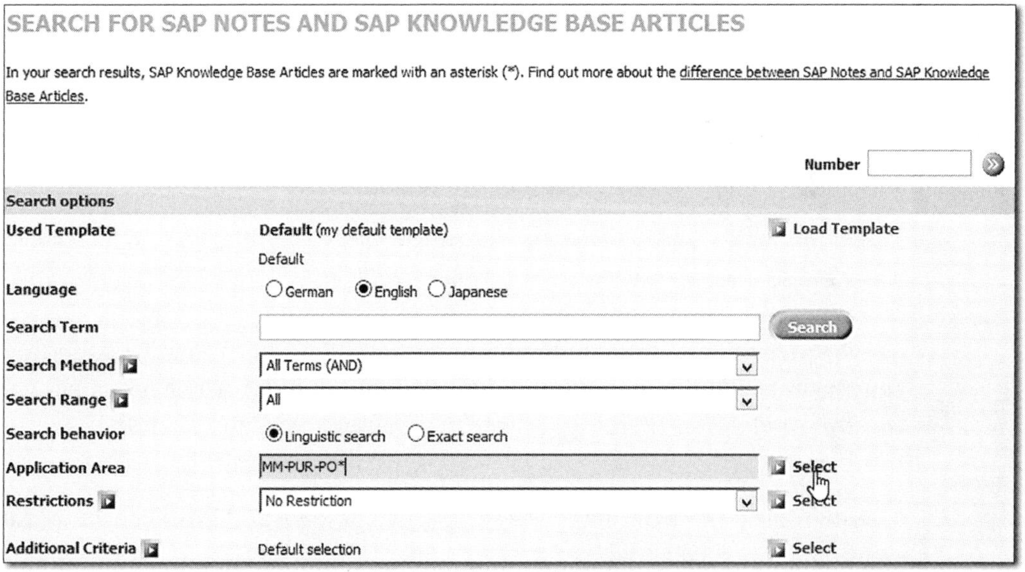

Figure 7.10 Searching for SAP Notes by Application Area (Part 1)

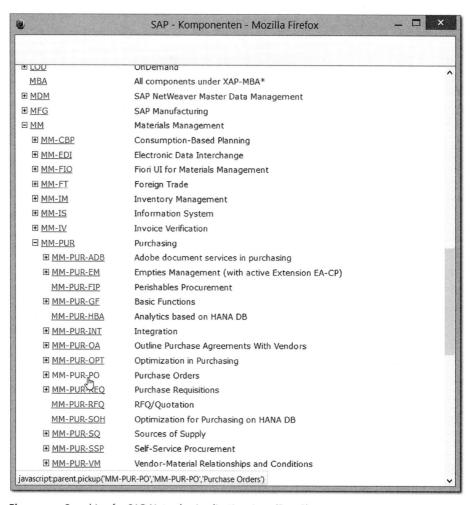

Figure 7.11 Searching for SAP Notes by Application Area (Part 2)

So what does all this have to do with packages? Well, since package definitions contain an application component attribute, we can technically align them with the SAP Application Hierarchy as well. This allows users to search for development objects by application area in a couple of different ways:

1. Within the REPOSITORY BROWSER perspective of the ABAP Workbench, we can search for particular types of development objects (e.g. classes) within a particular application component (or set of application components if we use the "*"

wildcard operator on the end of the search expression). This is demonstrated in the screen capture shown in Figure 7.12. Here, we're searching for custom employee classes created within the CA-HR application area (or subareas). Using this approach, we don't really have to guess at the naming convention of the classes, which package they might reside in, etc. Instead, we just look for classes in their logical application area and whittle down the list from there.

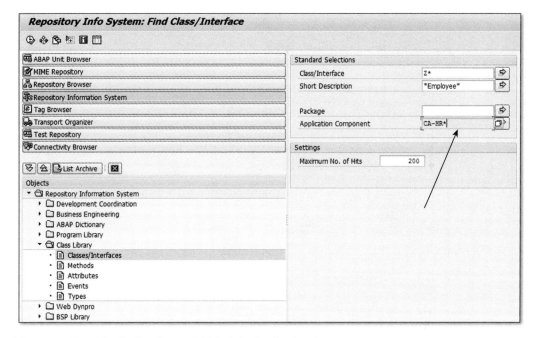

Figure 7.12 Searching for Development Objects by Application Area

2. If a more hierarchical search method is preferred, users can search for relevant development packages using the Application Hierarchy transaction (Transaction SE81). Here, the SAP application hierarchy is arranged in tree-like form, allowing users to drill into generic application areas and discover more specific sub-areas. Figure 7.13 demonstrates how we might use this transaction to pinpoint custom packages within the HR area. From here, we can double-click on the package names (e.g. ZEMPLOYEE_MODEL) and recursively search for the target development objects.

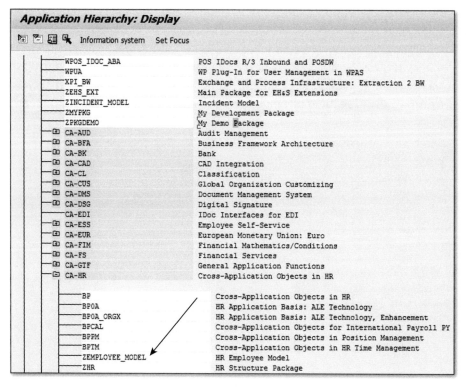

Figure 7.13 Searching within the Application Hierarchy

As you can see, this search capability is quite powerful and far superior to simply relying solely on naming conventions to identify objects. This is particularly the case for developers coming in off the street who need to orient themselves within a new customer landscape. Here, while a developer might not be familiar with naming conventions or object history, they should at least be able to navigate around within the application hierarchy and narrow down the scope of their search to objects within a particular application area.

7.2.4 Embedding Packages

In order to build out package hierarchies like the one shown in Figure 7.3, we must have a way to *embed* a package within another package. This can be achieved in several different ways:

▶ If we know the name of the superpackage we want to embed a new package in up front, we can specify its name in the SUPERPACKAGE attribute shown in Figure 7.8 (see Section 7.2.3 for a refresher on the package creation process).

▶ Otherwise, we can embed a package after it's initially created by opening up the superpackage in the Package Builder tool and navigating to the SUBPACKAGES tab shown in Figure 7.14. From here, we can embed the subpackage by clicking on the ADD EXISTING PACKAGE button and filling in the subpackage name in the ENTER PACKAGE dialog box that pops up. As soon as we click on the CONTINUE button, the subpackage will be added to the subpackage table contained within the SUBPACKAGES tab.

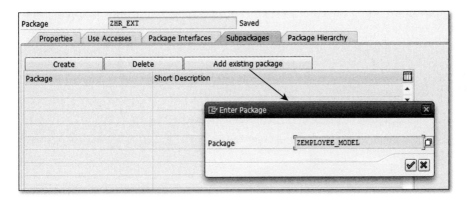

Figure 7.14 Embedding a Package in the Package Builder Transaction

▶ Another option is to create the subpackage directly within the SUBPACKAGES tab of the superpackage by clicking on the CREATE button (see Figure 7.14). This will bring up the familiar CREATE PACKAGE dialog box we reviewed in Section 7.2.3 with the superpackage pre-filled in.

▶ Finally, we can create subpackages directly within the ABAP Workbench by selecting the superpackage in the Repository Browser view and then right-clicking on the package name and choosing the CREATE • PACKAGES • PACKAGE context menu option shown in Figure 7.15. This also brings up the familiar CREATE PACKAGE dialog box we reviewed in Section 7.2.3 with the superpackage pre-filled in.

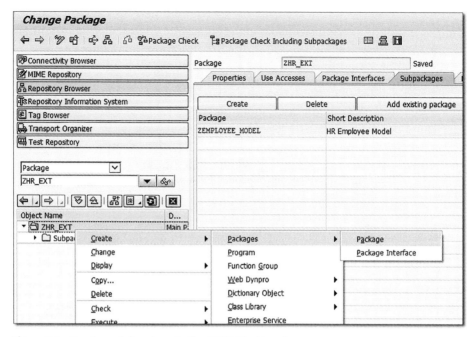

Figure 7.15 Creating a Subpackage in the ABAP Workbench

7.2.5 Defining Package Interfaces

Typically, we'll want to build our packages/components like *black boxes* and hide as much of the internal development object details as we can. This approach is partly meant to keep developers from getting their hands on internal objects that are subject to change, but more focused on highlighting the objects that we *do* want to share with clients. By adding these selected development objects to a package's interface, we can make it easier for external clients to understand how a library works without having to comb through each of the individual development objects.

To understand how this works, it's helpful to first see how package interfaces are created within the Package Builder. Here, the steps are relatively straightforward:

1. Within the Package Builder transaction, navigate to the PACKAGE INTERFACES tab and click on the CREATE button. This will open up the CREATE PACKAGE INTERFACE dialog box shown in Figure 7.16.

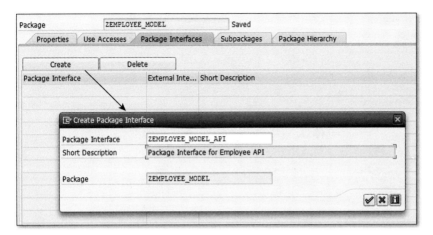

Figure 7.16 Creating a Package Interface (Part 1)

2. Within the Package Interface dialog box, we must provide a name for the package interface and a brief description. Since the package interface is defined as a separate object in the ABAP Repository, it's important that it be given the appropriate namespace prefix. Aside from that, we mainly want to ensure that we provide a name which conveys meaning. Click on the CONTINUE button to finish creating the package interface.

After the package interface is initially created, we can double-click on it to open up the CHANGE PACKAGE INTERFACE view of the Package Builder tool shown in Figure 7.17. Here, our focus will be mostly on adding/removing elements to the package interface on the VISIBLE ELEMENTS tab. From this tab page, we can use the toolbar buttons to maintain content (e.g. the ADD ELEMENT and REMOVE ELEMENT buttons) or we can use the drag-and-drop capabilities of the ABAP Workbench to drag over relevant objects from the object list (as demonstrated in Figure 7.17). Both approaches get us to the same place, though the drag-and-drop approach is generally faster and easier to work with.

In the case of nested package hierarchies, we can *promote* development objects from subpackages into the package interface of superpackages so that we can roll up related sub-objects into higher-level package interfaces. Here, the embedded objects get added to the From SUBPACKAGES folder shown in Figure 7.18. As is the case with regular development objects, we can use the toolbar buttons (e.g. the ADD PACKAGE INTERFACE button) or the drag-and-drop capabilities of the ABAP Workbench to add these sub-objects to the package interface (see Figure 7.18).

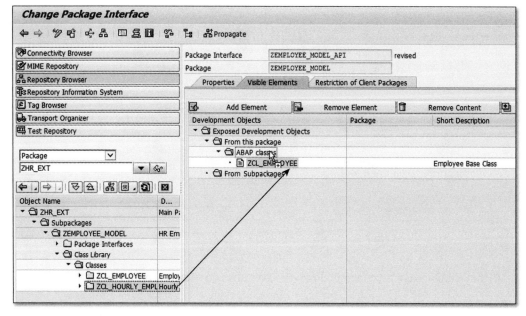

Figure 7.17 Adding Development Objects to a Package Interface

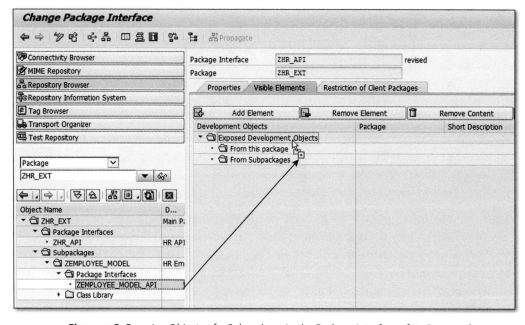

Figure 7.18 Exposing Objects of a Subpackage in the Package Interface of its Superpackage

When adding development objects to the package interface, we'll once again want to apply the *least privilege* principle described in Chapter 5. This is to say that we'll only want to add the minimum set of development objects outside packages will need to carry out their work. This approach, combined with the client restriction concept we'll explore in Section 7.2.6, allows us to very neatly lock down a package and ensure that only selected development objects are exposed. From a design perspective, this gives us the flexibility to change or remove internal development objects without having to worry about what kind of problems this might cause for other programs.

7.2.6 Creating Use Accesses

Frequently, development objects in one package depend on development objects defined in another package. Prior to the release of the Package Concept, such dependencies could be created at whim by developers without any restrictions whatsoever. From a logistics perspective, this was highly problematic since it was next to impossible to prevent developers from using development objects that they really shouldn't be using for one reason or another.

With the Package Concept, we can avoid this problem by creating explicit *use accesses* between packages. This can be achieved by performing the following steps:

1. First, we need to open up the package that contains the development object(s) that intend to use objects defined in another package in the Package Builder tool.

2. To create the use access, we need to navigate to the USE ACCESSES tab shown in Figure 7.19. Here, we can click on the CREATE button to create a new use access.

3. In the CREATE USE ACCESS dialog box, we specify the package interface which exposes the object(s) we want to leverage and choose an appropriate error severity. Normally, you'll want to select the default "No response" value here.

4. Finally, once the properties are set, we can click on the CONTINUE button to formally create the use access.

Once a use access is in place, the system now has information which tells it which packages plan on leveraging the publicly-exposed objects of other packages. In the next section, we'll see how this information can be used to enforce best practices on ABAP development projects.

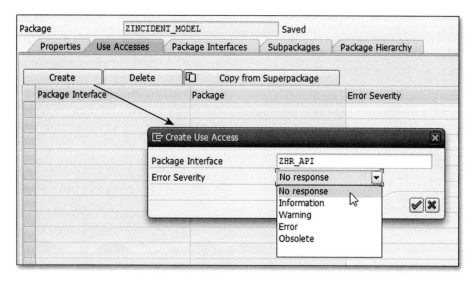

Figure 7.19 Creating Use Accesses in Packages

7.2.7 Performing Package Checks

By default, the package interfaces and use accesses we create serve little purpose other than to formally document a package's public interface and the way we intend for it to be used. While this is helpful up to a point, the real value of going to all this trouble is to be able to enforce best practices in the development process. Just as visibility sections lock down access to the components of ABAP Objects classes, we would like for package interfaces to be able to restrict access to internal development objects contained within packages.

To enable this kind of functionality, we must turn on the package check using the instructions provided with SAP Note #648898. Whenever this check is turned on, any unsolicited accesses to development objects between packages will result in a package check error.

To demonstrate how this works, imagine that we've created a package hierarchy to contain development objects related to the SAP standard *Environment, Health, and Safety* (EH&S) module. Among other things, our extensions to the EH&S module will include incident-related objects which have touch points to HR employee objects (employees might be involved in an incident record, for example). So, rather than reinventing the wheel, we want to leverage the ZCL_EMPLOYEE entity class we introduced in Chapter 5 in a utilities class called ZCL_PERSON_PROXY that's used to search for involved persons.

With the package check turned on though, we can't just arbitrarily access ZCL_EMPLOYEE from within our EH&S package hierarchy. That's because access to our employee package hierarchy is locked down to just include those elements we've purposefully exposed via the package interface(s). So, if we perform a package check on our ZCL_PERSON_PROXY class (by selecting the CLASS • CHECK • PACKAGE CHECK menu option in the Class Builder tool), we end up seeing an error report like the one shown in Figure 7.20. This error clearly tells us that we must create a use access for the ZCL_EMPLOYEE class before we can use it in our EH&S package.

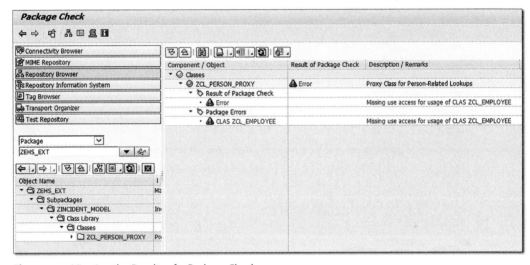

Figure 7.20 Viewing the Results of a Package Check

A Word of Caution

The extended package check is a system-wide setting which has can have widespread impacts if not configured carefully. For customers that have been violating these kinds of principles for years, the amount of effort required to clean up the custom packages/development objects might outweigh the benefits of turning on this check. This doesn't mean the check shouldn't be turned on, but we would strongly recommend that the development team work very closely with the Basis administrators to make sure that everyone's on the same page before proceeding. You can find further details concerning the impacts in SAP Note #648898.

To correct the package check error, we must go into the EH&S package hierarchy and define the relevant use accesses (see Figure 7.21). Once these use accesses are in place, the package check errors go away and everything is right again in the world.

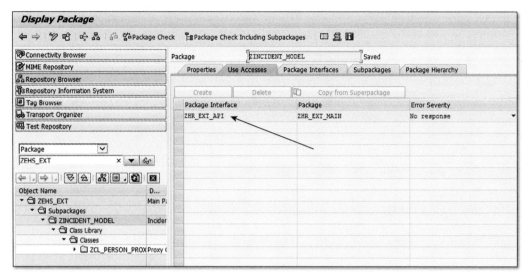

Figure 7.21 Adding Use Accesses to the HR API From the EH&S Package Hierarchy

In addition to manual package checks performed within the ABAP Workbench, package checks can also be triggered implicitly via the *Extended Program Check* tool (Transaction SLIN) and also via the CTS system during the transport release process. These checks are put into place to ensure that developers comply with best practices and declare their package dependencies up front. By doing so, development organizations can maintain clear visibility of dependencies and more quickly determine the impacts of migrating code libraries to other SAP Business Suite systems, assessing upgrade issues, and so forth.

7.2.8 Restriction of Client Packages

The use accesses we considered in Section 7.2.6 allow client packages to declare which provider packages they intend on using internally. Sometimes, we might want to go in the other direction and formally declare within the provider package which client packages we want to provide access to. While such tight coupling is somewhat rare, there will be times whenever it makes sense to lock access down to a handful of related packages.

Since use accesses are defined in terms of package interfaces, we must restrict access to client packages at this level. Here, the steps are as follows:

1. First, we first need to open up the target package interface and navigate to the PROPERTIES tab. Here, in the GENERAL PROPERTIES section, we can restrict access from client packages by checking the ENABLE RESTRICTION OF CLIENT PACKAGES checkbox as shown in Figure 7.22.

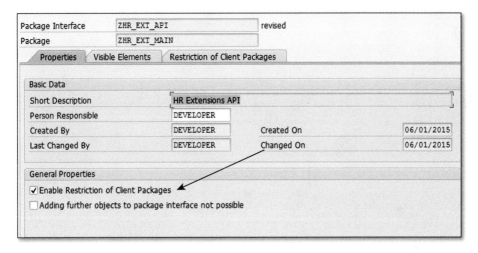

Figure 7.22 Restricting Access to Client Packages (Part 1)

2. As soon as we click on that checkbox, no client packages will be able to access the selected package – even if they have a defined use access. To enable access from client packages, we have to navigate over to the RESTRICTION OF CLIENT PACKAGES tab and plug in the packages we want to provide explicit access to (see Figure 7.23). Here, in addition to specifying the package itself, we also have a couple of checkboxes that we can utilize to further specify the nature of the relationship:

   ▸ POINT-TO-POINT ACCESS
   If this checkbox is selected, access is only granted to the target package; none of the package's superpackages receive implicit access.

▶ INCLUDE SUBPACKAGES

When this checkbox is selected, access is implicitly granted to the selected package's subpackages. This setting can come in handy whenever access is being provided to a super/main package whose subpackages are generally unknown to the provider package. In this way, access is inherited at the subpackage level and we don't have to constantly adjust the client package accesses within the provider package.

Package Interface	ZHR_EXT_API	revised		
Package	ZHR_EXT_MAIN			

Properties	Visible Elements	Restriction of Client Packages

Package	Short Description	Point-to-Point Access	Include Subpackages	
ZEHS_EXT	Main Package for EH&S Extensions	☐	☑	
		☐	☐	
		☐	☐	
		☐	☐	

Figure 7.23 Restricting Access to Client Packages (Part 2)

7.3 Package Design Concepts

As we've learned over the course of this chapter, the Package Concept is quite flexible. While such flexibility is obviously a good thing, it does make it a bit difficult to formulate a standards guide which determines when to use structured/main packages, how deep to define a package hierarchy, and so on. The answers to these questions really does depend on context, and as a result, are subject to change.

Rather than trying to place unnecessary restrictions around the package design process, we tend to let basic design principles guide our decision making. In his book *UML Distilled, Third Edition*, Martin Fowler identifies three basic principles that you can use to help you design your package architectures:

▶ The *Common Closure Principle* states that development objects within the same package should be changed for the same reasons. This basically re-affirms our goal of maintaining cohesiveness in software modules (whether they be packages, classes, or something else).

▶ The *Common Reuse Principle* suggests that development objects within a package should all be reused together.

▸ The *Static Dependencies Principle* advises you to consider how *stable* your package is if there are many dependencies flowing into it. For example, if ten packages are dependent on a single package, it's important for the interface(s) of that package to remain stable in order to avoid widespread rippling effects whenever a change occurs. Here, it's often useful to define the package interface in terms of interfaces and abstract classes as they provide the flexibility that's needed to adapt to changes.

Note

Mr. Fowler credits Robert Cecil Martin's *The Principles, Patterns, and Practices of Agile Software Development* when describing these principles.

Stick to these principles and we think that you'll remain on track. Also, bear in mind that you're not locked into a particular design if you eventually find that it's not working for your project. Package relationships, just like classes, sometimes require refactoring. Fortunately, the ABAP Workbench makes it easy for you to reassign a development object to another package: just right-click on the target object and select the ADDITIONAL FUNCTIONS • CHANGE PACKAGE ASSIGNMENT menu option as shown in Figure 7.24.

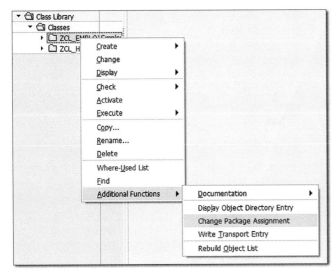

Figure 7.24 Changing the Package Assignment of Development Objects

7.4   UML Tutorial: Package Diagrams

The component design process can become quite involved, being heavily influenced by the subjective whims of developers that often have conflicting design goals. Typically, this process evolves over several iterations that gradually reshape the model to reflect the system that's being implemented. The UML supports the documentation of this design process with the *package diagram*. A package diagram allows you to group related classes and interfaces (and indeed, other development objects) into higher-level units called *packages*. It should be noted here that the overlap between the term "package" in the UML and the ABAP packages is purely coincidental. Generally speaking, a UML package is a logical concept that could be implemented in many different ways by various programming languages. However, as you'll see, the ABAP package concept does happen to align very closely with the UML package construct.

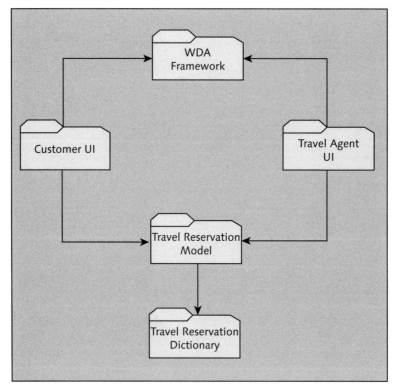

Figure 7.25 Package Diagram for a Web Dynpro ABAP Application

Figure 7.25 shows an example of a package diagram for a simple online travel reservation application built using the Web Dynpro ABAP web application development framework. Each of the folder-shaped icons in the diagram is intended to depict individual packages within the application architecture. The dotted lines between packages depict *dependencies* between the packages. The direction of the line indicates the direction of the dependency. For example the Customer UI and Travel Agent UI packages both depend on the WDA Framework and Travel Reservation Model packages. Similarly, objects within the Travel Reservation Model package depend on ABAP Dictionary objects defined within the Travel Reservation Dictionary package.

We could have used the formal ABAP package names in this diagram, but as you can see in Figure 7.26, this is optional in the UML. Like many diagrams in the UML, there are not a lot of restrictions in terms of the notation for a package diagram. For example, the package diagram in Figure 7.26 expands the basic notation to depict a few of the classes embedded within packages P1 and P2. The familiar "+" and "-" visibility tokens indicate whether or not the classes belong to the public or private interface of the package.

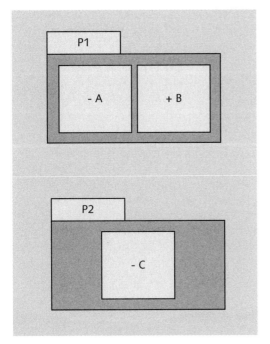

Figure 7.26 Including Classes in Package Diagrams

In the example shown in Figure 7.26, class B has been added to the package interface of package P1. This addition helps us better visualize the nature of the dependency between packages P1 and P2, perhaps showing us that class C is dependent upon the publicly-exposed class B.

Package diagrams are very useful in illustrating a system design in terms of its constituent components. If you find that the package diagram for your system looks like a plate of spaghetti, then it's likely that your packages are not well encapsulated and you probably need to refactor your package hierarchy. Consequently, updating your package diagrams periodically is a good way to gauge the effectiveness of your component designs over time.

7.5 Summary

In this chapter, we learned how to perform component-based software development in ABAP. Here, we learned how to apply the Package Concept to encapsulate related development objects together into logical software units with defined interfaces/dependencies. While this requires a little bit of work up front, we think that you'll find it very useful in keeping the software catalog clean and easy to manage. Plus, it aligns quite nicely with our end goal of improving the level of abstraction that want to deal with when building custom software.

In the next chapter, we'll take a look at the ABAP *class-based exception handling concept* and see how it's used to encapsulate exception scenarios and isolate exception handling logic from the normal program flow.

Software programs operate in an environment based on rules. However, as the saying goes, there's an exception to every rule. In this chapter, we'll explore ways of dealing with exception cases in ABAP programs using the class-based exception handling concept.

8 Error Handling with Exception Classes

No matter how hard we may try to improve the quality of our code, there's simply no way to avoid every type of error that might occur during the execution of an application. Indeed, some errors are accidentally introduced by programmers trying too hard to make their applications *error-proof*. Here, for instance, the error handling logic obscures the main purpose of the program flow, making the code harder to understand and maintain, and thus more susceptible to errors.

Generally speaking, error-handling logic is a *cross-cutting* concern that becomes tangled within the normal flow of the core application logic. Ideally, we'd like to be able to de-tangle error-handling logic from the main program flow so that these two orthogonal concerns can be managed separately. In this chapter, we will learn how to apply the ABAP *class-based exception handling concept* to achieve this kind of separation of concerns.

8.1 Lessons Learned from Prior Approaches

Prior to Release 6.10 of the SAP Web AS, there was not a comprehensive strategy for dealing with exceptions within the ABAP Objects language. Consequently, developers were forced to improvise, weaving custom exception-handling code into their normal program logic. Here, while developers did the best they could with what they had available to them at the time, the resultant solutions were less than optimal. In this section, we'll consider some of the lessons learned from these early approaches to exception handling in ABAP.

8.1.1 Lesson 1: Exception Handling Logic Gets in the Way

Without built-in language support for exception handling, developers were left to build out their exception handling logic using regular procedural code. While this works in principle, what we usually find is that the exception logic ends up getting in the way of the main program logic. To put this problem into perspective, consider the code excerpt contained in Listing 8.1. Here, you can see how error-handling logic has been added to a procedural report program that's calling a series of subroutines to perform various tasks. In a contrived example such as this, it's not too hard to follow what the program is doing. Still, notice that percentage-wise there are many more lines of code devoted to dealing with exceptions than the actual program logic. In larger production programs the problem becomes even more pronounced.

```
DATA lv_retcode TYPE sy-subrc.
PERFORM sub1 CHANGING lv_retcode.
IF lv_retcode NE 0.
  "Error handling logic...
ENDIF.

PERFORM sub2 CHANGING lv_retcode.
CASE lv_retcode.
  WHEN 0.
    "Operation was successful...
  WHEN 1.
    "Error handling logic...
  WHEN 2.
    "Error handling logic...
  WHEN OTHERS.
    "Error handling logic...
ENDCASE.

PERFORM sub3 CHANGING lv_retcode.
IF lv_retcode NE 0.
  "Yet more error handling logic...
ENDIF.
```
Listing 8.1 Handling Exceptions Using a Manual Approach

Ideally, we'd like to decouple the normal processing logic from the exception logic so that the two separate concerns remain separate. This makes the code easier to read and trace through. We'll explore ways of achieving this throughout this chapter.

8.1.2   Lesson 2: Exception Handling Requires Varying Amounts of Data

Looking at the code excerpt contained in Listing 8.1, we can see how the various subroutines are passing back a return code value which signifies whether or not an exception occurred. In this contrived example, that's probably all the information we need to deal with the error. However, in many cases, we need much more than just a simple return code; we may also require context about the source of the error, messages which explain what went wrong, and so forth.

Though we could conceivably add this data as exporting parameters to the subroutine/function/method signature, doing so clutters up the interface quite a bit. This problem is compounded by the fact that different developers may bundle up these exception parameters in different ways. For example, most BAPI function modules return an error message table that has the line type BAPIRET2. Internally, these BAPIs frequently call other standard function modules or subroutines that do not maintain message table parameters of this type. Consequently, additional code has to be written in the BAPI function to translate between the various message table types. In Section 8.3, we'll see how to develop exception classes that encapsulate these details much more efficiently.

8.1.3   Lesson 3: The Need for Transparency

Another problem with ad-hoc exception handling strategies is the fact that it can be very difficult to identify the types of errors that might occur within a given module without digging into the code. For instance, considering the subroutines contained in Listing 8.1, how would a client know what kind of errors might occur when these are called? Is sub1 dependent on some resource (e.g., a connection to an external SAP HANA database) that might not be available whenever it's called? What happens if sub2 attempts to divide by zero?

From a design perspective, we'd like for the interface of our modules to be more explicit about the types of errors that can occur within them. After all, exceptions are part of the API contract for a module, too. To some degree, certain previous concepts provide support for this requirement. For example, you can create named exceptions for methods and function modules using the EXCEPTIONS addition. However, these exceptions are essentially static error codes that have been assigned some semantic meaning inside the method/function module. The meaning of these exceptions tends to become obscured outside of the scope of the defining module, especially when new exceptions are added into the mix. Recognizing this, SAP decided to implement a new class-based concept for dealing with exceptions that could be used consistently in all ABAP contexts (i.e. programs, processing blocks, etc.). We'll learn more about this concept beginning in Section 8.2.

8.2   The Class-Based Exception Handling Concept

As the name suggests, the class-based exception handling concept uses a special types of ABAP Objects class called an *exception class* to encapsulate exception situations that may occur within a program. These classes are integrated into a framework that makes it easier for you to separate the exception-handling aspects of a program from the core functional aspects of the program. This framework is orchestrated by the TRY control structure whose form is given in Listing 8.2.

```
DATA lo_ex TYPE REF TO cx_exception_type.
DATA lo_root TYPE REF TO cx_root.
TRY.
  "Main programming logic goes here...
CATCH cx_exception_type INTO lo_ex.
  "Exception handler block
  lo_ex->...
CATCH cx_root INTO lo_root.
  "Exception handler block
  lo_root->...
CLEANUP.
  "Optional cleanup block
ENDTRY.
```

Listing 8.2 Basic Form of the TRY...ENDTRY Control Structure

The TRY statement separates the normal application flow from the exception-handling flow(s) by creating separate execution/processing blocks. The TRY block contains the normal application code that may trigger various types of exceptions along the way. These exceptions are handled by special exception handler blocks called CATCH blocks that contain code that is used to recover from a particular exception situation in some application-specific kind of way. After an exception is dealt with, you also have the option of adding a special CLEANUP block to do any sort of cleanup work that might need to be done before the TRY statement returns control to the normal program flow. This basic flow of a TRY statement is depicted in the diagram shown in Figure 8.1.

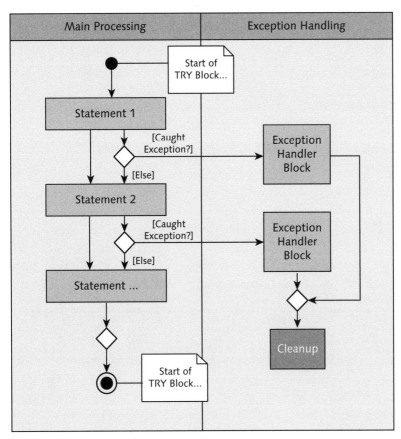

Figure 8.1 Flow Diagram for TRY Control Statement

In the upcoming sections, we'll see how all this plays out within various ABAP programming contexts.

Note
While the class-based exception handling concept does naturally utilize object-oriented concepts, we should point out that this does not preclude its use in procedural contexts, too. This is to say that class-based exceptions can be incorporated into subroutines, function modules, and even event blocks (e.g. the START-OF-SELECTION event in ABAP report programs).

8.3 Creating Exception Classes

Before we begin looking at how exception classes are used to handle exceptions, it's helpful to first take a moment to understand how these classesare defined. Therefore, in this section, we'll explore the anatomy of exception classes and also show you how to build your own custom exception classes.

8.3.1 Understanding Exception Class Types

At the end of the day, exception classes are basically just like any other ABAP Objects class. This is to say that exception classes have attributes and methods, are maintained in the Class Builder tool, and so on. However, unlike regular ABAP Objects classes which are descended from the generic OBJECT type, exception classes descend from one of the three abstract classes defined underneath the abstract CX_ROOT exception class depicted in Figure 8.2. Aside from this up-front constraint though, it's pretty much object-oriented ABAP as per usual.

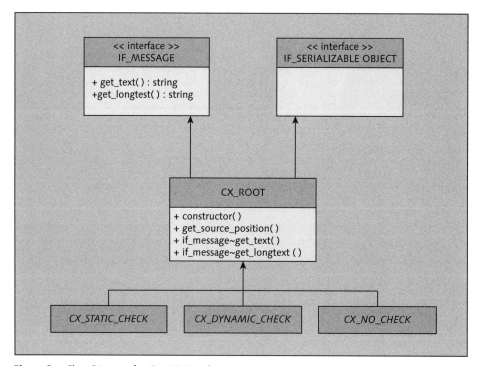

Figure 8.2 Class Diagram for CX_ROOT Inheritance Tree

In Section 8.3.2 and Section 8.3.3, we'll find that it's a pretty straightforward exercise to create custom exception types by subclassing one of the three abstract base types depicted at the bottom of the exception class hierarchy shown in Figure 8.2. For the most part, the biggest challenge here is in determining which base type to inherit from. Table 8.1 highlights the differences between these types so that you have a better sense for which type to use in particular circumstances.

Exception Class	Usage Type
CX_STATIC_CHECK	Exceptions of this type are used to represent checked error conditions that may occur within the logic of an application program. Such exceptions must either be explicitly declared in a procedure's interface using the RAISING addition or handled locally within a TRY statement. If an exception of this type is not properly handled, the compiler will issue a warning during the syntax check.
CX_DYNAMIC_CHECK	Exceptions of this type are used to represent unchecked error conditions that likely stem from errors in the program logic. For example, the standard exception class CX_SY_ZERODIVIDE is used to represent a situation where a division operation was attempted with a divisor whose value is 0. Realistically speaking, this kind of error should not happen, and if it does, it might not be possible to recover from it gracefully. Moreover, since a mathematics-intensive program could produce this kind of error in almost every statement, it's not practical to handle all of the possible exceptions that might occur. Therefore, exceptions of this type do not have to be explicitly handled and are not subject to static syntax checks at compilation time. Of course, failure to properly handle such an exception will ultimately result in a runtime error.
CX_NO_CHECK	Exceptions of this type are similar to ones deriving from CX_DYNAMIC_CHECK. The primary difference is that these kinds of exceptions are automatically forwarded if they are not explicitly handled locally in a TRY statement. In other words, the RAISING clause of a method, subroutine, etc. implicitly contains the CX_NO_CHECK addition in its signature, so it is not possible to add additional subordinate classes of this type to the signature of a procedure.

Table 8.1 Base-Level Exception Types in ABAP

Though there are many different schools of thought concerning the creation of exception types, we recommend that you define most of your custom exception types in terms of the CX_STATIC_CHECK superclass. Using this approach, you improve the readability/documentation of your code by explicitly calling out the types of exceptions that can be raised from within your module(s).

8.3.2 Local Exception Classes

Now that you have a sense for how exception classes are defined, let's take a look at what it takes to create a local exception class. Like any local class types, local exception types are non-reusable types that are unique to a particular application (i.e. a report).

As you can see in Listing 8.3, the syntax used to create a local exception type mirrors that of any local class definition which inherits from some base class type. This minimal syntax is all that's required to create the custom local exception type; the base-level functionality is inherited from CX_STATIC_CHECK in this case. Though it's technically possible to expand the definition of the subtype, SAP recommends that you do not define additional methods and/or redefine inherited methods in local exception classes.

```
CLASS lcx_local_excpetion DEFINITION
  INHERITING FROM cx_static_check.
ENDCLASS.
```

Listing 8.3 Defining a Local Exception Class

Looking at the class definition in Listing 8.3, you can see that the naming convention for local class types is LCX_{some_meaningful_name}. In this case, the LCX prefix is used to distinguish between local exception classes and regular local classes whose name starts with the LCL prefix.

8.3.3 Global Exception Classes

Most of the time, whenever we define exception classes, we'll prefer to create them globally in the ABAP Repository so that we can reuse them in other contexts. Global exception classes, like other global class types, are defined using the Class Builder tool, which adjusts to the *Exception Builder* perspective whenever you're editing an exception class.

As you can see in Figure 8.3, the CREATE CLASS dialog box looks a bit different whenever the EXCEPTION CLASS type is selected. Here, you enter a name for the exception class, the superclass (which must be defined as one of the three base exception class types CX_STATIC_CHECK, CX_DYNAMIC_CHECK, or CX_NO_CHECK or a subclass of those types), as well as some familiar fields that have been used to define other global classes. The WITH MESSAGE CLASS checkbox is used to include support for the integration of messages defined within a message class (i.e. in Transaction SE91). We will discuss this option in further detail in Section 8.3.4.

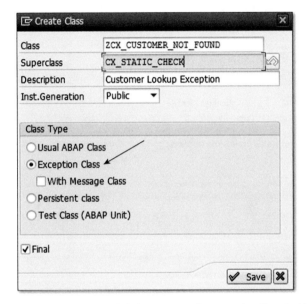

Figure 8.3 Creating Global Exception Classes in the Class Builder

Exception classes must be named according to the convention <namespace>CX_ {meaningful_name}. So, for example, when defining an exception class in the default customer namespace, the name would start with the prefix "YCX_" or "ZCX_".

Once an exception type is created, you can edit it using the Exception Builder perspective just as you would any normal global class type. For example, in Figure 8.4, you can see how all the same tab pages are provided when editing exception classes. With that being said, there are a couple of notable nuances to be aware of when editing exception class types:

▶ The auto-generated `constructor()` method cannot be edited like the `constructor()` methods of regular class types. This is by design since SAP wishes to guarantee that the constructor of any exception type contains a consistent interface that makes it possible to create new instances using the `RAISE EXCEPTION` statement.

▶ Any public attribute defined on the ATTRIBUTES tab will be dynamically added as an importing parameter to the auto-generated `constructor()` method. The implementation of the `constructor()` method will also be adjusted to ensure that the importing parameter value is mapped to the corresponding instance attribute at runtime.

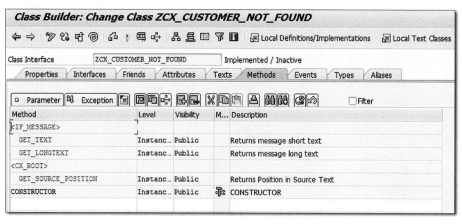

Figure 8.4 Editing an Exception Class Using the Exception Builder

Unlike local exception types which SAP recommends to keep pretty basic, there's nothing stopping us from expanding on global exception classes to better encapsulate specific exception conditions. Here, for example, we can define additional instance attributes to capture more details about the error condition as well as helper methods to lookup these details and generate formatted output messages. While the details will vary from exception class to exception class, the main takeaway from this is that you shouldn't be afraid to flex your new-found OOP skills towards the creation of exception class hierarchies and frameworks which make it easier to deal with exceptions. After all, what's the point of doing this object-oriented if we don't take advantage of OO techniques in the code?

8.3.4 Defining Exception Texts

Ideally, whenever an exception occurs, we'd like to be able to recover from it gracefully using logic defined within an exception handler block. Unfortunately, this is not always possible. Indeed, unexpected exception situations often require human intervention of some kind. Sometimes, this intervention comes in the form of an error message displayed on a screen; other times, a message is written to an error log. In either case, we need to be able to produce meaningful error messages in order for someone to be able to investigate the problem. The Exception Builder tool supports you in this endeavor by allowing you to configure *exception texts* for global classes.

Exception texts are maintained on the TEXTS tab of the Exception Builder (see Figure 8.5). However, behind the scenes, the actual text is stored in the *Online Text Repository* (OTR). The OTR is a central storage repository for texts that are defined within the AS ABAP. Like most reusable texts, OTR texts are translatable, making them ideally suited for implementing internationalized messages.

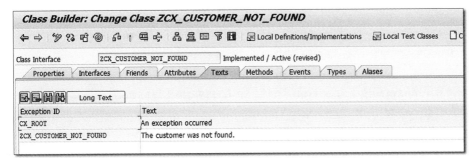

Figure 8.5 Defining Exception Texts in the Exception Builder

Within the Exception Builder, each exception text is defined using a unique exception text ID (i.e. ZCX_CUSTOMER_NOT_FOUND in Figure 8.5). The exception text ID correlates to a constant attribute with the same name that has the data type SOTR_CONC. These constant attributes belong to the same namespace as normal attributes, so it's a good idea to use the standard naming convention for constants (i.e., the CO_ prefix) when defining exception text IDs in the Exception Builder. If you look carefully, you'll notice that each constant attribute defined in relation to an exception text ID is initialized with a hexadecimal string value. This value is the globally unique key of the corresponding text object in the OTR.

You can define text parameters in your exception texts by surrounding elementary attribute names between ampersands. For example, the exception text READ_ERROR from exception class CX_SY_FILE_IO shown in Figure 8.6 contains three text parameters: FILENAME, ERRORCODE, and ERRORTEXT. At runtime, whenever an exception of this type is raised, the correspondingly named instance attributes will be used to generate the READ_ERROR text whenever the get_text() method is called. This approach naturally helps to produce message texts that are more meaningful to the end user.

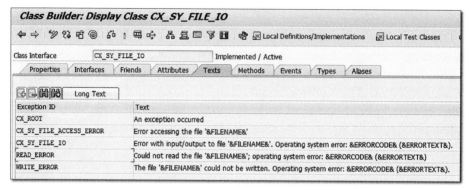

Figure 8.6 Defining Parameterized Texts

8.3.5 Mapping Exception Texts to Message Classes

Beginning with Release 7.00 of the AS ABAP, we now have the option of mapping exception texts to messages defined within messages classes. This functionality is enabled up front during the exception class creation process with the selection of the WITH MESSAGE CLASS checkbox (see Figure 8.3). Alternatively, you can add in this support after the fact for existing exception types by manually implementing the IF_T100_MESSAGE interface, though you may have to forcefully remove any pre-existing texts in the class to get this to work.

Once this functionality is turned on, we can maintain texts on the TEXTS tab by *mapping* an exception text to a message number in a message class. Such message classes are maintained outside of the Class Builder using the ABAP Workbench (Transaction SE80) or Message Maintenance (Transaction SE91). As you can see in Figure 8.7, the mapping process is pretty straightforward: we simply select a message class and message number and the text will be brought into context. If the message in question happens to define attributes, we can also map those attributes to instance attributes from the exception class.

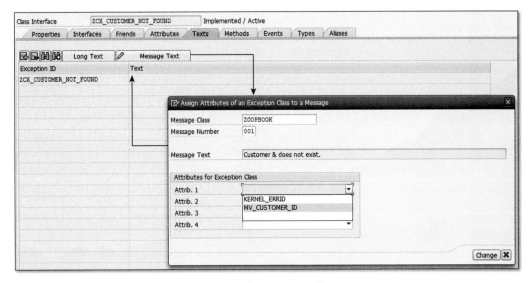

Figure 8.7 Mapping Exception Texts to Messages from Message Classes

The primary benefit for using the message mapping option with your exception classes is that you can leverage a pre-existing message base that is being maintained across the development landscape. Such messages can be maintained with long text and translated into other languages using the familiar tools provided with the Message Maintenance transaction.

8.4   Dealing with Exceptions

Whenever an ABAP program is executed, there are two different types of exceptions that can occur: exceptions that are raised explicitly using the RAISE EXCEPTION statement and exceptions that are raised implicitly by the ABAP runtime environment. In either case, we want to try to react to these exceptions and recover as gracefully as possible. With that in mind, in this section we'll consider how to use the TRY statement to trap exception conditions in ABAP programs.

8.4.1   Handling Exceptions

As we learned in Section 8.2, exceptions within the class-based exception handling concept are handled using CATCH blocks. These CATCH blocks are designed to handle exceptions of a particular type (or, as we'll learn, a family of related types). The exception type is defined in terms of an exception class that's part of an inheritance hierarchy based on the generic `CX_ROOT` superclass.

So how does this work? Well, let's imagine that a particular type of exception is raised at runtime. Whenever this exception is triggered, the ABAP runtime environment will look to see if the statement that triggered the exception is part of a `TRY` block. If it is, then it will look for a `CATCH` block which defines an exception type that matches that of the triggered exception. If no match is found, then the exception will be propagated up the call stack until a valid exception handler is found. Of course, if no valid handler is found after the call stack is completely unwound, then a runtime exception is triggered and the program abends/short dumps.

To put all this into perspective, let's consider some example code which triggers a class cast exception at runtime. In Listing 8.4, we've created a simple class hierarchy with a parent class called `LCL_PARENT` and a child class called `LCL_CHILD`. Within the main program logic, we create an instance of `LCL_PARENT` and then attempt to copy this reference into an object reference variable of type `LCL_CHILD`. At runtime, the ABAP runtime environment will detect the illegal widening cast and raise an exception of type `CX_SY_MOVE_CAST_ERROR`. From here, several things happen in short order:

1. First, the ABAP runtime environment implicitly creates an instance of the `CX_SY_MOVE_CAST_ERROR` class and fills it with pertinent information about the exception condition.

2. Next, a check is made to determine if there's an appropriate `CATCH` block which can handle the error.

3. Finally, since we did have our illegal cast wrapped up in a `TRY` statement with a corresponding `CATCH` block, control is immediately transferred to this `CATCH` block and a reference to the dynamically-generated exception object from the first item on this list is passed to the `lx_cast_error` variable defined within the `INTO` addition.

```
CLASS lcl_parent DEFINITION.
  PUBLIC SECTION.
    METHODS: a, b.
ENDCLASS.
```

```
CLASS lcl_parent IMPLEMENTATION.
  METHOD a.
  ENDMETHOD.

  METHOD b.
  ENDMETHOD.
ENDCLASS.

CLASS lcl_child DEFINITION INHERITING FROM lcl_parent.
  PUBLIC SECTION.
    METHODS: c.
ENDCLASS.

CLASS lcl_child IMPLEMENTATION.
  METHOD c.
  ENDMETHOD.
ENDCLASS.

DATA: lo_parent TYPE REF TO lcl_parent,
      lo_child TYPE REF TO lcl_child,
      lx_cast_error TYPE REF TO cx_sy_move_cast_error,
      lv_program_name TYPE syrepid,
      lv_include_name TYPE syrepid,
      lv_line_number TYPE I,
      lv_text TYPE string,
      lv_long_text TYPE string.

"Attempt a widening case where the dynamic type of the source
"object reference is not compatible with the static type of the
"target object reference:
TRY.
  CREATE OBJECT lo_parent.
  lo_child ?= lo_parent.
CATCH cx_sy_move_cast_error INTO lx_cast_error.
  "Retrieve information about the exception condition:
  lx_cast_error->get_source_position(
    IMPORTING
      program_name = lv_program_name
      include_name = lv_include_name
      source_line  = lv_line_number ).

  lv_text = lx_cast_error->get_text( ).
  lv_long_text = lx_cast_error->get_longtext( ).
  ...
ENDTRY.
```
Listing 8.4 Handling a Casting Exception Using the TRY Statement

As you can see in Listing 8.4, the CX_SY_MOVE_CAST_ERROR instance contains quite a bit of useful information about the nature of the exception and its origins. Naturally, the type of information carried within a given exception class will vary depending on the exception type. However, since all exception classes descend from the CX_ROOT superclass, every exception class is guaranteed to provide the get_text() and get_longtext() methods of the implemented IF_MESSAGE interface.

How Do I Know Which Exceptions to Catch?

Looking at the code excerpt contained in Listing 8.4, you might be wondering how we knew to catch the CX_SY_MOVE_CAST_ERROR exception type when performing our cast operation. Though some of this knowledge comes from experience working with the class-based exception handling concept, there are a couple of basic rules of thumb you can consider as you get started.

For exceptions that are triggered implicitly by the ABAP runtime environment, you can discover which exceptions are triggered for a particular statement when by looking at the ABAP Keyword Documentation. For example, if you were typing out the code contained in Listing 8.4 and wanted to know what would happen if a widening cast failed, you could put your cursor on the ?= operator and hit the F1 key to launch the ABAP Keyword Documentation. Within this context-sensitive documentation, there will be a section entitled *Exceptions* in which you can discover the types of catchable exceptions triggered by the ABAP runtime environment.

For all other exception class types, we must look within the code to figure out which exception types might be triggered. While this may seem like a daunting task, it's actually not as bad as it sounds provided that the code in question is developed using best practices. We'll take a closer look at all this in Section 8.5 when we learn how exception types are added to method signatures.

Handling Multiple Exceptions within a Single TRY Block

Technically speaking, we can include as many CATCH blocks as we want inside of a TRY block. So, for example, if we had a logical unit of work where there could be several different types of exceptions triggered, we might build our TRY block in similar fashion to the code excerpt contained in Listing 8.5. Here, if any of the statements within the TRY block raised an exception of type CX_XSLT_ABAP_CALL_ERROR, CX_XSLT_FORMAT_ERROR, or CX_XSLT_RUNTIME_ERROR, the ABAP runtime environment would kick in as per usual and scan through the CATCH blocks until an appropriate handler was found.

```
TRY.
  oref->method1( ).
  oref->method2( ).
  oref->method3( ).
CATCH cx_xslt_abap_call_error.
  ...
CATCH cx_xslt_format_error.
  ...
CATCH cx_xslt_runtime_error.
  ...
ENDTRY.
```
Listing 8.5 Handling Multiple Exception Types within a TRY Block

Implementing Generic CATCH Blocks

As you can see in Listing 8.5, we can get pretty granular with our exception handling, defining a CATCH block for any type of exception that might be triggered. Sometimes though, such granularity is overkill. For instance, in the code excerpt contained in Listing 8.5, each of the exception types that we're keying on are defined as subclasses of a superclass called CX_TRANSFORMATION_ERROR. Depending on the scenario, we may not care *why* a transformation failed, we just want to know an exception occurred so that we can deal with it in a generic kind of way. In these situations, we can refactor the TRY block to look something like the code excerpt contained in Listing 8.6.

```
TRY.
  CALL TRANSFORMATION xsl_test...
CATCH cx_transformation_error.
  ...
ENDTRY.
```
Listing 8.6 Implementing Generic CATCH Blocks

Whenever we set up CATCH blocks like the one shown in Listing 8.6, we're basically informing the ABAP runtime environment that we want to handle exceptions of type CX_TRANSFORMATION_ERROR *and* any exception types that are defined as a descendant of CX_TRANSFORMATION_ERROR. Note that we use the term "descendant" rather than "child" here because we can traverse far down the exception class hierarchy if we need to.

Bear in mind that the declaration of a generic CATCH block like the one shown in Listing 8.6 doesn't preclude us from also defining a selected number of specific exception blocks which have a higher precedence than the generic one. To understand how this works, consider the code excerpt contained in Listing 8.7. Here, whenever the CALL TRANSFORMATION statement is executed, there could be a number of exception types triggered. While we want to handle most of these exception types in a generic way, there could be one or two types that we want to handle differently. For instance, if an ABAP call from within the XSLT transformation fails, we might want to handle that differently from everything else. To achieve this separation, we simply define the more specific exception handlers *before* we define the more generic exception handler(s). That way, whenever an exception is triggered, the ABAP runtime environment will work its way through the CATCH blocks until it finds the most accurate match.

```
TRY.
  CALL TRANSFORMATION xsl_test...
CATCH cx_xslt_abap_call_error.
  ...
CATCH cx_transformation_error.
  ...
ENDTRY.
```

Listing 8.7 Picking and Choosing Specific Exception Types to Listen For

> **Note**
>
> When defining generic CATCH blocks like the ones demonstrated in Listing 8.7, it's important to note that generic exception types must be declared *after* any CATCH blocks that define exception handlers for subordinate classes. If you think about it, this makes sense as the more specific exception handlers would never be reached since the system would first find a matching exception handler for the superordinate class. Still, if all of this seems confusing, don't worry; the compiler will tell you where you've gone wrong.

Before we move on from this topic, we should warn that while generic CATCH blocks are highly useful, it's important not to get too carried away such that you start ignoring exceptions or throwing away useful information. There's a balance that must be struck here, so you really have to think from a defensive programming perspective how far you need to go to reasonably handle the types of exceptions that might crop up.

8.4.2 Cleaning Up the Mess

After we've recovered from an exception situation in a CATCH block, we may need to perform some additional cleanup tasks before we hand control back over to the normal program flow. For example, consider a program where you're writing some data to an output file. Inside a TRY block, you open up a file and start writing records to it. However, at some point an I/O exception occurs and processing halts in the TRY block before you get a chance to close the file. In this case, you can use the optional CLEANUP block to close the file since this block is guaranteed to be called by the ABAP runtime environment before the TRY statement is exited. A simplified example of this scenario is shown in Listing 8.8.

```
TRY.
    OPEN DATASET lv_file FOR OUTPUT IN TEXT MODE
                        ENCODING DEFAULT.

    LOOP AT lt_extract INTO ls_record.
      TRANSFER ls_record TO lv_file.
    ENDLOOP.

    CLOSE DATASET lv_file.
CATCH cx_sy_file_io.
    "Process I/O errors here...
CLEANUP.
    "Make sure that the file gets closed:
    CLOSE DATASET lv_file.
ENDTRY.
```

Listing 8.8 Recovering from an Exception Using the CLEANUP Block

Note that the CLEANUP block in a TRY statement is guaranteed to be called whenever an exception occurs regardless of whether or not the system can actually locate a suitable exception handler in that TRY statement. Prior to exiting, the CLEANUP block is executed to cleanup any local resources used within the context of the current TRY statement. As such, it's highly recommended that you only use the CLEANUP block for its intended purpose. We should also mention that you're not allowed to execute statements that are used to alter the control flow of a program such as RETURN, STOP, etc.

8.5   Raising and Forwarding Exceptions

As we noted in Section 8.4, exceptions can be raised either implicitly by the ABAP runtime environment or explicitly using the RAISE EXCEPTION statement. In this section, we'll take a closer look at these two different exception types and see how they're propagated to exception handlers.

8.5.1 System-Driven Exceptions

As we observed in the code examples contained in Section 8.3, there are a number of ABAP statements that may trigger an exception at runtime. For example, if an attempt to write to a file fails via the TRANSFER statement, the ABAP runtime environment will automatically raise an exception of type CX_SY_FILE_IO. Similarly, a division operation which attempts to divide by zero will raise an exception of type CX_SY_ZERODIVIDE.

Conceptually speaking, system-driving exceptions such as CX_SY_FILE_IO are classified as *unchecked exceptions* because they're not checked by the ABAP compiler at compile time. If you think about it, this makes sense since the ABAP compiler has no way of knowing if an I/O error might occur at runtime. From a development perspective, the main take-away from this is that we can't rely on the compiler to warn us that we might have a logic error, etc. Instead, we must follow best practices with regards to defensive programming and make sure we handle these exceptions on our own. Also, if you're new to the class-based exception handling concept, we'd highly recommend reading through the ABAP Keyword Documentation and make sure that you're familiar with the types of exceptions that particular statements might trigger.

8.5.2 Raising Exceptions Programmatically

While system-driven exceptions may occur from time to time, the majority of exceptions that we have to deal with are explicitly triggered from ABAP code using the RAISE EXCEPTION statement. Here, the focus is on dealing with application-level logic errors that might occur.

To illustrate how this works, let's imagine that you're tasked with building an API to lookup customer details such as a customer's credit rating. The input to this method is the customer's ID number; the output is the customer's credit score. A first cut of this method is provided in Listing 8.9. Here, the first step is to lookup the customer master record using the ID number provided via the importing IV_CUSTOMER_IDparameter. However, look at what happens whenever the provided customer ID is invalid. Since it's not possible for the method logic to continue without a valid customer number, a dummy credit rating (i.e. -1) is returned to the caller. Here, it's the responsibility of the caller to introspect the value and determine whether or not the credit rating was valid.

```
CLASS lcl_customer DEFINITION.
   PUBLIC SECTION.
      CLASS-METHODS:
         get_credit_rating IMPORTING iv_customer_id
                                     TYPE kunnr
                           RETURNING VALUE(rv_rating)
                                     TYPE i.
ENDCLASS.

CLASS lcl_customer IMPLEMENTATION.
   METHOD get_credit_rating.
      "Read the customer master record from the database:
      SELECT ...
        FROM but000
        WHERE partner EQ iv_customer_id.

      IF sy-subrc NE 0.
        rv_rating = -1.
        RETURN.
      ENDIF.
      ...
   ENDMETHOD.
ENDCLASS.
```

Listing 8.9 Handling Errors in Application Logic (Part 1)

As you can see in Listing 8.9, the exception handling approach taken is conceptually similar to the anti-pattern related to return code passing we observed in
Section 8.1.2. Here, we're effectively re-purposing the RV_RATING parameter as a
return code of sorts to inform the user of an error. Of course, we could have also
defined discrete exporting parameters to carry exception details separately, but
the main problem still persists – we need a better mechanism of raising a red
flag and making sure that the caller reacts appropriately. This is where the RAISE
EXCEPTION statement comes into play. With the RAISE EXCEPTION statement, we
can communicate these situations explicitly by raising particular types of exceptions.

The basic syntax for the RAISE EXCEPTION statement is given in Listing 8.10. One
on hand, the RAISE EXCEPTION statement behaves similarly to the CREATE OBJECT
statement in that it creates an instance of whatever exception type we specify
using the TYPE addition (e.g., CX_EXCEPTION_TYPE). Here, much like the CREATE
OBJECT statement, you have the option of specifying exporting parameters that
are passed into the constructor of the exception object. On the other hand, the

`RAISE EXCEPTION` statement also behaves like a control statement in the sense that it interrupts the normal program flow by causing the ABAP runtime environment to begin unwinding the call stack in search of an appropriate `CATCH` block to handle the exception.

```
RAISE EXCEPTION TYPE cx_exception_type
  [EXPORTING
      f1 = a1
      f2 = a2
      ...].
```

Listing 8.10 Basic Syntax of the RAISE EXCEPTION Statement

Now that we know how to raise exceptions, let's see how we could go back and rework the `get_credit_rating()` method from Listing 8.9 to include support for class-based exceptions. In Listing 8.11, we start by defining a simple exception class called `LCX_CUSTOMER_NOT_FOUND`. Then, after the introduction of the new exception class, the next major change you'll notice in the refactored code contained in Listing 8.11 is the amendment to the signature of the `get_credit_rating()` method. Here, we're using the `RAISING` addition to identify the exception type(s) that might be `raised` during this processing of this method. Though this is an optional addition to the code, it definitely improves the readability of the `get_credit_rating()` method.

```
CLASS lcx_customer_not_found DEFINITION
    INHERITING FROM cx_static_check.
ENDCLASS.

CLASS lcl_customer DEFINITION.
    PUBLIC SECTION.
        CLASS-METHODS:
            get_credit_rating
                IMPORTING iv_customer_id TYPE kunnr
                RETURNING VALUE(rv_rating) TYPE i
                    RAISING lcx_customer_not_found.
ENDCLASS.

CLASS lcl_customer IMPLEMENTATION.
    METHOD get_credit_rating.
        "Read the customer master record from the database:
        SELECT ...
          FROM knb1
          WHERE kunnr EQ iv_customer_id.
```

```
      IF sy-subrc NE 0.
        RAISE EXCEPTION TYPE lcx_customer_not_found.
      ENDIF.
      ...
    ENDMETHOD.
ENDCLASS.
```
Listing 8.11 Handling Errors in Application Logic (Part 2)

Within the method implementation itself, you can see how we're using the RAISE EXCEPTION statement to raise the exception whenever the lookup on the customer master data fails. As soon as we raise this exception, the method processing will halt and the exception will begin bubbling up the call stack until an appropriate exception handler is found. This forces clients to deal with the exception head on as demonstrated in the sample code contained in Listing 8.12.

```
DATA: lv_customer TYPE kunnr VALUE '1234567890',
      lv_credit_rating TYPE i.
      lo_customer_error TYPE REF TO lcx_customer_not_found.
TRY.
  lv_credit_rating =
    lcl_customer=>get_credit_rating( lv_customer ).
CATCH lcx_customer_not_found INTO lo_customer_error.
  "Handle the error in an application-specific way:
  MESSAGE lo_customer_error TYPE 'E'.
ENDTRY.
```
Listing 8.12 Handling Application-Specific Exception Types

Looking closely at the CATCH block in Listing 8.12, you can see how we're using a special variant of the MESSAGE statement to output the exception message. Whenever this statement is evaluated at runtime, the ABAP Runtime Environment will silently invoke the if_message~get_text() method to fetch the exception text and display it on the screen. For certain types of applications, this makes it very easy to relay error messages on to end users.

Raising Exceptions in the New COND and SWITCH Statements

In Release 7.40, SAP introduced a pair of constructor operators that can be used to evaluate logical conditions within the context of an initialization operation: COND and SWITCH. Though semantically similar to the more generalized conditional IF and CASE statements, the usage context for the COND and SWITCH statements is limited to introducing conditional logic in variable assignment expressions.

Depending on the type of assignment(s) we're performing it could be that the input data being evaluated doesn't match any particular pattern. In this case, we may not be able to reasonably initialize the target variable and therefore need to raise an exception. Whenever this occurs, we can raise an exception using the overloaded THROW statement.

The code excerpt contained in Listing 8.13 demonstrates how this syntax works for the COND statement. Here, we're evaluating a date value which provided in plain text format and trying to convert it to an internal ABAP date type. In this contrived example, we only support two input formats for the date: YYYYMMDD or MM/DD/YYYY. If the date value doesn't match up with this format, then an exception of type LCX_INVALID_DATE_FORMAT is raised using the THROW statement. Though we're not passing any parameters into the exception class's constructor method, we could have done so by entering the parameters within the parenthesis after the exception class name in the expression in the same way we would do so using the NEW operator reviewed in Chapter 2.

```
CLASS lcx_invalid_date_format DEFINITION
        INHERITING FROM cx_no_check.
ENDCLASS.

DATA(lv_raw_date) = `06/02/2015`.
DATA(lv_date) =
  COND d( WHEN cl_abap_matcher=>matches(
               pattern = `\d{8}`
                   text = lv_raw_date ) EQ abap_true
          THEN lv_raw_date
          WHEN cl_abap_matcher=>matches(
               pattern = `\d{2}[/.-]\d{2}[/.-]\d{4}`
                   text = lv_raw_date ) EQ abap_true
          THEN
             lv_raw_date+6(4) && lv_raw_date(2) &&
               lv_raw_date+3(2)
          ELSE
             THROW lcx_invalid_date_format( ) ).
```

Listing 8.13 Raising an Exception in a COND Statement Using the THROW Command

The code excerpt contained in Listing 8.14 shows how we can achieve similar results using the SWITCH statement. Since the syntax is largely the same in both cases, we won't re-hash the syntactical particulars of this statement here.

```
CLASS lcx_language_unknown DEFINITION
        INHERITING FROM cx_no_check.
ENDCLASS.
```

```
DATA(lv_message) =
  SWITCH string( sy-langu
    WHEN 'E'
      THEN `Welcome to ABAP Objects`
    WHEN 'S'
      THEN `Bienvenido a Objetos ABAP`
    WHEN 'D'
      THEN `Willkommen in ABAP Objects`
    ELSE
      THROW lcx_language_unknown( ) ).
```
Listing 8.14 Raising an Exception in a SWITCH Statement Using the THROW Command

8.5.3 Propagating Exceptions

Looking back on the customer credit rating check scenario introduced in Section 8.5.2 (and Listing 8.11), it's plain to see that there's really not much the get_credit_rating() method can do if the provided customer ID is invalid. Therefore, rather than swallowing up the exception or terminating silently in the background, the method explicitly raises an exception using the RAISE EXCEPTION statement. This exception is meant to propagate up the call stack so that the caller(s) can deal with it. Here, notice that we refer to callers in plural since the immediate caller(s) may also find that they too are unable to deal with the exception.

To put this into perspective, consider the LCL_CUSTOMER_REPORT class contained in Listing 8.15. This contrived class might be used to generate a customer output report leveraging features defined in the LCL_CUSTOMER utilities class we created earlier in this chapter. If you drill through the code, you'll find that the method which performs the majority of the heavy lifting –process_customer() – may encounter the LCX_CUSTOMER_NOT_FOUND exception defined in Listing 8.11. Whenever this occurs, there's really no point in continuing with the processing of the customer, so the method forwards it up the call stack using a hybrid form of the RAISE EXCEPTION statement. For all of the other exception types that might occur, it's assumed that the method is able to handle these internally, so we're using a generic catch block for CX_ROOT to swallow these up and prevent them from propagating back to the caller.

```
CLASS lcl_customer_report DEFINITION.
  PUBLIC SECTION.
    CLASS-METHODS:
      execute.

  PRIVATE SECTION.
    TYPES: BEGIN OF ty_customer,
```

```
            kunnr TYPE kunnr,
            ...
        END OF ty_customer.
    DATA mt_customers TYPE STANDARD TABLE OF ty_customer.

    METHODS:
      read_customer_data,
      process_customers,
      process_customer IMPORTING is_customer TYPE ty_customer
                       RAISING lcx_customer_not_found.
ENDCLASS.

CLASS lcl_customer_report IMPLEMENTATION.
  METHOD execute.
    DATA lo_report TYPE REF TO lcl_customer_report.
    CREATE OBJECT lo_report.

    lo_report->read_customer_data( ).

    lo_report->process_customers( ).
  ENDMETHOD.

  METHOD read_customer_data.
    ...
  ENDMETHOD.

  METHOD process_customers.
    FIELD-SYMBOLS <ls_customer> LIKE LINE OF me->mt_customers.
    DATA lx_root TYPE REF TO cx_root.

    LOOP AT me->mt_customers ASSIGNING <ls_customer>.
      TRY.
        process_customer( <ls_customer> ).
      CATCH cx_root INTO lx_root.
        MESSAGE lx_root TYPE 'E'.
      ENDTRY.
    ENDLOOP.
  ENDMETHOD.

  METHOD process_customer.
    DATA lx_customer_error TYPE REF TO lcx_customer_not_found.

    TRY.
      "Fetch the customer's credit rating:
      IF lcl_customer=>get_credit_rating( is_customer-kunnr )
         GT 550.
      ...
      ENDIF.

      "Perform other options which might raise
      "different exceptions that we want to handle internally...
    CATCH lcx_customer_not_found INTO lx_customer_error.
```

```
      "Forward the exception on to the caller:
      RAISE EXCEPTION lx_customer_error.
    CATCH cx_root.
      "Handle the error locally...
    ENDTRY.
  ENDMETHOD.
ENDCLASS.
```

Listing 8.15 Propagating Exceptions Using the RAISE EXCEPTION Statement

Any time we propagate exceptions from a method, it's usually a good idea to declare our intentions up front by including the target exception types in the RAISING clause of the method definition. Though we've seen some examples of this already, Listing 8.16 illustrates the syntax more clearly. Here, you can see that a given method can define many exception types as part of its signature.

```
METHOD some_method RAISING cx_ex1 cx_ex2 ...
```

Listing 8.16 Basic Syntax of the RAISING Addition

In practice, we probably want to keep the total number of exceptions within the RAISING clause to a handful of types. Indeed, if you're finding yourself defining more than a few exception types within a method's signature, it's a safe bet that your method is doing way too much and lacks cohesion.

For global classes maintained in the form-based view of the Class Builder tool, we can add exceptions to a method signature by selecting the method on the METHODS tab and clicking on the EXCEPTION button highlighted in Figure 8.8.

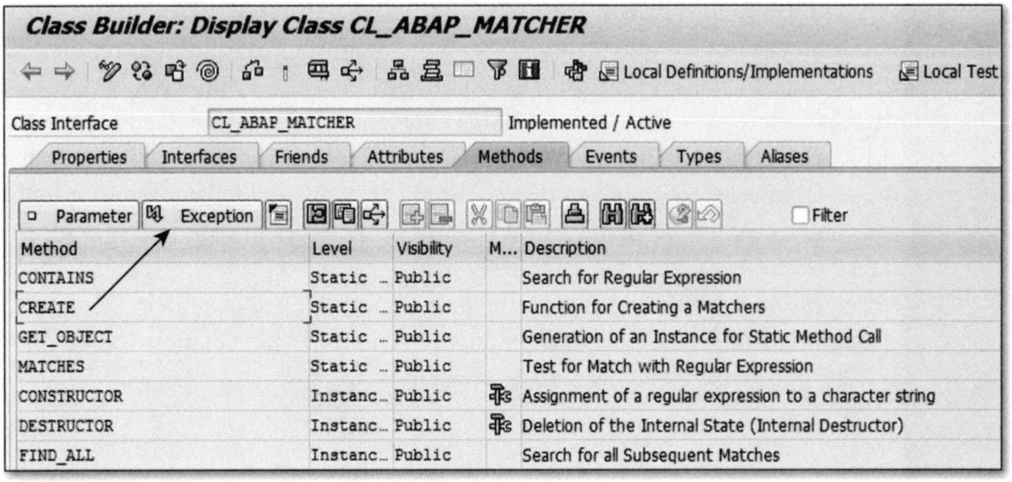

Figure 8.8 Adding Exceptions to the Signature of Methods in a Global Class (Part 1)

This brings up the editor page shown in Figure 8.9. From here, we can add the necessary global exception types to the signature by simply filling in the exception class names in the EXCEPTION column.

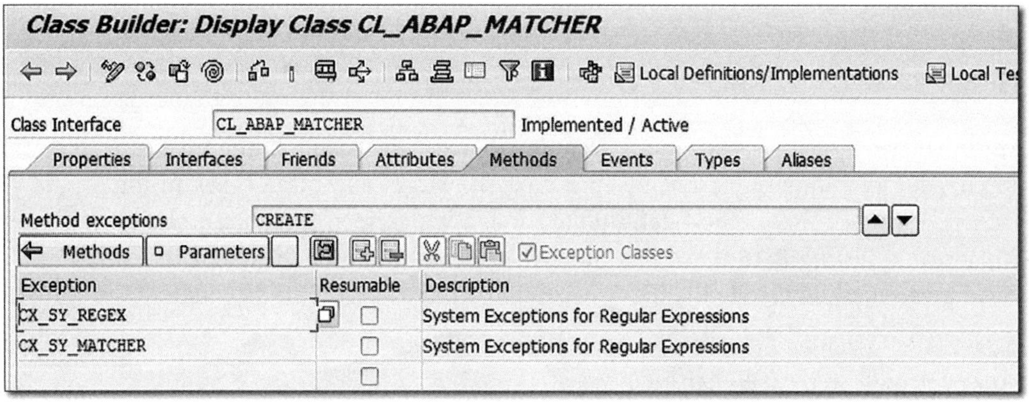

Figure 8.9 Adding Exceptions to the Signature of Methods in a Global Class (Part 2)

8.5.4 Resumable Exceptions

Beginning with Release 7.02 of the AS ABAP, SAP expanded the class-based exception handling concept to include support for *resumable exceptions*. As the name suggests, resumable exceptions are exceptions that can (usually) be dealt with cleanly enough that we can allow the program flow to *resume* after we clean up the mess in a CATCH block.

To demonstrate how this works, let's consider an example. In Listing 8.17, we've developed a simple report program which contains a couple of local test classes that are used to upload documents to some specialized document store. Though database agnostic, our document upload service is highly optimized for the SAP HANA database, making use of native features such as stored procedures. Within the code, checks are made to determine if the SAP HANA database is available (e.g. by reading the value of the built-in cl_db_sys=>is_in_memory_db attribute). If SAP HANA isn't available, then a resumable exception is raised to allow clients to determine if they want to continue on without SAP HANA or cease processing. Though admittedly contrived, this example gives us a useful demonstration of the syntax required to implement such a scenario.

```
REPORT zresumable_test.
CLASS lcx_doc_service_error DEFINITION
```

```
      INHERITING FROM cx_static_check.
ENDCLASS.

CLASS lcl_persistence_service DEFINITION.
   PUBLIC SECTION.
      METHODS:
         insert_document IMPORTING iv_file_name TYPE string
                                   iv_mime_type TYPE string
                                   iv_payload TYPE xstring
                         RAISING RESUMABLE(cx_sy_sql_error).
      ...
ENDCLASS.

CLASS lcl_persistence_service IMPLEMENTATION.
   METHOD insert_document.
      IF cl_db_sys=>is_in_memory_db EQ abap_true.
         "Call stored procedure to insert the document using AMDP...
      ELSE.
         RAISE RESUMABLE EXCEPTION TYPE cx_sy_sql_error
            EXPORTING
               sqlcode = 900
               sqlmsg = `SAP HANA is not available. ` &&
                        `Will process through OpenSQL instead.`.
      ENDIF.

      "Insert the document using OpenSQL instead...
      ...
   ENDMETHOD.
ENDCLASS.

CLASS lcl_document_service DEFINITION.
   PUBLIC SECTION.
      METHODS:
         constructor,
         upload_document IMPORTING iv_file_name TYPE string
                                   iv_mime_type TYPE string
                                   iv_payload TYPE xstring
                         RAISING lcx_doc_service_error.

   PRIVATE SECTION.
      DATA mv_session_id TYPE guid_16.
      DATA mo_persistence TYPE REF TO lcl_persistence_service.

      METHODS:
         log IMPORTING iv_message TYPE csequence.
ENDCLASS.

CLASS lcl_document_service IMPLEMENTATION.
   METHOD constructor.
      TRY.
```

```
      me->mv_session_id =
        cl_system_uuid=>create_uuid_x16_static( ).
      me->mo_persistence = NEW lcl_persistence_service( ).
    CATCH cx_uuid_error.
    ENDTRY.
  ENDMETHOD.

  METHOD upload_document.
    DATA lx_sql_error TYPE REF TO cx_sy_sql_error.
    TRY.
      mo_persistence->insert_document(
        iv_file_name = iv_file_name
        iv_mime_type = iv_mime_type
        iv_payload = iv_payload ).

      log( |File "{ iv_file_name }" was uploaded.| ).
    CATCH BEFORE UNWIND cx_sy_sql_error INTO lx_sql_error.
      "Test the nature of the exception to determine
      "if we should resume or abort:
      IF lx_sql_error->sqlcode EQ 900.
        log( lx_sql_error->sqlmsg ).
        RESUME.
      ELSE.
        RAISE EXCEPTION TYPE lcx_doc_service_error
          EXPORTING
            previous = lx_sql_error.
      ENDIF.
    ENDTRY.
  ENDMETHOD.

  METHOD log.
    WRITE: / iv_message.
  ENDMETHOD.
ENDCLASS.

START-OF-SELECTION.
DATA(lo_doc_service) = NEW lcl_document_service( ).
lo_doc_service->upload_document(
  EXPORTING
    iv_file_name = 'Test.txt'
    iv_mime_type = 'text/plain'
    iv_payload = CONV xstring( `This is a test.` ) ).
```

Listing 8.17 Working with Resumable Exceptions

Looking over the example code contained in Listing 8.17, we can see several new syntax elements on display that make this flow work:

▸ Within the definition section of the LCL_PERSISTENCE_SERVICE class, notice how the signature of the insert_document() method includes the RAISING

RESUMABLE(cx_sy_sql_error) addition. This addition declares that the insert_document() method may raise a resumable exception of type CX_SY_SQL_ERROR.

▶ Next, in the insert_document() method itself, we have a condition check on the cl_db_sys=>is_in_memory_db attribute to determine if the AS ABAP is running on top of the SAP HANA database. If not, an exception of type CX_SY_SQL_ERROR is raised using the RAISE RESUMABLE EXCEPTION statement. Here, the RESUMABLE addition tells the ABAP runtime environment that we *may* want to resume processing after this exception.

▶ In the calling upload_document() method of class LCL_DOCUMENT_SERVICE, we've wrapped the call to insert_document() inside of a TRY statement. Here, notice how we're using the BEFORE UNWIND addition of the CATCH statement to inform the ABAP runtime environment that we want to hang onto the processing context from which the exception was raised so that we can essentially pick up where things left off after we deal with the exception.

▶ Finally, within the CATCH block, you can see how we're assessing the nature of the error and determining if we should resume. In the case of a SAP HANA unavailable error, we use the RESUME statement to let the processing continue on to the failover section of the persistence service where we use regular Open-SQL to store the uploaded document.

Figure 8.10 contains a UML sequence diagram which illustrates the exception flow. As you can see, most of the magic happens between the point that we raise the resumable exception and the corresponding CATCH block decides to resume processing with the RESUME statement. After flow is resumed, the insert_document() method picks up right where it left off (with its local variables intact) and proceed on with the failover logic.

In summary, resumable exceptions provide a clean mechanism for trapping error conditions, recovering from them, and moving on as if the exception hadn't happened in the first place. This functionality can come in handy whenever we encounter situations where we need to build failover logic into our programs. With resumable exceptions, we can capture the exception conditions in an exception object, pass the information on to a CATCH block, and let the CATCH block determine whether or not we wish to proceed. This is preferable to having lots of IF statements scattered throughout the code to assess these conditions and (redundantly) react to them.

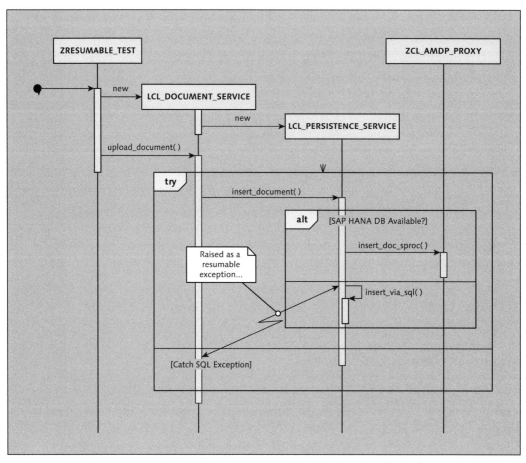

Figure 8.10 UML Sequence Diagram Showing Resumable Exception Flow

8.6 UML Tutorial: Activity Diagrams

The UML activity diagram is a behavioral diagram used to depict the high-level flow within a block of code. As such, activity diagrams share certain similarities with flow charts used in the procedural world. However, as you'll soon learn, there are certain things we can do with activity diagrams that we cannot do with flowcharts.

Figure 8.11 shows an example of an activity diagram that's being used to depict the flow of a simple ABAP extract program. The flow begins at the *initial node* action and proceeds to the very first action called Receive Query Parameters. Notice that the action names we have used here are fairly generic. For example, in the ABAP extract program, the Receive Query Parameters action would encompass the generation of a selection screen and the entry of selection parameters by a user. You can trace the control flow of an activity diagram by following the directed edges between actions. Eventually, the program flow proceeds all the way down to the *activity final* action (see Figure 8.11).

One significant addition to activity diagrams in the UML 2.0 standard was the specification of *protected nodes* and *handler blocks*. As you can see in Figure 8.11, the action Extract Data from Database is a protected node that might trigger an exception (i.e. Selection Failed). If no data is found in the database for the given selection criteria, control is transferred to the Display Error Message handler block.

It's also possible to group together multiple actions inside of a protected node. For example, all of the file I/O actions in Figure 8.11 were grouped together in a protected node that reacts to file I/O exceptions. Here, notice that flow from each handler block leads into a diamond-shaped node called a *merge*. Merges provide a convenient way of channeling multiple input flows into a common output flow.

Looking at the Write Record to File action in Figure 8.11, you'll notice that its boundary is depicted using a dotted line in lieu of the solid line used with all of the other normal actions. This dotted line marks an *expansion region* in the activity diagram. In the flow, the Write Record to File expansion region (along with the inputting tokens shown as small pins along the top of the action) represents a loop that takes the extract records from the database lookup and iteratively writes them to the extract file. This kind of notation is much more elegant than the typical use of conditionals in flowcharts to determine if there are more records to process, etc.

One of the beauties of activity diagrams is that they're extremely easy to read, oftentimes requiring little to no translation for non-technical members of the team. Consequently, they are an excellent communication tool for describing and refining a program flow with functional team members. Typically, once the process flow within an activity diagram is agreed upon, the design can be put in more technical terms in the form of interaction diagrams such as a sequence diagram, etc.

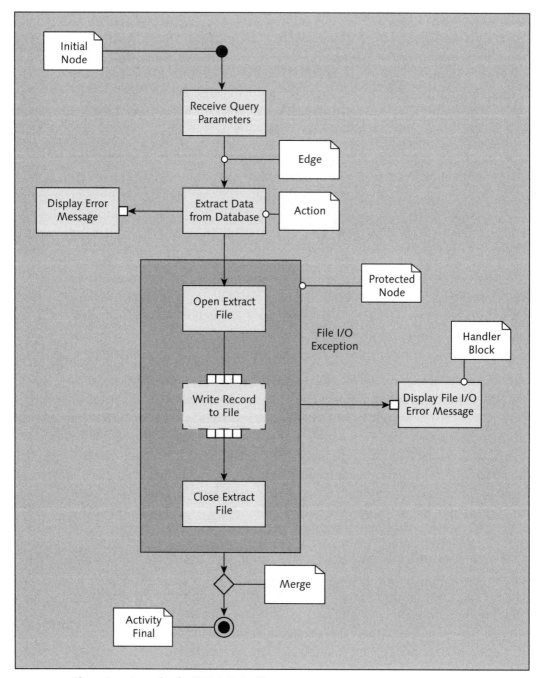

Figure 8.11 Example of a UML Activity Diagram

8.7   Summary

In this chapter, we were able to observe how the class-based exception handling concept greatly simplifies the process of dealing with errors that may occur within an application. The definition of a common framework for dealing with exceptions is essential for the development of reusable components since it provides a consistent model for relaying exceptions to users/clients.

In the next chapter we'll take a look at ABAP Unit and see how a test-driven approach to development can significantly improve the quality of your ABAP code.

ABAP Unit is a framework that assists developers in verifying outcomes and validating the results of paths throughout their code. In this chapter, we'll learn more about this framework and how it can be leveraged to facilitate the promotion of defect-free applications.

9   Unit Tests with ABAP Unit

An admirable objective for any ABAP developer would be to *always* write elegant, agile, and defect-free code. This lofty goal could prove to be more difficult than it seems if one were to rely solely on informal testing processes. Fortunately there are tools available that enable developers to improve the overall quality of their code while also allowing for confidence in any future refactoring efforts. An example of such a development tool is a robust automated unit testing framework.

A unit testing framework such as ABAP Unit allows a developer to write individual *unit tests* that target and verify the intended behavior of a specific "unit" of code. A code unit could be defined as the smallest testable part of an application but, more commonly, it's a method or function of a larger code container such as a class. If this seems a bit narrow in scope, ABAP Unit allows for organizing of unit tests into groups in order to adjust the extent of what is being tested. Each group may then be incorporated into a test run and set to run manually or automatically at specific points throughout the software development lifecycle to ensure that changes in code did not introduce any defects or software regressions.

One of the main goals of every unit test is to confirm that your individual modules are fulfilling the terms of their API contracts. Verifying this behavior early on helps to eliminate the tedious module-level bugs that prohibit integration and functional tests from running smoothly. In this chapter, you'll learn how the ABAP Unit test tool can support you in the process of developing and executing unit tests.

9.1   ABAP Unit Overview

In 1998 Kent Beck designed the first incarnation of a unit testing framework that could be used to provide some of the common elements necessary for building and running automated unit tests. The framework, created for the Smalltalk language, was called SUnit. Since that time, this same testing model (colloquially known as xUnit these days) has been adapted to create testing frameworks for other languages such as Java (JUnit), .NET (NUnit), and with the SAP NetWeaver 2004 release, ABAP Objects. The SAP implementation of the xUnit test framework is called ABAP Unit. In this section, we'll introduce the basic concepts of ABAP Unit and review how it works.

9.1.1   Unit Testing Terminology

To understand how to use ABAP Unit, it's important to define some of the basic terms that are used throughout the framework (see Table 9.1). These terms (and concepts they represent) are largely based on concepts outlined in the core xUnit framework.

Term	Description
Test Class	A test class defines an environment for running multiple related unit tests (implemented as test methods)
Test Method	Test methods are special instance methods of a test class that can be invoked to produce test results. In the xUnit framework, a test method represents a single unit test.
Fixture	A fixture defines an environment for running unit tests in the proper context. Fixtures are configured in special callback methods defined within a test class. You can insert code in these methods to obtain and clean up the resources (e.g., object instances, file handles, etc.) that are used within the unit test methods.
Test Task	A test task groups test classes together, allowing their methods to be executed together in a single test run.
Test Run	A test run controls the execution of a test task. Test runs produce test results that can be viewed in the ABAP Unit result display.
Assertion	Inside a test method, individual logical tests are made to assess the correctness of a particular piece of functionality. These logical tests that verify conditions via a true/false proposition are known as assertions.

Table 9.1 Basic ABAP Unit Terminology

9.1.2   Understanding How ABAP Unit Works

The ABAP Unit test framework is tightly integrated into the ABAP Workbench, making it very easy to set up and execute tests for a given ABAP program. The tests themselves are written in ABAP and are nothing more than local classes. This means that no additional language or interface skills are required to begin working with the ABAP Unit framework.

Each unit test class contains fixtures to help set up and tear down objects and resources necessary for executing each test. The runtime environment will search for a special method called `setup()` in the test class and, if the method exists, the runtime environment will call it *before* it calls any test method to ensure that the tests are set up properly. After the tests are complete, a `teardown()` method is called in similar fashion if it exists. The actual tests are performed by parameterless instance methods contained within the unit test class that verify results with utility methods from the class `CL_AUNIT_ASSERT`.

The outcomes of the various tests are shown in the ABAP UNIT RESULTS DISPLAY. The details shown in the ABAP UNIT RESULTS DISPLAY provide information about what went wrong, and where. The details are context-sensitive, allowing you to navigate within the ABAP Workbench to the source of the problem.

9.1.3   ABAP Unit and Production Code

The goal of the ABAP Unit framework is to allow for tests to be crafted and executed in order to ensure code performs as expected. These tests are expected to run throughout the development lifecycle to ensure that defects or software regressions are not introduced when code is promoted or transported to a production environment. In a live environment, tests could potentially cause problems if allowed to execute and, for this reason, ABAP does not generate byte code for ABAP Unit tests in production systems. This ensures that the test are not executable in these business critical environments and your test code cannot pose a potential strain or cause adverse side-effects.

9.2   Creating Unit Test Classes

For the most part, you define and implement test classes in the same way that you would build a regular ABAP Objects class. However, test classes and test methods must be defined using the FOR TESTING addition as shown in Listing 9.1. This addition effectively divides an application into two separate parts: test code and production code so that ABAP understands which code should not be generated in production systems as mentioned in Section 9.1.3.

```
CLASS ltc_my_test_class DEFINITION
      FOR TESTING.
[Risk Level {Critical|Dangerous|Harmless}]
[Duration {Short|Medium|Long}]
[...]
ENDCLASS.
```
Listing 9.1 Basic Form of ABAP Unit Test Classes

The following subsections contain a review of the pieces that you will need to assemble in order to create a unit test class along with a discussion of naming conventions and an introduction to the Test Class Generation Wizard that is available to help bootstrap your unit test development.

9.2.1 Unit Test Naming Conventions

Just as careful consideration of class, method and variable names is important in ABAP development, it should also be relevant in unit test construction. One important reason for this outside the scope of readability and maintenance is the fact that, if a unit test fails, the class and method names will appear in the failure message. If the class and method name provide adequate information on what is being tested, developers will be able to better identify and resolve problems with the code.

Although there are no binding naming conventions, SAP provides suggestions on ABAP Unit test class prefixes (Table 9.2).

Suggested Prefix	Type of Class
LTC_	Local ABAP Unit test class
LTD_	Local test double.
LTH_	Local test utilities class.

Table 9.2 SAP Suggested ABAP Unit Test Class Prefixes

It's ultimately up to the developer to write clean, understandable and organized unit tests. Many unit test naming strategies have been adopted throughout the development community across varied technologies. These strategies were created in order to allow for unit test names to express specific requirements, identify the targeted unit of work (methods, functions, class or combinations therein) and state the expected results. If there are not already naming conventions in place for your unit test methods, there are many online resources that you may explore to find a convention that suits your needs.

9.2.2 Test Attributes

When defining a test class, you *must* specify a couple of attributes that are used by the ABAP runtime environment during the execution of a test. These attributes are defined as statements in systems with release 7.02 or higher (see Listing 9.1 above) and as special *pseudo comments* in older systems (Listing 9.2). The two test attributes are the *risk level* and the *execution duration* of ABAP Unit tests and are added after the CLASS ... FOR TESTING statement.

```
CLASS … FOR TESTING.
"#AU Risk_Level Critical|Dangerous|Harmless
"#AU Duration Short|Medium|Long
```

Listing 9.2 Test Attributes in Systems with Earlier Release than 7.02

The RISK LEVEL attribute describes the effects that a test could have on the system. It's possible that test methods may invoke functionality that could make changes to system settings and/or the database. The three risk level values that may be assigned are CRITICAL, DANGEROUS and HARMLESS, with HARMLESS meaning that the test would *not* make changes to persistent data or impact the system in any negative way (see Table 9.3). Although there are two other choices outside of harmless, every test should be written with the objective of being "harmless" to the environment within which it's executed. Leveraging the dependency injection techniques described above, developers can prevent any unwanted consequences from running a unit test.

Risk Level	Potential Side Effects
CRITICAL	Could alter system settings, customizing and so on.
DANGEROUS	Could change records in the database.
HARMLESS	No side effects; the test is innocuous

Table 9.3 Risk Level Attribute Values

Test classes that introduce any risk over that of HARMLESS can be restricted for execution based on client customizing settings (defined in the Implementation Guide [IMG] or in Transaction SAUNIT_CLIENT_SETUP). This way, for example, you can protect a *golden client* from test side effects that could impact other project efforts.

The DURATION attribute specifies the expected execution duration of a test class. This attribute helps the ABAP runtime environment to know when a test has run too long (perhaps due to an error in the test code such as an infinite loop). The possible values of this attribute are SHORT , MEDIUM and LONG, and they have default values of 1 minute, 5 minutes, and an hour, respectively. These default values can also be adjusted in Transaction SAUNIT_CLIENT_SETUP.

The objective to keep in mind when writing unit tests is to keep your tests quick and lean. A test that has a noticeable duration, that greater than a few seconds, should be flagged for examination of both the test(s) and the target class under test for a potential refactoring effort. As you build up your unit test arsenal, you have to be confident that the lot of them could be executed at any time. If these tests are HARMLESS and have a SHORT duration, you can confidently make changes in the code and execute unit tests in order to ensure that no regressions or defects were introduced.

9.2.3   Test Methods

Test methods are defined as parameterless instance methods in a test class. The signature of these methods also requires the FOR TESTING addition (see Listing 9.3).

```
CLASS ltc_my_test_class DEFINITION FOR TESTING
      RISK LEVEL HARMLESS
      DURATION SHORT
      FINAL.
      PRIVATE SECTION.
  METHODS:
        test_method1 FOR TESTING.
        test_method2 FOR TESTING.
```

Listing 9.3 Defining Test Methods

Each test method in a test class corresponds to a single unit test. As described previously, a test method should concentrate on testing a single software unit (e.g., a method, a function module, etc.) rather than testing an entire application. It's important to keep unit tests granular so that we can focus in closely on potential bugs that might creep into various parts of the program. Most of the time, the implementation of a test method will simply consist of a single call to a module of the program under test followed by a status check using utility methods defined in class CL_ABAP_UNIT_ASSERT.

If you look closely at the code in Listing 9.3, you'll notice that the test methods have been defined in the private section of the test class. This is by design because test classes implicitly share a friendship relationship with the test driver of the ABAP runtime environment. Consequently, you should prefer to define your test methods in the private or protected (if it's inherited) sections of your test class.

9.2.4 Managing Fixtures

Test classes group related test methods (i.e., unit tests) together into a logical unit. In these classes, you can also define special fixture methods that help set up and teardown unit tests. These methods have predefined names that are automatically recognized by the ABAP runtime environment. Each method is defined in the private section of the class and has no parameters. Table 9.4 describes the various types of fixture methods that are supported by the ABAP Unit framework.

Method Name	Usage Type
setup()	This instance method is called prior to the invocation of every test method in the test class.
teardown()	This instance method is called after every invocation of a test method in the test class.
class_setup()	This class method is called once before any test methods are called in the test class.
class_teardown()	This class method is invoked after all of the test methods in the test class have been called.

Table 9.4 Fixture Methods and Their Usages

Fixture methods are an excellent place for defining common initialization code that is relevant for all of the test methods in a test class. In particular, the instance methods setup() and teardown() provide a useful hook for implementing code that ensures that each test is executed independently using the proper runtime configuration.

9.2.5 Test Class Generation Wizard

You can generate unit test classes for global classes using the test class generation tool provided with the Class Builder. To access this generation tool, put the cursor on the name of the object you with to create a unit test class for and select the menu path UTILITIES • TEST CLASSES • GENERATE or display the context menu and select CREATE • GENERATE TEST CLASS. This will launch the ABAP Test Class Generation Wizard as shown in Figure 9.1 below. Here, you are presented with options for specifying the unit test class attributes, generating fixtures, test methods, and so on. This is a way to quickly bootstrap a unit test class but you will obviously still be responsible in building setup and teardown operations along with implementing all of your unit test methods and assertions therein.

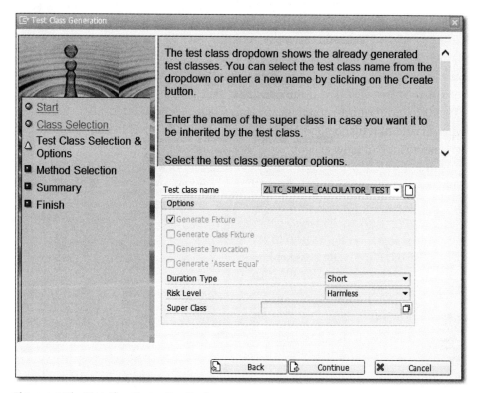

Figure 9.1 The Test Class Generation Tool

Once complete, you may access the generated test class by selecting GOTO • LOCAL TEST CLASSES in the menu path of the Class Editor screen of the Class Builder. The test class will also be available by drilling down to the LOCAL CLASSES folder under the object for which the class was associated with from within the Object Navigator (Transaction SE80).

9.2.6 Global Test Classes

Often times there is a need to design reusable pieces of logic that will be potentially be leveraged by many local unit test classes. These *global test classes* could take the form of a service or helper class to facilitate unit test creation or act as a parent to a unit test class in order to reuse logic by inheritance.

To create a *service class*, the only rules are that a service class must still contain the FOR TESTING option and will not implement any fixtures or unit test methods. This service class is essentially a standard ABAP class that needs to be associated with ABAP Unit.

A *parent unit test class* is created as an ABSTRACT class, also contains the FOR TESTING option and implements at least one fixture or test method. Local test classes may now inherit from this parent unit test class and reuse its logic while still maintaining their local relationship to the code they were intended to test. If a parent unit test class is not declared as ABSTRACT, then ABAP Unit will report a warning. For more information, please consult the online help documentation for ABAP Test and Analysis Tools: Correct Use of Global Test Classes (*http://help.sap.com*).

9.3 Assertions in ABAP Unit

An assertion can be defined as a verification of a condition using a true/false proposition. This condition is evaluated by code that is encapsulated within what ABAP Unit refers to as a *constraint*. The CL_ABAP_UNIT_ASSERT class contains many methods to test constraints and these methods should cover most of your needs when verifying outcomes within unit tests (see Table 9.5 for some examples of those methods). All of these methods expect a piece of data to be verified that is *actually* returned from the code that is under test (the act parameter). The assert_equals() also requires an expected piece of data (the exp parameter) which is used in a comparison against that data passed into the act parameter (Listing 9.4).

```
cl_abap_unit_assert=>assert_equals(
  EXPORTING
    act = lv_actual
    exp = lv_expected
    msg = 'Unit Test Test Failed' ).
```
Listing 9.4 Assertion Example

As expected, when all assertions within a test method evaluate true, the unit test has successfully passed and, based on the tested condition(s), the code path is functioning as expected. If any assertion fails in a unit test, that unit test will not pass and an error will occur in the ABAP UNIT RESULTS DISPLAY when executing the test. The severity `level` and any text passed into the `msg` optional import parameters of the assertion will show under the ALERTS AND MESSAGES panel in the upper-right portion of the screen (see Section 9.7).

Method Name	Description
assert_equals()	The two objects being evaluated must have a comparable type. This assertion will return true if the objects are equal and may be enhanced to perform *complex comparisons* by creating a class that implements `IF_AUNIT_OBJECT` (logic for comparison resides in the `equal_to()` method) and passing that class as the argument of the `exp` parameter of `assert_equals()`.
assert_bound()	Returns true if the reference of a reference variable has the ABAP property of `IS BOUND`.
assert_initial()	Returns true if an object has the ABAP property of `IS INITIAL`.
assert_subrc()	Returns true if a specific value is returned from `SY-SUBRC`.
assert_that()	Evaluates a specific conditions and is used in testing custom constraints (described below). The `exp` parameter expects an instance of a class that implements `IF_CONSTRAINT`.
fail()	Forces the test to fail.

Table 9.5 Examples of Some of the Methods of CL_ABAP_UNIT_ASSERT

9.3.1 Creating and Evaluating Custom Constraints

If there's ever a need to evaluate a condition outside the scope of the methods present within `CL_ABAP_UNIT_ASSERT`, ABAP Unit allow for *custom constraints* by creating a class that implements the `IF_CONSTRAINT` interface (Listing 9.5). This custom constraint class must, in turn, implement two methods defined by `IF_`

CONSTRAINT. These are the `is_valid()` method which contains the evaluation logic of the constraint and returns a Boolean result on whether the condition was met and the `get_description()` method which returns a message describing the test results. To utilize the user-defined constraint within unit tests, the `assert_that()` method of CL_ABAP_UNIT_ASSERT may be invoked and the custom constraint's methods may be passed in as the `exp` parameter. Any necessary parameters of your custom constraint must be passed in via the constructor of the class and set as attributes.

```
CLASS ltc_my_constraint DEFINITION.
     PUBLIC SECTION.
            INTERFACES if_constraint.
ENDCLASS.
```

Listing 9.5 Defining A Custom Constraint

9.3.2 Applying Multiple Constraints

If a more complex assertion is ever required, the CL_AUNIT_CONSTRAINTS class of ABAP Unit allows for multiple custom constraints to be combined via logical operators (AND, OR, NOT, XOR, etc.). These logical operators are represented as static methods of the CL_AUNIT_CONSTRAINTS class and return instances of objects that implement the IF_CONSTRAINT interface. The resulting combined constraint joined by this logical operator may, in turn, be passed to the `exp` parameter of the `assert_that()` method of CL_ABAP_UNIT_ASSERT (Listing 9.6).

```
DATA:
  " lo_first_constraint and lo_second_constraint implement
  " IF_CONSTRAINT interface
  lo_first_constraint     TYPE REF TO zltc_first_constraint,
  lo_second_constraint    TYPE REF TO zltc_second_constraint,
  lo_compound_constraint  TYPE REF TO if_constraint,
  lo_actual_results       TYPE REF TO data.

* Create instances of both custom constraints
CREATE OBJECT lo_first_constraint.
CREATE OBJECT lo_second_constraint.

* Make call to code under test to retrieve actual results
  ...
* Combine constraints using static method of cl_aunit_constraints
lo_compound_constraint = cl_aunit_constraints=>and(
  c1 = lo_first_constraint
```

```
  c2 = lo_second_constraint ).

* Utilize compound constraint in assertion
cl_abap_unit_assert=>assert_that(
  act = lo_actual_results  " Data to check from code under test
  exp = lo_compound_constraint ).
```

Listing 9.6 Combining Custom Constraints with CL_AUNIT_CONSTRAINTS

To leverage CL_AUNIT_CONSTRAINT, create an instance of each custom constraint, passing any required parameters via the class constructors (see Listing 9.6). A call can then be made to the required logical operator static method of CL_AUNIT_CON-STRAINT using your custom constraint objects as parameters. The static method will return a new instance of an object that implements IF_CONSTRAINT. This new instance will allow for a check against both custom constraints and evaluate those constraints based on the logical operation used to join them. The result is a class that can be used as the exp parameter of the assert_that() method of CL_ABAP_UNIT_ASSERT.

Multiple Assertions in a Unit Test

There are differing opinions on the number of assertions that should be present within each unit test or unit test method. One idea is that each test method should contain only one assertion in order to keep the code clean and easy to understand. There's no doubt that the number of assertions should be minimized and one assert per unit test is a good guideline to follow.

However, an alternative view is to restrict your unit tests to evaluate a single concept. If you're testing two independent outcomes, then two tests are necessary but, if you're testing a single concept that requires multiple assertions to cover specific dimensions of the outcome, a single test method or unit test will suffice.

9.4   Managing Dependencies

One of the positive side effects to adopting a unit testing framework and writing tests against ABAP objects is that these objects will require a break from outside dependencies in order to be properly tested. Database operations, function module calls, authorization checks and other services will need to be abstracted and encapsulated into specialized ABAP objects and set up to be "injectable" into ABAP classes.

The exercise described above is something known as dependency injection. In the following sections, we will briefly review some options on how to resolve dependencies in code and allow for more modularized, testable ABAP objects.

9.4.1 Dependency Injection

Dependency injection comes in many forms (see "Methods of Dependency Injection" below) and allows for encapsulated ABAP objects and services to be set for any dependent class. The goal is to allow for better software design and, in the context of ABAP Unit, to better isolate a "unit" of code by allowing for test doubles to be injected in place of normal production objects during unit testing.

These test doubles can take the form of a test stub or mocked object (among others), are usually simplified versions of their production counterparts and are set to return predictable data so that only the code under test may be targeted and evaluated properly. This helps to ensure that each test is now independent and repeatable in any environment. This is crucial for any unit test to be valid.

For more information on resolving dependencies and using test doubles or mocked objects in ABAP, please see *ABAP to the Future* (SAP PRESS, 2015).

Methods of Dependency Injection

The following is a list of standard techniques to decouple your object oriented application code from encapsulated services and other dependencies. Comparison of these methods is beyond the scope of this book but more information is available through the SAP online help documentation for Managing Dependencies in ABAP Unit Testing (*http://help.sap.com*) or other online resources.

- **Constructor Injection**: Needed ABAP objects or dependencies are passed as parameters to the class constructor.
- **Setter Injection**: This requires that the ABAP object provides setter method(s) for each dependency.
- **Interface Injection**: An interface defines the injection method or the setter methods of the class dependencies.

9.4.2 Private Dependency Injection

Another dependency injection method available in ABAP is *private dependency injection*, a technique that is better suited at substituting dependencies while writing unit tests in ABAP Unit. By associating a test class as a FRIEND to a class under test, the test class will have access to private and protected attributes of the class under test so that dependencies may be injected. This allows for breaking of dependencies but still protects the class under test from any outside manipulation. In order for this method to work properly, dependencies in the class under test must be resolved or set in methods outside of those that leverage them. In other words, the class constructor() would establish these dependencies and set them to private or protected attributes so that other methods of the class may use these objects in their logic.

You can find more information about private dependency injection in the SAP online help documentation for ABAP Test and Analysis Tools (*http://help.sap.com*). Sample code is provided to give an example of how one would implement this form of dependency injection.

9.4.3 Partially Implemented Interfaces

Release 7.40 added an improvement that removes the requirement of test classes to have to completely implement an inherited interface. Using the PARTIALLY IMPLEMENTED addition, you can now create classes that act as test doubles and only need to implement the pieces of the interface that the code under test requires (Listing 9.7). This removes that hassle of having to implement the entire contract that an interface presents or forcing you to add the pragma #needed to each empty method implementation. Again, this method of implementing an interface in a class can *only* be utilized in test classes.

```
CLASS ltd_test_double DEFINITION
      FOR TESTING.
      INTERFACES if_interface PARTIALLY IMPLEMENTED.
ENDCLASS.
```
Listing 9.7 Basic Form of a Partially Implemented Interface

9.4.4 Other Sources of Information

This may all seem a bit overwhelming for the uninitiated. It would also require a substantial refactoring effort to reshape legacy code that was not crafted with dependency encapsulation and injection in mind. The purpose of this section was to review some important software patterns that will aid in unit testing. It's not required that you completely understand all the techniques discussed above right away. These are complicated topics that go beyond the scope of this book. The good news is that there are many wonderful sources of information on topics such as dependency injection, software design patterns and *SOLID design principals* online and within other publications. See the *Recommended Reading* section at the end of this chapter for some of those sources.

SOLID Design Principals

S.O.L.I.D. is a mnemonic acronym for the first five object-oriented design (OOD) principles by Robert C. Martin (also known as Uncle Bob).

▶ **S** (Single-Responsibility Principle): A class should have only a single responsibility.

▶ **O** (Open-Closed Principle): Objects or entities should be open for extension, but closed for modification.

▶ **L** (Liskov Substitution Principle): Objects in a program should be replaceable with instances of their subtypes without altering the correctness of that program.

▶ **I** (Interface Segregation Principle): Many client-specific interfaces are better than one general-purpose interface.

▶ **D** (Dependency Inversion Principle): One should depend on abstractions and not upon concretions. Dependency Injection, covered in Section 9.4, is an example of this principle.

▶ See: *http://www.butunclebob.com/ArticleS.UncleBob.PrinciplesOfOod*

9.5   Case Study: Creating a Unit Test in ABAP Unit

Now that you have a basic understanding of how to create unit test classes, let's consider an example. The simple calculator class ZCL_SIMPLE_CALCULATOR in Listing 9.8 contains basic arithmetic operations in the form of methods. Accompanying this class is an ABAP Unit test class named ZLTC_SIMPLE_CALCULATOR_TEST with unit tests to cover one addition and subtraction condition along with testing whether the CX_SY_ZERODIVIDE exception is properly thrown by the divide() method when the divisor parameter is set to zero. The setup() fixture method within the unit test class instantiates and initializes the ZCL_SIMPLE_CALCULATOR object which is then used by each test method. The teardown then performs some clean up once every unit test has executed.

The MethodName_StateUnderTest_ExpectedBehavior naming convention was adopted for each of the unit tests outlined in Listing 9.8 but, as described in Section 9.2.1, other viable strategies have been made available by the development community.

```
* Class Under Test
CLASS zcl_simple_calculator DEFINITION
  PUBLIC
  FINAL
  CREATE PUBLIC.
  PUBLIC SECTION.
    TYPES:
      ty_quotient type p LENGTH 7 DECIMALS 4 .
    METHODS add
      IMPORTING
        iv_first_addend   TYPE int1
        iv_second_addend  TYPE int1
      RETURNING
        VALUE(rv_sum) TYPE int2.
    METHODS subtract
      IMPORTING
        iv_minuend      TYPE int1
        iv_subtrahend   TYPE int1
      RETURNING
        VALUE(rv_difference) TYPE int1.
    METHODS multiply
      IMPORTING
        iv_first_factor   TYPE int1
        iv_second_factor  TYPE int1
      RETURNING
        VALUE(rv_product) TYPE int4.
    METHODS divide
      IMPORTING
        iv_dividend   TYPE int1
        iv_divisor    TYPE int1
      RETURNING
        VALUE(rv_quotient) TYPE ty_quotient
      RAISING
        cx_sy_zerodivide.
ENDCLASS.

CLASS zcl_simple_calculator IMPLEMENTATION.
  METHOD add.
    rv_sum = iv_first_addend + iv_second_addend.
  ENDMETHOD.
  METHOD divide.
    rv_quotient = iv_dividend / iv_divisor.
  ENDMETHOD.
  METHOD multiply.
    rv_product = iv_first_factor * iv_second_factor.
  ENDMETHOD.
  METHOD subtract.
    rv_difference = iv_minuend - iv_subtrahend.
```

```abap
      ENDMETHOD.
ENDCLASS.

* Unit Test Class
CLASS zltc_simple_calculator_test definition FOR TESTING
  DURATION SHORT
  RISK LEVEL HARMLESS.
  PRIVATE SECTION.
    DATA mo_calculator TYPE REF TO zcl_simple_calculator.
    METHODS setup.
    METHODS add_2plus2_sum4 FOR TESTING.
    METHODS subtract_6minus2_dif4 FOR TESTING.
    METHODS divide_zerodivisor_exception FOR TESTING.
    METHODS teardown.
ENDCLASS.

CLASS ZLTC_SIMPLE_CALCULATOR_TEST IMPLEMENTATION.
  METHOD setup.
    CREATE OBJECT mo_calculator.
  ENDMETHOD.

  METHOD add_2plus2_sum4.
    DATA lv_expected      TYPE int2 VALUE 4.
    DATA lv_sum           TYPE int2.
    lv_sum = mo_calculator->add(
      EXPORTING
        iv_first_addend   = 2
        iv_second_addend  = 2 ).
    cl_abap_unit_assert=>assert_equals(
      EXPORTING
        act = lv_sum
        exp = lv_expected
        msg = 'Calculator Addition Test Failed' ).
  ENDMETHOD.

  METHOD subtract_6minus2_dif4.
    DATA lv_expected    TYPE int2 VALUE 4.
    DATA lv_difference  TYPE int2.
    lv_difference = mo_calculator->subtract(
      EXPORTING
        iv_minuend    = 6
        iv_subtrahend = 2 ).
    cl_abap_unit_assert=>assert_equals(
      EXPORTING
        act = lv_difference
        exp = lv_expected
        msg = 'Calculator Subtraction Test Failed' ).
  ENDMETHOD.
```

```
METHOD divide_zerodivisor_exception.
  TRY.
      mo_calculator->divide(
        EXPORTING
          iv_dividend = 5
          iv_divisor  = 0 ).
      cl_abap_unit_assert=>fail(
        msg   = 'CX_SY_ZERODIVIDE was not raised' ).
    CATCH cx_sy_zerodivide.
  ENDTRY.
ENDMETHOD.

METHOD teardown.
  CLEAR mo_calculator.
ENDMETHOD.
ENDCLASS.
```
Listing 9.8 A Simple Unit Test Example

Since CL_ABAP_UNIT_ASSERT has not defined an assertion method to cover exceptions, the divide_zerodivisor_exception() method in the unit test class in Listing 9.8 had to be implemented in an atypical manner. The method wraps a forced exception in a TRY block and sets the unit test to failed (via the fail() method of the CL_ABAP_UNIT_ASSERT class) if the exception is not thrown and caught (which would skip the fail method call entirely and skip to the CATCH statement).

9.6   Executing Unit Tests

After you've created your unit tests in ABAP Unit, you can run them in several different ways. In the following subsections, we will look at options for performing unit tests individually using the ABAP Workbench and in batch via the ABAP Unit Test Browser or Code Inspector Tool.

9.6.1   Integration with the ABAP Workbench

As we stated previously, the ABAP Unit test tool is tightly integrated into the ABAP Workbench. Therefore, it's easy to start test runs using standard menu options. For example, to initiate a test run for the ZLTC_SIMPLE_CALCULATOR_TEST test class defined in Listing 9.8, follow the context menu path of the ZLTC_SIM-PLE_CALCULATOR <OBJECT> • EXECUTE • UNIT TESTS. Upon execution, a window similar to what is seen in Figure 9.2 would display the results of the test run.

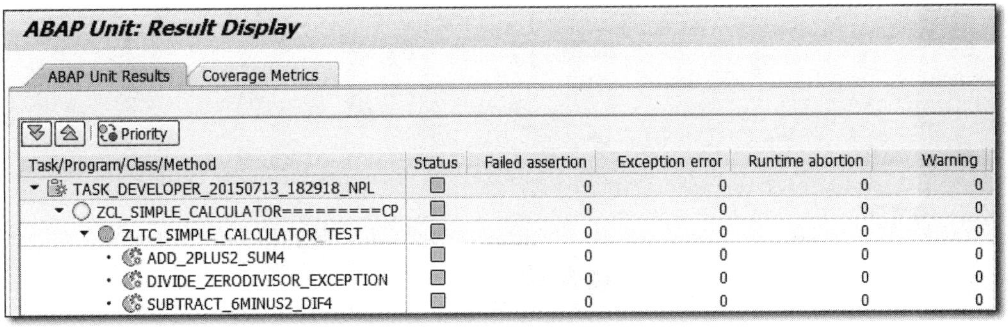

ABAP Unit: Result Display

| ABAP Unit Results | Coverage Metrics |

Task/Program/Class/Method	Status	Failed assertion	Exception error	Runtime abortion	Warning
▼ 📋 TASK_DEVELOPER_20150713_182918_NPL	☐	0	0	0	0
▼ ○ ZCL_SIMPLE_CALCULATOR=========CP	☐	0	0	0	0
▼ ◉ ZLTC_SIMPLE_CALCULATOR_TEST	☐	0	0	0	0
· 🔧 ADD_2PLUS2_SUM4	☐	0	0	0	0
· 🔧 DIVIDE_ZERODIVISOR_EXCEPTION	☐	0	0	0	0
· 🔧 SUBTRACT_6MINUS2_DIF4	☐	0	0	0	0

Figure 9.2 Executing The Simple Calculator Unit Tests

There's no predefined sequence in which the test methods are executed; after all, they are meant to be run independently. If the test(s) succeed, then a success message will appear in the status bar at the bottom of the screen. However, if there are errors in the unit test, then the ABAP Unit interface will be displayed. We'll look at the results of a test run with errors in Section 9.7.

9.6.2 Creating Favorites in the ABAP Unit Test Browser

The ABAP Unit Test Browser is integrated into the ABAP Workbench and, before you will be able to make use of it, you will need to select UTILITIES • SETTINGS… from the main menu path and select the WORKBENCH (GENERAL) tab. On that tab, ensure that the ABAP UNIT TEST BROWSER option is checked under BROWSER SELECTION.

With this browser enabled, unit tests may be grouped together into *favorites* and run as a whole or individually. First select ABAP UNIT BROWSER from the navigation menu on the left and make sure that FAVORITE is the value selected within the CHOOSE SELECTION CRITERIA field. You may now create a new favorite by clicking on the CREATE FAVORITE button and assigning it a name and title (Figure 9.3).

Once the favorite group is created, unit tests may be added by switching to edit mode and clicking on the ADD ELEMENTS button from the top navigation of the right-hand panel. You will be presented with a search screen to locate any objects and their associated unit tests to add to your favorite group. If you wish to control the way these favorites are executed, you may open up the SHOW/EDIT OPTIONS as shown in Figure 9.4. This allows you to restrict unit test runs by the risk level and duration of each test along with potentially displaying code coverage information (see Section 9.7).

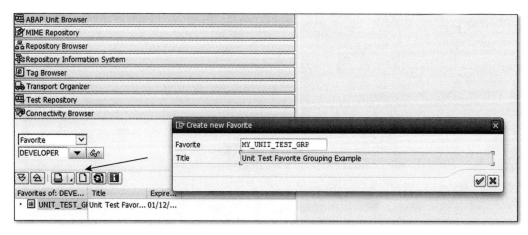

Figure 9.3 Creating A New ABAP Unit Browser Favorite (Group)

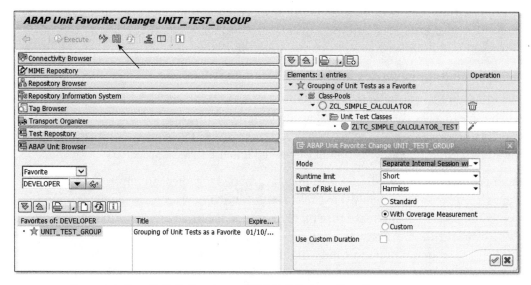

Figure 9.4 Show/Edit Options for an ABAP Unit Browser Favorite

9.6.3   Integration with the Code Inspector

You can also integrate ABAP Unit tests inside the Code Inspector tool (Transaction SCI). This tool is used to perform additional static checks for ABAP Repository objects. Examples of these checks include the verification of naming conventions for variables, the proper use of ABAP statements, and so on. Although the configuration and use of this tool is outside of the scope of this book, it is a very useful tool for implementing additional quality assurance steps in the development cycle. The integration of ABAP Unit inside the Code Inspector allows developers to automate the creation of the deliverables typically required by formal code reviews (i.e., proof of adherence to project coding standards and positive unit test results), speeding up the overall development process.

9.7   Evaluating Unit Test Results

Although unlikely, changes could be made to the ZCL_SIMPLE_CALCULATOR class (Listing 9.8) that would cause a method to return incorrect outcomes. If unit tests were present to cover these outcomes and their expected results, we would see something like Figure 9.5 in the ABAP UNIT RESULTS DISPLAY when executing our unit tests against the simple calculator class.

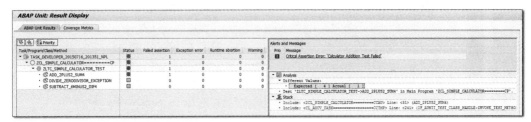

Figure 9.5 When A Unit Test Fails

ABAP Unit would indicate a problem by showing an error status for the failed test. The top-right ALERTS AND MESSAGES panel would also display the severity level and any message (both optional import parameters of methods of the CL_ ABAP_UNIT_ASSERT class) associated with the assertion(s) that failed. All of the unit tests created in this chapter did not pass in a severity level as a parameter so the default of CRITICAL was set. The bottom-right panel displays an analysis of the test with the expected and actual results (in this case) of the assertion(s) along with a stack trace. If the test task had been larger, there could have been more errors generated from other test methods. Therefore, the stack information provided in the bottom-right pane can be very useful in determining where a particular assertion failed. As you would expect, clicking on any line within the stack trace allows the user to dig into the test code to begin diagnosing why a unit test is failing.

Code Coverage

As more unit tests are written to cover specific code paths and outcomes, the degree of the application's code which is being tested by coded unit tests, or *code coverage*, increases. There are tools available that interpret and visualize this coverage which helps identify areas of an application that are lacking in unit tests or may not have any unit test coverage at all. Using this information, a developer is better able to target code for future unit testing development efforts.

One thing to understand about code coverage is that it's *not* an indication of the *quality* of the unit tests covering the application code. There's always the potential that a poorly written unit test gives the illusion that specific lines of code are less prone to software regressions. A unit test could even be created without an assertion and, thus, not test any condition of a unit of code but still contribute to the overall code coverage of that application.

While it would be optimal to achieve 100% code coverage across an application, a focus on writing quality unit tests that address the many outcomes of a unit of code may be more prudent. Since a program can have many more potential outcomes than lines of code, some code may require full coverage many times over. In other words, the goal in writing unit tests should not just be about attaining a specific percent in coverage but should be more about careful consideration of outcomes or results that should be tested when designing software units.

Your tests are just as important as any other code and should promote confidence when faced with a refactoring effort. If your code coverage is high but bugs still make their way to production or you are hesitant to refactor, then your unit test quality is not being held in high enough regard.

ABAP Unit: Result Display

Result Node	Total	Executed	Not Executed	Percentage	On/Off
ZCL_SIMPLE_CALCULATOR=========CP	8	5	3	62.50%	✓
ZCL_SIMPLE_CALCULATOR	8	5	3	62.50%	✓
ADD	2	2	0	100.00%	✓
DIVIDE	2	1	1	50.00%	✓
MULTIPLY	2	0	2	0.00%	✓
SUBTRACT	2	2	0	100.00%	✓

Figure 9.6 Simple Calculator Code Coverage Example

In AS ABAP Release 7.31 and greater, you can visualize code coverage by navigating to the ABAP Workbench (Transaction SE80) and following the context menu path of <OBJECT> • EXECUTE • EXECUTE TESTS WITH • COVERAGE. Under the COVERAGE METRICS tab (see Figure 9.6) you can view the degree of code coverage by branch, procedure and statement along with the option to drill down into code coverage by statement by double clicking on any of the methods of ZCL_SIMPLE_ CALCULATOR class.

9.8   Moving Towards Test-Driven Development

An advanced technique for developing unit tests involves writing a test *before* any new functionality or improvement is crafted. This software design technique is known as *test-driven development* (TDD) and allows for a unit test to "drive" development in small increments. TDD requires a developer to first write a failing unit test targeting a specific outcome in an automated testing environment such as ABAP Unit. When the test is complete the developer proceeds to write the minimal amount of code to make that unit test pass. This process of red (writing a small failing test) to green (writing the minimal functional code to make the test pass) to refactor (improve the design of the code while making sure that all tests continue to pass) is repeated over and over again until a new piece of functionality is complete.

Although the full-blown use of TDD (and indeed the extreme programming methodology from which it came) may be too controversial for your particular development team, the value of quality automated unit tests cannot be underestimated. It's imperative that you define your ABAP Unit tests as quickly as possible so that you can incorporate them into your normal development process. These tests will help keep you on target by providing immediate feedback whenever your individual modules begin to deviate from the terms of their API contracts. Unit tests will also shed light on areas of your design that need some work. For example, if you find that a given module is difficult to test, there's likely something wrong with it.

Finally, unit tests should inspire you with the confidence to take "risks" in your development. For instance, in Chapter 5, we discussed the concept of refactoring to improve the design of some existing code. Without unit testing, you might be hesitant to perform certain refactorings for fear of breaking some unforeseen dependent code. Similarly, you might also be cautious about implementing enhancements for the same reasons. However, with unit tests, you can apply the changes and know immediately whether or not you broke something in the system without having to conduct a full-scale regression test.

9.9   Behavior-Driven Development

The *behavior-driven development* (BDD) software development process is similar to that of test-driven development described above but has a focus on incorporating the domain (or business) experts along with the software developers when developing and writing unit tests. The following is a brief introduction to the topic of BDD. For more detailed information on behavior-driven development, see *Introducing BDD* by Dan North at *http://dannorth.net/introducing-bdd/*.

The goal in BDD is to adopt a more natural language in both unit test method naming and acceptance test definitions so all parties involved in development can understand intent and expected *behavior*. Unit test method names are generally written based on the outcomes that *should* occur (e.g.: `return_new_object_instance()` where the word should is implied or commented in ABAP due to the 30 character length restriction for method names). This naming convention helps in the understanding of what is being tested and the expected results (or what we *should* see as returned data in some cases).

In BDD, the following template is used to define the functional acceptance test scenarios and act as a guide in the creation of unit tests:

▶ Given some initial context (unit test setup),
▶ When an event occurs (calling the code under test),
▶ Then ensure some outcome(s) (a unit test assertion).

The idea here is to allow for mapping (as described above) of these scenario fragments to actual code. This more natural way of describing a test scenario helps *all* parties verify that the unit tests are meeting specifications and facilitates collaborative efforts in software development.

Recommended Reading

▶ ABAP Unit (Release 7.4): *http://help.sap.com*
▶ *Clean Code: A Handbook of Agile Software Craftsmanship* by Robert C. Martin (Prentice Hall, 2009)

▶ *ABAP to the Future* by Paul Hardy (SAP PRESS, 2015).

▶ *Principles of Object Oriented Design*: *http://www.butunclebob.com/ArticleS.Uncle-Bob.PrinciplesOfOod*

▶ *Head First Design Patterns* by Freeman et al. (O'Reilly Media, 2004)

9.10 UML Tutorial: Use Case Diagrams

Even if you haven't spent much time working with the UML before, it's likely that you may have heard the term *use case* used in various contexts at one time or another. Use cases are an important part of the UML standard, though ironically, the UML specification has very little to say about how to go about actually defining one. Instead, it focuses on the use case diagram, which only tells us a very small part of the story.

In *Writing Effective Use Cases*, Alistair Cockburn defines a use case as something that "...captures a contract between the stakeholders of a system about its behavior." In other words, you can think of a use case as a method for capturing the functional requirements of a system or module. A use case is fairly succinct, describing a single interaction scenario between a requesting user or system (referred to as an *actor*) and the system under discussion. Each use case defines a *main success scenario* that defines how an actor can achieve their goal. At each step within the main success scenario, it's highly possible that something might occur to cause the flow of the use case to deviate. These deviation scenarios are referred to as *extensions*. Separating these extension scenarios from the main success scenario makes the use case much easier to read.

Use case development is a collaborative process that requires a lot of communication within a project team. Most of the time, this process is driven heavily by business analysts that may not be familiar with the UML. Therefore, use case scenarios are often best represented in text form. We'll see an example of this form in Section 9.10.2.

9.10.1 Use Case Terminology

Before we proceed with the development of an example use case, it is important to understand some basic terminology. Table 9.6 provides a description of some of the most common terms used in use case parlance.

Term	Description
Actor	A user or system that interacts with the system under discussion. From the perspective of the system under discussion, an actor is defined in terms the role(s) it plays in the system.
Primary Actor	The primary actor is the actor that initiates the use case scenario.
Scope	The scope describes the system under discussion.
Preconditions	Preconditions describe what must be true before the use case can begin. For example, a precondition of a web application might be that the user has been properly authenticated. In this case, the precondition simplifies the prose in the use case scenario since we don't have to include steps to verify that a user is authenticated before executing a given step, etc.
Guarantees	A guarantee describes the invariants maintained by the system throughout a use case scenario. For example, a use case scenario describing a transfer of funds between two accounts in a banking system would have guarantees that ensure that both the source and target account are debited/credited correctly, etc.
Main Success Scenario	The primary scenario of the use case that describes how an actor will reach their goal. You can think of this scenario as the "sunny day" scenario for the use case.
Extension Scenarios	Extension scenarios are scenarios that describe alternative behavior within the main success scenario.

Table 9.6 Some Basic Use Case Terms

9.10.2 An Example Use Case

As we stated previously, there are no hard-and-fast rules for defining use cases. The use case example shown in Table 9.7 highlights some of the more common elements used when defining use case documents.

Use Case: Student Registering for a Training Class Online	
Primary Actor	Student
Scope	Online Course Registration website
Preconditions	Student has logged onto course website

Table 9.7 An Example Use Case Document

Use Case: Student Registering for a Training Class Online	
Main Success Scenario	
1. Student browses the course catalog and selects the course he wants to attend.	
2. Student clicks a button to register for the class.	
3. Student fills in basic contact information (i.e., name, email, etc.).	
4. Student fills in payment information (e.g., credit card, etc.).	
5. Student submits the registration request.	
6. System verifies that seats are available.	
7. System verifies payment information, authorizing the purchase.	
8. System displays success confirmation on the screen.	
9. System sends a follow-up email confirming the registration.	
Extensions	
6a. No seats are available	▸ System displays message indicating class is full ▸ Returns to main success scenario at Step 1.
7a. Payment information is valid	▸ Student can select another form of payment or cancel the process.

Table 9.7 An Example Use Case Document (Cont.)

Ideally, if we've done our job right, the use case in Table 9.7 should be very easy to follow. Here, we've documented a use case for registering for a training class online. Initially, we define the primary actor, the system under discussion, and some basic preconditions for executing the use case. Next, we proceed into the main success scenario, which is defined as a sequence of numbered steps. As you can see, each step is described using action words that are direct and to the point. To keep things succinct, you can reference other use cases by simply underlining a particular bit of action text. This is demonstrated in the first step where we defer a detailed discussion to the course catalog search to a separate use case. The use case in Table 9.7 also contains a couple of extension scenarios. These exception scenarios describe what happens whenever the class is full or if the provided payment details are invalid.

Keep in mind that the example shown in Table 9.7 is just one way of documenting a use case. Generally speaking, a use case is good so long as it accurately describes an interaction with the system. When you read a use case document, you should be able to quickly ascertain the *who*, the *what*, the *when*, the *where*, and the *why* of a particular interaction within the system. When it comes to use case documentation, less is more.

9.10.3 The Use Case Diagram

Figure 9.7 shows an example of a use case diagram for the use case outlined in Table 9.7. As you can see, the graphical notation for use cases in the UML is fairly simple, basically showing the relationships between actors and use cases. The use cases are drawn within a rectangular box that represents the boundaries of the system. Internally, use cases can define *include* relationships to depict their dependencies on other use cases.

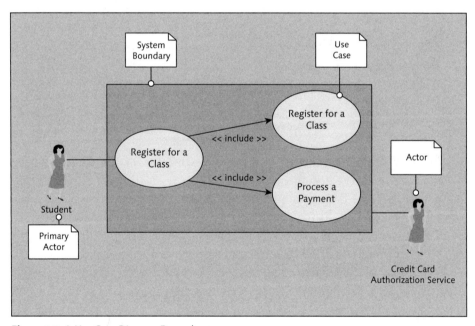

Figure 9.7 A Use Case Diagram Example

In his book *UML Distilled, 3rd Edition*, Martin Fowler suggests that one way to look at use case diagrams is as a type of graphical table of contents for a set of use case documents. For example, the use case diagram in Figure 9.7 shows a high-level overview of the course registration system, its use cases, and the relevant actors interacting with those use cases. For more information about any particular use case, we must consult detailed use case documentation such as that shown in Table 9.7.

9.10.4 Use Cases for Requirements Verification

Use cases are an excellent method for capturing functional requirements. Unfortunately, they are not widely used in SAP projects. Consequently, as an ABAP developer, you might be asking yourself why you should care about use cases. After all, most of the time the documentation of functional requirements falls under the purview of the business analysts working on a project.

Typically, in most waterfall methodologies employed on SAP projects, developers do not enter into the software development process until a functional specification is written. Here, developers are often expected to simply read through the functional specification and start the design process. However, before proceeding too far down this path, the smart developer will want to check back with the business analysts to make sure that their interpretation of the requirements is consistent with the vision of the business analysts so that nothing is lost in the translation of the functional requirements.

Use cases can be a very effective tool for documenting such interpretations. Moreover, by spending just a little bit of extra time documenting use cases, developers can make life much easier for themselves and others by distilling the requirements into a form that's straightforward and easy to interpret. This documentation becomes a vital part of a technical design document, saving future developers from having to try to interpret a complex functional design from scratch.

9.10.5 Use Cases and Testing

Use cases can also come in handy when you are ready to start developing unit or functional tests. Generally speaking, each action step in a main success or extension scenario probably represents a unit of work that should be tested independently. At the very least, it should give you an excellent start for narrowing down your test scenarios. When compared with the alternative of trying to comb through a large functional specification document in search of test scenarios, you can really see where the effort of documenting use cases is justified.

9.11 Summary

Unit tests are the last quality assurance checkpoint a development object must pass through before it is turned over to the wider project community. Consequently, it's important that you get them right so you can deliver quality development objects. The design of automated unit tests using the ABAP Unit testing framework simplifies this endeavor by facilitating the creation of robust test cases that produce repeatable results.

In the next chapter, we will shift gears and begin looking at some of the more typical places where ABAP Objects classes are used in common development efforts within an SAP project.

PART II

Case Studies

One of the great things about the Open SQL interface is that it makes it very easy to incorporate ABAP data objects such as structures and internal tables into routine database operations. Sadly, this ease of use doesn't extend to object instances—at least, not at the ABAP language level. In this chapter though, we'll see that there is an alternative to manual object-relational persistence as we explore the capabilities of the ABAP Object Services framework.

10   ABAP Object Services

For our first hands-on lesson, we'll be exploring the use of an ABAP Objects-based framework that has flown under the radar for many ABAP developers: *ABAP Object Services*. Besides offering developers a pure OO-based approach for implementing persistence, ABAP Object Services also presents us with an opportunity to see how core object-oriented concepts such as inheritance, polymorphism, and designing to interfaces are applied in real-world development frameworks.

As you follow along through this demonstration, we would invite you to spend some time understanding how all the pieces fit together within the ABAP Object Services framework. Even if you don't have any intentions of ever using this framework, simply grasping its main concepts will go a long way toward preparing you for advanced OO designs.

10.1   Introduction

As we learned in Chapter 4, object instances have a relatively short lifespan, existing within an internal program session from the time they're created (using the CREATE OBJECT statement) to the time they're garbage collected. For many types of objects, this sort of transient behavior is precisely what we want. On the other hand, if we're dealing with objects that model business entities, it's very likely

331

that we might want to store the data contained within those objects in the database so that we can retrieve it later on.

Since most ABAP developers are very comfortable working with SQL, it may not seem like a big deal to create a few methods to synchronize object data with a series of relational database tables and vice versa. However, this is definitely one of those areas where the devil is in the details.

In object-oriented circles, this phenomenon is described as the *object-relational impedance mismatch*. Here, the implication is that the relational data model gets in the way (or *impedes*) what we're trying to accomplish using object-oriented designs.

While we can't avoid such complications altogether, we can delegate the more tedious aspects of this exchange to a separate application layer that implements *object-relational mapping* (ORM) on our behalf. This is fundamentally what the ABAP Object Services framework brings to the table. In the sections that follow, we'll see how this framework makes it possible for us to implement persistence requirements without ever writing a single line of SQL.

10.1.1 Understanding Object-Relational Mapping (ORM) Concepts

As the name suggests, ORM tools are designed for one main purpose: to handle the synchronization of data stored in objects with relational database tables. Here, object instances and database rows become equivalent representations of the same data such that operations performed on an object are automatically reflected in the database and vice versa. This relationship is demonstrated in Figure 10.1 for a series of Book objects.

From a development perspective, the advantage of using an ORM tool over performing such translations by hand is that developers don't have to cross over from the OO world into the procedural world of SQL and relational databases. Besides saving time, this technique also makes the code much more flexible and readable.

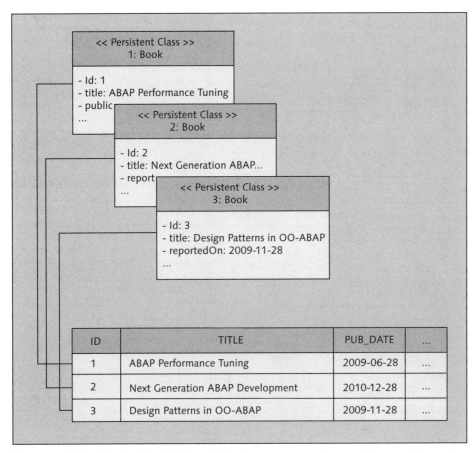

Figure 10.1 Understanding the ORM Translation Process

10.1.2 Services Overview

At this point, we've established that ABAP Object Services is a framework that allows us to implement object-relational persistence. To achieve this requirement, the framework defines three core services:

▶ **Persistence Service**

As you would expect, this service is at the core of the framework, implementing the low-level technical details/plumbing needed to synchronize object instances with relational database tables. We'll learn more about this service in Section 10.2.

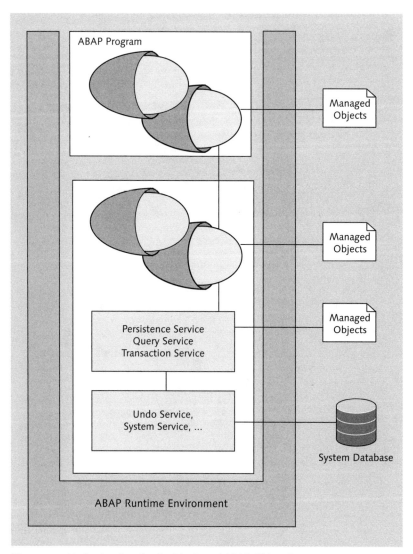

Figure 10.2 Understanding the Positioning of ABAP Object Services

► **Query Service**

The Query Service provides us with an object-oriented API that we can use to search for object instances within the database. Using this service, we can construct complex queries using the same kind of criteria that we would incorporate into a SQL SELECT statement. We'll learn more about these capabilities in Section 10.3.

▶ **Transaction Service**

If you've worked with database transactions and SAP logical units of work (LUWs) before, then you know that it can be very difficult to implement transactional requirements without having to get your hands dirty using a lot of procedural constructs. The Transaction Service allows us to skip over all that and stick with a pure OO approach. We'll see how this works in Section 10.5.

Figure 10.2 illustrates how these core services are positioned from an architectural perspective. Here, we can see how ABAP programs interface with the services layer to synchronize persistent objects with the database. As we progress throughout this chapter, we'll refer back to this diagram periodically to demonstrate how the various framework elements fit together.

10.2 Working with the Persistence Service

Now that you have a sense for how the Persistence Service is positioned from an ABAP development perspective, we're ready to start peeling back the layers to see how to utilize this service from a practical standpoint. Therefore, in this section, we'll see what it takes to create persistent classes and incorporate them into our ABAP programs.

10.2.1 Introducing Persistent Classes

Despite its sophistication, the Persistence Service is not able to store just any old object instance in the database. The reason for this makes sense when you think about it: normal object instances simply don't contain enough details for the Persistence Service to know where to store them, how to map their attributes to table columns, and so on. While different ORM tools go about solving this problem in different ways, SAP's approach was to create a distinct class type that's managed differently from normal ABAP Objects classes inside the Class Builder tool. These classes are referred to as *persistent classes*.

In order to understand the makeup of persistent classes, it's useful to look at one up close. So, with that being said, let's see what it takes to create a persistent class. The steps required here are as follows:

1. To begin, launch the class creation wizard within the ABAP Workbench (Transaction SE80). This will open up the CREATE CLASS dialog box shown in Figure

10.3. Here, we proceed with the creation of a new class as per usual. However, in the CLASS TYPE panel, we need to select the PERSISTENT CLASS radio button as opposed to the default USUAL ABAP CLASS option.

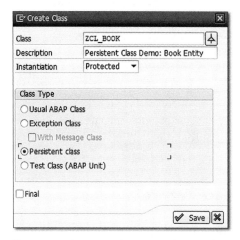

Figure 10.3 Creating a Persistent Class via the ABAP Workbench

2. After the attributes are set in the CREATE CLASS dialog box, we can create the persistent class by clicking on the SAVE button.

3. Once the persistent class is initially created, we'll find that the Class Builder has taken the liberty of automatically implementing the IF_OS_STATE interface within the persistent class. Aside from this pre-built functionality though, the class itself is basically empty until we define a persistence mapping. For now, we'll simply activate the shell class by clicking on the ACTIVATE button.

4. During the activation process, we're presented with the ACTIVATE PERSISTENT CLASSES prompt shown in Figure 10.4. Here, we're asked to choose whether or not we want to activate the persistent class's class actor. For now, simply choose the YES option.

After the dust settles on the persistent class creation process, we can observe that the Class Builder has also taken the liberty of creating a couple of other classes for us. This is demonstrated in Figure 10.5 where, in addition to the ZCL_BOOK persistent class, we also have ZCA_BOOK and ZCB_BOOK. The additional classes define the persistent class's class actor/agent. At runtime, these agent classes run interference between persistent objects and the ABAP Object Services layer (refer back to Figure 10.2 for an illustration of this relationship).

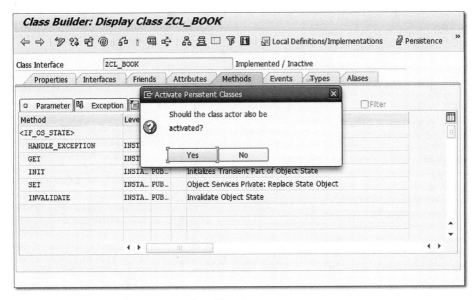

Figure 10.4 Activating the Persistent Class/Class Actor

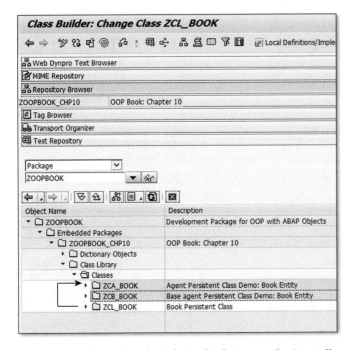

Figure 10.5 Understanding the Relationship between a Persistent Class and its Agent Classes

In just a moment, we'll delve into the mechanics of the class agent/persistent class relationship and see how this plays out in ABAP code. However, before we go there, we should point out another setting that the Class Builder automatically sets for persistent classes: the *instantiation context*. If you look closely at Figure 10.6, you can see that the instantiation context for persistent classes is automatically assigned the Protected value. As we learned in Chapter 4, this means that we cannot instantiate instances of our persistent class directly (e.g. using the CRE- ATE OBJECT statement). Instead, we'll have to work with the class agent to obtain persistent object instances from the ABAP Object Services layer.

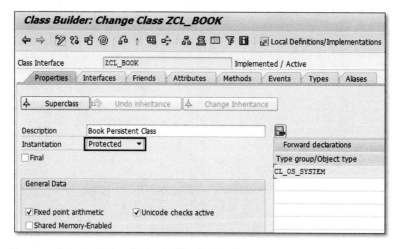

Figure 10.6 Instantiation Context of Persistent Classes

In order to comprehend the relationship between a persistent class and its class agent(s), consider the UML class diagram contained in Figure 10.7. This diagram illustrates the relationship(s) between a persistent class called CL_PERSISTENT and its agent classes: CA_PERSISTENT and CB_PERSISTENT.

As you can see in Figure 10.7, there's actually a little more to the persistent class hierarchy besides the persistent class and its agent classes. Using the UML class diagram as a guide, let's consider some of the more prominent relationships within this hierarchy:

- As we noted earlier, all persistent classes implement the IF_OS_STATE interface. This interface defines callback methods which allow a persistent class to respond to important lifecycle events. For example, the init() method can be used to initialize a persistent object after it's instantiated by the framework.

338

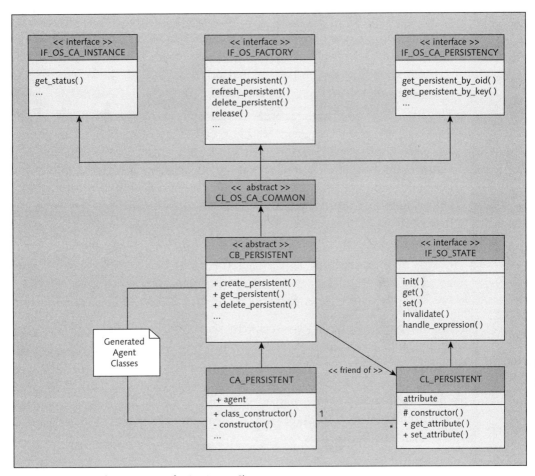

Figure 10.7 UML Class Diagram of a Persistent Class

▶ Next, we have the generated agent classes which are used to manage instances of the persistent class at runtime: CA_PERSISTENT and CB_PERSISTENT. The reason SAP decided to define two agent classes is so that developers would be able to selectively enhance an agent class without disturbing the base-level persistence logic generated by the Class Builder tool. At design time, this plays out as follows:

  ▸ The persistence logic that's generated by the Class Builder tool is written to the abstract CB_PERSISTENT class. This logic is protected against tampering by the Class Builder tool which prevents developers from editing the abstract class.

- ▶ The concrete CA_PERSISTENT class *inherits* the functionality of the abstract CB_PERSISTENT class. From here, we can tweak the agent class further as needed by selectively overriding methods. Such tweaks can be used to improve performance or perhaps expand the scope of the persistence (e.g. to sources other than the system database).

- ▶ The instrumentation methods of the class agent(s) are defined in the IF_OS_CA_INSTANCE, IF_OS_FACTORY, and IF_OS_CA_PERSISTENCY interfaces. These interfaces are implemented by the abstract CL_OS_CA_COMMON class that all agent classes inherit from. This implies that they're available for consumption from within the concrete ZCA_PERSISTENT agent class as shown in Figure 10.7. We'll get to know some of the more prominent methods defined by these interfaces in Section 10.2.3.

- ▶ Whenever the CL_PERSISTENT class was created, the abstract CB_PERSISTENT class is defined implicitly as a friend. This allows the CB_PERSISTENT class to access private attributes/methods of the persistent class as needed at runtime – one of the rare times whenever you see the friend concept applied in practice.

While the complexity of the class hierarchy shown in Figure 10.7 may seem overwhelming at first, rest assured that most of the intricacies of the class relationships are abstracted within the Persistence Service itself. For our part, we need only understand how persistent classes are created in the Class Builder tool and how to use the corresponding class agent to manage instances of them at runtime. We'll see examples of the latter in Section 10.2.3. In the meantime though, let's take a look at how to map persistent classes to database tables using the Class Builder tool.

10.2.2 Mapping Persistent Classes

In order for the Persistence Service to be able to manage persistent objects on our behalf, we need to provide it with some basic information: where we'd like the persistent objects to be stored, how to match up instance attributes with table columns, and so forth. Within the Class Builder, we can specify these mapping details using a tool designed specifically for persistent classes: the *Mapping Assistant*. In this section, we'll learn how to use this tool to define our data models.

Mapping Concepts Overview

In order to understand the mapping concepts used within the Persistence Service, it's helpful to see how such mappings are defined within the system. This approach will offer us some visual insight into how the concepts are applied within the Mapping Assistant tool. So, without further ado, let's start by launching the Mapping Assistant for the ZCL_BOOK entity class introduced in Section 10.2.1. Within the Class Builder tool, this can be achieved by opening the class in edit mode and clicking on the PERSISTENCE button in the editor toolbar (see Figure 10.8).

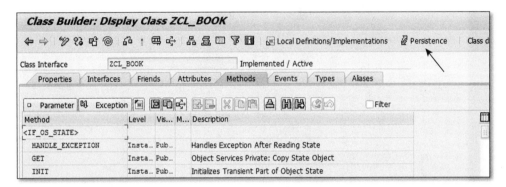

Figure 10.8 Opening the Mapping Assistant Within the Class Builder

This will open up the ADD TABLE/STRUCTURE dialog box shown in Figure 10.9. Within this dialog box, we must select an ABAP Dictionary object that we'll be mapping to. Here, we generally have three different dictionary object types to choose from:

► **Single-Table Mapping**
Most of the time, our objective is to perform a one-to-one mapping between a persistent class and an ABAP Dictionary table or view. So, in these cases, we can simply plug in the target table/view and begin mapping from there.

► **Multiple-Table Mapping**
Occasionally, a persistent class/object might provide an abstraction on top of several related tables. Though we could encapsulate this in a view, the Mapping Assistant also allows us to map multiple tables onto a single persistent class provided that the tables share the exact same primary key. At runtime, the Persistence Service is smart enough to connect the relevant attributes used in the mapping with their associated tables so that the object data is correctly distributed across each of the tables.

► **Structure Mappings**
If the data we're trying to map doesn't fit into one of the other two categories, then the third option would be to model the data the way we want it in an

ABAP Dictionary structure and then base our persistent class mapping off of that. The downside to this approach is that we can't rely on the Persistence Service to take care of persistence since there's no physical table/view to bind to. Instead, we have to write the persistence logic ourselves within the persistent class methods. We'll see an example of this in our book data model a little bit later on.

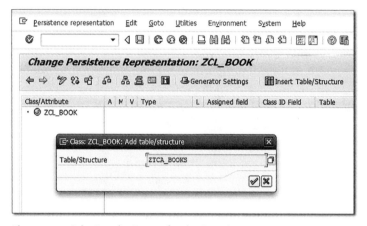

Figure 10.9 Selecting the Source for the Data Mapping

Note

The ABAP Dictionary object(s) that we try to map must exist *before* we leverage them in the Mapping Assistant tool; the Mapping Assistant is not equipped to generate such objects automatically.

Once we select the target dictionary type, the Mapping Assistant tool will be divided into two panels. In the top panel, we have the class/attribute mappings. The bottom panel contains the source dictionary object and its component fields. From here, our objective is simple: we need to figure out how to map component fields from the source dictionary object to persistent class attributes.

Logically, the mapping process starts with the mapping of the source entity's primary key field(s). In order to support the various kinds of data models developers might encounter during this process, SAP supports the three different mapping types described in Table 10.1. These mapping types provide us with the flexibility to tap into pre-existing relational data models, hybrid data models, or even brand new data models that are built from the ground up.

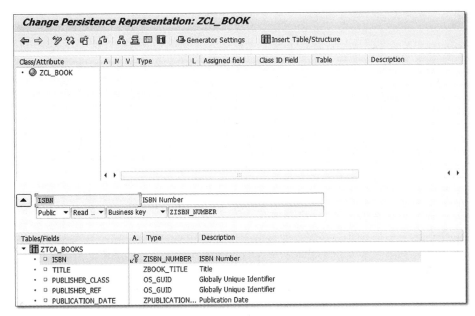

Figure 10.10 Defining the Persistence Mapping for a Simple Entity Type

Mapping Type	Description
By Business Key	This mapping type is normally used whenever we want to map pre-existing ABAP Dictionary tables which use semantic (or natural) primary keys. As the name suggests, a semantic key is a key which makes intuitive sense to the user.
	An example of a business key would be the PARTNER key field defined within the BUT000 business partner master table. The PARTNER field defines the business partner's ID, something that most users would immediately identify as a natural key for business partner records.
	Note that a business key can be comprised of multiple columns. For example, the BUT020 business partner address table has a composite key of PARTNER + ADDRNUMBER, where the ADDRNUMBER field represents the address number linked to the business partner.
By Instance-GUID	This mapping type is typically used whenever we're defining a persistence model from scratch. Here, we may find that it makes sense to define the primary key for certain entity types in terms of a system-generated *globally unique identifier* (or GUID) in situations there's not an obvious business key.

Table 10.1 Persistence Mapping Types

Mapping Type	Description
	For example, imagine that we're creating a data model for a phone directory application. Here, we might define a `Person` entity and a `ContactNumber` entity to model the relationship between a person in the directory and their various contact numbers. In the case of the `ContactNumber` entity, there's no real obvious business key because phone numbers change all the time.
	So, rather than defining an arbitrary sequential ID field that we have to supply using a number range of some kind, the preferred approach is to define a technical GUID using the `OS_GUID` type that will be automatically assigned and managed by the Persistence Service.
By Instance-GUID and Business Key	This mapping type combines both techniques so that we get the best of both worlds. Here, the mapped table has a semantic primary key as well as a non-key field of type `OS_GUID` that is defined as part of a unique secondary index in the table.
	The combination of these keys makes it possible to access persistent object instances by business keys or instance GUIDs depending on the usage scenario. Internally though, the Persistence Service will address such persistent objects using their instance GUIDs.

Table 10.1 Persistence Mapping Types (Cont.)

Once we identify the primary keys, the rest of the attributes usually map pretty easily. Indeed, in the next section, we'll find that the Mapping Assistant is usually smart enough to map these attributes automatically.

Defining Basic Mappings

In order to demonstrate how to map various types of entities using the Mapping Assistant tool, let's consider a database schema that might be defined for an online bookstore application.

> **Note**
>
> This data model is included with the book's source code bundle, so you don't have to recreate the tables in the ABAP Dictionary. Plus, we've included a sample program called `ZOOPBOOK_BOOK_MODEL_LOADER` that can be used to pre-fill the data model with some sample data to test with.

The entity-relationship (E-R) diagram contained in Figure 10.11 highlights some of the primary entities that might exist within this schema. Here, we can observe the following:

▶ The books maintained in the bookstore inventory are contained in the ZTCA_ BOOKS table. This table uses the book's ISBN number as a business key.

▶ Publishers are contained in the ZTCA_PUBLISHERS table. A given publisher may publish many books (but a book can only be published by a single publisher).

▶ Books can have one or more authors. These authors are stored in the ZTCA_ AUTHORS table. Since a particular author may write many books, there's a many-to-many relationship between books and authors. Therefore, our database schema introduces an association table which links the two entities: ZTCA_ BOOKAUTHORS.

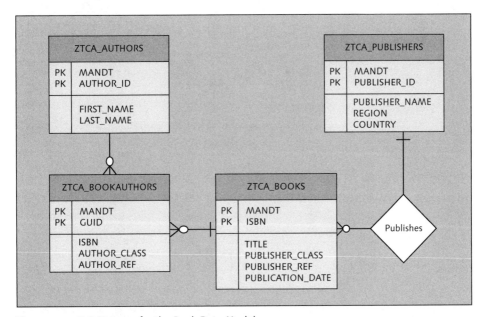

Figure 10.11 E-R Diagram for the Book Data Model

At the end of the day, our goal with ORM is to translate relational data models like the one shown in Figure 10.11 into a persistent class models like the one shown in Figure 10.12. Since we already know how to create persistent classes, our focus in this section will be on entity/attribute mapping.

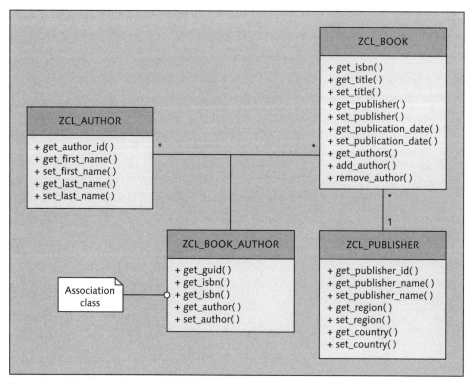

Figure 10.12 Persistent Class Representation of the Book Data Model

As we (briefly) observed in the previous section, persistence mappings are carried out using the Mapping Assistant tool built into the Class Builder. Once we determine the source table/view/structure that we want to map from, we can begin mapping individual attributes by selecting from the list of fields in the lower half of the screen as shown in Figure 10.13. This will load the field into the attribute editor form contained in the middle of the screen. Here, working from left-to-right, top-to-bottom, we can map a field from the source table/structure to a persistent class attribute by specifying the following properties:

▶ **Name**
This property is used to specify the persistent attribute's name.

▶ **Description**
This property contains the attribute's short text description.

346

▶ **Visibility**

Here, we can specify the visibility of the attribute (e.g. PUBLIC, PROTECTED, or PRIVATE).

▶ **Accessibility**

This property can be used to determine if the attribute is changeable from outside the class. If we set this property to read-only, then only a getter method will be exposed in the public interface. Otherwise, both a setter and getter method will be generated.

▶ **Assignment Type**

This property allows us to specify the type of field/attribute being mapped. Table 10.2 describes the different assignment type options in further detail.

▶ **Type**

This property allows us to specify the attribute's type. Though this is normally auto-filled in terms of the source field's type, this property will be used to define complex attributes which map object references.

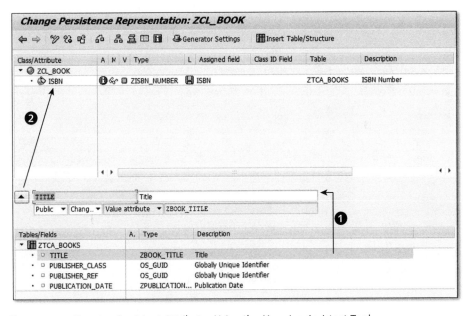

Figure 10.13 Mapping Persistent Attributes Using the Mapping Assistant Tool

Assignment Type	Meaning
Business Key	This assignment type is auto-derived by the Mapping Assistant for the primary key fields of an ABAP Dictionary table that has a semantic primary key. This assignment type cannot be overwritten.
GUID	This assignment type is auto-derived by the Mapping Assistant for the primary key field of an ABAP Dictionary table that uses an instance GUID as its primary key. This assignment type cannot be overwritten.
Class Identifier / Object Reference	These two assignment types are used to uniquely identify an object reference. We'll learn how this works in the next section.
Value Attribute	This is the default assignment type for non-key attributes.

Table 10.2 Persistent Attribute Assignment Types

After we specify an attribute's properties, we can add it to the persistent class definition by clicking on the button with the up arrow icon on it as shown in Figure 10.13. Then, once all of the source table/structure fields are mapped, we can save our changes by clicking on the SAVE button and then click the BACK button to return to the normal Class Builder view.

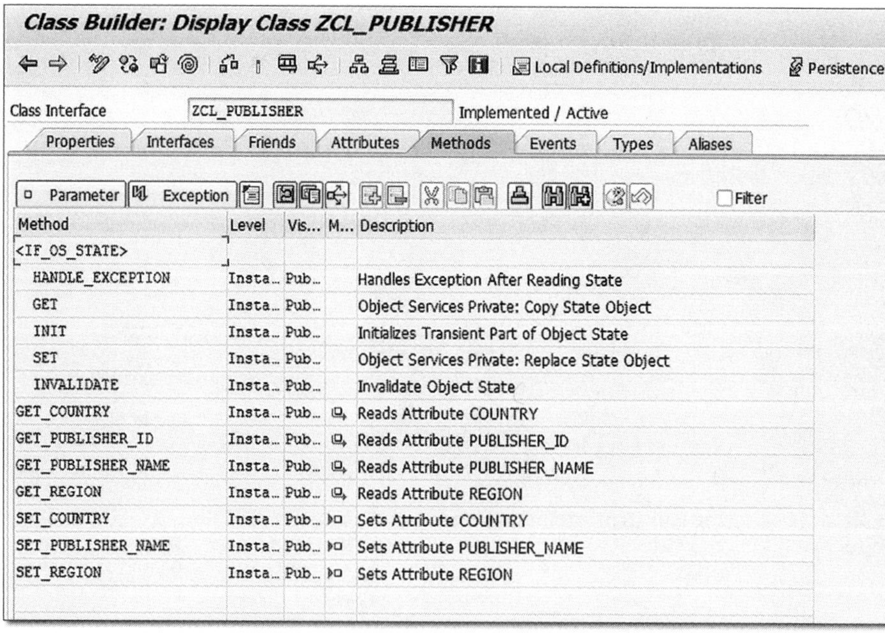

Figure 10.14 Viewing the Generated Methods of a Persistent Class

Figure 10.14 shows the finished product for the ZCL_PUBLISHER class defined in our persistent class model. Here, notice that the public interface of the class has been enhanced to include a number of getter/setter methods which correspond with the mapped persistence attributes. These methods are used at runtime to read/write the attributes as needed.

For simple entities like the ZCL_PUBLISHER entity, we can navigate through the mapping process pretty quickly, accepting all the default values proposed by the Mapping Assistant. However, matters are a bit more complicated for entities that maintain relationships with other entities. In the next section, we'll learn how to model these relationships.

Modeling Simple Entity Relationships

Looking at the persistent class model diagram contained in Figure 10.12, we can see that several of the entities are associated with one another in various ways. For example, the ZCL_BOOK class defines an association to the ZCL_PUBLISHER class in order to model the relationship between a book and its publisher. Similarly, the association between the ZCL_BOOK and ZCL_AUTHOR entities allows us to model the relationship between a book and its authors (and also an author and the books they write).

What's the significance of all this from an ORM perspective? Well, if we remember that our goal is to build a pure OO-based data model, then we need to figure out a way for consumers of our data model to navigate these relationships without having to write a lot of procedural SQL code. Indeed, in an ideal world, we'd like for users to be able to traverse these relationships using method calls. Though we could certainly build out such methods by hand, it turns out that the Mapping Assistant is able to generate this logic automatically in most cases.

To demonstrate how this works, let's take a closer look at the mapping of the ZCL_BOOK class. As you can see in Figure 10.15, the ISBN primary key field and the TITLE/ PUBLICATION_DATE value fields map pretty cleanly. This leaves us with the PUBLISHER_CLASS and PUBLISHER_REF fields, both of which are defined using the OS_GUID data type in the ZTCA_BOOKS table. Collectively, the PUBLISHER_CLASS and PUBLISHER_REF fields are meant to uniquely identify an instance of the ZCL_PUB-LISHER entity. Here, the PUBLISHER_CLASS field is used to store an identifier for the target persistent class (i.e. ZCL_PUBLISHER) and the PUBLISHER_REF field is used to store the primary key of the target publisher record.

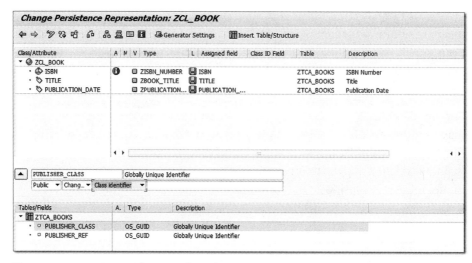

Figure 10.15 Mapping an Object Attribute (Part 1)

To merge these fields into a single persistence attribute, all we have to do is map both fields using the same attribute name (e.g. PUBLISHER). This approach is demonstrated in Figure 10.16 and Figure 10.17, respectively.

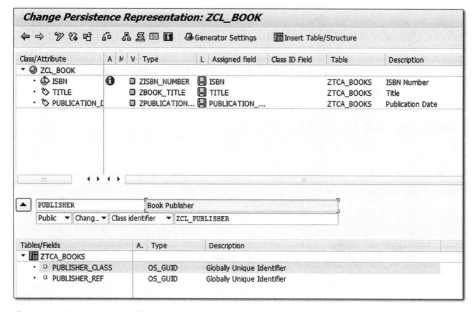

Figure 10.16 Mapping an Object Attribute (Part 2)

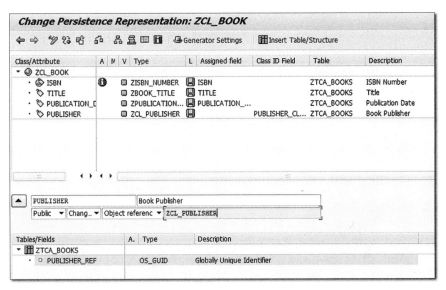

Figure 10.17 Mapping an Object Attribute (Part 3)

As you can see, we've mapped both fields to a persistent attribute called PUB-LISHER and set the attribute's type as ZCL_PUBLISHER. After the persistent class is regenerated, we can see that the getter/setter methods for this attribute are defined in terms of the persistent class type (see Figure 10.18).

Figure 10.18 Mapping an Object Attribute (Part 4)

Defining the PUBLISHER attribute this way means that we can bind an instance of the ZCL_PUBLISHER class by simply passing that instance as a parameter to the ZCL_BOOK class's set_publisher() method. Similarly, we can use the get_pub-lisher() method to lookup a book's publisher and then use the getter methods of the ZCL_PUBLISHER class to find out more about that particular publisher. To the consumer of our persistent data model, all this is achieved using OO programming techniques as per usual.

In Section 10.4, we'll take a look at some entity relationship types which are too complex for the Mapping Assistant to handle on its own. In the meantime, we need to spend some time learning how to interface with persistent objects from an API perspective.

10.2.3 Working with Persistent Objects

Having seen how persistent classes are designed and configured in the previous sections, let's now switch gears and see how we can get our hands dirty with persistent objects from a consumer perspective. Here, we'll demonstrate how to use the class agent API to perform basic CRUD (*Create*, *Read*, *Update*, and *Delete*) operations against persistent objects.

Understanding the Class Agent API

As we noted in Section 10.2.1, the instantiation context for persistent classes is set as Protected. This means that clients can't directly create instances of persistent classes using the familiar CREATE OBJECT statement. Instead, clients have to go through the persistent class's class agent in order to obtain these instances. From a client's perspective, this layer of indirection raises a couple of questions:

1. How can clients get their hands on a persistent class's class agent?
2. Once a client gets its hands on a class agent reference, how is the class agent used to interact with persistent objects?

The answer to the first question is fairly straightforward. Looking closely at the UML class diagram contained in Figure 10.7, we can see that a persistent class's agent class (e.g. CA_PERSISTENT) defines a public class attribute called AGENT which exposes this reference. This is to say that class agents are defined as *singletons*.

With the class agent instance in hand, clients can begin interfacing with persistent objects using the public instance methods of the agent class. For the most part, we think you'll find that the names of these methods are fairly intuitive. For example, if we want to create an instance of a persistent class, we use the create_persistent() method. Similarly, we can use the get_persistent() and delete_persistent() methods to fetch and delete said instances after they're created.

The complete set of methods provided by the class agent include methods defined by the core Persistence Service interfaces (e.g. IF_OS_FACTORY, IF_OS_CA_ SERVICE, IF_OS_CA_PERSISTENCY, and IF_OS_CA_INSTANCE) as well as agent-specific methods which are generated by the Mapping Assistant tool based on the persistent class mapping definitions. We'll explore some of the more prominent methods available here in the upcoming sections. A complete list of methods and their usage scenarios is provided in the SAP NetWeaver Library documentation available online at *http://help.sap.com* in the section entitled *Components of the Persistence Service*.

Creating Persistent Object Instances

Knowing what you now know about the relationship between a persistent object and its class agent, let's see how we can use the class agent to create a persistent object instance. Here, rather than speaking in general terms, we'll look at what it takes to create an author instance in our fictitious bookstore data model. As you can see in the code excerpt contained in Listing 10.1, this operation is accomplished using the create_persistent() method that's generated for the author's class agent (i.e. class ZCA_AGENT).

```
DATA lo_author TYPE REF TO zcl_author.
DATA lx_os_ex TYPE REF TO cx_os_object_existing.

TRY.
  lo_author =
    zca_author=>agent->create_persistent(
      i_first_name = 'Paige'
      i_last_name = 'Wood' ).
  COMMIT WORK.
CATCH cx_os_object_existing INTO lx_os_ex.
  "TODO: Error handling goes here...
ENDTRY.
```

Listing 10.1 Creating a Persistent Object Using the Class Agent API

Looking closely at the code excerpt contained in Listing 10.1, you can see that we were actually able to pass in all of the author details in one go via the call to create_persistent(). One notable omission in this parameter list is the key of the author entity (i.e. the AUTHOR_ID field). Since the ZCL_AUTHOR class is mapped using the "By Instance-GUID" mapping type, the Persistence Service will take care of allocating this key on our behalf behind the scenes. The other parameters are optional and are merely provided as a matter of convenience. If we wanted to, we could also omit the first/last name parameters and fill in the attributes after the fact using the appropriate setter methods of the ZCL_AUTHOR class.

Enhancing the Signature of Persistent Object Creation Methods

Looking at the call to create_persistent() in Listing 10.1, you might be wondering where the I_FIRST_NAME and I_LAST_NAME parameters came from. These parameters are created behind the scenes by the Mapping Assistant as it goes through the process of generating the persistent class's agent class methods.

You can control this behavior within the Mapping Assistant tool by clicking on the GENERATOR SETTINGS button and toggling the MINIMUM INTERFACE FOR METHODS CREATE_PERSISTENT AND CREATE_TRANSIENT checkbox field as shown in Figure 10.19. By turning this checkbox off for the ZCL_AUTHOR class, we've effectively given the Mapping Assistant the green light to enhance the signature of the create_persistent() method to include the optional I_FIRST_NAME and I_LAST_NAME parameters. Alternatively, if we turn the checkbox on, the method signature will be stripped down to just the essentials (e.g. the primary key in the case of business key mappings).

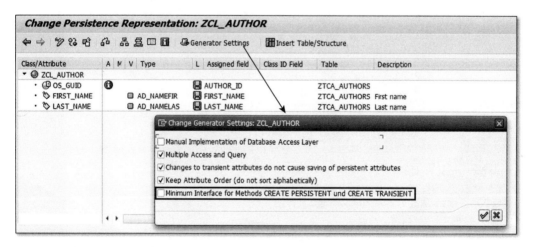

Figure 10.19 Configuring the Signature of the CREATE_PERSISTENT( ) Method

After the call to create_persistent(), a persistent object instance will be created as expected, but at this point, it exist only in memory. In order to persist the record, we must follow this method call with the familiar COMMIT WORK statement. This will cause the Persistence Service to convert the in-memory record into a record in the ZTCA_AUTHORS table as shown in Figure 10.20.

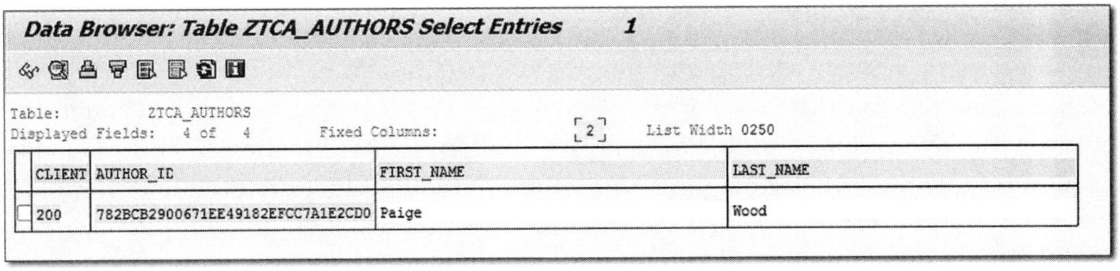
Data Browser: Table ZTCA_AUTHORS Select Entries 1
Table: ZTCA_AUTHORS
Displayed Fields: 4 of 4
Fixed Columns: 2
List Width 0250
CLIENT
AUTHOR_ID
FIRST_NAME
LAST_NAME
200
782BCB2900671EE49182EFCC7A1E2CD0
Paige
Wood

Figure 10.20 Viewing the Persistent Object Instance in the Database

Reading Persistent Object Instances

If a persistent class is defined using the "By Business Key" mapping type, then we can use the generated `get_persistent()` method to fetch persistent object instances of that class from the database. Listing 10.2 demonstrate this approach for the `ZCL_BOOK` persistent class. Here, you can see how we're looking up a book by its ISBN number. Once we have an instance of the persistent object in hand, we can query its attributes using the getter methods created by the Mapping Assistant (e.g. the `get_title()` method demonstrated in Listing 10.2).

```
DATA lo_book TYPE REF TO zcl_book.
DATA lv_title TYPE zbook_title.
DATA lx_obj_not_found TYPE REF TO cx_os_object_not_found.

TRY.
  lo_book =
    zca_book=>agent->get_persistent( '9781592294169' ).
  lv_title = lo_book->get_title( ).
  WRITE: / 'Title is:', lv_title.
CATCH cx_os_object_not_found INTO lx_obj_not_found.
  "TODO: Exception handling goes here...
ENDTRY.
```

Listing 10.2 Reading Persistent Objects Using the Class Agent API

As you browse through the sample code contained in Listing 10.2, you might be wondering how to read object instances whose persistent classes don't use the "By Business Key" mapping type. Since it's very unlikely that you would happen to know the GUID of such objects, lookups using a method like `get_persistent()` don't really make sense. Instead, the normal use case is to fetch such objects using a query of some kind. We'll learn how to implement such queries in Section 10.3.

Updating Persistent Objects

As we've noted throughout this section, persistent object instances are obtained indirectly via the class agent of the corresponding persistent class. Though this indirection may seem like a nuisance at first, there is a major benefit to this approach: by brokering all object instance requests through the class agent, SAP ensures that any time we get our hands on a persistent object, it's a live instance that's ready to be manipulated. In other words, if we want to update a persistent object, all we have to do is load the instance and start calling its setter methods.

This approach is demonstrated in the code excerpt contained in Listing 10.3. In this example, we're updating a book record's publisher reference by calling the set_publisher() method defined in the ZCL_BOOK persistent class. Here, notice how we're passing an instance of the ZCL_PUBLISHER class to set_publisher(). Internally, the Persistence Service will unpack this request and apply the results to the PUBLISHER_CLASS and PUBLISHER_REF fields of table ZTCA_BOOKS.

```abap
DATA lo_publisher TYPE REF TO zcl_publisher.
DATA lo_book TYPE REF TO zcl_book.
DATA lx_os_ex TYPE REF TO cx_os_object_existing.
DATA lx_obj_not_found TYPE REF TO cx_os_object_not_found.

TRY.
  lo_publisher =
    zca_publisher=>agent->create_persistent( ).
  lo_publisher->set_publisher_name( 'SAP Press' ).
  lo_publisher->set_region( 'MA' ).
  lo_publisher->set_country( 'US' ).

  lo_book =
    zca_book=>agent->get_persistent( '9781592294169' ).
  lo_book->set_publisher( lo_publisher ).

  COMMIT WORK.
CATCH cx_os_object_existing INTO lx_os_ex.
  "TODO: Error Handling goes here...
CATCH cx_os_object_not_found INTO lx_obj_not_found.
  "TODO: Error Handling goes here...
ENDTRY.
```

Listing 10.3 Updating Persistent Objects Using the Class Agent API

Looking closely at the code excerpt contained in Listing 10.3, you can see that we're once again issuing the COMMIT WORK statement to commit our changes to the database. Without this statement, all of the updates applied via the setter method calls would be lost.

Deleting Persistent Objects

In order to delete a persistent object instance, we must call the `delete_per-sistent()` method defined in the `IF_OS_FACTORY` interface that's implemented by a persistent class's class agent. This method is demonstrated in Listing 10.4. Here, we simply lookup the target persistent object and pass it to the `delete_per-sistent()` method. Then, as is the case for any permanent change, we issue the `COMMIT WORK` statement to commit the changes.

```
DATA lo_book TYPE REF TO zcl_book.
DATA lx_os_ex TYPE REF TO cx_os_object_existing.
DATA lx_obj_not_found TYPE REF TO cx_os_object_not_found.

TRY.
  lo_book =
    zca_book=>agent->get_persistent( '9781592294169' ).
  zca_book=>agent->if_os_factory~delete_persistent( lo_book ).
  COMMIT WORK.
CATCH cx_os_object_existing INTO lx_os_ex.
  "TODO: Error Handling goes here...
CATCH cx_os_object_not_found INTO lx_obj_not_found.
  "TODO: Error Handling goes here...
ENDTRY.
```
Listing 10.4 Deleting Persistent Objects Using the Class Agent API

10.3 Querying Persistent Objects with the Query Service

In the previous section, we learned how the class agent API allows us to perform basic CRUD operations on individual persistent objects. However, you may have noticed that the API isn't necessarily optimized for bulk operations. For example, what if we want to apply updates to all books that were published on or before a given date? Or, what if we don't happen to know the primary key of an object instance?

In the SQL world, these types of queries are executed using the familiar `SELECT` statement. Here, we can build various logical expressions using the `WHERE` clause to refine the selection and pull back the records we want to work with. Within the context of ABAP Object Services, such queries are built and executed via the

Query Service. In this section, we'll take a look at how this service can be used to fetch persistent object instances.

10.3.1 Technical Overview

From a client's perspective, the Query Service API is fairly concise, consisting of two main interfaces: IF_OS_QUERY_MANAGER and IF_OS_QUERY, respectively. The relationships between these interfaces and the CL_OS_SYSTEM class that grants us access to the Query Service are illustrated in the UML class diagram contained in Figure 10.21.

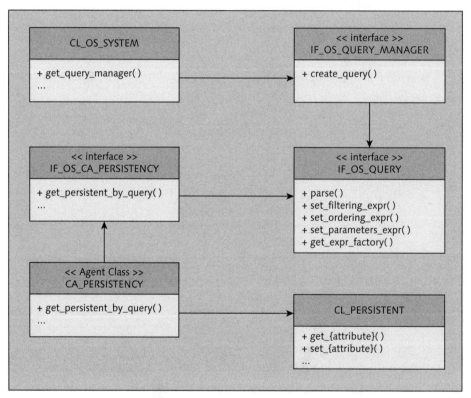

Figure 10.21 UML Class Diagram for Query Service API

Following the class diagram contained in Figure 10.21, we can see that basic call sequence for interfacing with the Query Service is as follows:

1. First, we call the static `get_query_manager()` method of class `CL_OS_SYSTEM` to obtain an object reference that implements the `IF_OS_QUERY_MANAGER` interface.

2. Next, we use the query manager instance to create a query by calling the `create_query()` method of the `IF_OS_QUERY_MANAGER` interface. Here, several optional parameters are provided to pre-define the query up front. We can choose to specify the query details here or at a later step using the instance methods defined by the `IF_OS_QUERY` interface.

3. Once the query object is created, we can use it to lookup persistent objects by calling the generic `get_persistent_by_query()` method that the target persistent class's class actor inherits from the `IF_OS_CA_PERSISTENCY` interface. This method will return a table containing all the persistent object references found by the query.

4. Finally, we can manipulate the objects returned by the query just as we would any normal persistent object using the class agent API.

For the most part, queries really are that simple. Of course, formulating the query conditions themselves can be a little tricky. Therefore, in the next section, we'll spend some time looking at how to build query expressions.

10.3.2 Building Query Expressions

To a large extent, query expressions within the Query Service are constructed in much the same way that we would construct the `WHERE` clause in an SQL `SELECT` statement. Indeed, as you can see in Table 10.3, most of the operators used to build query expressions are identical to the ones we have available via Open SQL. These standard operators are then supplemented with some Query Service-specific operators used to evaluate persistent object relationships.

Operator / Expression	Description
Relational Operators (=, <>, <, <=, >, >=)	As is the case with Open SQL, we can use the familiar SQL relational operators to build logical expressions, etc. Examples: `name = 'Xander'` `count >= 100`

Table 10.3 Elements Used to Build Filter Conditions in the Query Service

359

Operator / Expression	Description

Pattern Searches	This type of expression can be used to implement fuzzy search logic based on text patterns.
	Examples:
	`fname LIKE 'And%'`
	`lname NOT LIKE '%Wood%'`

Logical Operators
(AND, OR, NOT)
	These logical operators can be used to build complex expressions based on Boolean logic conditions.
	Example:
	`fname = 'Paige' AND`
	`lname = 'Wood'`

Null Checks IS [NOT] NULL	Whenever we're dealing with complex relationships between persistent classes, the `IS NULL` expression can be used to build join expressions based on the presence (or absence) of object references. Example: `Publisher IS NULL`
Object Reference Equality EQUALSREF	The `EQUALSREF` operator can be used to compare object references in much the same way that the equality (=) operator is used to evaluate the equality of elementary types. Here, the operand on the left-hand side of the expression is the object reference attribute in the target persistent class, and the operand on the right-hand side of the expression is an object reference that we want to compare against. Example: `publisher EQUALSREF par1`

Table 10.3 Elements Used to Build Filter Conditions in the Query Service (Cont.)

Collectively, the operators/expressions described in Table 10.3 are used to build one long filter condition string that we pass into the `create_query()` method of the `IF_OS_QUERY_MANAGER` interface. This approach is demonstrated in the code excerpt contained in Listing 10.5. Here, we're looking for any book records where the title contains the term "ABAP" and the publication date is greater than or equal to January 1st, 2010. If we wanted to be even more specific, we could continue expanding the `lv_filter` string to include the appropriate filter conditions, but you get the idea.

```
DATA: lo_query_mgr TYPE REF TO if_os_query_manager,
      lv_filter TYPE string,
      lo_query TYPE REF TO if_os_query,
      lo_agent TYPE REF TO if_os_ca_persistency,
      lt_books TYPE osreftab,
      lo_record TYPE REF TO object,
      lo_book TYPE REF TO zcl_book,
      lv_title TYPE string.

lo_query_mgr = cl_os_system->get_query_manager( ).
lv_filter =
  |PUBLICATION_DATE >= '20100101' AND TITLE LIKE '%ABAP%'|.
lo_query =
  lo_query_mgr->create_query(
    i_filter = lv_filter ).

lo_agent = zca_book=>agent.
lt_books =
  lo_agent->get_persistent_by_query( i_query = lo_query ).

LOOP AT lt_books INTO lo_record.
  lo_book ?= lo_record.
  lv_title = lo_book->get_title( ).
  WRITE: / lv_title.
ENDLOOP.
```
Listing 10.5 Working with the Query Service

As you can see in Listing 10.5, the result set returned from the get_persistent_
by_query() method is a generic object table of type OSREFTAB. In order to access
the persistent objects contained within, we must downcast the generic OBJECT
references into the appropriate persistent class type using the familiar ?= operator. Once we perform the downcast, it's business as usual from a Persistence Ser-
vice/Class Agent API perspective.

Besides specifying filter conditions in a query, the Query Service also allows us to
define sorting criteria for the result set that's returned to us. Here, we can sort the
results table by attributes in much the same way that we would specify an ORDER
BY clause in an SQL SELECT statement. For example, in Listing 10.6, you can see
how we re-worked our book query to sort the results by the PUBLICATION_DATE
attribute in ascending order.

```
DATA: lo_query_mgr TYPE REF TO if_os_query_manager,
      lv_filter TYPE string,
      lv_sort TYPE string,
      ...
```

```
lo_query_mgr = cl_os_system=>get_query_manager( ).
lv_filter =
  |PUBLICATION_DATE >= '20100101' AND TITLE LIKE '%ABAP%'|.
lv_sort = |PUBLICATION_DATE ASCENDING|.
lo_query =
  lo_query_mgr->create_query(
    i_filter = lv_filter
    i_ordering = lv_sort ).
...
```

Listing 10.6 Specifying Sort Conditions in a Query

Hopefully this section has provided you with a basic understanding of how to construct and execute queries using the Query Service. Realistically, there are so many features provided with this service that we can't reasonably cover them all in a book like this. However, if you're interested in finding more information about the capabilities of the Query Service, please check out the ABAP Object Services documentation available online in the SAP Help Portal for your particular SAP NetWeaver release.

10.4 Modeling Complex Entity Relationships

In Section 10.2.2, we observed how easy it is to model simple 1-to-1 relationships like a book-to-publisher relationship using the Mapping Assistant tool. However, you might be wondering how we deal with more complex relationships such as the 1-to-many relationship between a book and its contributing authors or the relationship between a publisher and the books they publish. Rest assured that it's definitely possible to model such relationships in persistent classes; we just have to work at it a bit more. This section will show you what's involved from a development perspective.

10.4.1 Performing Reverse Lookups

As our first case study, let's see what it would take to produce a list of books published by a particular publisher. In this scenario, our challenge lies in the fact that publisher entities don't maintain foreign keys to the books they publish. Therefore, we can't define the relationship within the ZCL_PUBLISHER class using the graphical Mapping Assistant tool.

The alternative is to utilize the Query Service to perform a reverse lookup for book objects whose publisher matches the publisher object driving the selection. This approach is demonstrated in the LIST_BOOKS() method that we defined in the ZCL_PUBLISHER class. As you can see in Listing 10.7, this custom method is designed to return a table of ZCL_BOOK objects where the publisher matches the driving ZCL_PUBLISHER instance. Here, we're using the EQUALSREF operator to define the relationship. Behind the scenes, the Query Service will unpack the source/target object references and use a SQL query to match up the keys.

```
CLASS zcl_publisher...
method LIST_BOOKS. "RETURNING VALUE(rt_books) TYPE zttca_books
  DATA: lo_query_mgr TYPE REF TO if_os_query_manager,
        lo_query TYPE REF TO if_os_query,
        lo_book_agent TYPE REF TO if_os_ca_persistency,
        lv_filter TYPE string,
        lt_parameters TYPE osdreftab,
        ls_parameter LIKE LINE OF lt_parameters,
        lt_results TYPE osreftab,
        lo_result TYPE REF TO object,
        lo_book TYPE REF TO zcl_book.

  "Perform a query to find all books matching this
  "publisher instance:
  lo_query_mgr = cl_os_system=>get_query_manager( ).
  lo_book_agent = zca_book=>agent.

  lv_filter = |publisher EQUALSREF par1|.

  lo_query =
    lo_query_mgr->create_query( i_filter = lv_filter ).

  GET REFERENCE OF me INTO ls_parameter.
  APPEND ls_parameter TO lt_parameters.

  lt_results =
    lo_book_agent->get_persistent_by_query(
      i_query = lo_query
      i_parameter_tab = lt_parameters ).

  "Copy over the results:
  LOOP AT lt_results INTO lo_result.
    lo_book ?= lo_result.
    APPEND lo_book TO rt_books.
  ENDLOOP.
endmethod.
ENDCLASS.
```

Listing 10.7 Performing a Reverse Lookup Using the Query Service

As you can see in Listing 10.7, the code contained within the LIST_BOOKS() method is rather unremarkable. The important thing to note though is that we can enhance persistent classes with helper methods where needed. And, with the Query Service, we don't necessarily have to write SQL to traverse these complex relationships. Oftentimes, we can write a simple query and connect the dots from there.

10.4.2 Navigating N-to-M Relationships

Looking back at the E-R diagram for our fictitious book data model in Figure 10.11, you can see that in order to model the complex many-to-many relationship between books and the authors that write them, we had to introduce an association table called ZTCA_BOOKAUTHORS. This table is basically a cross-reference table whose sole purpose is to link books with authors.

In the relational paradigm, we can use association tables like ZTCA_BOOKAUTHORS as the glue for a SQL JOIN statement that links book records with their corresponding author records. To achieve the same results in an object-based model, we employ to use the tried-and-true composition technique.

This starts with the creation of a persistence mapping on top of the ZTCA_BOOKAU-THORS table. As you can see in Figure 10.22, this table is mapped to the ZCL_BOOK_AUTHOR class using the GUID assignment type with two value attributes: ISBN to link the mapped book and AUTHOR to link to the mapped author instance.

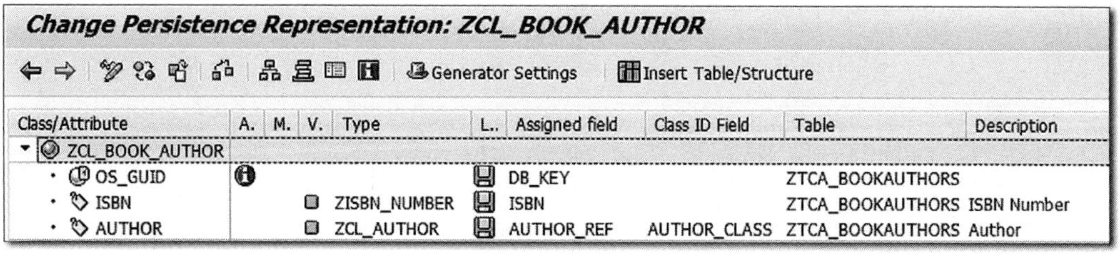

Class/Attribute	A.	M.	V.	Type	L..	Assigned field	Class ID Field	Table	Description
▾ ZCL_BOOK_AUTHOR									
· OS_GUID						DB_KEY		ZTCA_BOOKAUTHORS	
· ISBN				ZISBN_NUMBER		ISBN		ZTCA_BOOKAUTHORS	ISBN Number
· AUTHOR				ZCL_AUTHOR		AUTHOR_REF	AUTHOR_CLASS	ZTCA_BOOKAUTHORS	Author

Change Persistence Representation: ZCL_BOOK_AUTHOR

Generator Settings   Insert Table/Structure

Figure 10.22 Defining the Persistence Mapping for ZTCA_BOOKAUTHORS

With the ZCL_BOOK_AUTHOR persistent class in place, we can begin linking books to authors using the ZCL_BOOK_AUTHOR class's agent. Though this works in principle, it's not exactly what we want from an API perspective. Ideally, we want to be able to add/remove/display the authors associated with a particular book directly via the book instance. For instance, when defining a new book, it would be convenient to call a method like `add_author()` to create the linkage since this is more intuitive to the client than having to go through a (technical) construct like the `ZCL_BOOK_AUTHOR` association class. Indeed, in an ideal world, the details of this association would be encapsulated from the outside world (e.g. via package interfaces). The desired end result is illustrated in the enhanced class diagram for the `ZCL_BOOK` class contained in Figure 10.23.

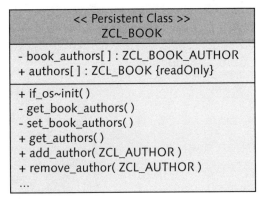

<< Persistent Class >> ZCL_BOOK
- book_authors[ ] : ZCL_BOOK_AUTHOR + authors[ ] : ZCL_BOOK {readOnly}
+ if_os~init( ) - get_book_authors( ) - set_book_authors( ) + get_authors( ) + add_author(ZCL_AUTHOR) + remove_author(ZCL_AUTHOR) ...

Figure 10.23 Enhanced Class Diagram for the ZCL_BOOK Persistent Class

With the UML class diagram contained in Figure 10.23 as our guide, let's walk through the elements we need/want to add to the `ZCL_BOOK` class in order to directly access the book-to-author relationship from book instances:

1. First, you can see how we've defined two instance attributes called `BOOK_AUTHORS` and `AUTHORS` which contain `ZCL_BOOK_AUTHOR` and `ZCL_AUTHOR` objects, respectively. These internal table attributes are used to keep track of author assignments within a `ZCL_BOOK` instance. Here, note that the `BOOK_AUTHORS` attribute (and corresponding getter/setter methods) as not exposed as part of the `ZCL_BOOK` class's public interface. Again, our goal is to shield clients from the intricacies of this complex relationship, so it makes good sense to hide it in the private section of the class.

2. In order to pre-fill the `BOOK_AUTHORS` and `AUTHORS` attributes such that a `ZCL_BOOK` instance is always consistent, we need to override the `init()` method that's inherited from the `IF_OS_STATE` interface. In just a moment, we'll see how to use the Query Service to fetch these instances at runtime.

3. Lastly, we have the `add_author()` and `remove_author()` methods which are used to add and remove contributing authors from a book record, respectively.

Listing 10.8 shows how we're initializing the `BOOK_AUTHORS` and `AUTHORS` instance attributes in the `ZCL_BOOK` class using the `if_os_state~init()`method. Since the Persistence Service calls this method immediately after loading the attributes of the book persistent object, it represents the ideal place to pre-fill the authors who collaborated on the book. From an implementation perspective, all we really have to do here is use the Query Service to lookup `ZCL_BOOK_AUTHOR` instances matching the book's `ISBN` attribute and store any found object references internally in the `BOOK_AUTHORS` and `AUTHORS` instance attributes. Once this operation is complete, our book instance is fully loaded and ready for business.

```
method IF_OS_STATE~INIT.
  DATA: lo_query_mgr TYPE REF TO if_os_query_manager,
        lo_query TYPE REF TO if_os_query,
        lo_agent TYPE REF TO if_os_ca_persistency,
        lt_book_authors TYPE osreftab,
        lo_result TYPE REF TO object,
        lo_book_author TYPE REF TO zcl_book_author,
        lo_author TYPE REF TO zcl_author.

  "Run a query to find all of the matching book authors:
  lo_query_mgr = cl_os_system=>get_query_manager( ).
  lo_query =
    lo_query_mgr->create_query( i_filter = 'ISBN = PAR1' ).

  lo_agent = zca_book_author=>agent.
  lt_book_authors =
    lo_agent->get_persistent_by_query(
      i_query = lo_query
      i_par1 = me->isbn ).

  "Copy the results into the AUTHORS attribute:
  LOOP AT lt_book_authors INTO lo_result.
    lo_book_author ?= lo_result.
    APPEND lo_book_author TO me->book_authors.

    lo_author = lo_book_author->get_author( ).
    APPEND lo_author TO me->authors.
  ENDLOOP.
endmethod.
```

Listing 10.8 Pre-filling the Authors of a Book Using the INIT( ) Method

With everything pre-configured, the implementation details for the `add_author()` method are fairly straightforward. Here, we simply pair the incoming author object with the book object's `ISBN` attribute, create a `ZCL_BOOK_AUTHOR` instance, and cache the results. As you can see in Listing 10.9 though, we first need to check to make sure that the author's not already associated with the book. This task is accomplished by looking up the author's GUID value using the `get_oid_by_ref()` method. With this value in hand, we can compare the GUID of the new author instance with those currently stored in the `AUTHORS` cache.

```
method ADD_AUTHOR.
  DATA: lo_author_agent TYPE REF TO if_os_ca_service,
        lv_author_guid TYPE os_guid,
        lo_temp_author TYPE REF TO zcl_author,
        lv_temp_guid TYPE os_guid,
        lo_book_author TYPE REF TO zcl_book_author.

  "Determine the GUID of the new author object:
  lo_author_agent = zca_author=>agent.
  lv_author_guid =
    lo_author_agent->get_oid_by_ref( io_author ).

  "Check to see if the author is already assigned
  "to the book:
  LOOP AT me->book_authors INTO lo_book_author.
    lo_temp_author = lo_book_author->get_author( ).
    lv_temp_guid =
      lo_author_agent->get_oid_by_ref( lo_temp_author ).

    IF lv_author_guid EQ lv_temp_guid.
      RAISE EXCEPTION TYPE cx_os_object_existing
        EXPORTING
          object = lo_book_author.
    ENDIF.
  ENDLOOP.

  "If not, go ahead and assign it:
  lo_book_author =
    zca_book_author=>agent->create_persistent( ).
  lo_book_author->set_isbn( me->isbn ).
  lo_book_author->set_author( io_author ).

  "Cache the results:
  APPEND io_author TO me->authors.
  APPEND lo_book_author TO me->book_authors.
endmethod.
```

Listing 10.9 Adding an Author to a Book Instance

For the most part, the remove_author() method simply reverses the steps we carry out in the add_author() method, removing the selected author instance from both the Persistence Service cache as well as the internal object cache defined by the ZCL_BOOK class. In both cases, it's worth noting that none of the changes are committed directly within the methods (e.g. with a COMMIT WORK statement). This is not an omission; rather, it's a design choice which allows our API to be incorporated into batch operations as needed. To get a sense for how this works, we're recommend that you check out the ZOOPBOOK_BOOK_MODEL_LOADER program that's included in the book's source code bundle for this chapter.

```abap
method REMOVE_AUTHOR.
  DATA: lo_author_agent TYPE REF TO if_os_ca_service,
        lv_author_guid TYPE os_guid,
        lo_book_author TYPE REF TO zcl_book_author,
        lo_author TYPE REF TO zcl_author,
        lv_temp_guid TYPE os_guid,
        lo_assoc_agent TYPE REF TO if_os_factory.

  "Determine the GUID of the target author object:
  lo_author_agent = zca_author=>agent.
  lv_author_guid =
    lo_author_agent->get_oid_by_ref( io_author ).

  "Check to see if the author is already assigned to
  "the book:
  LOOP AT me->book_authors INTO lo_book_author.
    lo_author = lo_book_author->get_author( ).
    lv_temp_guid =
      lo_author_agent->get_oid_by_ref( lo_author ).

    "If it is, remove it:
    IF lv_author_guid EQ lv_temp_guid.
      "First from the database layer:
      lo_assoc_agent = zca_book_author=>agent.
      lo_assoc_agent->delete_persistent( lo_book_author ).

      "And then from the cache:
      DELETE me->book_authors.

      LOOP AT me->authors INTO lo_author.
        lv_temp_guid =
          lo_author_agent->get_oid_by_ref( lo_author ).
        IF lv_temp_guid EQ lv_author_guid.
          DELETE me->authors.
        ENDIF.
      ENDLOOP.
```

```
    ENDIF.
  ENDLOOP.
endmethod.
```
Listing 10.10 Removing an Author from a Book Instance

10.5 Transaction Handling with the Transaction Service

With all of the abstraction layers provided by the Persistence Service, it can be easy to lose sight of the fact that the operations we perform using the class agent API, etc. result in SQL commands being issued to the underlying system database. Though this is of course the point with ORM tools, it's important to ensure that the updates we trigger are processed safely and reliably within transactions. In this section, we'll see how the *Transaction Service* makes it possible for us to achieve this while remaining in a purely OO context.

10.5.1 Technical Overview

So what is the Transaction Service you might ask? Well, in essence, it's an extension of the ABAP Object Services framework which provides an abstraction around the *SAP transaction concept*. Behind the scenes, the Transaction Service works in conjunction with the Persistence Service to enroll changes to persistent objects in an *SAP Logical Unit of Work* (LUW) so that a series of related operations can be committed or rolled back as a single unit/transaction.

Though we could technically achieve all this using elements of the SAP transaction concept (e.g. update function modules and/or subroutines), it's much more convenient to be able to utilize the features of the Transaction Service so that we don't have to mix-and-match OO programming with procedural constructs.

The UML class diagram contained in Figure 10.24 highlights the main elements of the Transaction Service. At the core of this is the IF_OS_TRANSACTION interface which encapsulates individual transactions. Here, we're provided with methods to start/stop transactions, rollback transactions, and so on. A detailed method-by-method description of this interface is provided in the SAP Help Library documentation available online at *http://help.sap.com* in the section entitled *Components of the Transaction Service*.

369

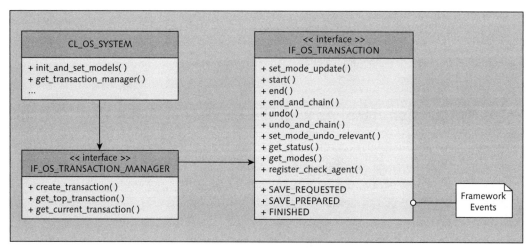

Figure 10.24 UML Class Diagram of Transaction Service Components

10.5.2 Processing Transactions

From a client's perspective, the Transaction Service is very easy to consume. To process updates to persistent objects inside of a transaction, the order of operations is as follows:

1. First, we initialize the Transaction Service by calling the static `init_and_set_modes()` method of class `CL_OS_SYSTEM`. This method accepts two parameters which are used to specify the mode of the Transaction Service:

    ▶ `I_EXTERNAL_COMMIT`
    This Boolean parameter determines whether or not the transaction commit happens externally or internally. In the former (default) case, we must follow a transaction commit with a `COMMIT WORK` statement to persist the changes. If we set the parameter to false, then we can process the transaction exclusively through the Transaction Service – which is usually what we want.

    ▶ `I_UPDATE_MODE`
    This parameter allows us to determine the update mode of the transaction. As you read through the online help documentation, you can see that the parameter options here correspond with options utilized within the SAP transaction concept (e.g. direct updates vs. updates via the asynchronous update task).

2. After the Transaction Service is initialized, the next step is to obtain a transaction manager instance which will be used to manage transactions. This is achieved by calling the static get_transaction_manager() method of class CL_OS_SYSTEM. This method will return an object of type IF_OS_TRANSACTION_MANAGER (see Figure 10.24).

3. To create the actual transaction, we call the create_transaction() instance method on the transaction manager retrieved from the second step. This method will return an object of type IF_OS_TRANSACTION.

4. Before we start the transaction, we have the option of registering event handlers to listen for the framework events shown in Figure 10.24. These callback methods are frequently useful for preparing for or reacting to key transaction processing milestone events.

5. To start the transaction, we then call the start() method defined by the IF_OS_TRANSACTION interface.

6. Once we have a live transaction running, we can begin performing updates to persistent objects as per usual.

7. Finally, we complete the transaction by calling either the end() method or the end_and_chain() method on the transaction instance. In the latter case, the transaction is committed and a new transaction is started in the same context. Alternatively, if we determine that something's gone awry, we can roll back the transaction by calling the undo() method.

To see how all this plays out in code, consider the ZTRANS_DEMO report program contained in Listing 10.11. Here, we're using the Transaction Service to group together the updates required to define a new book instance in our book data model. As you can see, aside from a bit of initial setup, the Transaction Service does a good job of getting out of our way and allowing us to work with persistent objects as per usual.

```
REPORT ztrans_demo.
CLASS lcl_loader DEFINITION.
  PUBLIC SECTION.
    CLASS-METHODS:
      class_constructor,
      execute.

    METHODS:
      handle_save_requested FOR EVENT save_requested
                               OF if_os_transaction,
      handle_save_prepared  FOR EVENT save_prepared
```

```
                                    OF if_os_transaction,
         handle_finished           FOR EVENT finished
                                    OF if_os_transaction
                                    IMPORTING status.
ENDCLASS.

CLASS lcl_loader IMPLEMENTATION.
  METHOD class_constructor.
    "Initialize the Transaction Service:
    CALL METHOD cl_os_system=>init_and_set_modes
      EXPORTING
        i_external_commit = oscon_false
        i_update_mode     = oscon_dmode_update_task.
  ENDMETHOD.

  METHOD execute.
    DATA: lo_loader    TYPE REF TO lcl_loader,
          lo_txn_mgr   TYPE REF TO if_os_transaction_manager,
          lo_txn       TYPE REF TO if_os_transaction,
          lo_author1   TYPE REF TO zcl_author,
          lo_author2   TYPE REF TO zcl_author,
          lo_publisher TYPE REF TO zcl_publisher,
          lo_book      TYPE REF TO zcl_book.

    "Initialization:
    CREATE OBJECT lo_loader.
    lo_txn_mgr =
      cl_os_system=>get_transaction_manager( ).
    lo_txn = lo_txn_mgr->create_transaction( ).

    SET HANDLER lo_loader->handle_save_requested
          FOR lo_txn.
    SET HANDLER lo_loader->handle_save_prepared
          FOR lo_txn.
    SET HANDLER lo_loader->handle_finished
          FOR lo_txn.

    TRY.
      "Start the transaction:
      lo_txn->start( ).

      "Create a publisher instance:
      lo_publisher =
        zca_publisher=>agent->create_persistent(
          i_country        = 'US'
          i_publisher_name = 'SAP Press, Inc.'
          i_region         = 'MA' ).

      "Create a couple of authors:
      lo_author1 =
        zca_author=>agent->create_persistent(
```

```
              i_first_name = 'Horst'
              i_last_name  = 'Keller' ).

      lo_author2 =
        zca_author=>agent->create_persistent(
            i_first_name = 'Sascha'
            i_last_name  = 'Krüger' ).


      "Create a book:
      lo_book =
        zca_book=>agent->create _persistent(
            i_isbn            = '9781592290796'
            i_publication_date = '20070315'
            i_publisher       = lo_publisher
            i_title           =
              'ABAP Objects: ABAP Programming in NetWeaver' ).

      "Assign authors to the book:
      lo_book->add_author( lo_author1 ).
      lo_book->add_author( lo_author2 ).

      "Commit the transaction:
      lo_txn->end( ).

    CATCH cx_root.
    ENDTRY.
  ENDMETHOD.

  METHOD handle_save_requested.
    WRITE: /
      'Save requested, perform any last-minute updates...'.
  ENDMETHOD.

  METHOD handle_save_prepared.
    WRITE: /
      'Save prepared, COMMIT WORK happens next...'.
  ENDMETHOD.

  METHOD handle_finished.
    IF status EQ OSCON_TSTATUS_FIN_SUCCESS.
      WRITE: / 'Transaction processed successfully.'.
    ENDIF.
  ENDMETHOD.
ENDCLASS.

START-OF-SELECTION.
  lcl_loader=>execute( ).
```

Listing 10.11 Processing Persistent Object Updates in a Transaction

10.5.3 Influencing the Transaction Lifecycle

By the time we decide to end/commit a transaction, each of the persistent objects enrolled in the transaction *should* be in a consistent state. However, it never hurts to have an additional checkpoint to ensure that each of the objects involved in the transaction are in a consistent state. That's why the Transaction Service allows us to register *check agents* with transactions so that a consistency check will be carried out before the transaction is committed. Within this check agent, we have the power to veto the transaction if something has gone awry.

From a technical perspective, a check agent is an object instance that implements the IF_OS_CHECK interface. This interface defines a single Boolean callback method called is_consistent() that gets called right before a transaction is committed. Here, we get to decide whether or not we want to pass or fail the transaction.

To demonstrate how this works, consider the code excerpt contained in Listing 10.12. Here, we've implemented the IF_OS_CHECK interface in our ZCL_BOOK class so that we can perform consistency checks for books before they're committed. In larger data models, we might want to externalize this functionality into a service manager or some such in order to enforce integrity checks on a more macro level, but you get the idea.

```
CLASS zcl_book...
  METHOD if_os_check~is_consistent.
    "Make sure a book instance has at least one author
    "before saving:
    IF lines( me->authors ) GT 0.
      result = abap_true.
    ELSE.
      result = abap_false.
    ENDIF.
  ENDMETHOD.
ENDCLASS.
```
Listing 10.12 Implementing the IS_CONSISTENT() Method

The code excerpt contained in Listing 10.13 shows how we can incorporate our check agent into the transaction used to manage the book creation process. As you can see, the check agent registration occurs via a call to the register_check_agent() method defined by the IF_OS_TRANSACTION interface.

```
CLASS lcl_loader...
  ...
  METHOD execute.
```

```
   ...
   TRY.
     "Start the transaction:
     lo_txn->start( ).
     ...
     "Create a book:
     lo_book = ...

     "Register the check agent:
     lo_txn->register_check_agent( lo_book ).

     "Commit the transaction:
     lo_txn->end( ).

   CATCH cx_root.
   ENDTRY.
   ENDMETHOD.
   ...
ENDLCASS.
```

Listing 10.13 Registering a Check Agent in a Transaction

10.6 UML Tutorial: Communication Diagrams

One of the most difficult stages of the Object-Oriented Analysis and Design (OOAD) process is the point at which we begin to try to assign roles and responsibilities to the classes identified during the structural analysis phase. At this point in the process, all that we have to work with are high-level behavioural diagrams (e.g. activity diagrams, use cases, etc.) as well as some class and object diagrams that describe the classes we have modelled. Certainly, associations in class diagrams help us to understand the relationships between these classes, but they aren't very useful in describing the *behavior* of a system in terms of these classes.

Frequently, this kind of detailed behavior is captured in a sequence diagram as we saw in Chapter 3. Sequence diagrams are an example of an *interaction diagram*. Interaction diagrams emphasize the flow of data and control between objects interacting in a system. In this section, we will look at another type of interaction diagram in the UML called the *communication diagram*.

Communication diagrams (formerly known as *collaboration diagrams* in UML 1.x), blend elements from class, object, sequence, and use case diagrams together in the graph notation shown in Figure 10.25. This communication diagram depicts the same Withdraw Cash interaction that we considered in Chapter 3 when we looked at sequence diagrams. As you can see, there are a lot of similarities between both of these diagrams. Indeed, whether you use one notation or the other is mainly a matter of preference. However, many developers like to use communication diagrams to whiteboard their ideas since they are generally easier to sketch than sequence diagrams. In fact, one way to develop communication diagrams is to begin overlaying an object diagram with messages.

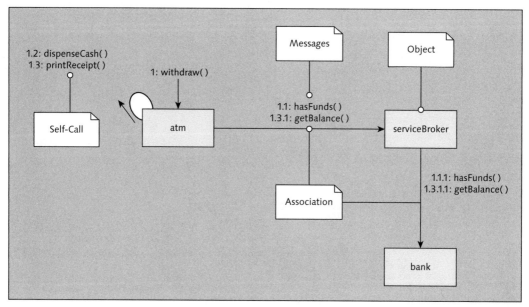

Figure 10.25 Example UML Communication Diagram

One challenge of working with communication diagrams is the nested decimal numbering scheme shown in Figure 10.25. For this reason, it's important that you keep a communication diagram small so that the message numbers don't become too nested and hard to read.

Perhaps the most valuable aspect of a communication diagram is the fact that it keeps static associations in focus as you begin to develop the interactions between classes. This visualization is important since it helps you to keep your architectural vision intact as you begin to connect the dots between your classes at runtime.

10.7   Summary

This concludes our whirlwind introduction to the ABAP Object Services framework. Whether you intend to utilize this framework in your day-to-day development tasks or not, we hope that you've found this exploratory journey to be worthwhile. Indeed, perhaps nowhere else in an ABAP system will you find so many object-oriented concepts on display. From inheritance and polymorphism, to designing to interfaces and even friendship relationships, there really is a little bit of everything. So, if nothing else, you can at least pick up on some design techniques that you can incorporate into your own OO-based frameworks.

In the next chapter, we'll take a look at another ABAP-based framework that makes heavy use of OO concepts: the *Business Object Processing Framework* (BOPF). Here, we'll learn how to build large-scale business objects that can be used to achieve component-based application designs.

Up till now, we've looked at techniques for encapsulating business logic on a micro scale, focusing our attention on handful of classes at a time. In this chapter, we'll broaden our scope and look at ways of encapsulating business logic within coarse-grained reusable business objects.

11   Business Object Development with the BOPF

In many ways, enterprise software development resembles one big game of chess in that the pieces are constantly in motion. Objectives change, processes evolve, and the only way for IT departments to keep pace is to have a good set of flexible business objects that can be molded, adapted and mixed and matched to develop business solutions. Here, business objects are rather like LEGO® blocks that can be stacked on top of one another to construct new solutions.

Knowing what you now know about object-oriented design, you probably already have lots of ideas for creating new business objects and implementing component-based architectures. However, while it's certainly possible to build such solutions from scratch, it turns out that SAP provides a very powerful framework which makes this process a whole lot easier: the *Business Object Processing Framework* (BOPF). In this chapter, we'll get to know the BOPF and see how it can be used in tandem with your new-found object-oriented skills to build powerful business solutions.

11.1   What is the BOPF?

If you haven't heard of the BOPF before, then a brief introduction is in order. As the name suggests, the BOPF is a framework for working with business objects (BOs). This framework was designed from the ground up to manage the entire lifecycle of BO development, saving you from having the reinvent the wheel each time you need to develop a new BO.

At a high-level, we can organize the services and functionality of the BOPF into two basic categories:

▶ **Design Time**
At design time, the BOPF provides a series of workbench tools that are used to model and construct BOs. Here, graphical editor screens and wizards are furnished to guide developers through the various stages of the BO development process.

▶ **Runtime**
At runtime, the BOPF provides a runtime framework which manages business object instances. Here, there's built-in functionality for automatic persistence, transaction and lifecycle management, caching, and much, much more.

The block diagram in Figure 11.1 illustrates how these pieces fit together within an application.

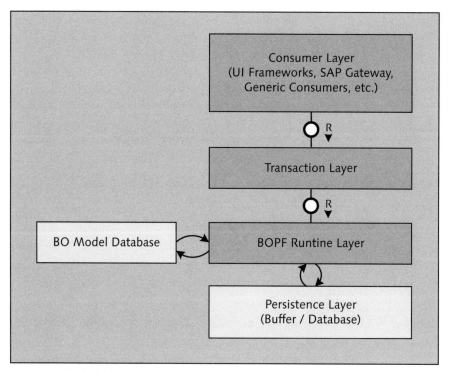

Figure 11.1 FMC Block Diagram Depicting High-Level BOPF Architecture

As you can see in Figure 11.1, BOPF application design calls for a layered approach to development:

- **Consumer Layer**
  At the consumer layer, clients can utilize the BOPF's object-oriented API to interface with BOs. Because this API is generic, it's very easy to develop universal consumer frameworks that sit on top of the BOPF. A couple of the more notable consumer frameworks at the time of this writing include the *FPM-BOPF Integration* (FBI) and *Gateway-BOPF Integration* (GBI) frameworks which integrate the BOPF with the *Floorplan Manager* (FPM) and SAP Gateway toolsets, respectively. These integration frameworks make it very easy to develop UI-centric applications using the FPM and SAPUI5 UI frameworks.

- **Transaction Layer**
  Client sessions are managed through a centralized transaction layer which handles low-level transaction handling details such as object locking and commit handling.

- **BOPF Runtime Layer**
  The core of the BOPF functionality exists within the BOPF runtime which is implemented via a series of standard-delivered classes provided by SAP. This layer contains all of the functionality needed to instantiate BOs, handle lifecycle events, and respond to client-level interactions.

- **Persistence Layer**
  As you might expect, the persistence layer provides the low-level functionality needed to persist BO instances to the database. Here, services are provided to implement performance optimizations such as buffering and caching. Over time, SAP continues to deliver innovations in this layer in order to improve performance and expand the overall feature set.

Though it's hard to really wrap your head around these concepts without seeing how all this plays out from a technical point-of-view, the major take-away for now is that the BOPF introduces consistency and predictability into the BO development process. With the BOPF, everything has its place and the framework makes it rather difficult for developers to stray too far off the beaten path.

Besides improving the quality of the components being developed, such standardization also leads to interesting innovations as patterns emerge. We'll see some examples of this over the course of this chapter. For now though, let's turn our attention to the inner workings of BOPF BOs.

11.2   Anatomy of a Business Object

In the help documentation for the SAP BOPF Enhancement Workbench SAP says BOs within the BOPF are "a representation of a type of uniquely identifiable business entity described by a structural model and an internal process model." This is to say that BOPF BOs:

▸ Have a structured component model.

▸ Have a well-defined process model which governs the BO lifecycle, behaviors, and so on.

In this regard, the BOPF BO concept is similar to other popular component models in the enterprise software space such as Enterprise JavaBeans (EJBs) in the Java world and COM+ in the Microsoft.NET world. Closer to home, the BOPF shares some similarities with previous ABAP-based business object frameworks like the *Business Object Layer* (BOL)/*Generic Interaction Layer* (GenIL) frameworks.

In just a moment, we'll delve into the various types of elements you can create when modeling BOPF BOs. However, before we go there, let's first take a moment to understand how business entities are modeled within the BOPF. Here, it's helpful to have a visual frame of reference to work with. So, with that in mind, consider the /BOBF/DEMO_SALES_ORDER demo BO shown in Figure 11.2. You can review the setup of this BO in your own local system using Transaction /BOBF/CONF_UI.

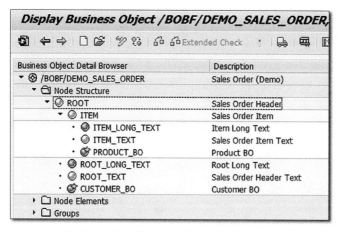

Figure 11.2 Understanding the Node Hierarchy Concept of BOPF BOs

As you can see in Figure 11.2, the basic modeling unit for BOPF BOs is the *node*. Within a BO, nodes are organized into a hierarchical node structure that mirrors the structure of elements in an XML document. This is to say that there are defined parent-child relationships which give the BO its structure. For instance, in the /BOBF/DEMO_SALES_ORDER BO, data is organized under the top-level ROOT node. Underneath the ROOT node, a node hierarchy is built off of child nodes such as ITEM, ROOT_TEXT, and so on. This process of nesting child nodes continues until all aspects of the business entity in question are properly modeled.

In the sections that follow, we'll investigate how we can use node hierarchies like the one shown in Figure 11.2 to model the various aspects of real world business entities.

11.2.1 Nodes

So at this point, we know that BOPF BOs are organized hierarchically into nodes. However, since the term "node" is rather generic, you're probably wondering what a node is exactly. The answer's complicated by the fact that the term takes on different meanings depending on the context:

- **Design Time**
  At design time, nodes are used to model the data and behavior of an individual aspect of a business object. For instance, in the sample /BOBF/DEMO_SALES_ORDER BO the ITEM node defines all aspects of a sales order line item: data, behaviors, linkages to other sales order-related entities, and so on.

- **Runtime**
  At runtime, nodes are containers (think internal tables) which group together object-like instances called *node rows*. Depending on the design-time definition of a node, we can perform operations on individual node rows or the node collection as a whole. The diagram contained in Figure 11.3 illustrates what an instance of the /BOBF/DEMO_SALES_ORDER BO might look like from a runtime perspective.

As you can see in Figure 11.3, each node/node row within a BO instance defines one or more *attributes*. For example, the ITEM node defines attributes such as ITEM_NO, AMOUNT, and so on. Collectively, these attributes describe the various aspects of sales order line item that we want to capture in our model.

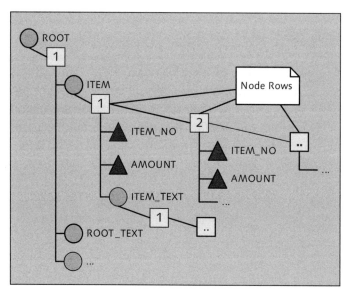

Figure 11.3 Snapshot of a /BOBF/DEMO_SALES_ORDER Instance at Runtime

Node and Attribute Types

From a data modeling perspective, nodes and node attributes are organized into two distinct categories: persistent nodes/attributes and transient nodes/attributes. As the name suggests, persistent nodes/attributes are *persisted* to the system database. From a developer perspective, we needn't worry about how this persistence takes place; this will be handled automatically on our behalf by the BOPF runtime environment. The important point to remember from a modeling perspective is that persistent nodes and their corresponding attributes are mapped to database tables and should therefore adhere to good normalization practices.

Transient nodes/attributes represent elements of the data model that are looked up and/or calculated on the fly. For example, let's say that we wanted to include within our data model details about the sales staff member who recorded the order. In an ERP system like SAP, basic employee details for this staff member are likely already recorded in the HR database. So, rather than redundantly store such data within the context of the sales order BO, it makes sense to read the data from the HR system on the fly at runtime. Not only does this eliminate data redundancy, it also ensures that the data remains fresh over time.

Depending on the usage scenario, we can establish such lookups at the node level or the attribute level. In our HR lookup scenario, it would make sense to pull the data into a separate transient node. On the other hand, if we're only looking up a handful of fields, we might just want to make those fields transient attributes. For example, in the ITEM node of the there's a persistent attribute called PRODUCT_ID which contains a foreign key to a product object maintained elsewhere. If we wanted to pull in the product description into our model, we wouldn't want to redundantly store that description in a persistent attribute. Instead, we'd want to perform an ad hoc lookup for the product description on demand and copy the value into a transient attribute. A similar approach would be used for calculated values such as the overall value of the sales order (which is calculated by summing up the AMOUNT attribute for each of the node rows within the ITEM node).

Understanding the Node Data Model

Figure 11.4 illustrates the data model of a BOPF node in further detail. Here, we find that there are several attributes that must be configured to build out the data model:

▸ Whenever a node is initially created, we must specify at the outset whether or not the node will be classified as persistent or transient. If the latter is selected, the TRANSIENT NODE checkbox will be checked.

▸ Within the DATA MODEL section, node attributes are defined as follows:

  ▸ The DATA STRUCTURE field points to an ABAP Dictionary structure which contains all of the persistent attributes defined within the node.

  ▸ The (optional) TRANSIENT STRUCTURE field points to an ABAP Dictionary structure which contains all of the transient attributes defined within the node.

  ▸ In Section 11.3, we'll find that the BOPF client API doesn't really distinguish between persistent and transient attributes. As a result, the API works with the combined structure type specified in the COMBINED STRUCTURE field. This combined structure collects persistent and transient attributes in a singular structure.

  ▸ The COMBINED TABLE TYPE field defines a table type whose line type is defined in terms of the combined structure type. This table type is used in API calls which pull back multiple node rows at a time.

▶ Lastly, in the DATA ACCESS section, we can see the transparent dictionary table where persistent node data is stored in the DATABASE TABLE field. These auto-generated tables will be defined in terms of the persistent attribute structure contained in the DATA STRUCTURE field. The key for any such table is an auto-generated UUID field called DB_KEY. For sub-nodes, there will also be a foreign key field called PARENT_KEY which can be used to traverse from the child node to its parent. Though such relationships are normally navigated using a node element called an *association*, the presence of this field can be used to implement SQL-based lookups of node data as needed.

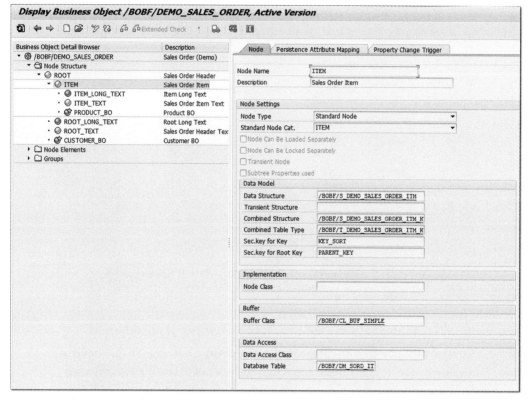

Figure 11.4 Understanding the Node Data Model

Putting it all Together

Before we move on, let's briefly summarize what we've learned in this section. So far, we know that BOs within the BOPF are organized into a node structure/hierarchy. Each node within this hierarchy is meant to model a particular aspect of a business entity. At the node level, we can fill out this model by defining persistent and/or transient attributes as we see fit.

When you think about it, this node-based modeling process is not unlike the one we use to build object models in a pure OO context. Indeed, in many respects, it's appropriate to think of a node definition as being rather like a class definition. Taking this a step further, we can think of BOs as being like composite classes in that they group together nodes and sub-nodes via associations.

If we get the node/data model right up front, the remaining elements required to accurately model a business entity should follow quite naturally. With that being said, let's peel back another layer of the BOPF component model and being looking at *node elements*. These elements allow us to weave in behavioral aspects into nodes so that they can become more than simple data structures.

11.2.2 Actions

If we think of nodes as being like classes, then it follows that we should be able to define operations/methods within a node to encapsulate node-specific behaviors. Within the BOPF node, such operations are called *actions*.

Though conceptually similar to methods in a pure OO context, the scope of the operations carried out with BOPF actions tends to be much larger than the average instance method in an OO class. This is because most attribute level updates are brokered through standard API methods defined by the BOPF core framework. As a result, you won't see lots of getter and setter methods in BOPF node definitions. Instead, BOPF actions are utilized more for encapsulating larger-scale business operations together in a callable package.

To put this idea into perspective, consider the `DELIVER` action defined in the `ROOT` node of the `/BOBF/DEMO_SALES_ORDER` sample BO shown in Figure 11.5. As the name suggests, this action is used to trigger the delivery of one or more sales orders. Internally, this processing will result in the update of pertinent node attributes (e.g. the `DELIVERY_STATUS` attribute) as well as other downstream updates. In a real-world scenario, this action might also trigger a chain of BOPF action calls between the sales order BO, delivery BOs, and so on. To the outside world though, the complexities of this task flow are abstracted behind an action with an obvious purpose — to process the delivery of a sales order.

Though there's nothing stopping us from defining lots of fine-grained actions within a node, it's important to remember that while BOs bear many similarities to classes, the interface cut is different. With BOs, the goal is to develop a model that closely resembles a business entity. Therefore the individual nodes and the actions they define should be defined in higher-level terms. That doesn't mean that the technical layers don't exist, it's just that we want to insulate clients from these details as much as we can.

Shifting away from the conceptual side of things, let's take a closer look at an action definition from a technical perspective. Looking at the DELIVER action shown in Figure 11.5, we can see that there are several attributes that contribute to the design of an action's signature. Some of the more notable attributes here include:

▶ **Node**
This attribute is used to bind the action with its corresponding node. While such a designation might seem obvious within the graphical design time tools, this specification is needed by the BOPF runtime to facilitate action processing at runtime.

▶ **Action Cardinality**
This attribute is used to identify the number of node row instances expected to be processed by the action. Most of the time, we'll choose between the SINGLE NODE INSTANCE and MULTIPLE NODE INSTANCES options depending on whether or not we plan to perform bulk operations. The other option is the STATIC ACTION option which effectively models the action as a static action. This option would make sense if we wanted to define utility actions and the like.

▶ **Class / Interface**
In this attribute, we must plug in an ABAP Objects class that defines the action logic. This class must implement the /BOBF/IF_FRW_ACTION interface. Here, the actual ABAP implementation code goes into the execute() method which comes pre-configured with contextual information that can be used to determine the node row(s) that are to be processed, etc.

▶ **Parameter Structure**
This optional attribute can be used to expand the signature of a BOPF action to include input/output parameters as needed. All of the fields are encapsulated inside of an ABAP Dictionary structure which is defined outside of the BOPF. At runtime, this parameter structure is passed by reference to the action implementation class so that attributes can be read and updated where appropriate.

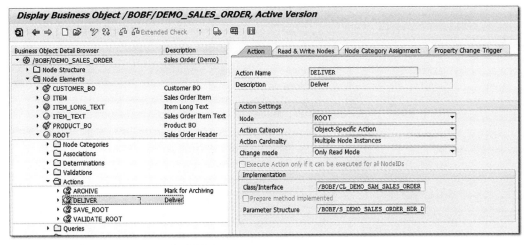

Figure 11.5 Defining an Action in the BOPF

In many respects, the attributes used to define an action are similar to the ones used to define a method of an ABAP Objects class in the form-based view of the Class Builder tool. Once the basic signature is defined, the rest of the focus is on the underlying action implementation class which is implemented using regular ABAP Objects code.

11.2.3 Determinations

During the lifecycle of a business object instance, there will be key milestone events that we may need to react to. For example, if data changes in one node, the update could have a cascading effect on other related nodes. Or, right before a BO instance is saved, there might be some last-second housekeeping that we need to take care of to ensure that the instance is persisted correctly. For these situations, and others, the BOPF object model provides us with *determinations*.

In the help documentation for the SAP BOPF Enhancement Workbench, SAP defines a determination as "an element assigned to a business object node that describes the internal changing logic on the business object. Like a database trigger, a determination is automatically executed by the BOPF as soon as the BOPF triggering condition is fulfilled."

The internal changing logic referenced in this definition is realized in the form of an ABAP Objects class which implements the /BOBF/IF_FRW_DETERMINATION interface. Whenever determinations are defined, these implementation classes are basically registered to run whenever specific triggering conditions are met. Table 11.1 shows the types of triggering conditions (or patterns) supported by the BOPF object model at the time of this writing.

Triggering Condition / Pattern	Description
Derive Dependent Data Immediately After Modification	This pattern is used to perform cascading updates whenever a node instance is created/updated/deleted. Some possible scenarios where this pattern would apply include: ▶ Setting default values for attributes of newly-created node rows. ▶ Updating related attributes and/or sub-nodes whenever node attributes change. ▶ Applying state transition rules to ensure that the object remains in a consistent state.
Derive Dependent Data Before Saving	This pattern is used to interject some custom logic right before a node instance is saved. Here, we might apply last-minute updates to a node row (e.g. updating date/time audit fields) or fire events which trigger downstream processing outside of the BOPF.
Fill Transient Attributes of Persistent Nodes	Determinations following this pattern are used to perform lookups/calculations of transient attributes defined within a node. This pattern can also be used to set runtime properties on BOPF nodes as needed.
Derive Instances of Transient Nodes	This pattern is used in cases where we need to allocate transient nodes on demand. Determinations following this pattern will be launched during the retrieve operation to build the requested transient node instances on the fly.

Table 11.1 Determination Patterns within the BOPF Object Model

Aside from selecting the appropriate determination pattern, the process for defining a determination is pretty straightforward. As you can see in Figure 11.6, a determination definition mainly consists of a determination name, the appropriate pattern (or category as it's sometimes called), and an implementation class. As noted earlier, the implementation class is a regular ABAP Objects class that implements the /BOBF/IF_FRW_DETERMINATION interface.

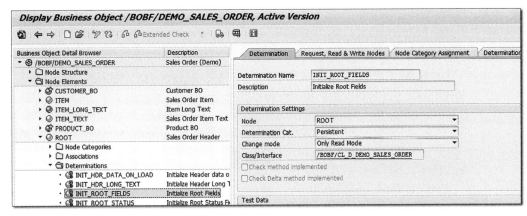

Figure 11.6 Defining a Determination in the BOPF

11.2.4 Validations

In Section 11.3, we'll learn that updates to nodes/attributes are carried out via a generic OO-based API. Here, a client is generally free to pass in whatever data they like—even if the data is incorrect. Thinking back on our encapsulation discussions from Chapter 3, you might naturally assume that this is a violation of basic encapsulation rules. However, as it turns out, there's a method to the BOPF's madness here.

Rather than encoding validation rules into individual setter methods and the like, the BOPF allows us to group business validation rules together in separate node elements called *validations*. Within these validations, we can enforce our consistency checks and ensure that the integrity of BO nodes and the BO as a whole remains intact. At specific milestone events (e.g. right before a BO instance is saved), the BOPF runtime automatically trigger these validations and ensure that any invalid data updates are prevented from slipping through the cracks. As such, validations represent the last line of defense for BO nodes.

In Figure 11.7, you can see an example of a validation called CHECK_ITEM within the /BOBF/DEMO_SALES_ORDER BO. This validation performs a consistency check to ensure that ITEM node instances remain consistent. As you can see in the screenshot, a validation definition consists of three main attributes:

▶ **Validation Name**
  This attribute defines the validation name, which is an identifier maintained

internally within the BOPF. Since validations are not callable objects, the name has little meaning outside of the BOPF framework from a runtime perspective.

▶ **Validation Category**
Here, we can choose between one of two options. The default CONSISTENCY CHECK option classifies the validation as an entity used to perform consistency checks before a node instance is saved, etc. The ACTION CHECK option can be used as a means to ensure that a node instance is ready to have an action performed against it.

▶ **Class/Interface**
This attribute defines the validation implementation class, which is a plain ABAP Objects class that implements the /BOBF/IF_FRW_VALIDATION interface. Within this validation class, we can perform the relevant checks and report any errors that might crop up using the EO_MESSAGE and ET_FAILED_KEY exporting parameters.

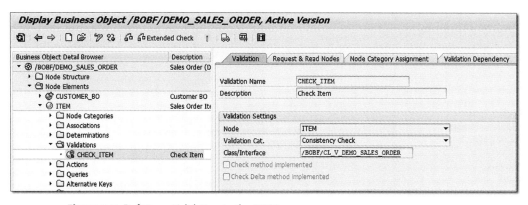

Figure 11.7 Defining a Validation in the BOPF

11.2.5 Associations

When processing BOs, we must be able to navigate through the nodes that make up the BO's node hierarchy. While this may seem like a given, the implementation details are more complex than you might think when you consider the fact that the BOPF runtime has to navigate through these relationships by evaluating node rows that are cached in shared memory. For this task, the BOPF runtime needs to know how to relate a pair of nodes with one another. Within the object model, these relationships are specified in the form of *associations*.

Figure 11.8 illustrates what an association definition looks like in the /BOBF/ CONF_UI transaction. This particular association defines the relationship between the sales order's ROOT node and the ITEM child node. As you can see in the ASSOCIATION SETTINGS section, the types of details specified here include the source/target nodes in the relationship, the cardinality of the relationship, and the resolving node. Naturally, the details will vary here depending on the types of nodes that are being associated with one another. Associations like the ITEM association shown in Figure 11.8 are defined automatically by the BOPF design time tools as we create new BOs. In general, there are three types of associations that will be created automatically by the BOPF design time tools:

- Simple associations from a given node to each of its child nodes. These associations will have a name which corresponds with the name of the child node.

- Associations from a child node to its parent node. These associations will go by the name TO_PARENT.

- Associations from a child node to the root node. These associations will go by the name TO_ROOT.

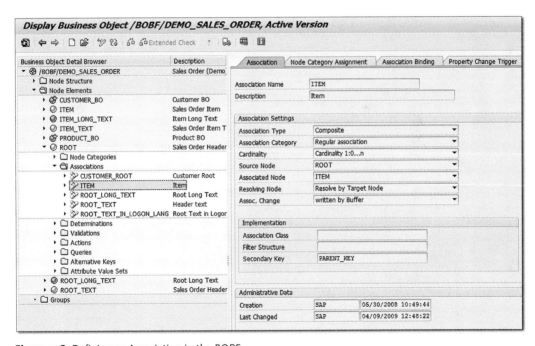

Figure 11.8 Defining an Association in the BOPF

Aside from these standard-delivered associations, we also have the option of creating custom associations which simplify node traversal. For example, consider the ROOT_TEXT_IN_LOGON_LANG association shown in Figure 11.9. This association basically serves the same purpose as the default ROOT_TEXT association, linking the ROOT node with its child ROOT_TEXT node. The difference in this case though is that the list of node rows returned by the association is filtered by the user's logon language. In essence, this is a convenience association which saves clients from having to parse through ROOT_TEXT rows in order to find the instance matching the user's logon language.

In order to implement custom associations like the ROOT_TEXT_IN_LOGON_LANG association shown in Figure 11.9, we must specify the filter criteria in one of two ways:

▶ If the join conditions are relatively static in nature, then we can define them graphically on the ASSOCIATION BINDING tab shown in Figure 11.9.

▶ Otherwise, we have to specify the join/filter conditions in an association class which implements the /BOBF/IF_FRW_ASSOCIATION interface. This class is then plugged into the ASSOCIATION CLASS field in the IMPLEMENTATION section shown in Figure 11.9 (e.g. the /BOBF/CL_DEMO_C_LANGUAGE1 class).

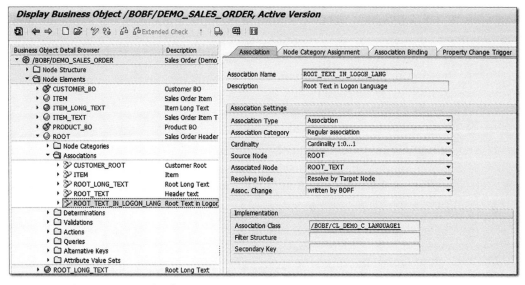

Figure 11.9 Example of a Custom Association

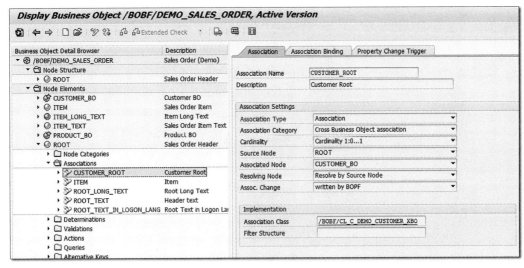

Figure 11.10 Example of an XBO Association

Before we wrap this section on associations, we should point out that the BOPF also allows us to define associations between nodes of different BOs as needed. An example of this is the CUSTOMER_ROOT association shown in Figure 11.10. This association allows us to traverse from the sales order ROOT node to the ROOT node of the /BOBF/DEMO_CUSTOMER BO. From a configuration perspective, cross-business object (XBO) associations are defined as follows:

1. First, the ROOT node of the linked BO must be mapped as a child node of the source node (e.g. the ROOT node of the /BOBF/DEMO_SALES_ORDER BO in this case). As you can see in Figure 11.11, the node type is BUSINESS OBJECT REPRESENTATION NODE. This type allows us to model a transient node which points to the ROOT node of the associated BO.

2. Once the BO representation node is in place, we can define the XBO association by mapping the source node to the delegate node as shown in Figure 11.10. In this case, the association category is CROSS BUSINESS OBJECT ASSOCIATION. Otherwise, it's pretty much business as usual.

XBO associations like the CUSTOMER_ROOT association represent one of the primary ways that we can achieve reuse within the BOPF. Here, rather than redundantly define customer details within the /BOBF/DEMO_SALES_ORDER BO, it makes sense to simply link the two BO instances together and create a composite. Over time, as the BO library expands, productivity will increase since developers won't constantly be re-building/re-applying business logic in new contexts.

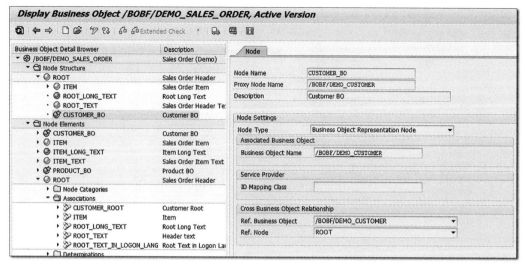

Figure 11.11 Example of an XBO Representation Node Definition

11.2.6 Queries

The last BO node element that we'll be looking at is *queries*. As you would expect, queries allow us to encapsulate node/BO lookup logic in callable modules that clients can use to search for BO instances. Within the BOPF object model, there are two different types of queries that can be defined:

▸ **Node Attribute Queries**

These types of queries are modeled queries whose logic is defined within the BOPF runtime. No custom coding is required to implement this type of query.

▸ **Custom Queries**

Custom queries are used to handle complex query requirements which exceed the capabilities of the canned node attribute queries. The query logic is encapsulated in a custom ABAP Objects class that implements the /BOBF/IF_FRW_ QUERY interface.

Figure 11.12 demonstrates the definition of a query within the /BOBF/CONF_UI transaction. As you can see, the attributes required to define a query are pretty straightforward. For modeled queries, we don't really have to specify anything as the BOPF framework will implement all of the necessary details for us. For implemented queries, the primary attribute we must specify is the query class.

Display Business Object /BOBF/DEMO_CUSTOMER, Active Version

Business Object Detail Browser	Description	Query	Property Change Trigger
▼ ⊗ /BOBF/DEMO_CUSTOMER	Customer (Demo)		
▸ ☐ Node Structure		Query Name	SELECT_BY_ATTRIBUTES
▼ ⊟ Node Elements		Description	Select By Attributes
▼ ⊘ ROOT	Customer Header		
▸ ☐ Node Categories		Query Settings	
▸ ☐ Associations		Node	ROOT
▸ ☐ Determinations		Query Category	Implemented
▸ ☐ Validations			Modeled
▸ ☐ Actions			Implemented
▼ ⊟ Queries		Implementation	
▸ ⑥ SELECT_ALL	Select All		
▸ ⑥ SELECT_BY_ATTRIBUTES	Select By Attributes	Query Class	/BOBF/CL_Q_DEMO_CUSTOMER
▸ ⑥ SELECT_BY_ELEMENTS	Select By Elements	Filter Structure	/BOBF/S_DEMO_CUSTOMER_HDR_QA
▸ ☐ Alternative Keys			
▸ ☐ Attribute Value Sets		Query Result Types	
▸ ⊘ ROOT_LONG_TEXT	Root Long Text	Result Type	
▸ ⊘ ROOT_TEXT	Customer Header Text	Result Table Type	
▸ ☐ Groups			

Figure 11.12 Defining a Query in the BOPF

Within a query implementation class, we can invoke other (modeled) queries or dynamically generate SQL code to lookup the relevant entries. The results of the query are passed back via an exporting parameter called ET_KEY which, as you'd expect, contains the keys of the node rows that we find during the course of the query execution. In Section 11.3, we'll learn how to use these keys in BOPF client API calls to fetch and update BOs as needed.

11.3   Working with the BOPF Client API

Now that you're familiar with the makeup of BOPF BOs, let's see how we can create instances of these BOs and manipulate them from within ABAP programs. Here, we'll find that SAP has provided us with a rich and flexible object-oriented API that's fairly easy to work with once you get the hang of it.

11.3.1   API Overview

For the most part, the BOPF API can be distilled down to three main object types (see the UML class diagram contained in Figure 11.13):

▸ /BOBF/IF_TRA_SERVICE_MANAGER
This interface defines the core API methods needed to interface with BO node elements. Here, methods are provided to execute queries, traverse through node hierarchies, execute actions, perform node updates, and more.

▶ /BOBF/IF_TRA_TRANSACTION_MGR

This interface provides a façade around BOPF transaction managers which are used to manage transactions. Such transactions could contain a single step (i.e. updates to a single node row) or multiple steps (e.g. adding/updating multiple node rows, calling actions, and so on). During the course of the transaction processing, we can use the interface methods to commit and/or rollback the current transaction as needed.

▶ /BOBF/IF_FRW_CONFIGURATION

This interface provides us with access to the BOPF configuration store where all of the design-time BO configuration metadata is stored. We can use the API methods defined by this interface to introspect BOs and determine node data types, etc. This information can be used in conjunction with the *ABAP Runtime Type Services* (RTTS) API to build generic BO processing logic as needed.

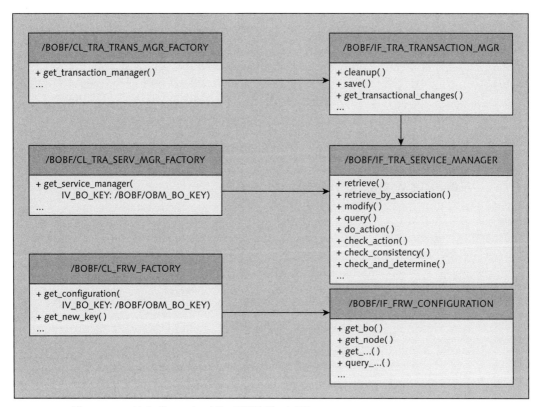

Figure 11.13 Main Elements of the BOPF Client API

As you can see in Figure 11.13, the internals of the BOPF runtime environment are abstracted away behind the three main interfaces described above. In order to get our hands on objects that implement these interfaces at runtime, we must go through the factory classes highlighted in Figure 11.13. Then, once we have our hands on these instances, we're basically off and running.

BO Keys and Constants Interfaces

Looking closely at the signature of the factory methods of the /BOBF/CL_TRA_ SERV_MGR_FACTORY and /BOBF/CL_FRW_FACTORY classes shown in Figure 11.13, you'll notice that these methods expect to receive a BO key. What is this BO key? Well, it's basically a key that's used to lookup BO metadata from the BOPF configuration store. The BOPF service manager and configuration managers need to have this information in context in order to understand how to respond to requests such as "perform this action" or "tell me the data type associated with this particular node". From this, we can glean an important truth about BOPF service managers and configuration managers: if we're going to be working with multiple BOs, we'll need separate service/configuration manager instances for each BO type that we're working with.

Since BO keys are auto-generated by the BOPF design-time configuration tools, you're not expected to simply know the BO key offhand. Instead, each BO has a generated constants interface associated with it that makes it easy to address the BO key as well as various BO node elements. For a given BO type, you can find the constants interface in the /BOBF/CONF_UI transaction by double-clicking on the BO and looking in the CONSTANTS INTERFACE field in the BUSINESS OBJECT SETTINGS panel of the default BUSINESS OBJECT tab (see Figure 11.14).

Within the /BOBF/CONF_UI transaction, the CONSTANTS INTERFACE field is context-sensitive, so you can double-click on it to open up the interface in the Class Builder tool. Figure 11.15 shows what the constants interface looks like for a given BO. Here, you can see the target BO key field exposed via the SC_BO_KEY constant. In addition to the key, you can see that there are quite a few other constants provided to address defined actions, queries, associations, and so forth. These constants are constantly being updated to reflect the current state of the BO. So, for example, if a new query is created in a BO node, the SC_QUERY constant would be updated accordingly. In the upcoming sections, we'll see how these other constants are used in API calls.

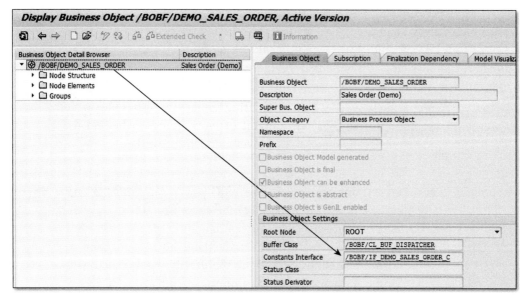

Figure 11.14 Accessing the Constants Interface for a BO (Part 1)

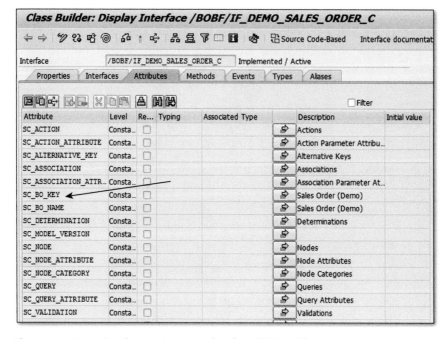

Figure 11.15 Accessing the Constants Interface for a BO (Part 2)

Bootstrapping the API

Having reviewed the basic architecture of the BOPF API, let's now take a look at what it takes to bootstrap the API using ABAP code. For the purposes of this demonstration, we'll be working with the /BOBF/DEMO_SALES_ORDER BO which is generally available in most SAP Business Suite systems. In Listing 11.1, you can see how we're preparing to work with this BO using the factory classes illustrated in Figure 11.13. Though there's a fair amount of work going on behind the scenes, the client-side API calls themselves are very straightforward.

```
DATA lo_svc_mngr TYPE REF TO /bobf/if_tra_service_manager.
DATA lo_txn_mngr TYPE REF TO /bobf/if_tra_transaction_mgr.
DATA lo_conf_mngr TYPE REF TO /bobf/if_frw_configuration.

TRY.
  lo_txn_mngr =
    /bobf/cl_tra_trans_mgr_factory=>get_transaction_manager( ).

  lo_svc_mngr =
    /bobf/cl_tra_serv_mgr_factory=>get_service_manager(
      /BOBF/IF_DEMO_SALES_ORDER_C=>SC_BO_KEY ).

  lo_conf_mngr =
    /bobf/cl_frw_factory=>get_configuration(
      /BOBF/IF_DEMO_SALES_ORDER_C=>SC_BO_KEY ).
CATCH /bobf/cx_frw.
  "TODO: Error handling...
ENDTRY.
```
Listing 11.1 Bootstrapping the BOPF API

In the upcoming sections, we'll start putting the API to work in performing basic CRUD operations on the /BOBF/DEMO_SALES_ORDER BO.

> **Note**
>
> You can find a fully developed version of this demonstration in the book's source code bundle.

11.3.2 Creating BO Instances and Node Rows

Much like the persistent objects we reviewed in Chapter 10, BOPF BOs are managed objects that must be created using the BOPF service manager. Here, most of the heavy lifting is carried out by the modify() method of the /BOBF/IF_TRA_SER-VICE_MANAGER interface. This method receives as its input an internal table called

IT_MODIFICATION that contains the nodes that we want to create. Create the right nodes, and you create a BO instance.

The code excerpt contained in Listing 11.2 demonstrates how we can use the modify() method to create an instance of the /BOBF/DEMO_SALES_ORDER BO.

> **Note**
>
> You can find a complete implementation of this code in the book's code bundle.

As you can see, the node creation process basically consists of creating a data reference, filling in the node data, and then adding the node as a record in the aforementioned IT_MODIFICATION table. Once this table is filled out, we can call the modify() method to apply the changes. Internally, the BOPF will process the request and carry out any validations/determinations configured to ensure that the integrity of the BO instance remains intact.

```
DATA lo_svc_mngr TYPE REF TO /bobf/if_tra_service_manager.
DATA lr_s_root TYPE REF TO /bobf/s_demo_sales_order_hdr_k.
DATA lr_s_root_text TYPE REF TO /bobf/s_demo_short_text_k.

DATA lt_mod TYPE /bobf/t_frw_modification.
FIELD-SYMBOLS <ls_mod> LIKE LINE OF lt_mod.
DATA lo_message TYPE REF TO /bobf/if_frw_message.
DATA lo_change TYPE REF TO /bobf/if_tra_change.

TRY.
  "Initialize the service manager:
  lo_svc_mngr =
    /bobf/cl_tra_serv_mgr_factory=>get_service_manager(
      /BOBF/IF_DEMO_SALES_ORDER_C=>SC_BO_KEY ).

  "Create the order ROOT node:
  CREATE DATA lr_s_root.
  lr_s_root->key = /bobf/cl_frw_factory=>get_new_key( ).
  lr_s_root->order_id = '1234567890'.
  ...
  lr_s_root->sales_org = 'AMER'.
  lr_s_root->amount = '250.00'.
  lr_s_root->amount_curr = 'USD'.

  APPEND INITIAL LINE TO lt_mod ASSIGNING <ls_mod>.
  <ls_mod>-node = /bobf/if_demo_sales_order_c=>sc_node-root.
  <ls_mod>-change_mode = /bobf/if_frw_c=>sc_modify_create.
  <ls_mod>-key = lr_s_root->key.
  <ls_mod>-data = lr_s_root.
```

```
"Create the order description:
CREATE DATA lr_s_root_text.
lr_s_root_text->key = /bobf/cl_frw_factory=>get_new_key( ).
lr_s_root_text->language = sy-langu.
lr_s_root_text->text = |Order # { lr_s_root->order_id }|.

APPEND INITIAL LINE TO lt_mod ASSIGNING <ls_mod>.
<ls_mod>-node = /bobf/if_demo_sales_order_c=>sc_node-root_text.
<ls_mod> change_mode = /bobf/if_frw_c=>sc_modify create.
<ls_mod>-source_node =
  /bobf/if_demo_sales_order_c=>sc_node-root.
<ls_mod>-association =
  /bobf/if_demo_sales_order_c=>sc_association-root-root_text.
<ls_mod>-source_key = lr_s_root->key.
<ls_mod>-key = lr_s_root_text->key.
<ls_mod>-data = lr_s_root_text.

"Apply the changes:
lo_svc_mngr->modify(
  EXPORTING
    it_modification = lt_mod
  IMPORTING
    eo_change       = lo_change
    eo_message      = lo_message ).

"Check the results:
IF lo_message IS BOUND AND lo_message->check( ) EQ    abap_true.
  "TODO: Error handling...
ENDIF.
CATCH /bobf/cx_frw.
  "TODO: Error handling...
ENDTRY.
```

Listing 11.2 Creating a Sales Order Instance Using the BOPF API

After the modify() method is finished, we can check the results using the following exporting parameters from the method signature:

▶ EO_CHANGE

This object reference parameter provides us with a handle that we can use to query the status of the updates and check for any failures that might have occurred. For more details about the types of operations you can perform, check out the documentation for interface /BOBF/IF_TRA_CHANGE.

▶ EO_MESSAGE

This object reference contains any human-readable messages generated during the update process. This includes messages issued from validations or determinations defined against the nodes being created. For more information about how to consume these messages, check out the documentation for interface /BOBF/IF_FRW_MESSAGE.

Assuming the modification process goes off without a hitch, the code excerpt contained in Listing 11.2 will generate a new sales order BO instance. However, it's worth noting that this instance only exists in shared memory. To persist this instance to the database, we must commit the in-flight transaction using the BOPF transaction manager. We'll see how to accomplish this in Section 11.3.6.

11.3.3   Searching for BO Instances

As we learned in Section 11.2.1, BOPF node rows are keyed by a UUID field called KEY. Though it's certainly efficient to access such rows by their key, many times we may not know the key offhand. In these situations, we can utilize BOPF queries to locate the node rows that we want to operate on.

The code excerpt contained in Listing 11.3 demonstrates how to utilize a BOPF query called SELECT_BY_ELEMENTS to search for a sales order instance using its ID. Using this same query, we could have searched for sales orders based on the sold-to customer, delivery status, and so on. We simply have to specify the search criteria by filling in a table of type /BOBF/T_FRW_QUERY_SELPARAM. This table type has a similar look and feel to ABAP range tables.

```
DATA lo_svc_mngr TYPE REF TO /bobf/if_tra_service_manager.
DATA lt_params TYPE /bobf/t_frw_query_selparam.
FIELD-SYMBOLS <ls_param> LIKE LINE OF lt_params.
DATA lt_key TYPE /bobf/t_frw_key.
FIELD-SYMBOLS <ls_key> LIKE LINE OF lt_key.
DATA lt_root TYPE /bobf/t_demo_sales_order_hdr_k.

APPEND INITIAL LINE TO lt_params ASSIGNING <ls_param>.
<ls_param>-attribute_name = 'ORDER_ID'.
<ls_param>-sign = 'I'.
<ls_param>-option = 'EQ'.
<ls_param>-low = '1234567890'.

lo_svc_mngr->query(
  EXPORTING
    iv_query_key =
    /bobf/if_demo_sales_order_c=>sc_query-root-select_by_elements
    it_selection_parameters = lt_params
    iv_fill_data = abap_true
  IMPORTING
```

```
      et_data = lt_root
      et_key = lt_key ).

READ TABLE lt_root...
```
Listing 11.3 Searching for BO Instances Using BOPF Queries

As you can see in Listing 11.3, there are two output parameters defined by the
`query()` method:

▶ `ET_DATA`
If the `IV_FILL_DATA` Boolean input parameter is set to true, then the actual node
row data for any found rows will be returned via the `ET_DATA` exporting parameter.

▶ `ET_KEY`
This table parameter passes back the keys of any found node row matching the
selection criteria.

So, depending on our use case, we can either fetch the keys of records that match
some selection criteria, or we can retrieve the actual node row data. In the next
section, we'll see how we can do productive things with this data once we
retrieve it using the BOPF service manager.

11.3.4 Updating and Deleting BO Node Rows

Once we get our hands on BO node rows, the process of applying updates to
these nodes is almost identical to the one we used to create the node rows in the
first place (refer back to Section 11.3.2). This is demonstrated in the code excerpt
contained in Listing 11.4. Here, we're updating the sales order `ROOT` node by
adjusting the overall amount. Then, we tell the BOPF we want to apply the update
by mapping the appropriate value in the `CHANGE_MODE` attribute highlighted in
Listing 11.4. Had we wanted to delete this node row, we would have assigned the
value `/BOBF/IF_FRW_C=>SC_MODIFY_DELETE`. In either case, the BOPF uses the
`CHANGE_MODE` attribute in conjunction with the rest of the data contained in the
modification table to identify the target node row (via the `KEY` attribute) and process the update.

```
DATA lo_svc_mngr TYPE REF TO /bobf/if_tra_service_manager.
DATA lr_s_root TYPE REF TO /bobf/s_demo_sales_order_hdr_k.
DATA lt_mod TYPE /bobf/t_frw_modification.
FIELD-SYMBOLS <ls_mod> LIKE LINE OF lt_mod.
```

```
DATA lo_message TYPE REF TO /bobf/if_frw_message.

...
READ TABLE lt_root INDEX 1 REFERENCE INTO lr_s_root.
IF sy-subrc EQ 0.
  lr_s_root->amount = lr_s_root->amount + '20.00'.

  APPEND INITIAL LINE TO lt_mod ASSIGNING <ls_mod>.
  <ls_mod>-node = /bobf/if_demo_sales_order_c=>sc_node-root.
  <ls_mod>-change_mode = /bobf/if_frw_c=>sc_modify_update.

  <ls_mod>-key = lr_s_root->key.
  <ls_mod>-data = lr_s_root.

  APPEND 'AMOUNT' TO <ls_mod>-changed_fields.
ENDIF.

IF lines( lt_mod ) GT 0.
  lo_svc_mngr->modify(
    EXPORTING
      it_modification = lt_mod
    IMPORTING
      eo_message      = lo_message ).

  "TODO: Error handling...
ENDIF.
```

Listing 11.4 Updating BO Node Rows Using the BOPF API

As is the case with the creation operation, all of the updates/deletes we perform using the modify() method are merely staged in shared memory until we either commit the transaction or roll it back. When building UI applications, this feature comes in quite handy since it makes it easy to manage long-running stateful sessions with users.

11.3.5 Executing Actions

In order to invoke a BOPF action, we simply need to call the do_action() method of the /BOBF/IF_TRA_SERVICE_MANAGER interface. This is demonstrated in the code excerpt contained in Listing 11.5. Here, we're calling the DELIVER action defined for the ROOT node of the /BOBF/DEMO_SALES_ORDER BO. In order to invoke this action, we simply need to pass in the action key, the key(s) of the node rows we want to process, and optionally a parameter structure.

```
DATA lo_svc_mngr TYPE REF TO /bobf/if_tra_service_manager.
DATA lt_key TYPE /bobf/t_frw_key.
FIELD-SYMBOLS <ls_key> LIKE LINE OF lt_key.
DATA lo_message TYPE REF TO /bobf/if_frw_message.
DATA lt_failed_key TYPE /bobf/t_frw_key.

"Call the DELIVER action:
lo_svc_mngr->do_action(
  EXPORTING
    iv_act_key =
      /bobf/if_demo_sales_order_c=>sc_action-root-deliver
    it_key = lt_key
  IMPORTING
    eo_message = lo_message
    et_failed_key = lt_failed_key ).

"Check the results:
IF lines( et_failed_key ) GT 0.
  "TODO: Error handling...
ENDIF.
```

Listing 11.5 Calling an Action Using the BOPF API

If any errors occur during the action processing, the corresponding node row keys will be added to the ET_FAILED_KEY exporting parameter. We can use this information in conjunction with the EO_MESSAGE exporting parameter to determine what might have gone wrong with the action call.

11.3.6 Working with the Transaction Manager

As we noted previously, all updates that we perform via the BOPF service manager are staged in shared memory. To commit these changes, we must invoke the save() method of the BOPF transaction manager. The code excerpt contained in Listing 11.6 demonstrates how this works.

```
DATA lo_txn_mngr TYPE REF TO /bobf/if_tra_transaction_mgr.
DATA lo_svc_mngr TYPE REF TO /bobf/if_tra_service_manager.
DATA lo_message TYPE REF TO /bobf/if_frw_message.
DATA lv_rejected TYPE boole_d.

TRY.
  "Initialize the BOPF API:
  lo_txn_mngr =
    /bobf/cl_tra_trans_mgr_factory=>get_transaction_manager( ).

  lo_svc_mngr =
```

```
    /bobf/cl_tra_serv_mgr_factory=>get_service_manager(
      /BOBF/IF_DEMO_SALES_ORDER_C=>SC_BO_KEY ).

  "Perform various updates using the BOPF service manager:
  ...

  "Commit the changes:
  lo_txn_mngr->save(
    IMPORTING
      eo_message = lo_message
      ev_rejected = lv_rejected ).

  IF lv_rejected EQ abap_true.
    "TODO: Error handling...
  ENDIF.
CATCH /bobf/cx_frw.
  "TODO: Error handling...
ENDTRY.
```
Listing 11.6 Working with the BOPF Transaction Manager

As you can see in Listing 11.6, the transaction manager mostly sits off to the side while we're performing our basic updates. It's certainly keeping track of things behind-the-scenes but, from an API perspective, we don't really notice it. It only really comes into play whenever we determine we either need to commit or roll-back a set of changes. For commits, we call the `save()` method; for rollbacks, the `cleanup()` method. Note that in either case, we don't have to chase the call with a `COMMIT WORK` statement – this is handled implicitly within the BOPF internal framework layer.

If a save/commit request is rejected, the `EV_REJECTED` flag will be set to true. Assuming that's the case, we can use the `EO_MESSAGE` exporting parameter to determine what went wrong. Most of the time, the messages contained in this parameter will be generated via consistency checks/validations performed within the BOPF nodes staged for updates. This last-minute check ensures that nothing slips through the cracks.

11.4 Where to Go From Here

Now that you have a general sense for what the BOPF is all about, let's take a moment to digest what we've learned and see how it relates to OO-based development in ABAP.

11.4.1 Looking at the Big Picture

Thinking back on the code excerpts demonstrated in Section 11.3, you might be inclined to think that BOPF development is rather tedious. While this is true to a point, it's worth pointing out that the BOPF is rarely consumed directly as we demonstrated in this chapter. Instead, BOPF BOs are normally consumed through higher-level frameworks which abstract away the more wearisome aspects of the API. These frameworks make it easy to consume BOs using SAP Gateway/OData services, through Web Dynpro ABAP (WDA) UI applications based on Floorplan Manager (FPM), and so forth.

Since this book is focused on OOP concepts, we're not so concerned with the specifics of any one-off consumption framework. Instead, our focus is on reusable API designs. When you think about the BOPF API design, it's completely generic. Whether we're dealing with a sales order BO, or a business partner BO, or a custom BO or our choosing, the API call sequence remains the same. We simply supply the API with a BO key and we're up and running. So, what can we take away from all this? Well, in terms of API design, we can see that the BOPF certainly employs many of the best practices described throughout this book:

▶ **Encapsulation**
The core business logic for a BOPF BO is encapsulated within its internal node elements (e.g. as actions, determinations, and validations). This is encapsulation on a macro scale, encompassing every aspect of a particular BO/entity.

▶ **Designing to Interfaces**
Looking at the UML class diagram depicting the BOPF API in Figure 11.13, you can see that clients work with generic interfaces which provide a consistent interface for working with BOPF BOs. Indeed, with a little bit of up-front RTTI/introspection development, we can build agents that can consume/interact with any BO type.

▶ **Cohesiveness**
Because of its strong object model, BOPF BOs tend to have very high *cohesion*. This is to say that node elements focus on implementing modeling the business logic and not on how they might be consumed via clients and/or UIs.

▶ **Introspection/Discoverability**
Using the /BOBF/IF_FRW_CONFIGURATION interface, clients can discover any aspect of a given BO using just its key. This, combined with the ABAP RTTI API, makes it possible for clients to dynamically consume BO data or adapt it for use in data binding protocols.

At the end of the day, we're still employing OO concepts; it's just that with the BOPF we're doing it on a larger scale. Since our primary objective is to build a better abstraction, we can think of the BOPF as a means of applying our OO-based artifacts towards the development of reusable BOs/entities.

11.4.2 Building and Enhancing BOs

At the time of this writing, SAP has already built several applications on top of the BOPF, and several more are on the way. Over time, developers will find that the BOPF repository will continue to grow with a wider set of reusable BOs. In addition to the standard offering, we also have the opportunity to create and model our own BOs. Assuming your SAP system has the appropriate patch level (see the sidebar below), you can create new BOs using the *Business Object Builder* provided via Transaction BOB. This transaction provides a WYSIWYG editor for modeling BOs and defining nodes/node elements. The implementation code is maintained using the Class Builder as per usual.

> **Note**
>
> The BOPF framework as a whole was opened up for general-purpose use with the release of the SAP Business Suite EhP 5, SP 11 (and EhP 6, SP 5). You can find more information about this release via SAP Note 1760610.

Besides creating new BOs, we also have the option of enhancing/extending existing BO types. This can be achieved using the *BOPF Enhancement Workbench* provided via Transaction /BOBF/CUST_UI. Here, we enhance an extensible BO by creating an enhancement BO which effectively inherits its node hierarchy from the parent. From here, we can define new custom nodes or add custom node elements to existing nodes. For more information about the features provided here, we highly recommend that you spend some time reading over the BOPF Enhancement Workbench help documentation.

11.4.3 Finding BOPF-Related Resources

These days, there are a lot of useful resources out there related to the BOPF. For the most part, these resources are consolidated on the BOPF Application Framework community page on the SAP SCN. You can access this page via the URL *http://scn.sap.com/community/abap/bopf*.

11.5   UML Tutorial: Advanced Sequence Diagrams

In this section, we'll look at some advanced features of UML sequence diagrams. As a frame of reference for this discussion, we've revised the sequence diagram example from Chapter 3 in Figure 11.16 to include some of the more advanced features that will be discussed in the upcoming subsections.

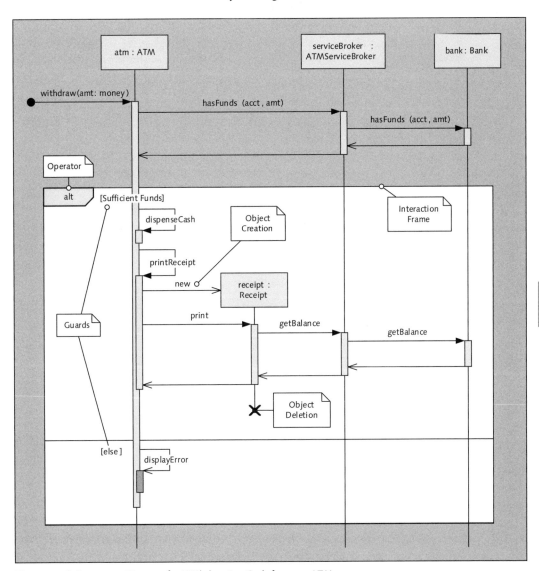

Figure 11.16 Sequence Diagram for Withdrawing Cash from an ATM

11.5.1 Creating and Deleting Objects

Within a given activation, it's not uncommon for a method to need to dynamically create another object in order to carry out a particular task. As you can see in Figure 11.16, the creation of an object is initiated by a special new message. The message name is actually optional, but the general convention is to name the message new. Here, notice that the object box for the receipt object is aligned with the creation message. This notation helps to clarify the fact that the object did not exist whenever the interaction began. Once an object is created, you can send messages to it just like any of the other objects in the sequence diagram.

If the created object is a temporary object (e.g. a local variable inside a method, etc.), then you can depict the deletion of the object by terminating the object lifeline with an X (see Figure 11.16). It's also possible for one object to explicitly delete another object by mapping a message from the requesting object to an X on the target object's lifeline.

11.5.2 Depicting Control Logic with Interaction Frames

As a rule, you typically do not want to depict a lot of control logic in a sequence diagram. However, it's sometimes helpful to include some high-level logic so that the interaction between the objects is more clear. In UML 2.0, this control flow is depicted using *interaction frames*.

An interaction frame partitions off a portion of the sequence diagram inside of a rectangular boundary. The functionality depicted in an interaction frame is described by an *operator* that is listed in the upper left-hand corner of the frame. For example, the sequence diagram in Figure 11.16 shows an interaction frame that is using the alt operator. The alt operator is used to depict conditional logic such as an IF...ELSE or CASE statement. The branches of this conditional logic are divided by a horizontal dashed line. Furthermore, each branch of the logic also contains a conditional expression called a *guard*. As you would expect, guards control whether or not the control flows to a particular branch of the conditional logic. For instance, in the sequence diagram shown in Figure 11.16, the atm object will only dispense cash if there are sufficient funds in the account. Otherwise, an error message will be displayed on the console.

Table 11.2 describes some of the basic operators that can be used with interaction frames. Again, we want to stress the fact that interaction frames should be used very sparingly. If you need to depict more complex logic, consider using an activity diagram or even some basic pseudocode.

Operator	Usage Type
alt	Used to depict conditional logic such as an IF...ELSE or CASE statement.
opt	Used to depict an optional piece of logic such as a basic IF statement.
par	Used to depict parallel behavior. In this case, each fragment in the interaction frame runs in parallel.
loop	Used to depict various types of looping structures (i.e. LOOP, DO, etc.).
ref	Used to reference an interaction defined on another sequence diagram.
sd	Used to surround an embedded sequence diagram within the current sequence diagram.

Table 11.2 Interaction Frame Operators

11.6 Summary

This concludes our introduction to the BOPF. Whether or not you plan to utilize the BOPF in your own custom developments, we hope that you'll have found this introduction useful in that it shows you how OO concepts can be applied on a wider scale within a reusable framework. This is an important concept to consider as your OO designs mature beyond a handful of classes. As designs increase in scope, it's useful to have a framework like the BOPF to organize development objects and provide an abstraction around common tasks such as transaction handling, persistence, and so on.

In the next chapter, we'll take a look at report development using the popular *SAP List Viewer* (ALV) framework. With this framework as a baseline, we'll develop our own report development framework which makes it easy for any ABAP developer to come along and build reports without any pre-existing ALV knowledge.

This chapter explores the OO-based enhancements added to the SAP List Viewer framework used to build interactive reports in ABAP. Here, we'll see how core OO concepts are applied to interface with the SAP standard components and build a flexible reporting framework on top of them.

12 Working with the SAP List Viewer

In the early days of ABAP Objects, the use of OO extensions was pretty much limited to a handful of specialized use cases. While customers were free to create their own classes and really embrace the OO mindset, SAP wasn't exactly leading the charge by delivering lots of OO-based content. However, in recent years, this trend has changed quite a bit.

Nowadays, SAP best practices call for the development of any new content to be based on OO concepts. So, whether you're building UIs with Web Dynpro for ABAP (WDA) or the Floorplan Manager (FPM) framework, interfacing with business objects, or creating enhancements, classes are at the heart of most everything.

In this chapter, we'll look at one area in particular where an OO-based approach has greatly simplified the implementation effort: interactive reporting with the *SAP List Viewer* (ALV). Here, we'll learn how SAP's *ALV Object Model* allows ABAP developers to greatly reduce the amount of code it takes to create an interactive report. Once you get the hang of the ALV Object Model, we'll see how we can expand on this foundation to create our own reporting framework which makes it possible for ABAP developers who don't know anything about ALV to quickly create a fully-functional report.

12.1 What is the SAP List Viewer?

Even though ALV technology has been around for a while, many readers may not be familiar with it so a brief introduction is in order. This introduction will also be of some interest to more experienced ABAP developers who may not realize all of the recent changes applied to the SAP List Viewer.

SAP List Viewer = ABAP List Viewer = ALV

Many ABAP developers may know the SAP List Viewer framework by a different name: the *ABAP List Viewer* (ALV). For many years, ALV was the catch-all term used to describe the functionality we now know as the SAP List Viewer. In recent years, SAP decided to re-brand the framework as SAP List Viewer in order to more broadly encompass ALV-based functionality that was ported to Web Dynpro ABAP and Web Dynpro Java. For the purposes of this book, we'll use the ALV abbreviation as this is consistent with SAP help documentation, etc.

As the name suggests, ALV is a framework that can be used to build *lists*. Here, we're talking about reports that contain a list/table of items such as a list of customers who have overdue payments, a list of materials based on some set of characteristics, and so forth. Such reports can be very fancy with lots of bells and whistles or just a straight dump of data from some ABAP Dictionary table(s). As a generic framework, we can use ALV to produce lists from most any kind of structured data source imaginable.

Figure 12.1 contains an example of a simple flight listing created using the ALV table control. Here, you can see how the flight records are displayed in a 2D table which resembles a Microsoft Excel worksheet. Other ALV controls allow you to output the data in hierarchical fashion as trees or tree tables.

OOP Book: Flight Report Demo

Client	Airline	Flight No.	Flight Date	Airfare	Currency	Plane Type	Capacity	Occupied	Total	Capacity	Occupied	Capacity	Occupied
001	AA	17	12/17/2014	422.94	USD	747-400	385	375	193,897.10	31	31	21	19
001	AA	17	01/14/2015	422.94	USD	747-400	385	372	193,106.22	31	30	21	20
001	AA	17	02/11/2015	422.94	USD	747-400	385	367	190,860.36	31	28	21	21
001	AA	17	03/11/2015	422.94	USD	747-400	385	371	192,277.19	31	30	21	20
001	AA	17	04/08/2015	422.94	USD	747-400	385	369	192,615.59	31	31	21	21
001	AA	17	05/06/2015	422.94	USD	747-400	385	364	187,701.01	31	29	21	19
001	AA	17	06/03/2015	422.94	USD	747-400	385	366	192,772.05	31	31	21	21
001	AA	17	07/01/2015	422.94	USD	747-400	385	371	191,850.03	31	29	21	20
001	AA	17	07/29/2015	422.94	USD	747-400	385	373	194,979.73	31	31	21	20
001	AA	17	08/26/2015	422.94	USD	747-400	385	194	98,646.65	31	14	21	10
001	AA	17	09/23/2015	422.94	USD	747-400	385	149	76,467.72	31	12	21	8
001	AA	17	10/21/2015	422.94	USD	747-400	385	107	56,018.50	31	9	21	6
001	AA	17	11/18/2015	422.94	USD	747-400	385	70	36,770.41	31	6	21	4
001	AA	17	12/16/2015	422.94	USD	747-400	385	11	6,386.39	31	1	21	1
001	AA	17	01/13/2016	422.94	USD	747-400	385	17	9,220.12	31	2	21	1
001	AA	64	12/19/2014	422.94	USD	A310-300	280	269	134,380.85	22	22	10	10
001	AA	64	01/16/2015	422.94	USD	A310-300	280	268	133,801.46	22	22	10	10
001	AA	64	02/13/2015	422.94	USD	A310-300	280	271	134,220.11	22	22	10	9
001	AA	64	03/13/2015	422.94	USD	A310-300	280	271	134,135.51	22	22	10	9
001	AA	64	04/10/2015	422.94	USD	A310-300	280	271	134,262.46	22	21	10	10

Figure 12.1 An Example SAP List Viewer Report

As you can see in Figure 12.1, ALV controls includes a host of toolbar functions which allow end users to sort the data, filter it, export it to desktop applications, and so on. These functions are implemented within the framework itself; there's no special coding required to enable this functionality. Internally, these function requests are primarily handled on the client side via SAP standard ActiveX/JavaBean controls and the SAP Control Framework. While the internals of all this is abstracted within the overall framework, the main take-away from this is that the functions are very responsive since the user doesn't have to wait on lengthy server roundtrips which exchange lots of data back and forth.

ALV: A Brief History

Over the years, the ALV programming model has seen many changes. To a large extent, these changes have had less to do with changes to the base-level functionality of the underlying ALV controls and more to do with the way ABAP developers prefer to interface with them.

All along, the ALV framework has been based on a series of client-side controls (e.g. ActiveX controls) which are loaded and managed from an ABAP context using the SAP Control Framework. Included in all this are a series of low-level ABAP Objects classes which provide a thin layer of abstraction on top of the client-side controls: CL_GUI_ALV_GRID and so on. While it's technically possible to interface directly with these classes, doing so requires some fairly specialized knowledge about classic Dynpro programming and the internal workings of ALV.

Recognizing this complexity, SAP has introduced several programming models over the years to provide developers with an abstraction that's easy to work with. This started with the REUSE* function modules which made it possible for procedural programmers to build ALV reports without having to put on their OOP hats. Included in this function suite was the REUSE_ALV_LIST_DISPLAY function used to create a simple tabular list and REUSE_ALV_HIERSEQ_LIST to build tree tables.

For years, ABAP developers have leveraged the REUSE* function modules to create ALV reports. Indeed, even now it's quite common to see new reports being built on this legacy programming model. While these modules still work, they're really starting to show their age. In particular, there are several pain points worth mentioning:

1. The REUSE* function modules are stateless function modules which don't provide developers with a handle for addressing the ALV control after the report is generated. This is fine for simple static reports, but problematic for complex interactive reports.

2. The interface of the REUSE* function modules is incredibly cluttered and can be overwhelming for new developers trying to figure out how to use these modules.

3. As an extension of the previous point, the function modules typically require you to specify much more than just the report data to bootstrap the report. Though enhanced recently, these modules generally require the manual creation of field catalogs and other settings which call for lots of redundant boilerplate code.

Historically, developers have gotten around these issues by creating "template" reports which other developers copy-and-paste to create a new report. However, beginning with Release 7.00 of the AS ABAP, SAP presented developers with a new OO-based programming model that encapsulates the basic functionality defined with these templates into easy-to-use classes: the *ALV object model*. In the next section, we'll learn about the ALV object model and see how it can be used to build interactive reports.

12.2   Introducing the ALV Object Model

If you've ever worked with the REUSE* function modules described in Section 12.1, then you can probably attest to the fact that there's lots of boiler plate code required to create a new report. With the ALV object model, all the same parameters are available, but encapsulated into smaller classes which are rather *opinionated*. Here, the term "opinionated" implies that the individual classes of the ALV object model are smart enough to specify default values on our behalf if we just want the report to exhibit common/standard behavior in a certain area.

For example, if we know we want to display all of the columns in an internal table in the list output, we don't have to pass the ALV object model a field catalog. Instead, we can let the ALV object model derive this field catalog internally by introspecting the internal table type definition using the *ABAP Run Time Type Ser-*

vices (RTTS) framework. Indeed, if all we want to do is create a report to display the contents of an internal table, we can use the ALV object model to get this done in less than 10 lines of ABAP code as demonstrated by the simple report contained in Listing 12.1.

```
REPORT zalvreport.
DATA gt_outtab TYPE STANDARD TABLE OF sflight.
DATA go_alv_table TYPE REF TO cl_salv_table.

START-OF-SELECTION.
  SELECT * FROM sflight INTO TABLE gt_outtab.

  cl_salv_table=>factory(
    IMPORTING
      r_salv_table = go_alv_table
    CHANGING
      t_table = gt_outtab ).

  go_alv_table->display( ).
```
Listing 12.1 A Simple Report Using the ALV Object Model

As you can see in Listing 12.1, the ALV object model makes it absurdly easy to create a simple ALV report. In this simple example, we produce the output in three easy steps:

1. First, we build an internal table using regular ABAP code (e.g. using the SELECT statement).

2. Then, we use the factory() method of class CL_SALV_TABLE to create an instance of the ALV table control, binding the control with the table we built in the first step.

3. Finally, we use the CL_SALV_TABLE instance's display() method to display the list control on the screen.

For more sophisticated reports, the model is generally the same only we include some additional formatting logic in between steps two and three. For this, we call on the various getter methods of the ALV control we're dealing with: CL_SALV_TABLE for two-dimensional tables and CL_SALV_HIERSEQ_TABLE for tree-tables. The class diagram contained in Figure 12.2 illustrates the relationships between the core classes of the ALV object model.

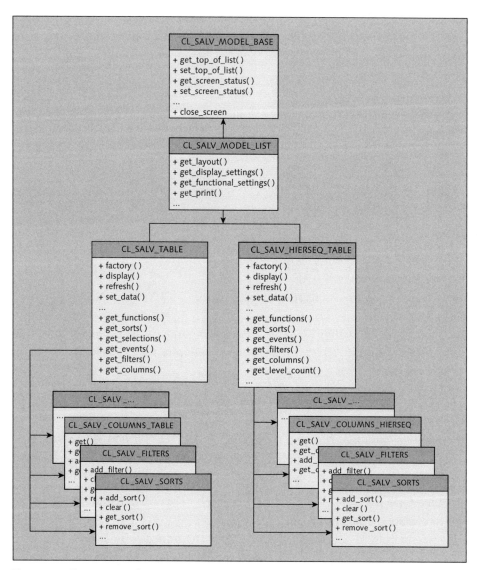

Figure 12.2 Class Diagram for ALV Object Model

As you can see in Figure 12.2, the getter methods in CL_SALV_TABLE and CL_SALV_ HIERSEQ_TABLE return instances of classes that encapsulate specific aspects of the ALV output. For example, if we want to adjust the sort conditions of the output, we can call on the get_sorts() method of either class to get an instance of type CL_SALV_SORTS. Using the methods defined in CL_SALV_SORTS, we can add/

remove sorting conditions, query the existing conditions, and so forth. The same general principles work for adjusting filter conditions, columns in the list layout, etc.

Finding the ALV Object Model Documentation

To find a comprehensive treatment of all the available classes and their methods, we would encourage you to look at the class documentation in the Class Builder tool as well as the online help documentation available at *http://help.sap.com*. From the landing page, click on TECHNOLOGY • SAP NETWEAVER PLATFORM • {YOUR CURRENT NETWEAVER RELEASE} • FUNCTION-ORIENTED VIEW • {YOUR LANGUAGE} to navigate to the SAP NetWeaver Library documentation. From here, click on UI TECHNOLOGIES IN SAP NETWEAVER • SAP GUI • SAP GUI TECHNOLOGY • SAP LIST VIEWER (ALV).

12.3 Developing a Reporting Framework on top of ALV

Historically, one of the hardest parts about working with classic Dynpro/SAP GUI technology is that it doesn't lend itself very well to pattern-oriented UI development using the *model-view-controller* (MVC) design pattern. This doesn't mean that it's impossible to achieve MVC when building ALV reports; it just means that we have to work at it a little bit more.

What that in mind, in this section, we'll attempt to build a framework which places some boundaries around the ALV report creation process and helps facilitate a clear separation of concerns between ALV-related output generation, data selection, and event handling. For the purposes of this demonstration, we'll focus on building reports using the CL_SALV_TABLE control, though we could have just as easily built a framework around the CL_SALV_HIERSEQ_TABLE.

Besides offering some utility for ALV report generation, the development of this framework will also allow us to exercise our OO minds and consider how concepts like encapsulation, designing to interfaces, and polymorphism can be applied in practical use case scenarios. So, without further ado, let's get started.

What is MVC?

MVC is a software design pattern which emphasizes a separation of concerns between the user interface (*view*) and the business/data model that's being edited in the view. This separation is desirable because the two layers tend to evolve differently over time:

> ► UI technology tends to change quite rapidly—so much so that a new UI application is almost outdated from the day it goes live. To put this into perspective, consider how many new UI technologies we've seen in the SAP world in the last 10-12 years: *Business Server Pages* (BSPs), Web Dynpro ABAP (WDA) and now the HTML5-based SAPUI5 framework.
>
> ► On the other hand, the business logic/data model behind a UI application may change in more subtle ways as new processes are rolled out, enhancements are made, and so forth.
>
> Ideally, we'd like to keep these two layers separate so that they can vary independently. For example, if we want to switch from a WDA-based UI to an SAPUI5-based UI, we should be able to do this without affecting the underlying business model. In effect, we're just putting a different face on the application. Similarly, the view shouldn't be impacted by changes to the implementation of the business model. For example, if a company decides to refactor the data model to take advantages of new technology innovations provided by SAP HANA, the view really shouldn't be impacted by this. Again, this is another example of "design-by-contract" in action.
>
> To achieve this separation, we must set up boundaries between the view and model layers and let an intermediary (the controller) broker the data exchange behind the scenes. This keeps the UI application architecture flexible and easy to reuse as technology/requirements change.
>
> Whether we're developing in cutting edge UI technology or classic Dynpro and ALV, the strategy remains the same—we want to maintain a clear separation of concerns with our UI designs.

12.3.1 Step 1: Identifying the Key Classes and Interfaces

As we observed in Section 12.2, the ALV object model does a good job of encapsulating view-level concerns such as rendering the ALV list, etc. So, rather than reinventing the wheel, our framework will leverage the ALV object model as-is to handle view-level concerns. With that foundation in place, our focus will be on building out the controller and model layers—keeping in mind that we're going to want to eventually integrate them into an ABAP report program.

The UML class diagram contained in Figure 12.3 identifies the classes/interfaces that we've introduced with our custom reporting framework. Moving from left-to-right, we can identify these types as follows:

► `ZCL_ALV_REPORT_CONTROLLER`
This class provides the base-level controller for the framework, providing integration between the ABAP report program, the ALV table control, and a report *feeder class*.

▶ ZIF_ALV_REPORT_FEEDER

This interface provides the basic blueprint for the aforementioned report feeder class. Here, we're drawing inspiration from SAP's *Floorplan Manager* (FPM) and *Personal Object Worklist* (POWL) frameworks which have similar constructs in place to provide instance-specific extensions of the controller that facilitate simplified integration with the model layer.

▶ ZCL_ALV_TABLE_EVENT

This class encapsulates all of the various types of events that might be fired by the CL_SALV_TABLE control (e.g., double-clicking on a cell, clicking on a toolbar function, or printing out the top of the page). By encapsulating these events centrally, we can define a single event handler method in the feeder class called process_event() in which consumers of the framework can quickly build up eventing scenarios. It also allows us to abstract the event registration process which is normally required when working with the ALV object model.

▶ ZCL_ALV_RPT_PARAMETERS

This class encapsulates the various parameters passed by the CL_SALV_TABLE control whenever an event is fired. Consumers can access this object instance (which is automatically provisioned by the ZCL_ALV_REPORT_CONTROLLER class) via the ZCL_ALV_TABLE_EVENT object reference passed into the process_event() method of the feeder class.

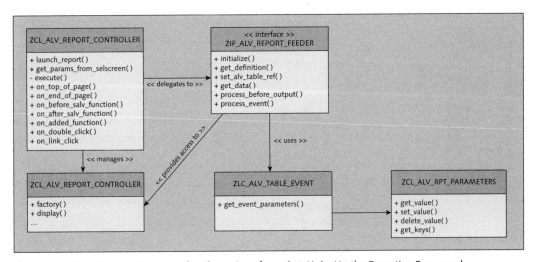

Figure 12.3 Class Diagram Depicting the Classes/Interfaces that Make Up the Reporting Framework

12.3.2 Step 2: Integrating the Framework into an ABAP Report Program

Now that you have a sense for the key classes/interfaces that make up the framework, let's take a look at how we can incorporate these elements into a functional report program. To guide us through this process, we'll re-create the simple flights report we created in Listing 12.1.

The code excerpt contained in Listing 12.2 shows how we're integrating the ZCL_ ALV_REPORT_CONTROLLER class into an ABAP report program. As you can see, there's not much code required to bootstrap the framework. We basically just need to collect any selection screen parameters we'd like to pass on to the model layer and then call the static launch_report() method of the ZCL_ALV_REPORT_ CONTROLLER class to start the report processing.

```
REPORT zflights_report.
TABLES: sflight.
SELECT-OPTIONS:
  s_carrid FOR sflight-carrid,
  s_connid FOR sflight-connid,
  s_fldate FOR sflight-fldate.

DATA gt_params TYPE
  zif_alv_report_feeder=>ty_selection_param_tab.

AT SELECTION-SCREEN.
  zcl_alv_report_controller=>get_params_from_selscreen(
    EXPORTING
      iv_program_name = sy-repid
      iv_screen_number = sy-dynnr
    IMPORTING
      et_parameters = gt_params ).

START-OF-SELECTION.
  zcl_alv_report_controller=>launch_report(
    EXPORTING
      iv_feeder_class = 'ZCL_FLIGHT_FEEDER'
      it_selection_params = gt_params ).
```

Listing 12.2 Recreating the Flights Report Using the Custom Framework

Looking closely at the code excerpt contained in Listing 12.2, you can see how the first parameter we're passing to the launch_report() method is the name of our custom feeder class. We'll learn how to build out this feeder class in Section 12.3.3, but for now, just note that this is how we're injecting custom report logic into the framework.

Aside from the feeder class, we're also passing a parameter list to the optional IT_ SELECTION_PARAMS parameter of the launch_report() method. Since parameters/ select-options in ABAP are treated like global variables within the defining report program, we wanted to capture these values in a format that's easier to exchange from an OO context. This logic is encapsulated in the get_params_from_ selscreen() utility method provided with the ZCL_ALV_REPORT_CONTROLLER class.

After we bundle up the selection screen parameters and identify the feeder class, we can effectively transfer control from the ABAP report program to the framework. This frees us from having to worry about the impedance mismatch between ABAP event-based reports on one hand and the OO-based framework on the other.

12.3.3 Step 3: Creating Custom Report Feeder Classes

With the basic framework in place, all that's left is to build out the report-specific logic in the custom feeder classes. For this, we create a regular ABAP Objects class that implements the ZIF_ALV_REPORT_FEEDER interface.

For simple reports, there are generally two main methods in the ZIF_ALV_REPORT_ FEEDER interface that we need to provide a concrete implementation for:

▶ get_definition()
In this method, we need to generate a descriptor object which informs the framework about the type of data we plan on representing via the report. Here, we must use the CL_ABAP_TABLEDESCR class of the ABAP RTTS API to describe the internal table type that we'll be returning via the get_data() method.

▶ get_data()
In this method, we implement the integration logic required to fetch report data from the underlying model layer. For simple reports, this could be as simple as a SELECT statement, but normally we'd prefer to delegate to a more sophisticated business objects layer (e.g., the BOPF, for instance).

By simply implementing these two methods, we have enough functionality in place to produce a working report like the one shown in Figure 12.1. The code excerpt contained in Listing 12.3 demonstrates how we might implement the default reporting logic in the ZCL_FLIGHT_FEEDER class. As you can see, the hardest part of all this is parsing the selection screen parameters into ABAP range tables—everything else is basic ABAP without any specialized ALV knowledge required.

```
CLASS zcl_flight_feeder DEFINITION.
  PUBLIC SECTION.
    INTERFACES zif_alv_report_feeder.
    TYPES ty_flights_tab TYPE STANDARD TABLE OF slfight.

  PRIVATE SECTION.
    DATA mr_t_data TYPE REF TO data.
ENDCLASS.

CLASS zcl_flight_feeder IMPLEMENTATION.
  METHOD zif_alv_report_feeder~get_definition.
    DATA lt_flights TYPE zcl_flight_feeder=>ty_flights_tab.
    eo_field_catalog ?=
      cl_abap_tabledescr=>describe_by_data( lt_flights ).
  ENDMETHOD.

  METHOD zif_alv_report_feeder~get_data.
    DATA: BEGIN OF ls_search,
            carrid TYPE RANGE OF sflight-carrid,
            connid TYPE RANGE OF sflight-connid,
            fldate TYPE RANGE OF sflight-fldate,
          END OF ls_search.
    FIELD-SYMBOLS <ls_param> LIKE LINE OF it_selection_params.
    FIELD-SYMBOLS <ls_temp> TYPE any.
    TYPES ty_flights_tab TYPE STANDARD TABLE OF sflight.
    FIELD-SYMBOLS <lt_data> TYPE ty_flights_tab.

    GET REFERENCE OF ct_data INTO me->mr_t_data.
    ASSIGN me->mr_t_data->* TO <lt_data>.

    LOOP AT it_selection_params ASSIGNING <ls_param>.
      CASE <ls_param>-attribute_name.
        WHEN 'S_CARRID'.
          APPEND INITIAL LINE TO ls_search-carrid
                    ASSIGNING <ls_temp>.
          MOVE-CORRESPONDING <ls_param> TO <ls_temp>.
        WHEN 'S_CONNID'.
          APPEND INITIAL LINE TO ls_search-connid
                    ASSIGNING <ls_temp>.
          MOVE-CORRESPONDING <ls_param> TO <ls_temp>.
        WHEN 'S_FLDATE'.
          APPEND INITIAL LINE TO ls_search-fldate
                    ASSIGNING <ls_temp>.
          MOVE-CORRESPONDING <ls_param> TO <ls_temp>.
      ENDCASE.
    ENDLOOP.

    "Search the flights database:
```

```
    SELECT *
      INTO TABLE <lt_data>
      FROM sflight
     WHERE carrid IN ls_search-carrid
       AND connid IN ls_search-connid
       AND fldate IN ls_search-fldate.
  ENDMETHOD.
  ...
ENDCLASS.
```

Listing 12.3 Implementing the Flights Report Feeder Class

With this foundation in place, we can begin splicing in more advanced functionality into our feeder class. In the upcoming subsections, we'll demonstrate how this works.

Adjusting Output Properties on the ALV List

By default, the ZCL_ALV_REPORT_CONTROLLER class will apply various defaults to make sure the ALV object model is instantiated properly. Here, it will optimize the column layout, make sure that the default toolbar functions are enabled, etc. While this is enough to bootstrap the framework, there may be times that we want to tweak the output further. In these situations, we can leverage the process_before_output() method of the feeder class to apply any last-minute formatting additions.

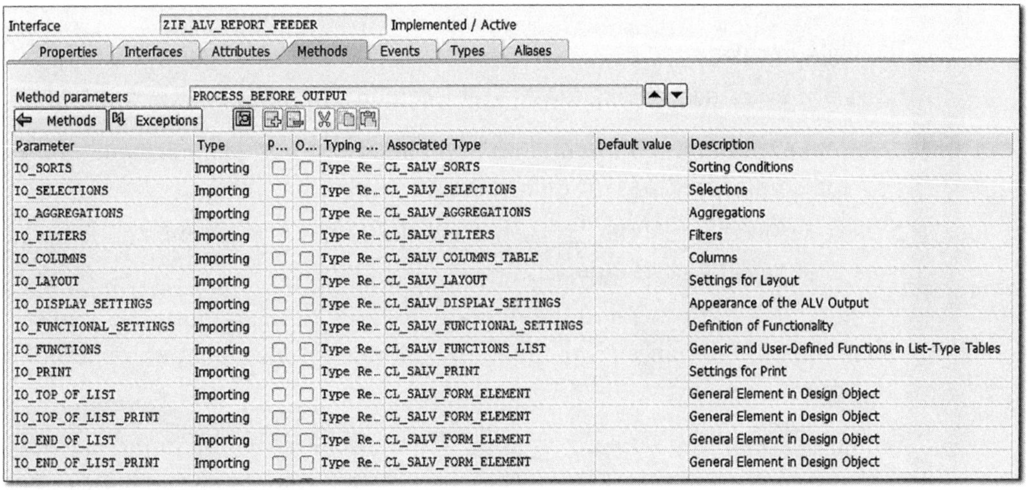

Parameter	Type	P...	O...	Typing ...	Associated Type	Default value	Description
IO_SORTS	Importing	☐	☐	Type Re...	CL_SALV_SORTS		Sorting Conditions
IO_SELECTIONS	Importing	☐	☐	Type Re...	CL_SALV_SELECTIONS		Selections
IO_AGGREGATIONS	Importing	☐	☐	Type Re...	CL_SALV_AGGREGATIONS		Aggregations
IO_FILTERS	Importing	☐	☐	Type Re...	CL_SALV_FILTERS		Filters
IO_COLUMNS	Importing	☐	☐	Type Re...	CL_SALV_COLUMNS_TABLE		Columns
IO_LAYOUT	Importing	☐	☐	Type Re...	CL_SALV_LAYOUT		Settings for Layout
IO_DISPLAY_SETTINGS	Importing	☐	☐	Type Re...	CL_SALV_DISPLAY_SETTINGS		Appearance of the ALV Output
IO_FUNCTIONAL_SETTINGS	Importing	☐	☐	Type Re...	CL_SALV_FUNCTIONAL_SETTINGS		Definition of Functionality
IO_FUNCTIONS	Importing	☐	☐	Type Re...	CL_SALV_FUNCTIONS_LIST		Generic and User-Defined Functions in List-Type Tables
IO_PRINT	Importing	☐	☐	Type Re...	CL_SALV_PRINT		Settings for Print
IO_TOP_OF_LIST	Importing	☐	☐	Type Re...	CL_SALV_FORM_ELEMENT		General Element in Design Object
IO_TOP_OF_LIST_PRINT	Importing	☐	☐	Type Re...	CL_SALV_FORM_ELEMENT		General Element in Design Object
IO_END_OF_LIST	Importing	☐	☐	Type Re...	CL_SALV_FORM_ELEMENT		General Element in Design Object
IO_END_OF_LIST_PRINT	Importing	☐	☐	Type Re...	CL_SALV_FORM_ELEMENT		General Element in Design Object

The table above also shows:
- Interface: ZIF_ALV_REPORT_FEEDER — Implemented / Active
- Tabs: Properties, Interfaces, Attributes, Methods, Events, Types, Aliases
- Method parameters: PROCESS_BEFORE_OUTPUT
- Methods, Exceptions

Figure 12.4 Signature of the process_before_output() Method

To demonstrate how this works, let's imagine that we want to sort the flight list in descending order based on the flight date. Under normal circumstances, these conditions would be defined in the ABAP report layer by calling the CL_SALV_ TABLE class's get_sorts() method and then manipulating the returned CL_SALV_ SORTS instance to build the sort conditions. As you can see in Figure 12.4, the framework provides us with a shortcut here by automatically passing the sorts handle as a parameter (IO_SORTS). Of course, we're not limited to just sorting here, we also have IO_FILTERS to define filters, IO_COLUMNS to adjust the column layout, and so forth.

The code excerpt contained in Listing 12.4 illustrates how we can implement the sort condition. At runtime, the ZCL_ALV_REPORT_CONTROLLER class will invoke the process_before_output() method polymorphically right before the report is displayed. So, we can use this method to implement any and all tweaks to the ALV output before the list is rendered.

```
CLASS zcl_flight_feeder IMPLEMENTATION.
  ...
  METHOD zif_alv_report_feeder~process_before_output.
    "Sort by flight date in descending order:
    io_sorts->add_sort( columnname = 'FLDATE'
                        sequence = IF_SALV_C_SORT=>SORT_DOWN ).
  ENDMETHOD.
ENDCLASS.
```
Listing 12.4 Defining Sort Conditions in the Feeder Class

Handling Events

Normally, event handling in the ALV object model requires several steps:

1. First, we have to define/identify an event handler class and implement separate event handler methods for each event we want to listen for.
2. Next, we have to call the CL_SALV_TABLE class's get_event() method to obtain an object reference of type CL_SALV_EVENTS_TABLE.
3. Finally, we have to register the event handler methods with the CL_SALV_ EVENTS_TABLE instance using the ABAP SET HANDLER statement we reviewed in Chapter 2.

Within our reporting framework, we abstract this event wiring in the base-level controller class ZCL_ALV_REPORT_CONTROLLER. Here, you can see how we're performing the steps above in method register_event_handlers(). At runtime, whenever an event is fired from the ALV control, the registered event handler methods in the controller class wrap up the event in an instance of class ZCL_ALV_ TABLE_EVENT and pass it to the feeder class via a polymorphic call to the process_ event() method.

Within the process event method, we can determine the type of event triggered by comparing the public mv_event_id attribute against the various constants defined in the CO_EVENT_TYPE constant. For example, the code excerpt contained in Listing 12.5 shows how we're sorting out event handling logic for using a simple ABAP CASE statement. Here, we're reacting to the ALV table control's double-click event by determining the selected table row and opening up transaction BC_ GLOBAL_SBOOK_CREA so that a user can create a flight booking in reference to an available flight. Though the code's pretty straightforward, notice how we're using the get_event_parameters() method of the ZCL_ALV_TABLE_EVENT class to fetch the table row index which was originally passed via the standard event definition.

```
CLASS zcl_flight_feeder IMPLEMENTATION.
  ...
  METHOD zif_alv_report_feeder~process_event.
    FIELD-SYMBOLS <lt_data> TYPE ty_flights_tab.
    FIELD-SYMBOLS <ls_data> TYPE sflight.
    DATA lv_row TYPE sy-tabix.

    CASE io_event->mv_event_id.
      WHEN zcl_alv_table_event=>co_event_type-double_click.
        "Read the selected flight record:
        IF me->mr_t_data IS BOUND.
          ASSIGN me->mr_t_data->* TO <lt_data>.
          io_event->get_event_parameters( )->get_value(
            EXPORTING
              iv_key = 'ROW'
            IMPORTING
              ev_value = lv_row ).

          READ TABLE <lt_data> INDEX lv_row ASSIGNING <ls_data>.
          IF sy-subrc NE 0.
            RETURN.
          ENDIF.
        ELSE.
          RETURN.
        ENDIF.

        "Open up a transaction to create a flight booking:
        SET PARAMETER ID 'CAR' FIELD <ls_data>-carrid.
        SET PARAMETER ID 'CON' FIELD <ls_data>-connid.
        SET PARAMETER ID 'DAY' FIELD <ls_data>-fldate.
```

```
        CALL TRANSACTION 'BC_GLOBAL_SBOOK_CREA'.
      ENDCASE.
    ENDMETHOD.
ENDCLASS.
```
Listing 12.5 Defining Event Handler Logic in the Feeder Class

12.4 UML Tutorial: Advanced Activity Diagrams

In Chapter 8, we learned how to model basic process flows using activity diagrams. In this section, we 'll expand upon these basic capabilities and look at some of the more advanced flow control elements provided for activity diagrams in the UML 2 standard.

The activity diagram shown in Figure 12.5 depicts an employee leave request workflow process. To effectively trace this process across all of the relevant parties/systems, we chose to split the diagram into rectangular swim lanes called *partitions*. Partitions can be labelled to depict a class, a person/role, a system, an organization, etc. The basic idea here is to show who does what in the process flow. In this case, an *Employee* initiates the workflow process by creating a leave request. Looking closely at the Create Leave Request action, you'll notice that there's a little "fork-like" icon on the left-hand side of the action icon. This notation indicates that the Create Leave Request action is actually a sub-activity whose details are described in another activity diagram.

Tracing the flow in Figure 12.5, you'll notice that once the leave request is created, the next action is to submit the request to a workflow engine. This submission process is depicted using a special action type called a *signal*. The use of signals here helps to signify the fact that the workflow process receives the request from an external process. Signals can also be used to depict other complex synchronous and asynchronous messaging scenarios.

Once the leave request is received by the workflow engine, it's forwarded to the employee's supervisor (via e-mail, for instance). At this point in time, the workflow process is in a holding pattern as it waits on a couple of potential outcomes. This holding pattern is depicted using a *fork* element. Here, one of two things can happen. Ideally, the supervisor will receive the request (again via a signal action), process it, and send a response back to the workflow engine. However, if the supervisor hasn't responded within 24 hours, the process should terminate. This 24 hour watch period is depicted using a *time signal* (i.e. the "bow-tie" icon shown in Figure 12.5). In either case, the process comes together again in a *join* element. From here, an e-mail response message (favorable or otherwise) is forwarded back to the initiating employee and the process terminates as per usual.

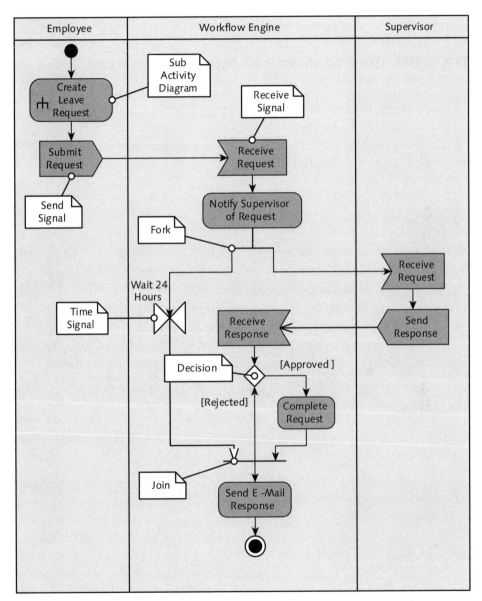

Figure 12.5 A More Advanced UML Activity Diagram

Another element of the activity diagram that we've not yet considered is the diamond-shaped *decision* node shown in Figure 12.5. This node looks just like the *merge* node described in Chapter 8. However, in this case, there's one input and multiple outputs as opposed to multiple inputs and a single output. Each of the outputs of a decision node are marked with a special guard text (e.g. [Approved] or [Rejected]) that describes the condition(s) in which that particular output path is selected. As you might expect, decision nodes are very good for depicting an IF/ELSE or CASE statement in a flow.

In many ways, even the advanced elements described in this section barely scratch the surface with regards to the types of things you can model using activity diagrams. To learn more about activity diagrams, we highly recommend Martin Fowler's *UML Distilled, Third Edition*.

12.5 Summary

In this chapter, we were able to demonstrate how to use the SAP List Viewer framework to build a custom reporting framework using OO-based concepts. Here, we were able to accomplish quite a bit using a handful of strategically positioned classes and interfaces, but that's really just the beginning. Over time, it's likely that this framework might evolve to include built-in model integration, families of feeder classes that pre-define reusable logic, and so forth. The sky's really the limit here—it just takes a proper foundation to get things started.

In the next chapter, we'll reflect on many of these concepts and look ahead to next steps in your OO journey.

In this chapter, we look at additional topics/resources that you can use to further hone your skills and master OO development concepts.

13   Where to Go From Here

In many respects, OOP can be distilled down into a handful of basic elements/concepts:

- The creation of abstract data types based on classes/interfaces
- Encapsulation
- Inheritance
- Polymorphism

Though it takes a little while wrap your head around these concepts such that you "think" in object-oriented terms, once you get the hang of it, you're well on your way to becoming a master. In this chapter, we'll look at some further topics/resources that you can utilize to move in this direction.

13.1   Object-Oriented Analysis and Design

As we've seen over the course of this book, the mechanics of OOP in a language like ABAP Objects are fairly easy to grasp once you understand basic syntax elements. After you get past this initial learning curve, reading and understanding how existing classes work should be fairly straightforward. However, learning to see the world around you using OO lenses takes some time.

For practical advice here, we'd encourage you to look at some of the many great resources out there related to the topic of *object-oriented analysis and design* (OOAD). Most resources in this space are largely language-agnostic, focusing more on pure design concepts rather than implementation details specific to Java, C++, or ABAP Objects. Some recommended titles here include:

▸ *Head First Object-Oriented Analysis and Design: A Brain Friendly Guide to OOA& D* (O'Reilly Media, 2006)

▸ *Domain-Driven Design: Tackling Complexity in the Heart of Software* (Addison-Wesley, 2003)

Within these books (and others like them), you'll find some practical advice for learning how to think in OO terms and ask the right questions during the requirements gathering process to make sure you don't end up on the wrong track during the design process.

13.2   Design Patterns

In the mid-1990s, a group of software engineers got together and published a classic title that really changed the way that developers thought about writing OO software: *Design Patterns: Elements of Reusable Object-Oriented Software*. This book drew inspiration from another classic title from the world of architectural design: Christopher Alexander's *A Pattern Language*. In *A Pattern Language*, Alexander says that patterns describe "a problem which occurs over and over again in our environment, and then describes the core of the solution to that problem, in such a way that you can use this solution a million times over, without ever doing it the same way twice."

By putting together a collection of reusable patterns, the authors of *Design Patterns* (colloquially referred to as the "Gang of Four") established a set of best practices which demonstrated how classes/interfaces could be used to implement solutions to common problems that might crop up during the design phase of a project. Here, rather than reinventing the wheel, developers were able to consult a patterns catalog which prescribed solutions which were generally more thorough than something they might come up with on their own.

In the 20+ years that have passed since the class *Design Patterns* title was first published, we've seen many resources come along to supplement the patterns catalog, simplify pattern explanations, or even provide language-specific cookbooks which make it easier to relate pattern concepts to developers who work exclusively in a particular language. Some recommended titles in this area include:

▸ *Pattern Hatching: Design Patterns Applied* (Addison-Wesley, 1998)

▸ *Design Patterns Explained: A New Perspective on Object-Oriented Design, 2nd Edition* (Addison Wesley, 2004)

- *Head First Design Patterns* (O'Reilly Media, 2004)
- *Refactoring to Patterns* (Addison-Wesley, 2004)
- *Patterns of Enterprise Application Architecture* (Addison-Wesley, 2002)
- *Design Patterns in Object-Oriented ABAP* (SAP PRESS, 2009)

If you're a new OO developer interested in learning how to apply the concepts you've learned in this book, we'd highly encourage you to check out these resources (or others) and work through some of the more common patterns. Once you get to this stage in your development process, the only way you get better is through experience, and you can save yourself a lot of heartache if you try to acquire this experience through the lessons learned by those who've already been where you are in the journey.

13.3   Reading and Writing ABAP Objects Code

In addition to academic-style learning, we'd strongly encourage you to read through as much ABAP Objects code as you can get your hands on – good or bad. These days, SAP provides a lot of OO-based libraries which you can use to come up with ideas and strategies. This is one step in the growth process that you can't really skip over—there are simply no substitutes for experience. Much like learning foreign languages, immersion is by far the most effective way to learn.

Note that this immersion process also extends to day-to-day development. ABAP Objects can generally be used for any kind of development task. Whether you're building a report program as demonstrated in Chapter 12, creating UIs with Web Dynpro ABAP (WDA), building workflows, or implementing enhancements, classes can (and should) be at the center of everything you do.

This is about more than just writing ABAP Objects classes for the sake of it. Even the simplest of tasks, which might seem easier to implement using quick-and-dirty procedural techniques, can usually benefit from an OO-based approach. For example, imagine an enhancement requirement which starts off with a simple enhancement implementation that defines some business rules. Over time, this enhancement implementation swells into many lines of code which become difficult to maintain. Plus, the same logic ends up getting replicated over to other enhancement implementations.

The moral of this story is this: what starts off as something simple often grows into something large and unmanageable if you don't stick to the core principles of encapsulation. The old adage of "find what varies and encapsulate it" applies whether we're talking about a small user exit or a complete UI application. Taking the extra time to identify the appropriate classes and define appropriate roles and responsibilities can make all the difference in the long run.

The more you do this, the easier the OO growth process will be. Plus, you'll find that many of these scenarios present you with excellent learning opportunities which really reinforce core concepts.

13.4 Summary

This concludes our exploration of OO development using ABAP Objects. We hope that you've enjoyed this book and that you feel empowered to get out there and apply what you've learned. The future of ABAP remains bright, and there are ample opportunities out there for developers who understand how to work with object-oriented ABAP.

Appendices

A   Installing the Eclipse IDE

Installing the ABAP Development Tools for Eclipse (ADT) is not too difficult once you understand the various steps involved. In this appendix, we'll walk through these steps and show you how to install the ADT on your local machine.

A.1   Installing the Java SDK

The Eclipse environment runs on top of the *Java Runtime Environment* (JRE), a virtual machine which can run Java code on top of most any OS environment: Microsoft Windows, Mac OS, Linux, and so forth. Though you can technically run Eclipse using the standalone JRE, we recommend that you install the complete Java SDK as this contains features that can come in handy for some of the other SAP-related plug-ins you might wish to install alongside your Eclipse installation.

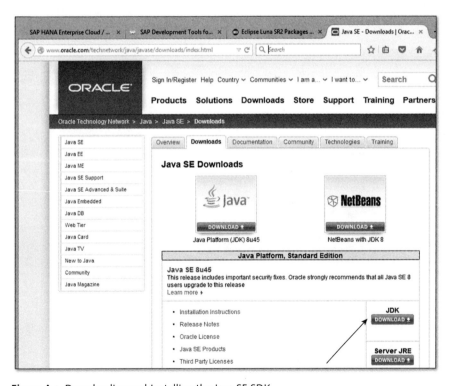

Figure A.1 Downloading and Installing the Java SE SDK

The Java SDK can be downloaded from the Oracle Technology Network online at *http://www.oracle.com/technetwork/java/javase/downloads/index.html*. From here, you can click on the DOWNLOAD button highlighted in Figure A.1.

From here, you'll be routed to a DOWNLOADS page where you can download the setup executable for your particular OS/environment. The installation process takes moments and is straightforward to complete.

A.2   Installing Eclipse

Once the Java SDK is in place, you can proceed with the installation of the Eclipse IDE itself. To find the appropriate installation package, browse to *https://tools.hana.ondemand.com/#abap* and find the recommended distribution which is compatible with the latest innovation of the ABAP development tools. Figure A.2 shows how you can locate the recommended version to install.

Figure A.2 Downloading the Eclipse IDE (Part 1)

Once you find the appropriate installation for your environment, follow the hyperlink to the Eclipse downloads page as shown in Figure A.3. From here, you can download either the Eclipse IDE for Java Developers or the Eclipse IDE for Java EE Developers. Both installations work just fine for ABAP-related development, so you can't go wrong with either installation. The Java EE edition just contains more plug-ins for Java EE development and therefore can also be used to develop custom applications for the SAP HANA Cloud Platform, etc.

Figure A.3 Downloading the Eclipse IDE (Part 2)

After you download Eclipse, you can install it by simply unpacking the ZIP archive into a directory on your local machine. From here, you can launch Eclipse the first time by running the Eclipse executable from the root directory of the program installation folder.

> **Tip**
>
> For a variety of reasons, we recommend that you avoid unpacking the Eclipse installation folder too deep within your folder structure. Since some of the Java-related artifacts have long folder/file names, some plug-ins have problems if the Eclipse installation is buried underneath too many folders.

The first time Eclipse runs, it will prompt you to select a *workspace* folder where projects and related metadata are stored (see Figure A.4). Here, we suggest that you pick a directory path that you'll remember (and keep backed up). While you can of course change this selection after the fact, it's much easier to get it right up front.

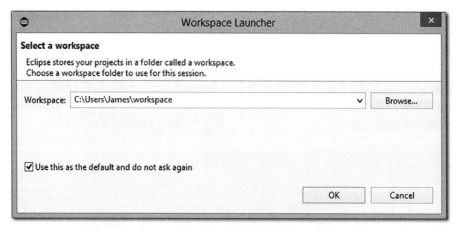

Figure A.4 Determining the Eclipse Workspace Folder

A.3 Installing the ABAP Development Tools

With the Eclipse installation in place, all that's left is to install the ADT plug-ins. This can be achieved within the Eclipse IDE itself by performing the following steps:

1. First, select the HELP • INSTALL NEW SOFTWARE... menu option as shown in Figure A.5.

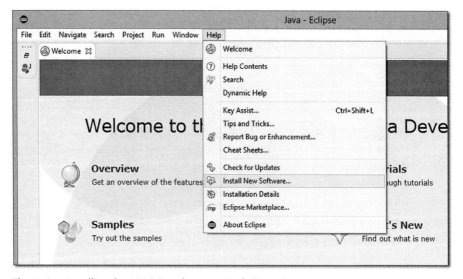

Figure A.5 Installing the ABAP Development Tools (Part 1)

2. This will open up the INSTALL dialog box shown in Figure A.6. Here, we must configure a *software site* which points to the ADT-related plug-ins. You can find the relevant software site for your particular Eclipse distribution via the SAP Development Tools for Eclipse home page available online at *https:// tools.hana.ondemand.com/#abap* (see Figure A.2). Once you identify this URL, plug it into the LOCATION field, give the installation repository a name, and click the OK button.

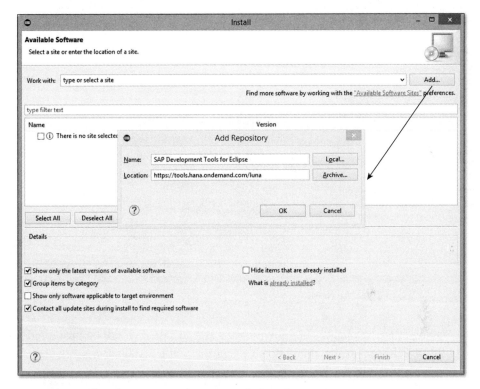

Figure A.6 Installing the ABAP Development Tools (Part 2)

3. At this point, Eclipse will connect to the software site and find a list of provided installation items. As you can see in Figure A.7, the ADT-related plug-ins are included in this list, among other things. Here, you can select as many of the items as you like (they're compatible with one another) and then proceed through the rest of the wizard steps to complete the installation.

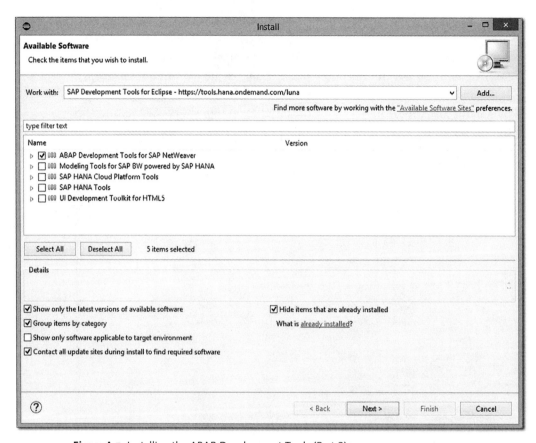

Figure A.7 Installing the ABAP Development Tools (Part 3)

4. Finally, after the plug-ins are downloaded and installed, you'll be prompted to re-start Eclipse. Go ahead and do so to complete the installation.

Assuming the installation runs smoothly, Eclipse will re-start and the Welcome page will be updated to include various ABAP-related links. You can click on these links to view tutorials, find supporting documentation, and more.

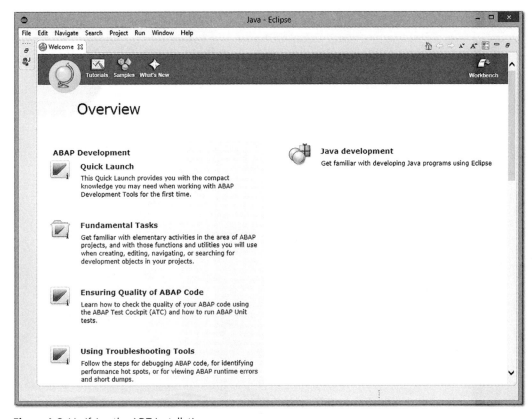

Figure A.8 Verifying the ADT Installation

A.4 Where to Go to Find Help

If the installation process fails for some reason, you can find links to forums and supporting documentation online at *https://tools.hana.ondemand.com/#abap*.

B Debugging Objects

As you begin working with objects in your programs, it's useful to be able to step interactively through a program to see the values assigned to various attributes, and trace through the program logic. In this appendix, we'll learn how to use the ABAP Debugger tool to perform these tasks. Here, we'll assume that you have some familiarity for debugging programs using the ABAP Debugger tool. If you haven't used the debugger before, we recommend that you read through the online help documentation since we won't be covering basic concepts here.

B.1 Understanding Debugger Types

Prior to Release 6.40 of the SAP Web AS, there was only one type of debugger tool available to developers. However, over time, certain limitations in this tool prompted SAP to implement a new debugger tool using a different and more flexible architecture. While the details of the differences between these two debugger types is beyond the scope of this book, we've separated our discussion of debugging objects into two sections so that you'll understand how to use both tools to debug objects.

B.2 Debugging Objects Using the Classic Debugger

For the most part, you'll find that dealing with objects in a debugger session is quite similar to working with normal data objects, procedures, etc. Nevertheless, there are elements of the debugging process that are unique to objects. Therefore, in this section, we'll highlight some of these particular concepts.

B.2.1 Displaying and Editing Attributes

Within a debugger session, you can inspect an object reference by performing the following steps:

1. If you're not already in the FIELDS display mode, select this display mode by clicking on the corresponding button underneath the application toolbar.

2. Select the object reference variable that points to the object you wish to inspect by double-clicking on the reference variable name in the ABAP program code display. Alternatively, you can enter the reference variable name in the FIELD NAMES section and press the ⌷Enter⌷ key (see Figure B.1).

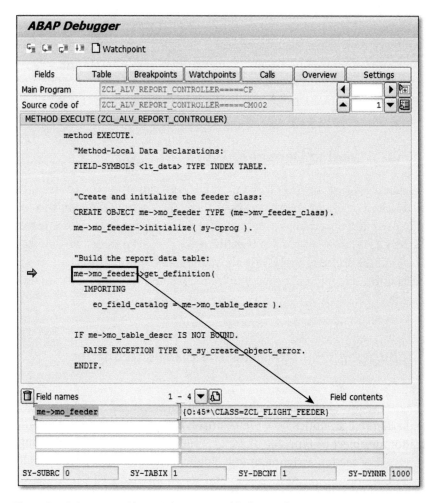

Figure B.1 Selecting an Object Reference Variable for Display

3. As you can see in Figure B.1, the FIELD CONTENTS display for an object reference variable only shows the internal object ID of the object pointed to by the object reference variable. To view the values of the attributes in this object, you

must double-click on the object ID. This will open up the OBJECT display mode view shown in Figure B.2.

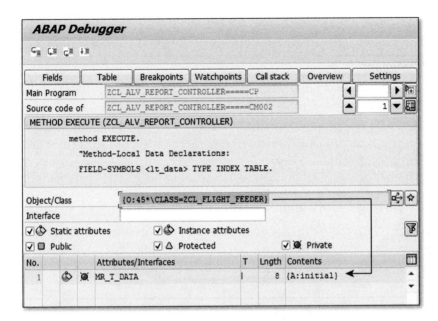

Figure B.2 Displaying the Attributes of an Object/Class

Once you're in the OBJECT display mode, you can edit individual primitive attributes by double-clicking their name in the ATTRIBUTES/INTERFACES column. Similarly, you can edit complex types by drilling into structures, internal tables, and indeed embedded objects.

You also have the option of filtering the display to specific types of attributes. For example, in Figure B.2, notice how we're displaying both the static and instance attributes for an object of type ZCL_FLIGHT_FEEDER. We can also filter attributes based on visibility section assignment (e.g. Public, Private, or Protected). Finally, if the class of the object in question implements an interface, you can filter the attribute list to just those fields defined within the interface.

B.2.2 Tracing Through Methods

The process of tracing method logic is no different than tracing through a subroutine or function module. Prior to a method invocation, you can select the SINGLE

STEP button to debug the method's implementation code. Inside the method, you can continue to step into or step over individual lines of code as per usual. Similarly, if you wish to exit from the method and resume debugging after the method call, you can select the RETURN button. Of course, if you wish to step over the method implementation entirely, you can select the EXECUTE button to execute the method.

One thing that we should point out is the fact that constructor methods do not behave in the same way as normal methods in the debugger. If you step into the CREATE OBJECT statement, the debugger will begin tracing through the constructor method. This is not the case, however, with class constructors. Here, you must explicitly set a breakpoint in order to debug the class constructor logic.

B.2.3   Displaying Events and Event Handler Methods

To display the registered events for an object/class, you open up the OBJECT display mode in the debugger. Here, you can click on the EVENTS button to switch from object mode to events mode (see Figure B.3).

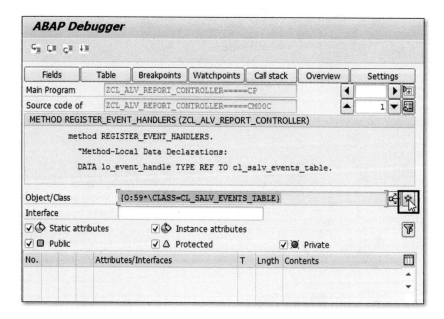

Figure B.3 Displaying the Registered Events for an Object (Part 1)

This view will show you all of the events defined for the object/class as well as any registered handling objects for the events. You can navigate to the objects shown in the HANDLING OBJECT column to set breakpoints in the event handler methods to debug event handling scenarios. This can be sometimes useful in frameworks where you're not real clear where event handlers are registered, etc.

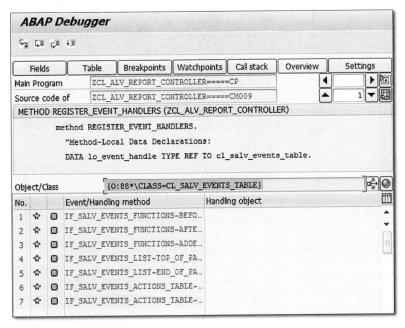

Figure B.4 Displaying the Registered Events for an Object (Part 2)

B.2.4 Viewing Reference Assignments for an Object

Sometimes, you may encounter situations where an object is manipulated in ways that you didn't expect. Here, it's possible that more than one reference to the object exists. You can identify the set of references to an object by selecting GOTO • SYSTEM • FIND REFERENCE in the menu area. This menu option will open up a dialog box showing you all of the references to the object in question in the system (see Figure B.5).

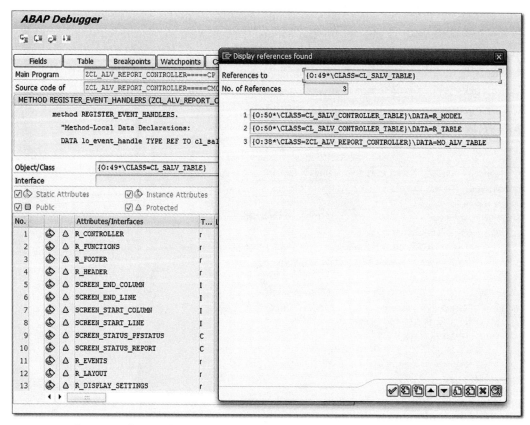

Figure B.5 Showing the Reference Assignments for an Object

B.2.5 Troubleshooting Class-Based Exceptions

Whenever an exception is triggered by a statement during a debugging session, the ABAP debugger will trace the exception propagation process back to the exception handler block that captures the exception—assuming there was one. Oftentimes, you'll encounter debugging scenarios where a developer chose not to capture the exception situation in an exception object. This information can be crucial for debugging complex exception situations. Therefore, you can modify the debugger session settings to dynamically generate an exception object that you can use to troubleshoot an error. To configure this setting, select the SETTINGS display mode and click on the ALWAYS CREATE EXCEPTION OBJECT checkbox (see Figure B.6).

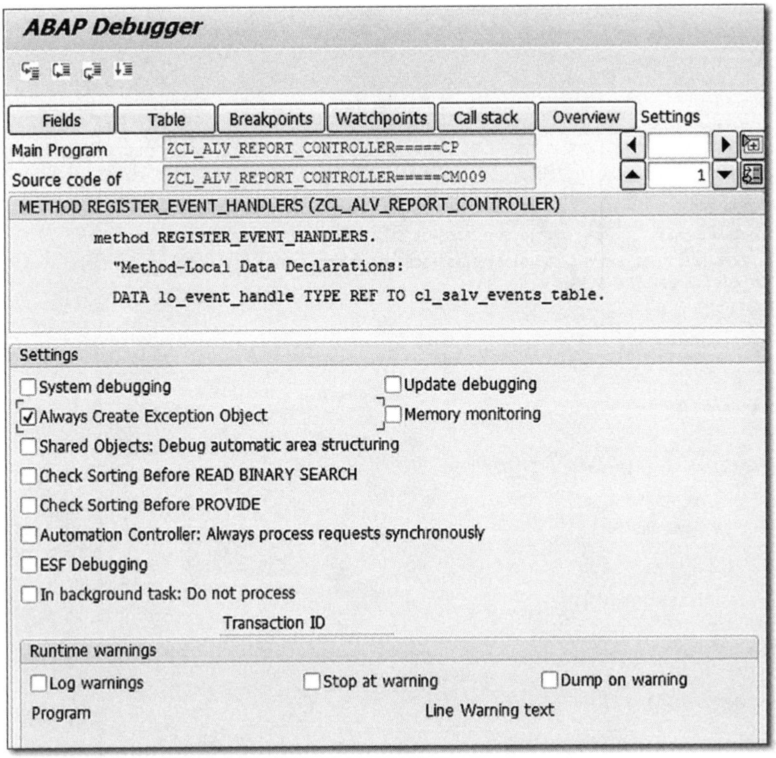

Figure B.6 Turning on the Automatic Creation of Exception Objects

After the exception is triggered, the cursor will be placed at the beginning of the CATCH block defined to handle the exception. If this CATCH block is not defined using the INTO addition, then you can display the exception object by clicking on the DISPLAY EXCEPTION OBJECT button (see Figure B.7). Otherwise, you can double-click on the exception object reference just as you would for any normal object reference variable.

453

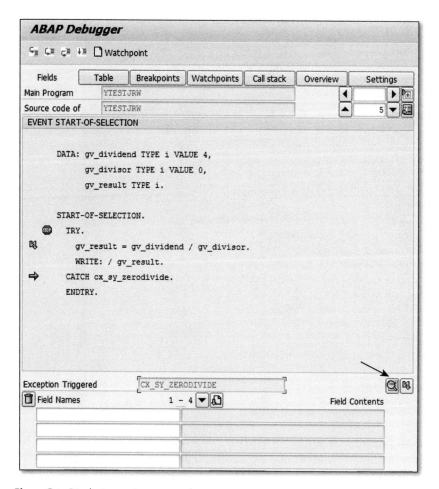

Figure B.7 Displaying an Exception Object (Part 1)

The exception object is displayed in the OBJECT display mode just like any other object type. Here, you can trace the exception chain via the PREVIOUS attribute in addition to any custom attributes that further define the exception situation (see Figure B.8).

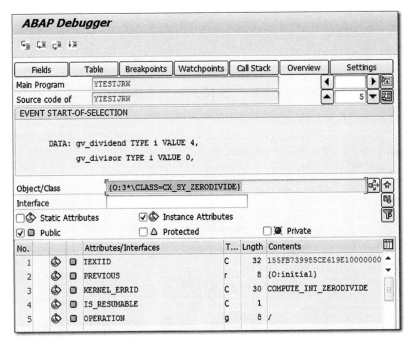

Figure B.8 Displaying an Exception Object (Part 2)

B.3 Debugging Objects Using the New Debugger

In most respects, the process of debugging objects in the New ABAP Debugger is quite similar to the process of debugging objects in the Classic ABAP Debugger. The primary difference is in the layout of the OBJECT display area. Context-sensitive access to this view is provided in all of the various variable display sections within the debugger window. For example, by double-clicking the object ID in the VALUE column shown in Figure B.9, we were taken to the OBJECT display shown in Figure B.10.

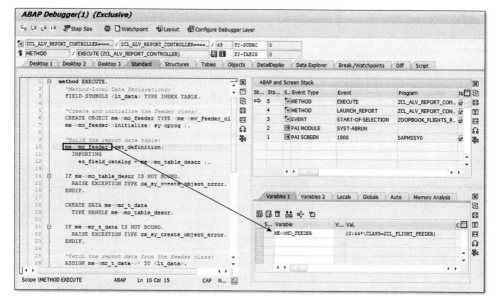

Figure B.9 Basic Layout of the New ABAP Debugger

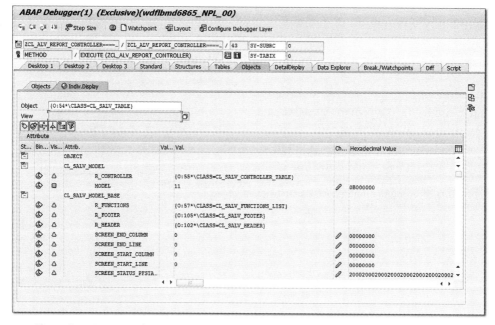

Figure B.10 Viewing Objects in the New ABAP Debugger

As you can see in Figure B.10, the OBJECT display in the New ABAP Debugger is much more streamlined. Here, by default, you can see the attributes of the object/class in question arranged hierarchically according to the inheritance hierarchy. You can turn this feature off by selecting the SUPERCLASSES ON/OFF button directly above the attribute display. Events and their registered event handler methods are displayed using the EVENTS button. References to the object in question can be viewed using the DISPLAY REFERENCES button.

In addition to all of the standard features carried over from the classic debugger, the new debugger also provides a function to display the inheritance hierarchy of a given object at runtime. This function can be accessed by clicking on the DISPLAY INHERITANCE HIERARCHY button. Figure B.11 shows the INHERITANCE RELATIONSHIP view for an object of type CL_SALV_TABLE.

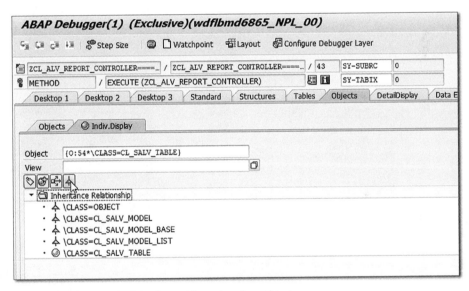

Figure B.11 Showing the Inheritance Hierarchy of an Object

C   Bibliography

Alexander, Christopher. *A Pattern Language* (Oxford University Press, 1977)

Arnold, Ken, James Goslin, and David Holmes. *The Java Programming Language*, *4th Edition* (Addison-Wesley Professional, 2006)

Cockburn, Alistair. *Writing Effective Use Cases* (Addison-Wesley Professional, 2000)

Eckel, Bruce. *Thinking in C++, 2nd Edition* (Prentice Hall, 2000)

Fowler, Martin. *Refactoring: Improving the Design of Existing Code* (Addison-Wesley Professional, 1999)

Fowler, Martin. *UML Distilled: A Brief Guide to the Standard Object Modeling Language, 3rd Edition* (Addison-Wesley Professional, 2003)

Gamma, Erich, Richard Helm, Ralph Johnson, John Vlissides. *Design Patterns: Elements of Reusable Object-Oriented Software* (Addison-Wesley Professional, 1994)

Kerievsky, Joshua. *Refactoring to Patterns* (Addison-Wesley Professional, 2004)

Meyer, Bertrand. *Object-Oriented Software Construction, 2nd Edition* (Prentice Hall, 1997)

Shalloway, Alan. *Design Patterns Explained: A New Perspective on Object-Oriented Design, 2nd Edition* (Addison-Wesley Professional, 2004)

D   The Authors

James Wood is the founder and principal consultant of Bowdark Consulting, Inc., an SAP consulting firm specializing in custom development and training. James is also an SAP Mentor and the author of several best-selling SAP-related titles.

Before starting Bowdark in 2006, James was a consultant at SAP America, Inc. and IBM Corporation where was involved in many large-scale SAP implementations. To learn more about James and the book, please check out *http://www.bowdark.com*.

Joe Rupert is a senior technical consultant at Bowdark Consulting, Inc. Before joining Bowdark, Joe worked for several health care technology companies building complex search engines for querying biomedical research, patient lab and clinical data.

Index

- ▶ Discover the latest and greatest features in the ABAP universe

- ▶ Explore the new worlds of SAP HANA, BRFplus, BOPF, and more

- ▶ Propel your code and your career into the future

Paul Hardy

ABAP to the Future

ABAP has been around for a while, but that doesn't mean your programming has to be stuck in the past. Want to master test-driven development? Decipher BOPF? Manage BRF+? Explore ABAP 7.4? With clear explanations, engaging examples, and downloadable code, this book is your ride to the future. After all: If you're going to build something with ABAP, why not do it with some style?

727 pages, 2015, $69.95/€69.95
ISBN 978-1-4932-1161-6
www.sap-press.com/3680

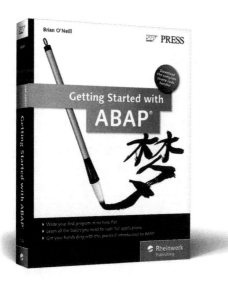

- ▶ Learn the basics of ABAP and write your first program

- ▶ Set up an ABAP trial system and master the integrated development environment (IDE)

- ▶ Develop an example application using strings and text, dates and times, and more

Brian O'Neill

Getting Started with ABAP

Learn to code in ABAP, SAP's programming language! This book is a beginner's guide to all things ABAP. You'll become familiar with core language concepts, develop your first application, and learn key advanced programming techniques. Step-by-step instructions and hands-on exercises help ensure that you can apply the skills you learn to real-life scenarios.

452 pages, 2016, $49.95/€49.95
ISBN 978-1-4932-1242-2
www.sap-press.com/3869

Interested in reading more?

Please visit our website for all new
book and e-book releases from SAP PRESS.

www.sap-press.com